# Studies in Economic History

**Aims and Scope**

This series from Springer provides a platform for works in economic history that truly integrate economics and history. Books on a wide range of related topics are welcomed and encouraged, including those in macro-economic history, financial history, labor history, industrial history, agricultural history, the history of institutions and organizations, spatial economic history, law and economic history, political economic history, historical demography, and environmental history.

Economic history studies have greatly developed over the past several decades through application of economics and econometrics. Particularly in recent years, a variety of new economic theories and sophisticated econometric techniques—including game theory, spatial economics, and generalized method of moment (GMM)—have been introduced for the great benefit of economic historians and the research community.

At the same time, a good economic history study should contribute more than just an application of economics and econometrics to past data. It raises novel research questions, proposes a new view of history, and/or provides rich documentation. This series is intended to integrate data analysis, close examination of archival works, and application of theoretical frameworks to offer new insights and even provide opportunities to rethink theories.

The purview of this new Springer series is truly global, encompassing all nations and areas of the world as well as all eras from ancient times to the present. The editorial board, who are internationally renowned leaders among economic historians, carefully evaluate and judge each manuscript, referring to reports from expert reviewers. The series publishes contributions by university professors and others well established in the academic community, as well as work deemed to be of equivalent merit.

All books and chapters in the Studies in Economic History book series are indexed in Scopus.

Zhiwu Chen · Cameron Campbell · Debin Ma
Editors

# Quantitative History of China

## State Capacity, Institutions and Development

Springer

*Editors*
Zhiwu Chen
Faculty of Business and Economics
The University of Hong Kong
Hong Kong, China

Cameron Campbell
Division of Social Science
The Hong Kong University of Science and Technology
Hong Kong, China

Debin Ma
School of Economics
Fudan University
Shanghai, China

ISSN 2364-1797 ISSN 2364-1800 (electronic)
Studies in Economic History
ISBN 978-981-96-8271-3 ISBN 978-981-96-8272-0 (eBook)
https://doi.org/10.1007/978-981-96-8272-0

The work described in this edited volume was substantially supported by a grant from the Research Grants Council of the Hong Kong Special Administrative Region, China (Project Reference Number: AoE/B-704/22-R).



This Springer imprint is published by the registered company Springer Nature Singapore Pte Ltd.
The registered company address is: 152 Beach Road, #21-01/04 Gateway East, Singapore 189721, Singapore

# Contents

# About the Editors

**Zhiwu Chen** is Chair and Cheng Yu-Tung Professor in Finance at the University of Hong Kong (HKU). He currently serves as director of both Hong Kong Institute for the Humanities and Social Sciences (HKIHSS) and Centre for Quantitative History (CQH). His research covers finance theory, the sociology of finance, economic history, quantitative history, emerging markets, as well as China's economy and capital markets. He was a former Professor of Finance at Yale University (1999–2017) and a Special-Term Visiting Professor at Peking University and Tsinghua University.

He started his career by publishing research papers in top economics and finance journals on topics related to financial markets and theories of asset pricing. Around 2001, he began to expand research beyond mature markets by investigating market development and institution-building issues in the context of China's transition process and other emerging markets. He successfully led efforts to construct historical financial and social databases from China's historical archives and has written on economic/social history topics. In 2013, he started the annual Summer School for Quantitative History cum International Symposium on Quantitative History at Tsinghua University and continued to organize them at Peking University, with the goal of promoting quantitative research on the history of China and beyond. In 2022, his Quantitative History of China project was awarded HK$67.32 million (over US$8.5 million) under the Areas of Excellence (AoE) Scheme funded by the Research Grants Council (RGC) of Hong Kong.

He is a frequent contributor to media publications in China on topics of economic policy, market development, institutional reform, and historical research. His work has been widely published and regularly featured in major newspapers and magazines in the United States, Hong Kong, China, and many other countries. His Chinese books include: *How Is Wealth Created*? (2005), *Media, Law and Markets* (2005), *Why are the Chinese Industrious and Yet Not Rich* (2008), *Irrational Overconfidence* (2008), *The Logic of Finance* (2009), *24 Wealth Lectures* (2009), *Assessing China's Economic Growth of the Past 30*

*Years* (2010), *On the China Model* (2010), *The Logic of Finance 2: Path to Individual Freedom* (2015), *Introduction to Finance* (2018), and *Introduction to Investment* (2019). He recently published a two-volume book in Chinese, titled *Logic of Civilization*, that explores a number of human innovations, including mythology or magic and supernatural beliefs, technologies, social structures, cultural norms, religions, financial markets, and the welfare state. He has received research awards including the Graham and Dodd Award (2013), the Pacesetter Research Award (1999), the Merton Miller Prize (1994), and the Chicago Board Options Exchange Competitive Research Award (1994). He has also received a number of book awards in China and Hong Kong, among which are 23 awards for *The Logic of Finance* in China and Hong Kong.

He received his Ph.D. in financial economics from Yale University in 1990; MS in systems engineering from Changsha Institute of Technology in 1986; and BS in computer science from Central-South University in 1983. He was Assistant Professor of Finance at University of Wisconsin–Madison (1990-95); Associate Professor of Finance at Ohio State University (1995–99); and Professor of Finance at Yale University.

**Cameron Campbell** is Chair Professor in the Division of Social Science at the Hong Kong University of Science and Technology (HKUST). Before joining HKUST in 2013, he was a Professor of Sociology at UCLA, starting as an Assistant Professor there in 1996. He has published in *American Journal of Sociology*, *Demography*, *American Sociological Review*, *Population Studies* and other journals. Since 2020, he has been a Distinguished Professor in the School of History and Culture at Central China Normal University.

His research focuses on demography, stratification, and inequality in historical China and in comparative perspective. In his current projects, he studies official, educational, and professional elites in China from the middle of the eighteenth century to the present. For this, he and his collaborators in the Lee-Campbell Group have constructed a family of 'big data' studies of specific categories of elites using datasets we have constructed ourselves from archival sources. In connection with this, he leads the study of the Qing civil service from the middle of the eighteenth century to the beginning of the twentieth century by construction and analysis of a database of office holders we call the China Government Employee Database-Qing (CGED-Q). He participates in two other major projects with the Lee-Campbell Group that involve the creation and analysis of large, longitudinal, individual-level databases from archival records: a study of the social origins and careers of university students, professionals, and other elites in the first half of the twentieth century and a study of rural society in mainland China from 1949 to the mid-1960s using village-level microdata.

He continues to conduct research on kinship, inequality, and demographic behavior in historical China and in comparative perspective using large multi-generational population databases that my collaborators and I constructed, most notably the China Multigenerational Panel Datasets (CMGPD). He has published on a wide variety of topics using these data, including economic, family, and social influences on demographic outcomes such as birth, marriage, migration, and death, fertility limitation in historical China, and the role of kin networks in shaping social mobility. He also published related books at MIT Press and Cambridge University Press. He has publicly released the CMGPD and they are available at ICPSR.

He was a Fellow of the Center for Advanced Study in the Behavioral Sciences at Stanford 2022-23. He was awarded a Guggenheim Fellowship in 2004. He was a Changjiang Scholar at Central China Normal University from 2017 to 2020.

He earned his Ph.D. in Sociology and Demography from the University of Pennsylvania in 1995, and his BS in Engineering and Applied Science and in History from Caltech in 1989.

**Debin Ma** is a Professor of Economics at Fudan University, Shanghai, China, and a Quondam Fellow at All Souls College, Oxford University. His main expertise is in the long-term economic growth of East Asia, especially China. His research interests include global history; the international comparison of living standards; institutions, legal traditions, and ideology; human capital and productivity; and the economic history of the silk industry. He has published widely on Asian and comparative economic history and is the co-editor of the *Cambridge Economic History of China.*

# Chapter 1
# Editorial Introduction: Quantitative History of China: State Capacity, Institutions and Development

**Zhiwu Chen, Cameron Campbell, and Debin Ma**

## 1.1 Introduction

Record keeping in China dates to the Shang dynasty (1600–1046 BCE). While limited at the beginning, the scope of coverage expanded tremendously over the subsequent three millennia, including not just matters of imperial importance but also topics of concern to ordinary people and crucial to their livelihoods. As a result, historians of China have enjoyed access to a wealth of archival resources mostly unmatched by other countries. For example, there are about 100,000 surviving local gazetteers across China, compiled during different dynasties, which amounts to roughly 1.5 billion pages of content if we assume an average number of 100 volumes per gazetteer and 150 pages per volume. There are almost as many pages of clan genealogy books and millions of official documents from the national and local levels of government. As voluminous as these sources are, traditional historians have been unable to fully exploit their potential because the qualitative methodologies they employ, especially case studies, are labor intensive and reading all or even most of the pages is not humanly possible.

In the twentieth century, however, historians began to apply quantitative methods to these sources to carry out pioneering but by today's standards small-scale studies of China's social, political, economic, and demographic history. The earliest studies

Z. Chen
Centre for Quantitative History, Faculty of Business and Economics; Hong Kong Institute for the Humanities and Social Sciences, The University of Hong Kong, Hong Kong, China
e-mail: zhiwu.chen@hku.hk

C. Campbell
Division of Social Science, The Hong Kong University of Science and Technology, Hong Kong, China
e-mail: camcam@ust.hk

D. Ma (✉)
School of Economics, Fudan University, Shanghai, China



Z. Chen et al. (eds.), *Quantitative History of China*, Studies in Economic History,
https://doi.org/10.1007/978-981-96-8272-0_1

made use of relatively small samples because in the absence of the computing technology that is now widely available, tabulations and other calculations had to be manual. One of the earliest was Ho Ping-ti's (1962)classic *Ladder of Success in Imperial China*, in which Ho tabulated information on the family backgrounds of examination degree holders in the Ming and Qing to study elite social mobility. Li and Zhou (1974) collected information about the appointments of local officials in historical gazetteers and calculated the lengths of their appointments and other basic parameters of their careers. As computing technology became more widely available, demographic historians began to produce estimates of birth, death, and marriage rates in the Chinese past by analysis of databases of household registers and genealogies (e.g. Wolf and Huang 1980; Lee and Campbell 1997; Liu 1978). Since the databases used by these studies were constructed by manual transcription, these early efforts could only make use of a small fraction of the existing archival sources. In the last two decades, database construction has moved from bespoke efforts for specific projects to systematic undertakings exhausting all available documents in each category.

We are entering a new era in terms of the possibilities for the use of these sources because recent advances in computing and machine learning technology have led to the massive growth in the transcription and organization of historical archives in China. These developments offer historians of China a golden opportunity. In the past, it was simply not possible for any scholar to make use of such vast amounts of historical and archeological data in an analysis. It is not humanly possible for any historian to read and digest even a reasonable fraction of the abundant historical resources that are already, or will soon be, digitized. The quantitative methods employed in early studies, most commonly tabulation and other basic calculations, are not sufficient to fully realize the potential of these vast and complex datasets. Taking advantage of the opportunity offered by these new data, therefore, requires new methodologies. Fortunately, social scientists have developed methods for the analysis of large and complex datasets that are now the mainstay for quantitative studies of contemporary society and economy. Application of these methods to the analysis of China's vast corpus of historical sources will open up a wide range of possibilities for the study of past social, economic, and political phenomena.

Recognizing an opportunity to develop the quantitative study of Chinese history into a field, Zhiwu Chen and his associates established the Centre for Quantitative History (CQH) at the University of Hong Kong as a hub for researchers with related interests from Hong Kong, mainland China, Taiwan, and the rest of the world. Generously supported by funding from the Hong Kong Research Grants Council Area of Excellence Scheme, CQH has held conferences on quantitative history and organized summer schools and other training programs. The group has made ambitious efforts to create vast new databases from diverse sources that will transform the quantitative study of Chinese history and make Hong Kong a center for such research, promoting dialogues between social science historians and traditional historians. Our goal is to inspire new approaches to the investigation of the historical roots of modern China by making use of cutting-edge quantitative methods developed by social scientists studying contemporary society, economics, and politics that complement more traditional historical approaches. The topics covered include, but are not limited to, economic, demographic, social, institutional, and political processes and phenomena that are difficult or impossible to study by application of traditional methods.

This volume is among the first fruits of these efforts. The studies included here were first presented at a conference at the University of Hong Kong, organized by CQH in October 2023. Collectively, they showcase the range of the research being carried out by the scholars associated with CQH, including the East–West Great Divergence debate, unification versus segmentation as drivers of, or the lack thereof, competition, determinants of demand for new technology, historical patterns of regicide, historical roots of regional variation in warrior culture, spatial distributions of place of origin and deployment for military officers, impact of disasters on the careers of officials, fiscal and financial development and state capacity, and the influence of Christian missionaries on agricultural development. The studies make use of diverse sources: archeological excavation reports, dynastic histories, information extracted from local gazetteers, official documents, rosters of civil officials and military officers, records of missionaries, and painstakingly reconstructed war, climate event, revenue, price, and wage data. Taken together, they demonstrate the potential of advanced quantitative methods applied to novel historical sources to transform our understanding of Chinese history.

The remaining chapters are organized into four parts. Part I discusses the role of inter-state conflicts, or war, in generating demand for and incentivizing the development of new technology. It addresses the Needham Puzzle that prior to and including the Song dynasty (960–1279 CE), China had many inventions but did not translate these inventions into productive applications and that after the Song, even inventions became less frequent (Needham 1954). Part II focuses on the relationship between the rulers and the governing elites (especially the military elites), including the role of the emperor, power-sharing institutions (and the lack thereof), rise of warrior culture, and the recruitment of military officers. Part III considers state capacity, with a specific emphasis on fiscal and financial development. Its chapters take a critical look at imperial China's revenue-raising mechanisms and financial development, and in one chapter, the state's enforcement of its regulations related to personnel management. Part IV looks at the influence of religion on economic development.

## 1.2 Part I: War, Technology, and the Needham Puzzle

One of the most prominent questions facing comparative historians generally and historians of China particularly is why the Industrial Revolution of the late eighteenth century started in Europe but not China. According to the so-called Needham (1954) Puzzle, from the sixth century BCE to the fourteenth century CE, even though China's inventions in science and technology were unmatched by any other country, many of them were never translated into useful applications on the battlefield or in agricultural and other goods production. In other words, China could have had an Industrial Revolution well before Europe did but did not. Thereafter, the West took the lead in technology, eventually culminating in the so-called Great Divergence in economic and other performance measures in the late eighteenth century, and possibly earlier. The chapters in Part I investigate the Needham Puzzle. In contrast with previous studies that have investigated the roles of culture and institutions, these chapters focus on the negative impact of unification on China's demand for military technology.

Chapter 2 examines the negative impact of unification on China's demand for military technology. The three co-authors—Zhiwu Chen, Senhao Hu, and Zhan Lin—make two assumptions. First, innovations in technology can take place due to either supply or demand. The fact that China had many inventions but did not make widespread use of them suggests that the Needham Puzzle cannot be explained using supply-side arguments and that one must look for answers from the demand side. Second, for much of China's history, war threats occupied a dominating position in the minds of the elites and their advisors, so that if there was one place to look for evidence of demand for technological innovations or the lack thereof, the battlefield would be the first to consider as it had immediate implications for both personal and national survival. Based on these two assumptions, the co-authors choose to focus on how unification reduced the frequency of war and whether reduced war threats indeed stifled the demand for technology.

Chapter 2 makes use of national-level historical data on war and military technological innovations to show that foreign wars, not internal rebellions, stimulated technological innovations. External war, in other words, was the crucial channel through which inter-state competition forced each nation to innovate technology and apply it; by the same token, the unification of many otherwise independent nations into a single state would remove the pre-existing inter-state competition, which would translate into less demand for technological innovations. For their empirical exercise, they adopt the Herfindahl–Hirschman Index (HHI), which is widely used in economics and finance to measure the level of concentration in a given industry, to capture the degree of unification in China. Used in this way, the HHI offers an objective measure of the extent to which China was fully, partially, or not unified at each historical time.

They show that since 770 BCE, periods with a higher unification index had lower frequencies of external war and fewer military technological innovations per 10 million population per 100 years, confirming that unification depressed the demand for new technology by reducing the threat of foreign war. External war threats thus had a positive effect on military technological innovations. Internal conflicts had, however, a negative impact on military technological innovations, possibly because domestic rebellions could be addressed through governance reforms rather than hardware innovations.

In Chapter 3, Zhiwu Chen, Senhao Hu, and Zhan Lin take another approach to investigating the importance of external conflict in generating demand for military technology. They show that regions that experienced more external wars during the prehistoric or early historic period had a higher share of bronze grave goods that were military, implying that these war-torn regions prioritized the application of military bronze technology, which at the time was the state-of-the-art metal-making technology, on the battlefield. In contrast, war experience had no effect on the extent of bronze and iron applications in farming. The chapter's key innovation is the use of the new China Archaeological Database (CADB) at the University of Hong Kong, to define a proxy for the extent of each region's demand for new technology during the prehistoric era when no written record is available. This database includes military grave goods excavated from 8000 BCE to 1911 CE. Their analysis shows that regions facing higher war threats adopted new technology more quickly, especially on the battlefield.

Taken together, these two chapters suggest that at least one of the keys to resolving the Needham Puzzle is the inverse relationship between unification and innovation. Europe's division after the fall of the Roman Empire into states that fought incessantly has been argued to be responsible for not only technological innovation but also fiscal and bureaucratic innovations (Fernández-Villaverde et al. 2023). China's persistent unification, by contrast, reduced the military and other inter-state competition that in Europe drove innovation in multiple directions, leading to lower demand for technology, and slower innovation in historical China.

## 1.3 Part II: Rulers, Institutions, and the Military

From prehistoric to modern times, statecraft has been a preoccupation of Chinese elites, so Part II turns to the institutions by which the state maintained and exercised its power. It examines rulers, power-sharing institutions, the military, and the bureaucracy in historical China. In Chapter 4, Zhiwu Chen and Zhan Lin investigate how emperors died in historical China, with a focus on regicide. As reflected in countless novels, plays, and other works of fiction, rulers in China and beyond were preoccupied with the possibility that someone might take their life and hence took extraordinary measures to protect themselves. According to Chapter 4, regicide was common overall, but rulers in later dynasties were more successful at avoiding unnatural death. Chapter 5 examines factors that influence the emergence and persistence of a warrior culture, showing that prefectures that in the past experienced frequent wars produced more military exam (*wuju*) degree holders in the Qing and still have more martial art academies per million population today, favoring the use of *wu*, or force, over that of *wen*, or negotiation, to resolve conflicts. Chapter 6 examines the provinces of origin and deployment of Qing military officers in the nineteenth century, demonstrating that there was a long-term trend toward reallocating officers back from the northwest frontiers to the southeast coastal provinces and that the rise of the Hunan army faction played a role in this reallocation and other changes. Chapter 7 turns to personnel management for civil officials, examining whether and how the Qing state enforced its own rules for the termination of officials for poor performance. The authors in this part of the book show through different angles and with detailed data analyses how imperial China worked and who governed the middle kingdom in the nineteenth century.

In Chapter 4, Chen and Lin make use of detailed information on each ruler since the beginning of the Zhou dynasty (1046–221 BCE) to analyze their vulnerability to regicide. Some scholars have argued that China's imperial institutions were static, even stagnant, over centuries or even millennia, with little change until the end of the Qing. One widely acknowledged feature of imperial institutions was that the government was autocratic, with the emperor at the center, and at least in principle holding absolute power. Whether and how the power of the emperor changed, and whether such changes had any effect, has been a preoccupation in the study of Chinese history, especially its history of institutional development. In the existing literature on China, studies of the exercise of power by historical rulers are often based on the experience of a single emperor or dynasty, and few studies cover the entire imperial period. More generally, even though Aristotle hypothesized millennia ago that in an autocracy, both the inner court and the masses are motivated to kill the ruler, there have been few studies prior to this one that examine which of the two groups poses a bigger threat to the ruler's life. With detailed data on regicide in historical China, Chen and Lin address this hypothesis empirically.

Chapter 4 treats the regicide rate as a measure of the quality of governance institutions that captures the trade-off between the ruler's power and the checks and balances on his power by the imperial institutions. A high regicide rate reflects a situation where unchecked power makes assassination the only option for ambitious rivals. A low regicide rate implies that there are enough checks and balances on the ruler's power that rivals have other options for advancing their agenda, possibly limiting the effectiveness of his rule. By the same token, changes in the regicide rate can be viewed as an indicator of institutional development. Their analysis includes all the 1948 kings and emperors (hereinafter rulers) from the entire period of 1046 BCE–1911 CE. They show that during this time, regicide was common: of the 1948 rulers of 448 states that covered the area of what we now know as China, 35.7% died unnaturally, implying a regicide rate of 2,899.8 deaths per 100,000 ruler-years. This death rate is almost five times as high as that on a modern battlefield.

According to the results, members of the court, relatives and trusted ministers, were the most likely to perpetrate regicide, along with invading armies. From the seventh to sixteenth centuries, China's regicide rate was generally higher and more volatile than those of European kings, but lower than those of Islamic sultans. Several factors influenced the chances of being the victim of regicide. Current or past uncertainty about succession was a clear threat to a ruler's life: rulers who appointed a successor were less likely to be assassinated, but rulers subject to a regency at the time of their ascension or whose predecessor died unnaturally were more likely to be assassinated. War, drought, flood and other natural disasters—as well as the number of co-existing competing states—also increased the probability of unnatural death for the ruler. Perhaps most importantly, after the Tang dynasty (618–907 CE), the chances of a ruler being assassinated gradually declined, reflecting improvements in the institutional design based on lessons learned.

The composition of the civil and military elites who exercised power in terms of their regional or provincial origin has been of longstanding interest in Chinese history. Certain regions had reputations for producing officials or soldiers. For example, some mostly eastern and southern provinces such as Jiangsu, Zhejiang, and Anhui had such a track record of producing successful examination degree candidates who went on to become officials that quotas were introduced to ensure that candidates from northern and interior provinces could also obtain degrees. As for military affairs, Shaanxi and Gansu had a longstanding reputation for producing talented officers and soldiers. At specific points in time, specific regional factions emerged. One of the most notable was the veterans of the Hunan Army who dominated the civil and military hierarchy after the Taiping Rebellion. Such patterns are important because officials from the same place often formed factions and looked after each other's interests. If they were overrepresented among political elites, they could have disproportionate influence, and their home regions might benefit. Despite this, there have been relatively few large-scale quantitative studies of the provinces of origin of elites, especially ones who held power in the military.

To investigate the determinants of the spatial distribution of military elites in historical China, Chapter 5 focuses on the origins of military degree (*wuju*) holders in the Qing dynasty as well as the historical roots of regional variation in warrior culture, as represented by military-career aspirations and a preference for the use of force to resolve disputes. A common view among historians is that due to Confucian orthodoxy, Chinese society prized the civilian over the martial, or the *wen* over the *wu*, for the exercise of state power as well as for the resolution of disputes. In this view, young Chinese men were not supposed to have any aspiration for the acquisition of warrior skills or a preference for a military career, which would make it hard for the imperial government to recruit the needed warriors for defense. However, this view is not supported by empirical evidence. Young men in many prefectures studied martial arts and at least during the Qing prepared sat for the military service examinations that would qualify them for appointment as an officer. Every era produced military leaders and war heroes, providing role models for the young. These warriors were distributed unevenly across regions, with a disproportionate number coming from northern China. For example, as noted in Chapter 6, Shaanxi and Gansu had a reputation for producing soldiers and military leaders. Even though such variation is well-known, there are few systematic studies of its origins.

Chapter 5 demonstrates that more exposure to war in the past led to higher measures of warrior culture. Using data for 257 prefectures, the authors first show that there was a positive correlation between the frequency of war in the past and its production of military elites. The latter is measured by the number of passers of the Qing military exams (*wuju*) in the eighteenth and nineteenth centuries. Using each prefecture's distance to strategic locations as an instrumental variable, they show the link between a prefecture's past military conflicts and its number of passers to be causal. They also illustrate that during the Qing, the inhabitants of prefectures that had experienced more wars in the past exhibited a higher tendency to use violence to resolve conflicts (as reflected by a higher frequency of homicide cases), but that there were no significant differences between prefectures in economic development according to their historical frequency of wars, population density or the number of civil exam passers. Even today, regions with greater historical war exposure have more martial arts schools but fewer elementary and middle schools per million population, suggesting a persistent impact of past wars on warrior culture formation and on human capital investment.

Chapter 6 turns the focus from military degree holders to officers, examining the deployment and place of origin of Qing military officers by province. During the nineteenth century, the Qing experienced domestic turmoil and foreign incursions. Notable examples include the Taiping Rebellion (1850–1862) and the First Opium War (1839–1842). Previous studies of the military during this period have focused on such major figures as Zeng Guofan or Zuo Zongtang, the causes and consequences of major events like wars and rebellions, and the mostly unsuccessful late Qing efforts to reform the military. Chen and Campbell take a different approach, using comprehensive data on the high-, mid- and low-ranked military officers from 1786 to 1908, sourced from the quarterly rosters *Zhongshu Beilan,* to look at changes over time in where officers were from and where they were deployed. Geographic patterns of officer deployment provide insight into the military priorities of the Qing state. The number of officers deployed to a location is shown to be highly correlated with the number of troops stationed there, thus it is an index of resources.

Chen and Campbell show in Chapter 6 that even though the First Opium War exposed the vulnerability of the Qing to naval power, it did not result in a redeployment of military personnel to maritime defense and the coasts. It was only after the rise of the Hunan army veterans in the military and civil, established after the conclusion of the Taiping Rebellion, that there was a clear shift in the allocation of resources to the southeast coast, away from the frontiers in the west and northwest. The chapter also documents the influx of Hunan-origin officers into the different ranks following the end of the Taiping, and the implications of the changes over the nineteenth century for the implementation of the rule of avoidance for military officers, according to which mid-ranked and senior officers were not supposed to serve within 500 *li* of their hometown. They show that for the first half of the nineteenth century, enforcement of the rule of avoidance initially weakened, so that more officers were serving close to their place of origin. The rule was generally less likely to be enforced in frontier regions. The share of officers serving in their home provinces fell after the Taiping, but this was mainly due to the massive influx of Hunan-origin officers at every rank and in every location. Enforcement declined again after the wave of Hunan army veterans passed.

Chapter 7, by Cameron Campbell and Shuaiqi Gao, studies the operation of Qing bureaucracy, in particular, its ability or willingness to enforce its own rules for the evaluation and dismissal of civil officials. An orderly, rule-based bureaucracy is central to the state's ability to enforce its will. While the general impression is that in the nineteenth century, the Qing bureaucracy became less effective over time, most of the evidence is anecdotal, and there have been few large-scale studies over extended periods of time. The relationship between disasters and careers is a useful index of rule enforcement within the bureaucracy because personnel regulations specify the responsibility of county magistrates for preventing, reporting, and responding to disasters, and their response was assessed during their performance evaluations. The regulations were clearest for locust infestations since they were considered preventable. Their occurrence was regarded as *prima facie* evidence of poor performance and was supposed to result in immediate termination. The etiology of other disasters was more complex, and blame was harder to ascribe.

Accordingly, Chapter 7 investigates the influence of natural disasters including famines, floods, infestations, epidemics, and droughts on the careers of county magistrates in the Qing between 1830 and 1905 to see whether they increased the chances that a career would end and whether the effects changed over time. Specifically, it combines county-level annual data on disasters with information on the careers of civil officials from the *Jinshenlu* to examine whether the occurrence of one of these disasters raised the chances that a magistrate's career would end in the current or next year, whether these effects changed over time, and whether they were stronger for holders of exam degrees, or in counties regarded by the central government as more complex or difficult to administer and therefore subject to greater oversight. It finds that infestations and famines increased the chances of termination, at least before 1880, and that effects did not differ according to whether an official had an exam degree, or the county was subject to special attention. By this measure, in other words, the Qing did enforce some basic rules related to personnel management for much of the nineteenth century.

## 1.4 Part III: State Capacity, Fiscal and Financial Development

The four chapters in Part III study fiscal and financial development in imperial China over different time periods. State capacity is a recurring theme. As revenue and expenditure underpinned an imperial state's ability to achieve its goals, understanding them provides insights into state capacity. Chapter 8 examines the long-term impact of the fiscal and financial crises which followed three major defeats of the Song army between 1039 and 1042. Chapter 9 picks up where Chapter 8 leaves off. After the demise of the Song and Yuan dynasties, the Chinese path toward a fiscal state was largely reversed, retrogressing into a traditional agrarian structure during the Ming and Qing dynasties. Chapter 9 constructs a 500-year time series of fiscal revenue and expenditure, to help better understand this process.

Chapter 10 follows up on the issues covered in Chapters 8 and 9 by turning to the question of why Qing China failed to establish fiscal federalism between the central and local governments. Chapter 11 focuses on the rise and fall of the Shanxi traditional banks (*piaohao*) that played a role in the finances of the Qing Empire in the late nineteenth century and early twentieth century. Together, Chapters 10 and 11 show that the political and economic problems which had undermined the development of the Song fiscal state, such as the lack of credible commitments on the part of the government, became far more serious in the succeeding dynasties.

In Chapter 8, William Guanglin Liu and Kai Wan Kwan evaluate the state capacity of the Northern Song (960–1126 CE) in terms of its fiscal and financial capability, focusing on times of war in the eleventh century. By collecting quantitative and qualitative data from extensive historical materials, this chapter evaluates both the extent of fiscal and financial crises caused by the prolonged war with the Tangut state and the effectiveness of the changing fiscal and monetary policies of the Song state. In 1039 CE, the conflict between the Northern Song and the Western Xia (1038–1227 CE) escalated into a large-scale war on the northwestern frontier of Northern Song China. From 1039 to 1042 CE, the Song armies suffered three major defeats on the battlefield: Sanchuankou, Haoshuichuan, and Dingchuan Fort. While the Song state suffered catastrophic military defeats on the battlefield, it also experienced fiscal and financial crises directly provoked by the war. To cope with the war-induced fiscal crises, the Northern Song state developed the *ruzhong* provisioning system, under which the government bought grain and fodder for the military from civilian suppliers who were issued vouchers for salt, tea, and other monopoly commodities. These vouchers developed into a form of public debt for the government and security in the secondary market at Kaifeng.

While such fiscal and financial innovations were remarkable, the over-issuance of vouchers in the face of escalating crisis damaged the credibility of these financial instruments given the dwindling reserves of commodities and cash reserves. Although the Song state tried various means of controlling the issuance of vouchers and increased the amount of monopoly commodities or cash reserves to shore up the value of the vouchers, their efforts achieved only limited success. Ultimately, Northern Song's resort to the debasement of copper currencies led to significant inflation as well as a massive reduction in the value and popularity of vouchers in the market. As with technological innovation studied in Chapter 2 of this volume, the results of the chapter suggest that fiscal and financial innovation were also more likely to develop in times of political fragmentation, though these innovations were not always successful.

Chapter 9 by Hanhui Guan, Debin Ma, and Runzhuo Zhai examines the public finances of the Ming and Qing dynasties. They construct a nearly 500-year series of the central government's fiscal revenue and expenditure for Ming and Qing China. National total and per capita fiscal revenues, both in nominal and real terms, are estimated from historical documents, with the total revenue itemized by type: in-kind versus monetary revenue, land versus commercial taxes, direct versus indirect taxes, and seigniorage revenue. This work represents the first attempt to construct such a long-time series based on several primary sources.

The time series indicates a long-term trend of decline in real per capita fiscal revenue, an increasing trend for the ratio of land taxes, as well as a rising trend toward monetization of taxation. The 500-year time series also allows us to make a direct comparison with England, which emerged as the world's first modern fiscal state from the late seventeenth century onward. Converted into comparable measures, their estimates reveal that the divergence in fiscal state capacity between England and China had clearly emerged by the seventeenth century and only widened further thereafter.

For Chapter 10, Yu Hao and Kevin Zhengcheng Liu turn to the question of why Qing China failed to establish fiscal federalism between the central and local governments. They start with the premise that the ability to tax and provide public goods is essential for economic and political development. Fiscal capacity concerns not only tax collection but also fiscal budgeting and spending allocation among different layers of government. In these aspects, Qing China stood in stark contrast with the fiscal prowess that accompanied the emergence of the modern centralized fiscal state in the West. Economic historians now agree that the pre-modern Chinese state was much weaker in fiscal capacity than its European counterparts. In addition, the intra-government fiscal arrangement was characterized by a "dual-track fiscal system" in which a formal system with central revenue and expenditure coexisted with an informal local fiscal system based on miscellaneous extra-legal levies. Such fragmented local administration also impeded resource mobilization and the building of fiscal capacity. This chapter highlights the commitment problem between different levels of government. Due to the lack of formal institutions to constrain opportunistic behavior by higher-level governments, the latter often extracted lower-level revenues and at the same time pushed down spending responsibilities to the lower levels.

Chapter 11 by Wentian Diao, Jinyan Hu, and Chicheng Ma traces the rise and fall of Shanxi banks (*piaohao*) in the nineteenth and early twentieth centuries. It looks at how by engaging in long-distance financial transactions, these influential financial institutions promoted cross-regional trade and, consequently, foster economic development. However, the successful execution of long-distance financial transactions requires substantial market demand, reliable credit, and robust risk management. In modern society, legal systems that facilitate contract enforcement can provide credit support for financial institutions by protecting private property rights. Cross-regional instant communication technologies, such as telegrams and telephones, can assist financial institutions in promptly acquiring information to identify risks. Nevertheless, those modern legal systems and advanced communication technologies are products of the post-Industrial Revolution era, and they cannot explain the development of long-distance financial transactions and the expansion of cross-regional financial institutions that existed in pre-modern societies. Current studies have highlighted the important role of political connections.

While there is extensive anecdotal evidence, empirical evidence is still lacking on how political connections shaped the rise and fall of influential financial institutions and their long-distance transactions in pre-modern society. In pre-modern society, China already had developed financial markets without modern legal and technological supports, featuring not only the emergence of paper currency but also various financial institutions engaged in different financial activities. Among these institutions, Shanxi *piaohao*—stood out as the largest group of banking institutions with the most extensive network across the country. These banks were named for Shanxi, the home province of their operators. The nationwide branch networks reached as far as 2000 km away from their headquarters. Shanxi banks provided loans for small native banks and long-distance remittance for cross-regional merchants and played a crucial role in helping the provincial government transfer local tax revenues to Beijing, the national capital.

Despite this success, the Shanxi banks came to an end shortly after the collapse of the Qing Dynasty in 1911, just one hundred years after its first appearance in 1823. This chapter studies how political connections shaped the rise and fall of the Shanxi banks and finds that these institutions opened more branches in provinces where the provincial governors came from Shanxi. However, Shanxi banks declined after political connections were broken due to the collapse of the Qing dynasty in 1911, and the decline was faster in provinces that had been governed by more Shanxi officials than in the other regions. Exploring the reasons behind the rise and fall of these financial houses will help us understand banking development in a pre-modern society characterized by an authoritarian regime lacking legal and technological support.

## 1.5 Part V: Religion and Agricultural Development

Part V turns to culture and religion. In Chapter 12, Ying Bai and Xiaoyu Bian examine the impact of the diffusion of Protestantism on agricultural development in China, using a dataset at the prefecture level. Inspired by Max Weber's classic work, social scientists have studied the influence of Protestantism on economic prosperity. This research has shown that the impact of Protestantism on economic development extends beyond Protestant ethics and operates through various other channels. Considering that 80–90% of the total population in China at that time resided in rural areas and were engaged in agriculture, it is important to explore the influence of Protestantism on the rural and agricultural sectors of China. Like their efforts in the urban sector, Protestant missionaries also endeavored to disseminate knowledge in rural China from the middle nineteenth century onward, which had the potential to benefit agricultural development. The hope was that once witnessing agricultural productivity gains, farmers would embrace the Protestant faith with gratitude. Consequently, Protestant missionaries became a medium for spreading Western agricultural knowledge, to a certain extent.

Bai and Bian find a significantly positive effect of Protestantism on agricultural productivity, implying that Protestant missionaries did introduce useful Western knowledge that contributed to agricultural development. However, this effect is weaker once the impact of organic fertilizers, small plot sizes, and rice cultivation is controlled for, highlighting that the effectiveness of this "useful" knowledge differs in an environment that greatly contrasts with Europe and the US. These results align with the "inappropriate technology hypothesis," which suggests that customizing technology to local conditions hinders its diffusion and productivity benefits in other contexts. This work by Bai and Bian nonetheless enriches our understanding of how Christian missionaries contributed to China's modernization.

## 1.6 Conclusion

The quantitative history of China is at a crossroads. It is transitioning from relatively small-dataset studies based on manually constructed bespoke datasets using traditional econometric techniques to construction of large general-purpose datasets by application of OCR and AI, and analysis of them by novel econometric approaches. It is moving from narrowly focused studies of specific regions, eras, or phenomena, to large-scale comparative studies using national data spanning centuries or millennia. Taken together, the chapters in this volume exemplify this transition. They include more traditional studies, as well as studies that make use of large newly constructed datasets and which generalize at a national level, in some cases over long periods of time.

For this transition to be successful, we need to further develop infrastructure for recruitment, training, dataset construction and dissemination, and venues for sharing results. CQH has already taken the lead in the recruitment and training of the next generation of quantitative history researchers. Through its ongoing annual summer school programs since 2013, it has exposed many young scholars to quantitative history. Participants in these programs have gone on to conduct pioneering studies on interesting and important questions about the history of development in China from its very beginning. CQH and its affiliates are also leading efforts to construct massive new datasets and make them available to the field. We also look forward to additional conferences and workshops like the one that yielded this volume, so we can build a community of quantitative historians of China, and by involving scholars who work in other parts of the world, promote comparative research and increase the visibility of our own work.

**Acknowledgements** We gratefully acknowledge the financial support as part of the Areas of Excellence (AoE) Scheme (Project number: AoE/B-704/22-R) awarded by the Research Grants Council). This edited volume comes out of the AoE—Quantitative History Conference organized and held at the Centre for Quantitative History (CQH) on October 25-26, 2023. Our volume overall benefited from the special invited discussants Ting Chen, Jin Li, Tetsuji Okazaki, Paul Seabright, Tuan-Hwee Sng, and Duoduo Xu. Other participants also contributed to the conference including Chen Lin, Jed O. Kaplan, Ghassan Moazzin, Matthew Noellert, and Jiongyi Xue.

We would like to thank among others the enormous administrative support for both the conference and volume from Beth Kwok and Danni Lo at the CQH. Our special thanks go to George W. Russell who has provided superb and timely editorial assistance and feedback for the entire volume. At the Springer publisher, we want to thank the support from Tetsuji Okazaki, the Editor of the Studies in Economic History and Juno Kawakami, the Publishing Editor as well as two thoughtful review reports on our proposal and sample chapters.

## References

Basu, Susanto, and David N. Weil. 1998. Appropriate Technology and Growth. *The Quarterly Journal of Economics* 113 (4): 1025–1054.

Fernández-Villaverde, Jesús, Mark Koyama, Youhong Lin, Tuan-Hwee Sng. 2023. The Fractured-Land Hypothesis. *The Quarterly Journal of Economics* 138 (2): 1173–1231.

Ho, Ping-ti. 1962. *The Ladder of Success in Imperial China.* New York City: Columbia University Press.

李國祁 (Li Guoqi) and 周天生(Zhou Tiansheng). 1974. 清代基层地方人事嬗遞現象之量化分 (The Quantitative Analysis of Personnel Transition in Qing Local Governance). 國立台灣師範大學歷學報 *(History Journal of National Taiwan Normal University)* 2: 301–383.

Lee, James, and Cameron Campbell. 1997. *Fate and Fortune in Late Imperial China.* Cambridge: Cambridge University Press.
Liu, Ts'ui-jung. 1978. Chinese Genealogies as a Source for the Study of Historical Demography. *Studies and Essays in Commemoration of the Golden Jubilee of the Academia Sinica* (June): 849–870.
Needham, Joseph. 1954. *Science and Civilization in China,* vol. 1. Cambridge: Cambridge University Press.
Wolf, Arthur P., and Chieh-shang Huang. 1980. *Marriage and Adoption in China.* Stanford: Stanford University Press.

**Zhiwu Chen** is Chair and Cheng Yu-Tung Professor in Finance at The University of Hong Kong (HKU). He currently serves as director of both Hong Kong Institute for the Humanities and Social Sciences (HKIHSS) and Centre for Quantitative History (CQH). His research covers finance theory, the sociology of finance, economic history, quantitative history, emerging markets, as well as China's economy and capital markets. He was a former Professor of Finance at Yale University (1999–2017) and a Special-Term Visiting Professor at Peking University and Tsinghua University. In 2013, he started the annual Summer School for Quantitative History cum International Symposium on Quantitative History at Tsinghua University and continues to organize them at Peking University, with the goal of promoting quantitative research on the history of China and beyond.

**Cameron Campbell** is Chair Professor in the Division of Social Science at The Hong Kong University of Science and Technology (HKUST). He is also a Distinguished Professor in the School of History and Culture at Central China Normal University. His research focuses on demography, stratification and inequality in historical China and in comparative perspective. For his research, he and his collaborators in the Lee-Campbell Group construct, analyze, and publicly release datasets constructed from archival and other sources. He was a Fellow of the Center for Advanced Study in the Behavioral Sciences at Stanford 2022–23, and a Guggenheim Fellow in 2004–2005. He was a Changjiang Scholar at Central China Normal University from 2017 to 2020.

**Debin Ma** is a Professor of Economics at Fudan University, Shanghai China and a Quondam Fellow at All Souls College, Oxford University. His main expertise is on the long-term economic growth of East Asia, especially China. His research interests include global history; the international comparison of living standards; institutions, legal traditions, and ideology; human capital and productivity; and the economic history of the silk industry. He has published widely on Asian and comparative economic history and is the co-editor of the *Cambridge Economic History of China.*

# Part I
# War, Technology and the Needham Puzzle

# Chapter 2
# War and Demand for Technology: How Unification Disincentivized Innovations in Historical China

**Zhiwu Chen, Senhao Hu, and Zhan Lin**

## 2.1 Introduction

It has long been a fascination among comparative historians as to why the Industrial Revolution occurred in Britain in the late eighteenth century but not in China—the so-called Needham Puzzle. According to Needham (1954), China's inventions in science and technology were unmatched by any other country from the sixth century BCE to the fourteenth century CE; but, thereafter, it has been the West that led in technological advancement, culminating in the Great Divergence in economic and other performance measures between China and the West, starting before 1800 CE (Pomeranz 2001).

As Lowrey and Baumol (2013) note,

> For some sixteen centuries, … China was the source of … inventions that included a vast variety of prospectively valuable novelties as diverse as printing, the blast furnace, the spinning wheel, the wheelbarrow, and playing cards, in addition to the more widely recognized gunpowder and compass. … All of this gives rise to a great mystery, the apparent fact that none, or almost none, of these early Chinese inventions seems to have been put to effective use and employed to its full potential… (p. 2)

Z. Chen
Centre for Quantitative History, Faculty of Business and Economics; Hong Kong Institute for the Humanities and Social Sciences, The University of Hong Kong, Hong Kong, China
e-mail: zhiwu.chen@hku.hk

S. Hu (✉)
Hong Kong Institute for the Humanities and Social Sciences, The University of Hong Kong, Hong Kong, China
e-mail: senhao@connect.hku.hk

Z. Lin
Institute of Qing History, Renmin University of China, Beijing, China
e-mail: zhan.lin@ruc.edu.cn



Z. Chen et al. (eds.), *Quantitative History of China*, Studies in Economic History,
https://doi.org/10.1007/978-981-96-8272-0_2

So, it was not the supply of inventions that caused the Industrial Revolution to happen elsewhere, but the absence of demand. Why didn't Chinese society have innovative entrepreneurs to transform inventions into effective applications, even during its inventive heyday? Needham (1954)and Lin (1995) looked for answers in both the conservative Confucian culture and the civil service exams for government recruiting (*keju*), whereas Landes (1999) attributed it to the Chinese state that was limiting. Lowrey and Baumol claim China's scarcity of innovative entrepreneurs was due to its socioeconomic institutions that incentivized businessmen and upper-tail human capital to direct their efforts elsewhere, instead of promoting wider and deeper uses of technological discoveries.

In this and the chapter to follow, rather than searching through culture and institutions, we focus on the negative impact of unification on China's demand for military technology to explain the Needham Puzzle. Our analysis consists of two parts. First, the present chapter uses macro-level historical data on war and military technological innovations to demonstrate that since the Qin dynasty (221–206 BCE), China has remained largely unified (except for some temporary interruptions), which has generally meant fewer external wars per year. It was usually foreign wars, not internal conflicts, that stimulated technological innovations, which is why too much unification too early led to depressed demand for technology and hence fewer actual innovations. Thus, the war channel is crucial through which unification translated into less innovativeness on the technology front. Second, the next chapter relies on archaeological data on military grave goods from 1700 BCE to 589 CE to show, at the micro-level, that war frequency determined the level of demand for technology: regions facing higher war threats adopted new technology more actively in early historical China. Taken together, these two chapters suggest that, at least as one of the explanatory factors, China's persistent unification, as opposed to Europe's long-lasting division into many warring states since the fall of the Roman Empire in 476 CE, reduced the level of inter-state competition (military and otherwise), leading to lower demand for technology and fewer innovative entrepreneurs in historical China.

Why do we use inter-state military competition to explain the Needham Puzzle and shed light on the great divergence debate, especially by going back to early historical China? Understandably, if there is one place where the demand for applications of new technology should be the highest, it should be the battlefield "because the penalty for failing to do so can be immediate and fatal" (Parker 1996, 2). That is the case if and when war threats were so much at the center of human attention, such as for the residents of China during the Warring States (481–221 BCE) and the Eastern and Western Jin dynasties (266–420 CE) and of Europe in the late medieval and early modern times (Hoffman 2012; Andrade 2016). Indeed, "The story of the human race is War. Except for brief and precarious interludes there has never been peace in the world" (Churchill 2013). Hoffman (2012) also points out the importance of violence in explaining why Europe forged ahead of Eurasia in modern times: the desire to survive wars is what drove Europeans to engage in technological discovery and relentless applications of new innovations. Gross and Sampat (2022) document that as recently as in the twentieth century, World War II played a key role in mobilizing and stimulating research and development in technologies and medical treatments that not only helped win the war but also changed civilian life forever; the wartime research and application model was so successful that it has served as the template for the war and post-war innovation policies such as the Manhattan Project. The pattern that warfare triggered innovations, and their quick adoptions have been known to historians, who call the pattern the "challenge–response dynamic" (Parker 1996).

One might also find the choice of inter-state military competition in the context of historical China to be puzzling as the Chinese culture has been thought to be non-military or anti-military, based on readings of Warring States texts (e.g., Kierman and Fairbank 1974). For example, in *The Analects,* Confucius was, as quoted below, supposed to accept the need for warfare but play down its importance (Slingerland 2003, p. 128):

> Zigong asked about governing.
>
> The Master said, 'Simply make sure there is sufficient food, sufficient armaments, and that you have the confidence of the people.'
>
> Zigong said, 'If sacrificing one of these three things became unavoidable, which would you sacrifice first?'
>
> The Master replied, 'I would sacrifice the armaments.'
>
> Zigong said, 'If sacrificing one of the two remaining things became unavoidable, which would you sacrifice next?'
>
> The Master replied, 'I would sacrifice the food. Death has always been with us …'

This dialogue has been taken to exemplify the Confucian aversion to military action, prizing peace over violence, or the *wen* over the *wu*. However, this historical text-based view on Chinese culture is hardly supported by empirical evidence. For example, Chen et al. (2023) show that war triggered the emergence of Chinese civilization in the mid to late Neolithic (5000–1700 BCE) and warfare played as much of a role in China's development history as in the West. China has had a long history of military conflicts for it would otherwise have not been able to establish its long martial arts tradition (Chen et al. 2024, this volume) or maintain unification for so long.

In a related study, Andrade (2016) uses the comparative development history of gunpowder, firearm, and cannon technologies after the tenth century to showcase how the challenge–response dynamic worked to eventually create a divergence in military technology between China and Europe. In particular, he details how the intensive wars during the 1350–1450 CE transition from the Yuan (1271–1368 CE) to the Ming dynasty (1368–1644 CE) gave rise to heightened demand for firearms innovations, leading to their extensive adoption and use on battlefields. The early Ming even required 10% of the troops to carry guns and by the late 1400s, this proportion had risen to 30% (Andrade 2016, 4). However, for the subsequent century from 1450 to 1550, the Ming had relative peace with few external wars, while Europe was engaged in more frequent and more violent large-scale warfare, resulting in fewer gun innovations in China but fueling fast advancements in Europe.

In this and the subsequent chapter, we go beyond gunpowder technology, examine the evolution of broader military technological innovations in connection with war frequency, and conduct systematic testing on the "challenge–response dynamic". Our central claim is that from 221 BCE to 1840 CE, China was at least moderately unified for 1626 out of the 2061 years (78.89% of the time) but not so during the other years. Also, even during these moderately unified years, the degree of unification varied. Although China was not short of external wars during these years, unification did substantially reduce foreign war frequency, lowering the demand for new military technology, and stifling whatever dynamism there was for technological innovations and adoptions.

In Sect. 2.2, we present the unification measure, war threats, and technological innovations during different Chinese periods. Section 2.3 describes the co-moving trends of war frequency and inventiveness/innovativeness in historical China, providing macro evidence for our claim that the unification of China stifled the demand for military technology. Section 2.4 offers concluding remarks.

## 2.2 Quantifying Unification and Technological Innovations

Figure 2.1 presents each historical period's number of external wars per year, fraction of years with external wars and HHI of unification, spanning 770 BCE to 1840 CE, where the war data comes from China's Military History Editorial Committee (2003). Note that an "external war" (interchangeably, a "foreign war") is defined as a military conflict between a state within China Proper and another polity (either inside or outside China Proper).[1] For example, during the Song dynasty (960–1279 CE), any military conflict between the Song and the Dali state, as well as between the Liao and the Dali state, is counted toward the Song period's total number of external wars.

The HHI was invented in economics and finance to measure the degree of intra-industry concentration, defined as the sum of squared percentage market shares of all firms in a given industry and taking a value between 0 and 1, with 1 indicating absolute monopoly by one company and no competition within the industry (see Calkins 1983 for a more detailed discussion). Here, we extend this index to capture the degree of unification in China, calculated as the sum of squared percentage territorial shares of all independent states that are located within, or overlap with, the 1820 landmass of the Qing dynasty (1644–1911 CE).[2] Following the practice in economics, we consider China to be divided when a period's Herfindahl Index is below 0.25, moderately unified when the Index is between 0.25 and 0.4, and unified when it is greater than or equal to 0.4. Applying the HHI to measure China's extent

[1] China Proper refers to the 18 mainstream provinces of the Qing dynasty and excludes the periphery. A province is the administrative unit directly under the central government.

[2] One can of course use the territorial map of China at other historical times or of present-day China, which may change the HHI value for a given historical period but will not affect the general time trends of unification versus division from 770 BCE to the present. We follow a common practice to take the 1820 landmass of Qing China as the benchmark for the definition of unification (Bai and Kung 2011).

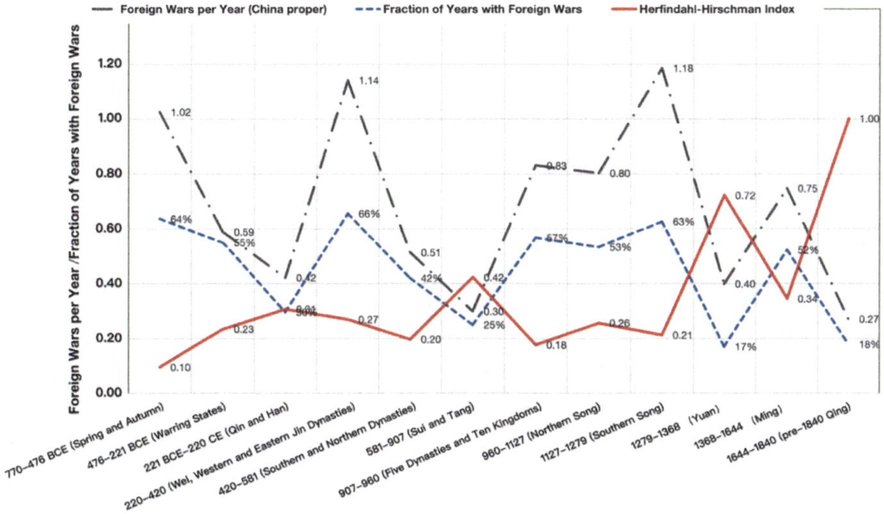


**Fig. 2.1** Degree of unification and foreign wars.[3] *Note* For each historical period, three measures are displayed: foreign wars per year and fraction of years with foreign wars, and the HHI (capturing the degree of China's unification, calculated as the sum of the squared percentage territorial shares of all independent states within the 1820 Qing China landmass, on a 0–1 scale), where each war that took place between a state inside the 1820 Qing landmass and any other state is counted as one toward to the period's total number of foreign wars. See Sect. 2.2 for the data sources

of unification helps avoid the ambiguity and vagueness caused by supplementing the traditional discourse with concrete data points.

Since historical war data does not start until 770 BCE, our periodization in Fig. 2.1 is as follows: the Spring and Autumn period (770–476 BCE), the Warring States (476–221 BCE), the Qin and Han (combining the Qin and Han dynasties 221 BCE-220 CE), the Wei, Western Jin, and Eastern Jin period (220–420 CE), the Southern and Northern Dynasties (420–581 CE), the Sui and Tang dynasties (581–906 CE), Five Dynasties and Ten Kingdoms (907–960 CE), the Northern Song (960–1127 CE), the Southern Song (1127–1279 CE), the Yuan (1279–1368 CE), the Ming (1368–1644 CE), and the pre-1840 Qing. We include only the Qing years up to 1840 as China became open to the outside world after the Opium War (1839–1842 CE), importing Western technologies and knowledge and entering a new era.

In Fig. 2.2, we introduce the main outcome variable of interest, the number of military technological innovations by period, to capture the country's innovativeness and inventiveness. Specifically, we divide each dynasty/period's total number of inventions and major innovations for battlefield weapons by its number of years of duration and by its population (of a time point in the given dynasty, depending on historical population availability for the period), normalized to "per 10 million

[3] In this chapter and Chap. 3, we use the time point 589 CE as the end of the Period of Division, following Lagerwey and Lü (2010). The Sui dynasty was established in 581 CE. Consequently, there are several years of overlap between the Period of Division and the Sui-Tang periods.

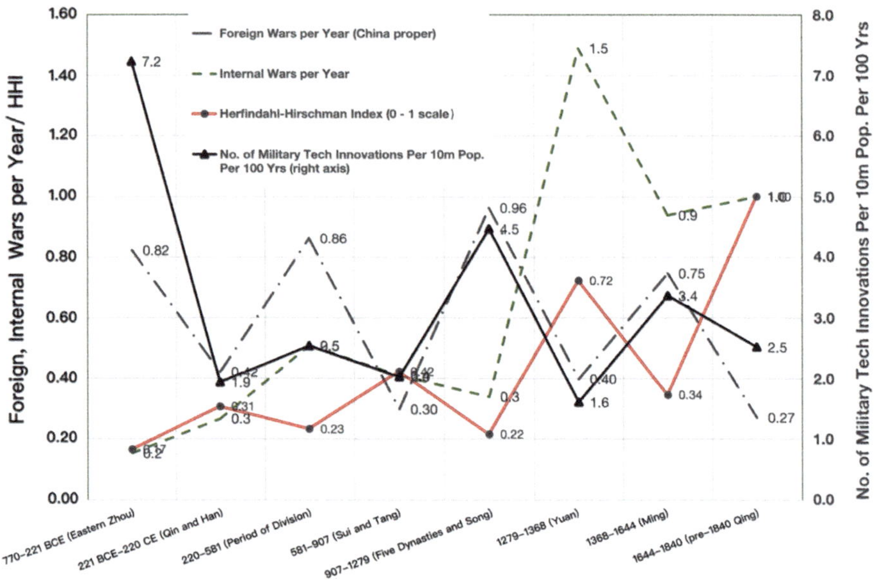


**Fig. 2.2** Foreign/internal wars and military technology innovations. *Note* For each historical period, four measures are displayed: foreign and internal wars per year, HHI of unification (on a 0–1 scale, with 1 indicating full unification relative to the 1820 Qing landmass), and number of military technological innovations per million population per 100 years. See the note to Fig. 2.1 for calculation methods and Sect. 2.2 for the data sources

population per 100 years" for the convenience of inter-dynasty comparability. The military technology data are from Wang (1998a, b), whereas the historical population data from Jiao (2007) for the 770–221 BCE period, Ge (2002) for pre-Ming periods, and Cao (2022) for the Ming and Qing dynasties. Because the timing resolution for many technological inventions and innovations is not precise, Fig. 2.2 is based on a coarser periodization: the Eastern Zhou (combining the Spring and Autumn and the Warring States periods, 770–221 BCE), the Qin and Han, the Period of Division (220 BCE–589 CE),[4] the Sui and Tang, the Five Dynasties and Song (907–1279 CE), the Yuan, the Ming, and pre-1840 Qing. Note that the Spring and Autumn period and the Warring States are treated as the Eastern Zhou dynasty as commonly referred in the literature and because many military technologies are only dated back to that overall period without further details.

[4] For the period after the collapse of the Han dynasties and before the reunification of China by the Sui dynasty, historians commonly use the term "Period of Division" to describe this war-torn era. (Lagerwey and Lü 2010).

## 2.3 Macro Evidence on War and Technological Innovations

With the main indices of interest constructed in Figs. 2.1 and 2.2, we can now discuss their correlations by going through each historical period and highlighting known innovations therein. Causality investigation is left for the next chapter.

### *2.3.1 Unification and Decline in War Threats*

The Western Zhou (1046–771 BCE) was powerful and able to hold its vassal states together. But, after King You of Zhou died in 771 BCE, his successor decided to move its capital to Luoyi in the following year, marking the end of the Western Zhou and the beginning of the Eastern Zhou. Soon after the move, the dynasty fell into a state of decline and chaos, with the new king losing control over the feudal states, resulting in those states gaining independence and fighting with each other. According to Chen (2009), there were 209 independent states at the peak level of division during the Spring and Autumn. For this period, China's HHI of unification is at 0.10 (i.e., 10% unification). With so many polities contending for domination and fighting over resources, it is no surprise that 301 inter-state wars are recorded for this period, which translates into 1.02 foreign conflicts per year, with 64% of the years having at least one inter-state war going on (Fig. 2.1).

By the early Warring States period, the number of remaining states shrank to about 35. Among them were the famous states of Qin, Chu, Jin, Qi, Song, Wu, Yue, Ba, Shu, Chen, Zheng, Cao, Cai, Lu, and Wei. As a result, the HHI of unification rose to 0.23, higher but still implying a high degree of division. This period records 150 inter-state wars, with 0.59 foreign conflicts per year and 55% of the years having at least one inter-state war. Thus, the Warring States period was substantially more peaceful than its predecessor, despite the name given to the period. The non-stop fighting led to the conquest of the weak states by the strong, continuously cutting the number of surviving states until the Qin state's final win over the Qi, to form the first moderately unified empire, the Qin dynasty, in 221 BCE.

The Qin dynasty was short-lived and full of intra-elite fighting, to be toppled by rebel forces in 206 BCE. After four years of chaotic civil wars, Liu Bang (256–195 BCE) came out victorious and founded the Han dynasty (202 BCE-220 CE) to unify the country again, ruling over a territory of 6.1 million $km^2$. As the Qin dynasty lasted only for 15 years, we combine the Qin and Han into one period, for which the HHI is 0.31, a moderate degree of unification of 31%. As a benefit of moderate unification, the Qin-Han dynasties faced much lower foreign threats with 185 external wars over the 441 years, yielding 0.42 foreign wars per year with 30% of the years in military conflicts with foreign states (Fig. 2.1). Thus, a higher degree of unification brought more peace to China, which gave the Han court and its bureaucracy more time to focus on institution-building for domestic governance. The reduced inter-state military competition of course meant lower demand for military technological innovations, which we will come back to in the next chapter.

After the Han fell in 220 CE, China was again disintegrated into multiple states, including the Three Kingdoms (220–280 CE) and the Western and Eastern Jin dynasties (266–420 CE), resulting in a decline in the HHI of unification to 0.27. The increased division created opportunities for more violent competition, recording 228 foreign wars at 1.14 wars per year and 66 of the years in such fighting, both at record highs.

The following period, the Southern and Northern dynasties (420–581 CE), marked a higher level of division, with its HHI of unification at 0.2, producing 82 inter-state wars, or 0.51 foreign wars per year, with 42 percent of the years in military conflict.

The Sui then unified the country in 581 CE but ended in 618 CE and was followed by the Tang dynasty (618–906 CE). The Tang expanded its territorial reach to 12.37 million $km^2$, bigger than any of its predecessors. Thus, its HHI rose to a new high of 42% unification. With so much land under its rule, the Sui and Tang fought 97 foreign wars at 0.3 wars per year (with 25% of the years in inter-state conflict), marking the most peaceful era since the beginning of Chinese history, which is a major reason for why this period is best known for its cultural creativity, with its residents famously indulging in poetry, painting, and other artistic expressions. However, its emperors suffered the highest regicide rate to date (Chen and Lin 2024, Chapter 4 in this volume), suggesting that the Tang may have had much peace from external threats but did not resolve its internal power-sharing challenges.

After the Tang ended in 906 CE, China entered a new period of chaos marked by the brief Five Dynasties and Ten Kingdoms (907–960 CE), with its HHI falling to 0.18, only 18% unification. It had 0.83 foreign wars per year and 57% of the years in external conflicts.

That brief episode of chaos was followed by a moderately unified Northern Song (960–1127 CE), which controlled only 22.6% of the Tang's territorial size, with 2.8 million $km^2$ in area, and co-existed with several competing states of almost equal power, including the Tangut Xi Xia (1038–1227 CE), the Jurchen Jin (1115–1234 CE), the Khitan Liao (916–1125 CE), and the Dali state (937–1253 CE). Its HHI of unification was 0.27, with 134 external wars at 0.8 wars per year and 53% of the years in such fighting.

The Song lost control of its northern half to the Jin state in 1127 CE and had to relocate its capital to Hangzhou, starting the Southern Song (1127–1279 CE). Its territory shrank to about 2 million $km^2$ as a result, which is why its HHI of unification declined to 0.21, implying that the Southern Song was really a "divided China", rather than a unified country. It recorded 180 external wars, with 1.18 foreign wars per year (the highest ever in Chinese history) and 63% of the years at war (Fig. 2.1).

The Yuan dynasty was established by the nomadic Mongols from the north and ruled China from 1271 to 1368 CE. As the Mongol empire is known to have expanded its reach as far as Europe and West Asia, it is no surprise that its territory was at a new high of 13.7 million $km^2$, leaving little room for foreign military conflicts. With a HHI of unification at 0.72 (a new peak), the Yuan recorded only 35 external wars, at 0.4 such conflicts per year and with 17% of the years at war. Some of these wars were self-inflicted as the Mongols attempted to extend their territorial control both westward toward Southeast Asia, West Asia, and Europe and eastward to Japan. Given that the Yuan court left international, especially maritime, trade alone, leading to a relative economic boom (Wang 1998a, b), this dynasty achieved more peace than its predecessors in terms of foreign threats but, as Fig. 2.2 shows, the Yuan experienced the highest frequency of internal conflicts (e.g., domestic revolts and peasant rebellions), at 1.5 occurrences per year, perhaps as a result of both the majority Han population being discontented and the ruling Mongols lacking experience in structuring and governing an ultra-large complex agrarian society.

Ultimately, the peasant uprising, known as the Red Turban Movement, led by Zhu Yuanzhang (1328–1398 CE), a Han Chinese peasant from Anhui, toppled the Yuan and established the Ming dynasty in 1368 CE. From the start, Zhu reversed the Mongol rulers' anti-Confucian policies and reinstated Confucianism as the state orthodoxy for structuring and governing society, which brought social stability domestically and widespread support for the Ming Empire, especially among ethnic-Han intellectuals. However, the Ming's territory was about 72.6% of the land area ruled under the Yuan, or 9.97 million km$^2$, with the HHI dropping to 0.34 (only a moderate unification of 34%), which exposed the Ming to more competing states along its borders. In addition, as the second half of the Ming was in the middle of the Little Ice Age, severe and long-lasting droughts not only caused more peasant rebellions internally but also prompted the steppe nomads north of China to attack the Central Plain and other parts of China (e.g., Bai and Kung 2011) in search of food. As a result, though China was moderately unified, the Ming experienced 206 foreign wars, at 0.75 wars per year and 52% of the years at war. Still, the Ming had more peace from foreign threats than the Song, though it suffered from more domestic instability as it experienced 0.9 internal conflicts per year, as opposed to the Song's 0.3 internal wars a year (Fig. 2.2).

The non-stop severe droughts from the late sixteenth to the mid-seventeenth century triggered so many peasant rebellions that the Ming was eventually overthrown by the rebel group led by peasant Li Zicheng (1606–1646 CE) in 1644 CE, whose army was in turn destroyed by the Manchurians who founded the Qing dynasty (1644–1911 CE). The Qing rulers were semi-nomads from Manchuria, whereas most of the Qing population was Han Chinese, which set up the stage for a tough early period as the Qing empire initially did not reign over all of China, with remnants of the Ming dynasty forming a rebel state called the Southern Ming (1644–1662 CE), plus a few peripheral frontier states. Fighting continued between them and the Qing as the latter tried to annex them. However, by the late seventeenth century, Qing China was unified again with a landmass of 13.16 million km$^2$ and a Herfindahl Index value of 1.00, making it even more externally peaceful than the Sui-Tang period. Prior to 1840, the Qing fought 53 external wars at 0.3 wars per year and with only 18% of the years in external conflict. However, the Qing had the second highest frequency of internal wars, with an average of 1.0 such wars per year.

Based on the above review, periods with higher unification levels are clearly associated with lower frequencies of external wars, supporting our hypothesis at the macro-level that higher unification brings more peace, a conclusion that should not be surprising as a major purpose of territorial unification was to reduce inter-state conflicts. In Table 2.1, we present the correlation matrix among the variables of interest, showing that over the historical periods, the HHI of unification has a correlation of −0.82 with the number of foreign wars, −0.71 with the number of foreign wars per year, and −0.82 with the fraction of years with external wars, but positive correlations with internal war measures (a correlation of 0.28 with the number of internal wars, 0.76 with the number of internal wars per year, and 0.59 with the fraction of years with internal wars). The significantly negative correlations between external and internal war measures suggest that a more unified China had fewer foreign wars per year (fewer foreign threats) but more internal conflicts (more internal threats as a bigger country made it more difficult to govern), implying the general difficulty of simultaneously cutting war threats internally and externally.

From Fig. 2.2, the total number of wars per year (including both external and internal conflicts) was the highest at 1.9 during the Yuan, followed by the Ming (1.6), the Period of Division (1.4), the Song and Qing (1.3), and the Eastern Zhou (1 war a year), whereas the Han and Tang dynasties were overall the most serene with 0.7 total wars per year. What may be surprising is the fact that once both types of war are considered, the Yuan and Ming dynasties were even more war-torn than the Warring States and the Period of Division, with the latter periods producing more external conflicts but higher tranquility domestically.

**Table 2.1** Correlation matrix among war measures and military technology innovations

| | No. of military tech innovations per 10 m pop. per 100 Yrs | No. of foreign wars | Foreign wars per year | Fraction of years with foreign wars | No. of internal wars | Internal wars per year | Fraction of years with internal Wars | Total no. of wars per year |
|---|---|---|---|---|---|---|---|---|
| No. of foreign wars | 0.84 | | | | | | | |
| Foreign wars per year | 0.62 | 0.87 | | | | | | |
| Fraction of years with foreign wars | 0.73 | 0.94 | 0.94 | | | | | |
| No. of internal wars | −0.32 | −0.30 | 0.00 | 0.01 | | | | |
| Internal wars per year | −0.50 | −0.72 | −0.42 | −0.59 | 0.43 | | | |
| Fraction of years with internal wars | −0.45 | −0.56 | −0.19 | −0.36 | 0.58 | 0.96 | | |
| Total no. of wars per year | −0.11 | −0.19 | 0.22 | 0.02 | 0.51 | 0.79 | 0.90 | |
| Herfindahl–Hirschman index | -0.50 | −0.82 | −0.71 | −0.82 | 0.28 | 0.76 | 0.59 | 0.32 |

### 2.3.2 Negative Impact of Unification on Demand for Technology

During historical times, survival from war and violence was the biggest challenge facing humanity, so military applications should have been a top priority for technological innovations. This is why we focus on the relation between war threats and weapon innovations to examine the claim that early unification depressed the demand for new technology. For each historical period, Fig. 2.2 displays the number of military technological inventions and innovations per 10 million population per 100 years, together with the HHI of unification and separate measures of external and internal wars per year, where China's military technological inventiveness and innovativeness are shown to be strongly positively correlated with each period's number of foreign wars (a correlation of 0.82 as presented in Table 2.1), frequency of foreign wars (0.62), and fraction of years with external wars (0.73), but negatively correlated with the degree of unification (−0.5) and number of internal wars per year (−0.5). It is interesting to note that external, but not internal, war threats caused more weapon innovations, perhaps because domestic conflicts could be resolved through governance and institutional reforms (rather than military hardware improvements), whereas foreign threats could be better addressed through weapon innovations.[5] Thus, at least at the macro-level, the data do suggest that unification depressed China's incentives to innovate in military technology.

Although a comprehensive review of China's extensive military technology history is beyond our scope, we would like to highlight relevant developments in each period, which will also help to provide the historical context for our quantitative analysis in the next chapter.

During China's Neolithic age (8000–1700 BCE), there were stone, jade, bone and wooden weapons. A breakthrough in battlefield instruments occurred with the introduction of bronze technology around 2000–1800 BCE (Andersson and Black 1925; Loehr 1949; Lee 2015). There is still some controversy as to whether this metallurgical technology was indigenously invented in China or adopted from abroad. However, with more archaeological sites excavated since the 1960s in Gansu, Qinghai and Xinjiang—regions near the Hexi Corridor and neighboring Central Asia, archaeologists have detected a close connection among the early second millennium BCE cultures in Central Asia, northwest China and the Central Plain, as demonstrated by

---

[5] Dincecco and Wang (2018) contrast the nature of war threats between Europe and China, to explain why democratic institutions developed in Europe while autocracy strengthened in China in history. In fragmented Europe, threats of conflict came both externally and internally, with the elites having plenty of exit options, forcing the ruler to make political concessions to the elites in order to retain their tax contributions and fight external threats. In unified autocratic China, however, the elites did not have exit options, so the emperor did not need to compromise but still taxed the elites heavily. Following their logic, we can also see why internal conflicts did not lead to military technological innovations, because the emperor could just repress domestic rebellions and other civil conflicts using some violence but not necessarily the best and most advanced weapons. In other words, internal conflicts were more of a governance challenge, whereas external threats were existential that required the deadliest response.

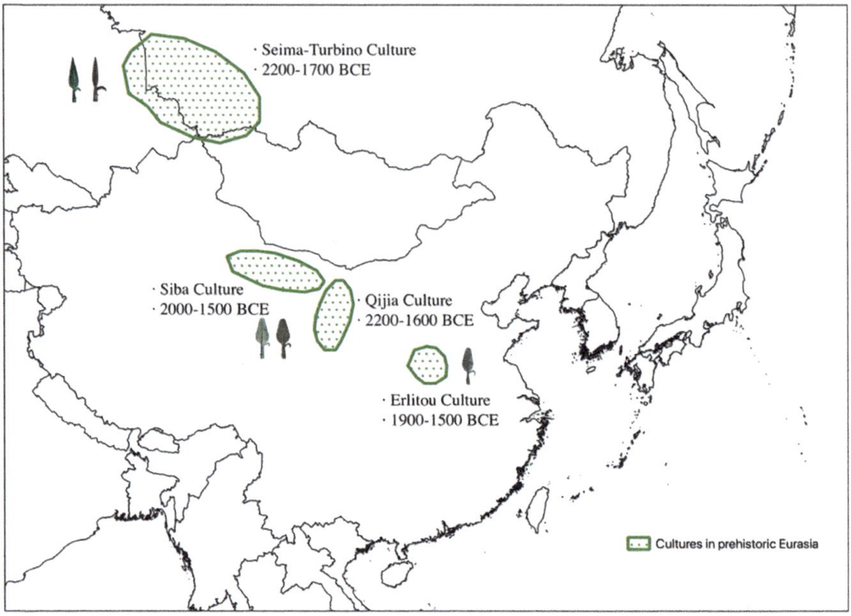


**Fig. 2.3** Cultures and Spread of Bronze Technology in Prehistoric Eurasia. *Note* For the exact locations of the cultures and spearheads in this figure, refer to Lin and Liu (2017). The country border shapefile is sourced from Esri (2022)

the close similarities in style among their bronze daggers and spearheads in Figs. 2.3 and 2.4.

In the 1960s, Chernykh (2010) collected archaeological evidence to indicate that the Seima-Turbino culture in the Altai Mountains of Central Asia was one of the earliest in eastern Eurasia to adopt metal goods and metalworking technologies from the Near East. An (1993) conducted a careful comparison of the bronze grave goods excavated from northwest China with their Central Asian counterparts (Fig. 2.4), to conjecture that bronze development by the Qijia culture (2300–1500 BCE) in Gansu and the Siba culture (1900–1500 BCE) in Qinghai must have been influenced by Central Asia through the proto-Silk Road (Fig. 2.3). By studying the bronze weapons of the Qijia and Erlitou culture (1900–1500 BCE), Fitzgerald-Huber (1995) not only corroborated An's conjecture but also pointed to a possible connection between Central Asia and Erlitou in the Central Plain. These discoveries were further confirmed by Sun and Han (1981)and Li (2000), who found the cultures of the early second millennium BCE along the Hexi corridor and of Central Asia to have made bronze using similar copper-arsenic alloys, as opposed to the later copper-tin alloys more commonly manufactured in China during the Shang (1600–1045 BCE) (Liu et al. 2016). Archaeologists have discovered at least 13 socketed spearheads with the Seima-Turbino culture genes in China, some of which are displayed in Fig. 2.4 (Lin and Liu 2017), where all ten spearheads share similar features, evidence that the

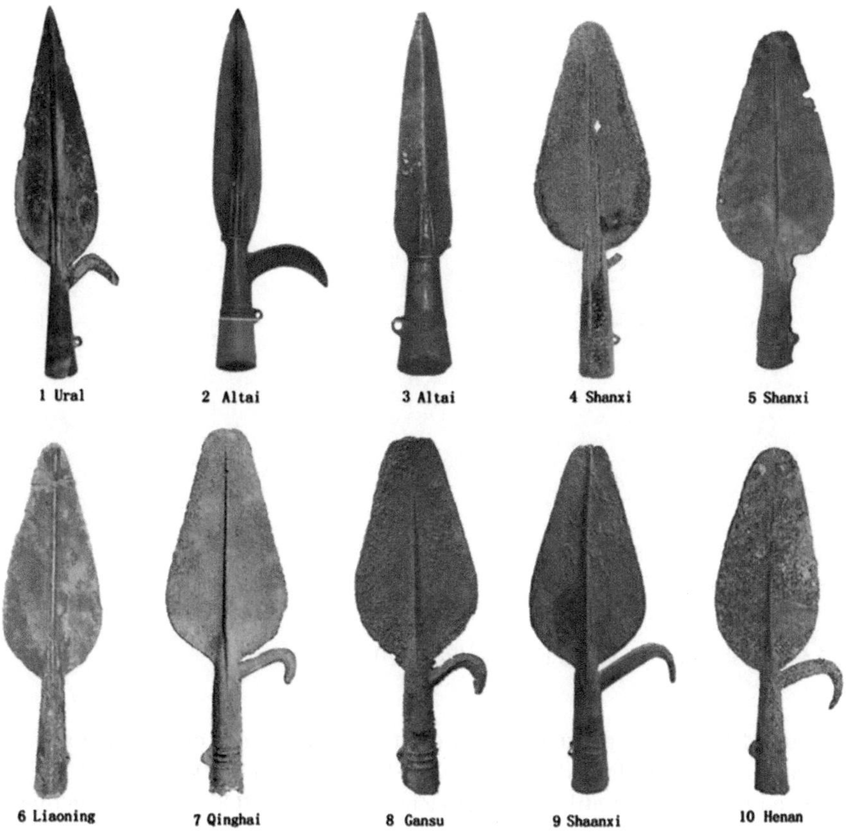


**Fig. 2.4** The Seima-Turbino spearheads from Ural Mountain and various imitations in northern China (Lin and Liu 2017)

metallurgical technology diffused and spread from Central Asia to China's Central Plain.[6]

Based on the China Archaeological Database (CADB),[7] about which more details are provided in the next chapter, we count each period's number of bronze grave goods excavated for each grid cell of 100 km $\times$ 100 km in area and plot its spatial distribution across all the cells in Fig. 2.5. From this figure, the time-sequential

[6] See Mei Jianjun (2000), *Copper and Bronze Metallurgy in Late Prehistoric Xinjiang: Its Cultural Context and Relationship with Neighbouring Regions.* BAR International Series 865, Oxford: Archaeopress; and Mei (2015), Qijia and Seima-Turbino: The Question of Early Contacts Between Northwest China and the Eurasian Steppe. *Bulletin-Museum of Far Eastern Antiquities* 75: 31–54.

[7] The China Archaeological Database (CADB), maintained at the Centre for Quantitative History at The University of Hong Kong, is an important source for our work in this and the next chapter. CADB compiles data from both available issues of the *Atlas of Chinese Cultural Relics* and all archaeological excavation reports published up to and including 2021. The database was still under construction at the time of writing this and the next chapter.

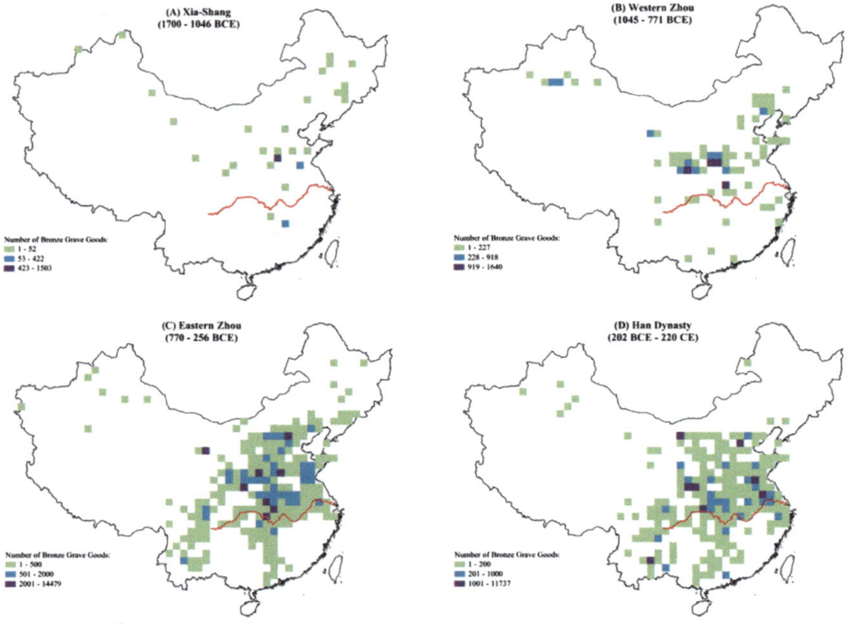


**Fig. 2.5** Distribution of bronze grave goods from 1700 BCE to 220 CE

evolution of the spatial distribution demonstrates that bronze objects first appeared in graves in northern China during the Xia-Shang period (1700–1046 BCE) and did not spread to the south until the Eastern Zhou (770–256 BCE); by the Han dynasty and especially during the Period of Division, they were everywhere across China.

The studies reviewed above also uncover a close connection between the introduction of bronze technology into China and battlefield applications, as these spearheads and daggers could not have been for production or daily-life purposes (see also Lee 2015, p. 70). To see this more systematically, in Fig. 2.6, we plot each grid cell's ratio of military bronze grave goods to all bronze grave goods, capturing the degree of the new technology's military application priority in the region, together with each cell's number of external wars, from 770 to 221 BCE. This chart illustrates a high positive correlation between the two: higher ratios of military bronze grave goods are associated with more foreign wars in the regions. Such early experience clearly hints at our broader claim about military applications being the first to consider for new technology development, even back in prehistoric and early historical times. Once bronze metallurgy was adopted for war-fighting purposes, it led to indigenous advancements in China, such as the invention of mold-casting technology (Mei 2000, 2015).

The chariot is another major military implement that is tied to the introduction of bronze technology. Initially invented between 3700 and 3200 BCE by the Maikop people living on the edges of the Caucasus mountains in Eastern Europe, this horse-drawn battle wagon quickly spread across the Eurasian steppes, including Central

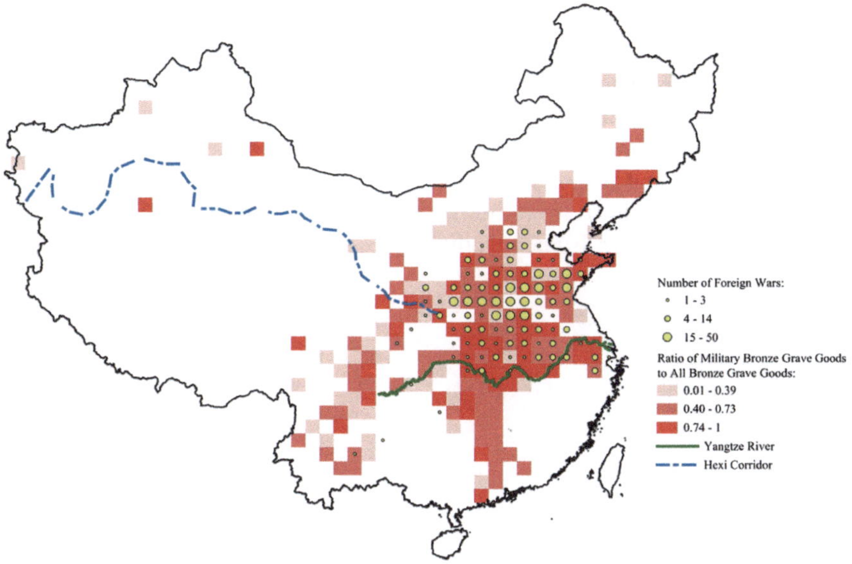


**Fig. 2.6** Foreign war and ratio of military to all bronze grave goods (770–221 BCE)

Asia; no later than 2100 BCE, some of the peoples southeast of the Ural mountains developed the chariot to maturity for long-range battlefield usage, carrying one to three bow-armed warriors while being pulled on two wheels by four horses; via the steppe peoples, the chariot came to China in its relatively mature form around 1200 BCE (Lee 2015). However, archaeological excavations have found chariot parts mostly in royal graves, suggesting narrow initial usage. Perhaps, "most Shang chariots must have been reserved for members of the ruling clan, high-ranking officials, and important officers dispersed across the battlefield" (Sawyer 2011, 365). Still, the Shang may have maintained a ratio of 30 infantrymen to one chariot, while this ratio expanded to about ten to one during the Zhou dynasty (1045–221 BCE). There is also speculation that chariot technology may have been responsible for the Zhou tribe's success in toppling the Shang dynasty around 1045 BCE, as the former was located on the Hexi corridor in northwest China and west of the Shang in the Central Plain, thus having better access to steppe-supplied horses (Lee 2015, 72).

Nonetheless, during the Spring and Autumn period (770–476 BCE), the fierce inter-state fighting (Fig. 2.1) generated heightened demand for advanced weapons, leading to the chariot and other bronze weapons playing a crucial role in the state armies (Lee 2015, 73). For example, Figs. 2.5 and 2.6 display the heavy battlefield applications of bronze technology during the Eastern Zhou and the Han dynasties.

Figure 2.7 illustrates bronze chariot fittings that have been excavated from the graves of different subperiods in the Autumn and Spring as well as the Warring States, where each feudal state's number of chariot fittings is shown together with its number of foreign wars, by subperiod. The two quantities are again highly correlated with one another. This episode of increased inter-state conflicts in some regions leading to intensified battlefield applications of the chariot supports our claim that war stimulates demand for technology.

We can also speculate that the spread of the chariot and other bronze weapons during the Western Zhou (1045–770 BCE) may have contributed to its own break-up in 770 BCE into multiple vassal states that continued their fighting during the subsequent Spring and Autumn and the Warring States periods, in which sense the new technology brought in from the Eurasian steppe, bronze making, changed the Chinese historical course. Ironically, the wide use of chariots increased interactions

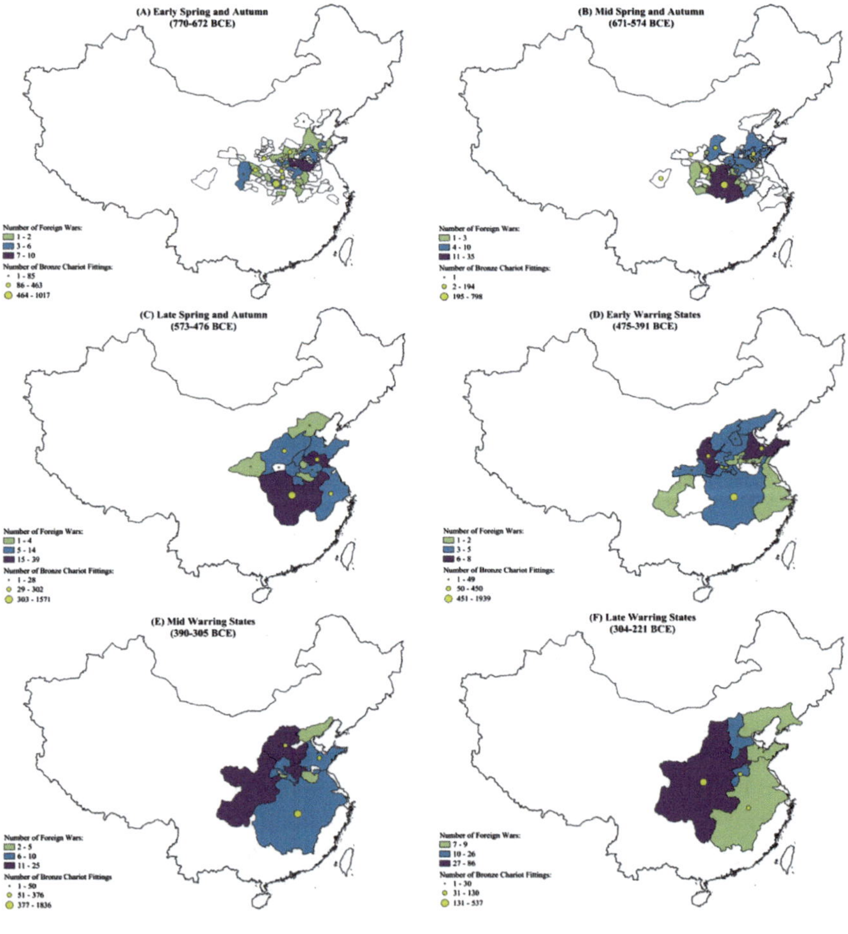


**Fig. 2.7** Distribution of foreign wars and bronze chariot fittings in Eastern Zhou (770–221 BCE). *Notes* The Eastern Zhou is divided into six subperiods: the early (770–672 BCE), middle (671–574 BCE), and late Spring and Autumn (573–476 BCE), and the early (475–391 BCE), middle (390–305 BCE), and late Warring States (304–221 BCE). The numbers of foreign wars and bronze chariot fittings are calculated for each feudal state by subperiod. The area map of each state in 770, 650, 505, 403, 305, and 230 BCE is used to represent the state's area during each respective subperiod.

between the settled and the nomadic steppe societies, making the farmer states in the Central Plain and other Chinese regions more dependent on the steppe for horses, and hence raising their chances of conflict with their nomadic neighbors in the north.

During the Warring States, significant structural improvements were made to the bronze halberd. Specifically, the blade end of the halberd was modified from a wide to a narrow shape, and from a straight to a curved design. Furthermore, the angle between the handle and the blade was increased to approximately 110 degrees. These changes served to enhance its hooking and killing effect. As a result, the halberd became widely used by infantry and cavalry fighters. In addition, in the southern vassal states of Wu, Yue, Chu, and others, a type of head with one or two spikes was affixed to the long handle. This innovation also enhanced the lethality of the halberd. Overall, these modifications proved to be highly effective in improving the functionality of the bronze halberd, making it a valuable weapon on the battlefield (Wang 1998a, b, 33).

The Eastern Zhou witnessed much progress in ironmaking technology, introducing new instruments of armament. Figure 2.8 demonstrates the spatial distribution of excavated iron grave goods by period based on our CADB, indicating possible steppe origins of this metal technology along the same route as for the bronze. By the Han dynasty (206–220 BCE), iron objects were all over China, marking the technology's full adoption everywhere.

As shown in Fig. 2.2, the Eastern Zhou was the most war-torn period that was also the most inventive as it yielded 7.2 military technological innovations per 10 million population per 100 years.

Thanks to advancements in metallurgy, especially ironmaking, the cavalry had become a major force by the Qin and Han, altering the roles of the chariot (Wang 1998a, b, 75). The excavation of Liu Sheng's grave of the Western Han dynasty (206 BCE-9 CE) in Mancheng County, Hebei province, uncovered 441 arrowheads, of which only 70 were crafted from bronze and the remaining 371 were made of iron, indicating that the use of iron far exceeded that of bronze by this time (Wang Zhaocun 1998b, 66). During the Western Han, a flat-bladed sword was created from solid carburized steel using a method introduced during the late Warring States.

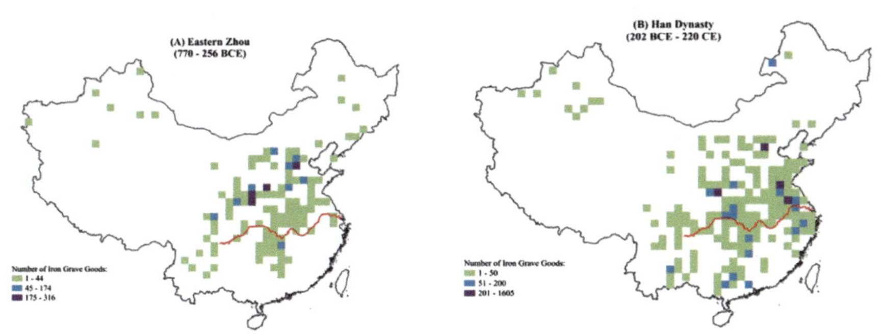


**Fig. 2.8** Distribution of iron grave goods from 770 BCE to 220 CE

Subsequently, tempered steel was developed for sword making during the Middle Western Han. Notably, Liu Sheng's sword, retrieved from the Han grave, boasts a length of 104.8 cm, with steel made using a technique that involved repeated heating, carburizing, folding, beating, and cooling, to harden and sharpen the blade. The sword struck an ideal balance between rigidity and softness, while the ridge was both tough and durable. During the Eastern Han (25–220 CE), iron swords were forged using the Hundred Refined Steel technique, which refers to the number of times the metal is folded and/or welded (Wang 1998a, b, 68).

Given the low frequency of 0.4 foreign wars per year during the Han, however, this period's overall technological inventiveness was 1.9 new innovations per 10 million population per 100 years (Fig. 2.2), much lower than during the Eastern Zhou.

During the ensuing Period of Division, China fell into a divided state again, with an HHI of 0.23 and a foreign war frequency of 0.9 per year, exceeding even that of the Eastern Zhou, which led to a higher level of inventiveness at 2.5 innovations per 10 million population per 100 years. As an example of new technology from this period, Ma Long, in 279 CE, introduced a flat wagon during a conflict with the Xianbei army, an innovative design that allowed it to function as a mobile camp in the wilderness, with antlers inserted into the perimeter of the defensive wagon to obstruct enemy riders. Additionally, on narrow roads or mountain tops, a flat box could be placed on the wagon to protect the soldiers within from enemy arrows and stones. As the demand from the battlefield grew, various military vehicles, including heavy auxiliary vehicles, were developed in response (Wang 1998b, 75).

The Sui and Tang dynasties raised China's unification to a new level, with an HHI of 0.42, reducing both the foreign war frequency (0.3 per year, a new low) and the incentive to innovate technologically (2 innovations per 10 million population per 100 years). Military innovations from the Tang include the *hai hu* (sea hawk) warship, featuring a low bow and a high stern, resembling the shape of a bird and lowering the risk of capsizing (Wang 1998, 90). It was armed with a 34-m-long crossbow, which could be extended with a winch so that it was capable of firing seven heavy arrows simultaneously that could reach a range of 700 steps, powerful enough to damage, or even demolish, castles and weaker city walls (p. 66).

After the fall of the Tang in 907 CE, China went through the divisive period of Five Dynasties and Ten Kingdoms (907–960 CE), followed by the Song dynasty. This period of 907–1279 CE had a low HHI of 0.22 and many foreign wars (1.0 war per year), with lots of weapon innovations (4.5 innovations per 10 million population per 100 years, the highest level of inventiveness since the Warring States). The experience of the Song precisely confirms Napoleon's statement that a country, when challenged militarily, responds with innovation, as this period "saw the most momentous developments in military technology in human history until the twentieth century" (Andrade 2016, 18). China brought out several well-known military inventions during this Song Warring States Period (Andrade 2016, 24–28), including gunpowder and many related application tools, such as the siege weapons, known as "bed crossbows", that could fire gunpowder arrows against targets as far away as 1.5 km, making them invaluable both offensively and defensively. In 1004 CE, the Song army used the bed crossbow to kill Xiao Ta, a general of the Khitan army (Wang 1998b, 112).

During the early Southern Song dynasty (1127–1279 CE), significant progress was made in the development of firearms, particularly muskets, based on the experience learned from gunpowder arrows and fireballs. As an example, the long bamboo musket was invented with a substantial body, and it was so heavy as to require three soldiers to operate it: one to hold the gun, one to fire, and one to assist. The artillery powder used in this firearm was markedly improved over that used during the Northern Song, resulting in faster speed and higher lethality. When combined with the right battlefield strategies, this invention led to devastating effects on the enemy (p. 108). The Song inventors also introduced double-acting pump flamethrowers, fast rapid-fire crossbow cartridges, large artillery crossbows and new techniques for forging swords, lances, and armor (Andrade 2016, 21).

With the Yuan dynasty's HHI of unification at a record high (0.72) and external war threats near the historical low (0.4 wars per year), it did not face much pressure to innovate until its final two decades, when fighting among the different rebel groups broke out, forcing the Yuan court to improve its arms again. Overall, the Yuan was the least inventive among all the dynastic periods, creating 1.6 military innovations per 10 million population per 100 years.

The Ming dynasty was more troubled as it faced high levels of war threats, both externally (0.7 external wars per year) and internally (0.9 internal wars per year). The Ming was only moderately unified with an HHI of 0.34, coupled with the challenges from the Little Ice Age that brought drought and food shortage frequently (Bai and Kung 2011). These drought episodes forced the steppe nomads in Central Asia to frequently attack the sedentary farming communities in China Proper, producing many inter-state wars (Bai and Kung 2011), and also triggering multiple domestic rebellions (Jia 2014). The Ming fought the Mongols in the north, peripheral states in the west, Vietnam in the southwest, and Japan to the east. External challenges produced many responses in innovation, with 3.4 military technological innovations per 10 million population per 100 years (Fig. 2.2). The Hongwu gun (*huo chong*), named after the founding emperor of the Ming, is a noticeable example, featuring numerous improvements over the gun inherited from the previous dynasty. Gun size varied from handguns (*shou chong*) to large pieces (*wankou chong*), whose manufacturing was much refined with a smoother surface and more uniform thickness for the gun bore and barrel, strengthening the gun body and improving shooting accuracy (Wang 1998a, 159). In the early Ming, about 10% of the official troops carried guns, and then this ratio rose to 20% by the 1430 s and 1440 s and to about 30% by 1466, making Ming China the first "Gunpowder empire of the world" (Andrade 2016, 55–56).

After the Ming collapsed in 1644, Qing China went through an early period of continuing conflicts to take down the remaining Ming rebel groups and peripheral states. By the early eighteenth century, the Qing succeeded in subduing the Mongols and other steppe nomads to the north, folded in the polities to the west and secured the southern coast, leading to very few external threats until the Opium War (1839–1842 CE). With a high level of unification and the resulting long peace (prior to 1840), the

Qing faced little pressure to innovate, having low demand for new technology and producing few innovations (Fig. 2.2).

The temporal macro evidence is thus supportive of our hypothesis that unification cut the demand for new technology, partly explaining the lack of innovative entrepreneurs in post-Qin historical China and the Needham Puzzle.

## 2.4 Concluding Remarks

There are for sure numerous causes and explanations for why China led the world with many inventions up to the Song dynasty but lagged subsequently and missed the opportunity to start its own Industrial Revolution in the fifteenth century or later. In this chapter, we approached this puzzle by focusing on the war channel, through which unification led to lower frequencies of external war and hence lower demand for new technology, which is true at least for battlefield technology. As commented earlier, military applications, rather than production applications, were central drivers of inventive and innovative efforts before the Industrial Revolution (Parker 1996; Hoffman 2012; Andrade 2016).

Bronze technology was introduced to China along the Hexi corridor during the early second millennium BCE, but was only slowly adopted and applied. It was during the middle centuries of the first millennium BCE when bronze finally became widely applied, as evidenced by the evolution of the spatial distribution of excavated bronze grave objects (Fig. 2.5). The charts in Fig. 2.5 show that bronze objects first spread in northern China where wars were, as demonstrated by Chen et al. (2023), frequent, indicating a close association between war threats and the adoption and application of this new technology. Figure 2.6 further demonstrates that, even by the Eastern Zhou (770–221 BCE), regions with more frequent wars had much higher ratios between military and all bronze grave goods, implying that these regions used bronze significantly more heavily in weapons, less in production and day-to-day tools. The next chapter conducts more rigorous tests on our claim made here using micro-level archaeological data.

## References


An, Zhimin. 1993. Shilu zhongguo de zaoqi tongqi [On the Bronze Grave Goods in Early China]. *Kaogu (Archaeology)* 12: 1110–1119.

Andersson, Johan G., and Davidson Black. 1925. *Preliminary Report on Archaeological Research in Kansu*. Peking: The Geological Survey of China, Ministry of Agriculture and Commerce.

Andrade, Tonio. 2016. *The Gunpowder Age: China, Military Innovations, and the Rise of the West in World History*. Princeton, NJ: Princeton University Press.

Bai, Ying, and James K. S. Kung. 2011. Climate Shocks and Sino-Nomadic Conflict. *The Review of Economics and Statistics* 93 (3): 970–981.

Calkins, Stephen. 1983. The New Merger Guidelines and the Herfindahl-Hirschman Index. *California Law Review* 71 (2): 402–429.

Cao, Shuji. 2022. Population Change. In *The Cambridge Economic History of China*, ed. Debin Ma and Richard Von Glahn, , vol. 1, 300–339. Cambridge: Cambridge University Press.

Chen, Pan. 2009. *A Record of Major Events during the Spring and Autumn Period, Listing the Noble Surnames of Each State and Their Rise and Fall, with Notes on Their Difference* (*Chunqiu dashi biao lieguo juexing ji cunmie biao zhuanyi*). Shanghai guji chuban she.

Chen, Yicheng, Zhiwu Chen, and Chicheng Ma. 2023. War Breeds Warriors: Impact of Historical Conflicts on Warrior Culture Formation. Working Paper. [Subsequently published as Chapter 5 in this edited volume.]

Chen, Zhiwu and Zhan Lin. 2024. Quantitative History of Regicide in China. Working Paper. [Subsequently published as Chapter 4 in this edited volume.]

Chen, Zhiwu, Peter Turchin, and Wanda Wang. 2023. War and the Origins of Chinese Civilization. Working Paper.

Chernykh, EvgeniĭN., and Sergeĭ V. Kuz'minykh. 2010. *Ouya dalu beibu de gudai yejin* [The Ancient Metallurgy in North Eurasia].trans. Minghua Li and Bo Wang. Beijing: Zhonghua shuju.

China's Military History Editorial Committee. 2003. *Zhongguo lidai zhanzheng nianbiao* [A Chronology of Warfare in Dynastic China]. Beijing: Jiefangjun chubanshe.

Churchill, Winston S. 2013. *The World Crisis*, Kindle edition, vol. 4. New York City: RosettaBooks.

Dincecco, Mark, and Yuhua Wang. 2018. Violent Conflict and Political Development Over the Long Run: China Versus Europe. *Annual Review of Political Science* 21 (1): 341–358.

Esri. 2022. World Administrative Divisions.. Accessed 25 September 2023. https://services.arcgis.com/P3ePLMYs2RVChkJx/arcgis/rest/services/World_Administrative_Divisions/FeatureServer/0

Fitzgerald-Huber, Louisa G. 1995. Qijia and Erlitou: The Question of Contacts with Distant Cultures. *Early China* 20 (20): 17–67.

Ge, Jianxiong. 2002. *Zhongguo renkou shi diyijuan* [Population History of China], vol. 1. Shanghai: Fudan chubanshe.

Gross, Daniel P., and Bhaven N. Sampat. 2022. The World War II Crisis Innovation Model: What Was It, and Where Does It Apply? NBER Working Paper No. 27909.

Hoffman, Philip. 2012. Why Was It Europeans Who Conquered the World? *The Journal of Economic History* 72 (3): 601–633.

Jiao, Peimin. 2007. Study on the Population of the Pre-Qin Period (Xianqin renkou yanjiu). PhD Dissertation, Zhengzhou University.

Jia, Ruixue. 2014. "Weather Shocks, Sweet Potatoes and Peasant Revolts in Historical China." *Economic Journal* 124 (575): 92–118.

Kierman, Frank A., and John K. Fairbank, eds. 1974. *Chinese Ways in Warfare*. Cambridge, MA: Harvard University Press.

Lagerwey, John, and Lü Pengzhi. 2010. *Early Chinese Religion. Part Two: The Period of Division (220–589 AD)*. Leiden and Boston: Brill.

Landes, David. 1999. *The Wealth and Poverty of Nations: Why Some Are So Rich and Some So Poor*. New York: W. W. Norton & Company.

Lee, Wayne. 2015. *Waging War: Conflict, Culture, and Innovation in World History*. New York: Oxford University Press.

Li, Shuicheng, and Shui Tao. 2000. Siba wenhua tongqi yanjiu [Study on the Bronze Grave Goods from Siba Culture]. *Wenwu [Cultural Relics]* 3: 36–43.

Lin, Justin. 1995. The Needham Puzzle: Why the Industrial Revolution Did Not Originate in China. *Economic Development and Cultural Change* 43 (2): 269–292.

Lin, Meicun, and Xiang Liu. 2017. The Origins of Metallurgy in China. *Antiquity* 91 (359): 1–6.

Liu, Rui, Jiangtao Gao, and Deming Kong. 2016. The Alloy Compositions of Seima-Turbino Socketed Spearheads With Single Side Hooks Discovered in China. *Chinese Cultural Relics [Minneapolis, Minn.]* 3 (1-002): 413–424.

Loehr, Max. 1949. Weapons and Tools from Anyang, and Siberian Analogies. *American Journal of Archaeology* 53 (2): 126–144.
Lowrey, Ying, and William Baumol. 2013. Rapid Invention, Slow Industrialization, and the Absent Innovative Entrepreneur in Medieval China. *Proceedings of the American Philosophical Society* 157 (1): 1–21.
Mei, Jianjun. 2000. *Copper and Bronze Metallurgy in Late Prehistoric Xinjiang: its Cultural Context and Relationship with Neighbouring Regions.* BAR International Series 865. Oxford: Archaeopress.
Mei, Jianjun. 2015. Qijia and Seima-Turbino: The Question of Early Contacts Between Northwest China and the Eurasian Steppe. *Bulletin-Museum of Far Eastern Antiquities* 75: 31–54.
Needham, Joseph. 1954. *Science and Civilisation in China.* Cambridge: Cambridge University Press.
Parker, Geoffrey. 1996. *The Military Revolution: Military Innovation and the Rise of the West, 1500–1800.* Cambridge: Cambridge University Press.
Pomeranz, Kenneth. 2001. *The Great Divergence: China, Europe, and the Making of the Modern World Economy.* Princeton, NJ: Princeton University Press.
Sawyer, Ralph D. 2011. *Ancient Chinese Warfare.* New York: Basic Books.
Slingerland, Edward. 2003. *Confucius: The Analects.* Indianapolis: Hackett.
Sun, Shuyun, and Han Rubin. 1981. Zhongguo zaoqi tongqi de chubu yanjiu [A Preliminary Study on the Bronze Grave Goods in Early China]. *Kaogu Xuebao [Journal of Archaeology]* 3: 287–302.
Wang, Gungwu. 1998a. *The Nanhai Trade: The Early History of Chinese Trade in the South China Sea.* Marshall Cavendish International.
Wang, Zhaochun. 1998b. (*Zhongguo kexue jishu shi: junshi jishu juan*) [History of Science and Technology in China, Military Technology Volume]. Beijing: Kexue chubanshe.

**Zhiwu Chen** is Chair and Cheng Yu-Tung Professor in Finance at The University of Hong Kong (HKU). He currently serves as director of both Hong Kong Institute for the Humanities and Social Sciences (HKIHSS) and Centre for Quantitative History (CQH). His research covers finance theory, the sociology of finance, economic history, quantitative history, emerging markets, as well as China's economy and capital markets. He was a former Professor of Finance at Yale University (1999–2017) and a Special-Term Visiting Professor at Peking University and Tsinghua University. In 2013, he started the annual Summer School for Quantitative History cum International Symposium on Quantitative History at Tsinghua University and continues to organize them at Peking University, with the goal of promoting quantitative research on the history of China and beyond.

**Senhao Hu** is a Ph.D. candidate at The University of Hong Kong, focusing his research on how war-related technological innovations, institutions, culture, and fiscal systems have influenced the development of the historical state and society in China. Collaborating with Prof. Zhiwu Chen and utilizing the rich archaeological data from the China Archaeological Database (CADB), he has conducted a series of studies exploring how military technological innovations and adoption have contributed to various aspects of Chinese development, particularly their impact on the rise of Chinese states. Additionally, in collaboration with Prof. Zhiwu Chen and Mr. Xinhao Li, he has researched the impact of Marco Polo on China's modernization through Christian missionaries. Senhao Hu holds a BBA from Shanghai Jiao Tong University, an MA from The Chinese University of Hong Kong, and an MPhil from Lingnan University in Hong Kong. From 2022 to 2023, he served as a research assistant at the Business School of The University of Hong Kong.

**Zhan Lin** is an Associate Professor of Chinese Economic History at the Renmin University of China. He received his Ph.D. in economics from Tsinghua University in 2014. He is the author of *The Logic of Usury: The Market Mechanisms in Private Lending in the Qing Dynasty and the Republic of China*, a Chinese book. Dr. Lin serves as the associate editor of the *Qing History*

*Journal* and on the editorial board of *Quantitative History Research.* Dr. Lin is also a Co-Principal Investigator of RGC's Area of Excellence (AoE) project, Quantitative History of China. He was the winner of the 10th Golden Fleece Award for Financial Books (2022) and the 2018 Sun YeFang Economics Papers Award (the top honorary prize in China's economics).

# Chapter 3
# War and Demand for Technology: Archaeological Evidence from Early China

**Zhiwu Chen, Senhao Hu, and Zhan Lin**

## 3.1 Introduction

In this chapter, we continue to address the question of why the Industrial Revolution occurred in the West but not in China, that is, the Needham Puzzle (Needham 1954). Based on macro-level historical data, the preceding time-series analysis shows that external, but not internal, war had a strong effect on military technological innovations in historical China. Specifically, since the Qin dynasty (221–206 BCE), periods of high levels of unification are shown to have experienced lower frequencies of external war, which stimulated fewer technological innovations. Thus, in contrast with the case of divided Europe (Fernández-Villaverde et al. 2023), too much unification too early in China depressed demand for technology, leading to a lower supply of actual innovations. However, while the macro evidence provided in the previous chapter highlights the general patterns at a helicopter level, the analysis does not go deep or detailed enough. It especially does not rule out the impact or channels of other confounding factors.

To dig deeper into the causality link, we now turn attention to micro-level evidence by focusing on how bronze, and later iron, technologies were adopted and applied after they were first introduced to China around 1800–1700 BCE. As reviewed in

Z. Chen
Centre for Quantitative History, Faculty of Business and Economics; Hong Kong Institute for the Humanities and Social Sciences, The University of Hong Kong, Hong Kong, China
e-mail: zhiwu.chen@hku.hk

S. Hu (✉)
Hong Kong Institute for the Humanities and Social Sciences, The University of Hong Kong, Hong Kong, China
e-mail: senhao@connect.hku.hk

Z. Lin
Institute of Qing History, Renmin University of China, Beijing, China
e-mail: zhan.lin@ruc.edu.cn



Z. Chen et al. (eds.), *Quantitative History of China*, Studies in Economic History,
https://doi.org/10.1007/978-981-96-8272-0_3

the preceding chapter, bronze technology was the newest technology until about the Eastern Zhou (770–221 BCE); hence, examining where this new technology was quickly adopted can shed light on when and where demand for new technology rose first. Our hypothesis to test is that regions facing higher war threats should adopt new technology more actively.

Section 3.2 introduces the archaeological and historical datasets used in this and the prior chapter, followed by definitions and explanations for our outcome, explanatory and control variables. Section 3.3 presents the baseline results and robustness checks. In Sect. 3.4, we conduct an instrumental variable analysis to further establish causality between war threats and demand for technology. Concluding remarks are offered in Sect. 3.5.

## 3.2 Archaeological Data and Historical Variables

### *3.2.1 Archaeological Data Source*

Since administrative zoning constantly changed and evolved in early historical China, we cannot rely on any administrative unit as the basis for our analysis. Instead, we divide contemporary China's landmass into 1004 grid cells of 100 km $\times$ 100 km to conduct our exercise.

The China Archaeological Database (CADB), maintained at the Centre for Quantitative History at The University of Hong Kong, is an important source for our work in this and the previous chapter. As described by Chen and Zhang (2022), CADB compiles data from both available issues of the *Atlas of Chinese Cultural Relics* and all archaeological excavation reports published up to and including 2021. Our focus of analysis is on the 1700 BCE–220 CE period (from the Xia-Shang to the Han dynasty), as it was during this time when bronze and, later, iron technologies first came to China, representing the newest technologies of the time that could be applied in various contexts, hence offering a unique "historical experiment" for testing our hypothesis on war-driven demand for technology. Grave-level archaeological data are available in the CADB for all the subperiods: the Xia-Shang period (1700–1046 BCE), the Western Zhou (1046–771 BCE), the Eastern Zhou, and the Han dynasty (202 BCE–220 CE). Although archaeological data are available for the Period of Division (220 CE–589 CE) and later dynasties, excavation efforts have been much less for post-Han periods due to lower funding available for excavation of later sites (Xu 2017). Thus, CADB's coverage is less comprehensive for post-Han dynasties. Also, by the Han dynasty, metallurgy was more developed with various types of metal being made and applied, making the research design more challenging.

### 3.2.2 Measures of Demand for New Technology

Since metal weapons are more lethal than those made from stone, bone, and wood (Vandkilde 2016), we expect regions with more war threats to apply metal technologies more widely and deeply on the battlefield, which allows us to use, for example, the ratio of military to all bronze grave goods to capture the extent of a region's demand for new technology. That is, after the introduction of bronze technology into China around 2000–1700 BCE, this technology became available across regions north of the Yangtze River, but who would use it, and for which purposes a region would apply it, should be functions of need and priority. Here, we assume that a region's composition (in terms of relative share) of burial goods across object types captures the relative importance of human activities, corresponding to each object type, to residents when they were alive. For example, if most grave goods excavated in a region are weapons, the locals who were alive at the time must have experienced many wars and threats, for they would otherwise have not cared so much about weapons that they would want to carry them into their graves after death. Likewise, higher ratios between military and all bronze grave goods mean that the locals prioritized the newest technology—bronze—in battlefield applications.

Figure 2.5 of Chapter 2 depicts the spatial distribution of each cell's total number of bronze grave goods archaeologically excavated by period, revealing the relatively widespread use of this technology from 1700 to 1045 BCE, especially by 1045–771 BCE. However, not every region applied this technology to the same extent for battlefield purposes, as Fig. 2.6 demonstrates large cross-regional variations in the ratio of military bronze grave goods, with northern regions exhibiting more battlefield applications (along and north of the Yangtze River basin). These spatial distributions indicate a high positive correlation between foreign war frequency and the ratio of military bronze grave goods. Figures 2.5 and 2.6 of Chapter 2 also suggest a clear north–south divide in both the number of metal grave goods and the ratio of military bronze weapons, with the North leading the South in new technology applications. Table 3.1 provides descriptive statistics on the number of metal grave goods by cell and by period, showing the highest average value for the ratio of military bronze grave goods reached in the Eastern Zhou (11.5%) and that for the ratio of military iron objects in the Han (8%). This means that between the Eastern Zhou and the Han, there was a systematic transition from bronze to iron weapons. In comparison, much fewer grave goods per grid cell have been discovered for the Period of Division, due to more limited funding for excavation work on post-Han dynasty sites, which is why our period of analysis ends at the Han dynasty.

### 3.2.3 Indicators of War Threats

The most authoritative and comprehensive historical war data at the time of writing are in the *Chronology of Chinese Wars* compiled by China's Military History Editorial

**Table 3.1** Summary statistics

| | N | mean | sd | min | max |
|---|---|---|---|---|---|
| **Panel A: Ratio of bronze weapons among all bronze grave goods** | | | | | |
| Xia-Shang | 1004 | 0.0140 | 0.100 | 0 | 1 |
| Western Zhou | 1004 | 0.0420 | 0.173 | 0 | 1 |
| Eastern Zhou | 1004 | 0.115 | 0.261 | 0 | 1 |
| Han Dynasty | 1004 | 0.0270 | 0.101 | 0 | 1 |
| Period of Division | 1004 | 0.0100 | 0.0670 | 0 | 1 |
| **Panel B: Ratio of iron weapons among all iron grave goods** | | | | | |
| Eastern Zhou | 1004 | 0.0430 | 0.172 | 0 | 1 |
| Han Dynasty | 1004 | 0.0800 | 0.221 | 0 | 1 |
| Period of Division | 1004 | 0.0600 | 0.202 | 0 | 1 |
| **Panel C: Military grave goods** | | | | | |
| Xia-Shang | 1004 | 2.580 | 55.55 | 0 | 1729 |
| Western Zhou | 1004 | 6.722 | 54.62 | 0 | 1018 |
| Eastern Zhou | 1004 | 50.35 | 306.0 | 0 | 6445 |
| Han Dynasty | 1004 | 9.641 | 91.67 | 0 | 2252 |
| Period of Division | 1004 | 1.830 | 16.25 | 0 | 329 |
| **Panel D: Foreign wars** | | | | | |
| Eastern Zhou | 1004 | 0.692 | 3.398 | 0 | 50 |
| Han Dynasty | 1004 | 0.600 | 1.981 | 0 | 25 |
| Period of Division | 1004 | 1.306 | 4.246 | 0 | 57 |
| **Panel E: Cities** | | | | | |
| Xia-Shang | 1004 | 0.0290 | 0.232 | 0 | 4 |
| Western Zhou | 1004 | 0.0660 | 0.345 | 0 | 4 |
| Eastern Zhou | 1004 | 0.654 | 2.592 | 0 | 38 |
| Han Dynasty | 1004 | 0.020 | 0.153 | 0 | 2 |
| Period of Division | 1004 | 0.235 | 0.635 | 0 | 6 |
| **Panel F: Control variables** | | | | | |
| Rice suitability | 1004 | 3634 | 7455 | 0 | 23,167 |
| Millet suitability | 1004 | 4130 | 5249 | 0 | 16,245 |
| Terrain ruggedness | 1004 | 658.5 | 541.9 | 4.677 | 2762 |
| Coast distance (km) | 1004 | 1372 | 991.5 | 0.111 | 3712 |
| River distance (km) | 1004 | 532.0 | 437.6 | 0.016 | 1748 |
| Steppe distance (km) | 1004 | 934 | 615 | 6 | 2571 |

Committee (2003). But its coverage only starts from 770 BCE. Thus, for the dynasties of 770 BCE–220 CE, we use each cell's number of external wars to capture its level of war threats during each period.

For the 1700–771 BCE period, as well as for the 770 BCE–589 CE subperiods for the purpose of robustness checks, we rely on two proxies for war threats: each cell's excavated military grave goods and its number of walled cities, from a given period.

Chen et al. (2023) propose to use archaeologically excavated military grave goods as a proxy for war threats faced by locals during their time. In essence, only if a region facing many war threats would the inhabitants care about weapons enough to even want to carry some into their graves upon death. Otherwise, they would not develop such an obsession with lethal tools. To the extent that the afterlife world was simply an extension of one's real-life experience, only in regions where the living did suffer from and fight frequent wars would the locals want to take weapons into graves to protect their afterlife. Thus, we use military grave goods as a proxy for war threats.

A cell's number of walled cities is utilized as an alternative proxy for war threats in a given period, where the data for walled cities are from Xu (2017) for the Xia-Shang (1700–1046 BCE), the Western Zhou (1046–771 BCE) and the Eastern Zhou, and from Guo (1996) for the Han (202 BCE–220 CE) and the Period of Division (220 CE–589 CE). According to Xu (2017), walls, moats, fences, and other physical barriers were constructed to defend the people within from enemy attacks. Therefore, war gave rise to early Chinese cities and civilization (Chen et al. 2023). For this reason, more walled cities in a cell signal higher war threats faced by the locals.

In Pre-Qin China, there was no unified empire so we can treat the war threats, measured respectively by military grave goods and walled cities, as foreign war threats. This assumption is reasonable given that there were hardly any internal wars recorded even for the Eastern Zhou. For the Eastern Zhou and the Han periods, we effectively employ three cell-level war-threat measures: military grave goods, walled cities, and foreign wars, for each of which Table 3.1 provides descriptive statistics.

There is a concern among historians that especially for early China, recorded wars may have a strong selection bias favoring northern and against southern China, since historians prior to the Song or even the Ming dynasty were mostly northerners who did not have much exposure to events in the south (Zhao 2015). If this was true, northern regions would have more wars recorded. In this sense, our proxies based on military grave goods and walled cities are not subject to such a bias as archaeological discoveries have been relatively evenly spread geographically, at least for regions within China Proper. Nonetheless, recorded wars remain one of the most reliable variables, capturing conflict levels in historical China, used by scholars (Bai and Kung 2011).

### 3.2.4 *Control Variables*

When testing the effect of external war on demand for technology, we include a host of controls that may confound the outcome, such as agricultural productivity (in terms of rice and millet suitability), terrain ruggedness, shortest distance to the coast, shortest distance to major rivers, longitude and latitude, with their summary statistics also included in Table 3.1.

#### 3.2.4.1 Rice and Millet Suitability

The role of agriculture in the rise of complex society is widely acknowledged (e.g., Diamond 1997; Scott 2017). We thus control for its potential impact on military technological innovations by including separate indices for rice and millet suitability at the grid cell level. Galor and Ozak (2016) have used these suitability indices to assess the agricultural productivity of each cell.

#### 3.2.4.2 Terrain Ruggedness

According to Chen et al. (2023), communities on flat land were easier to be attacked and more difficult to defend, making these settlements more subject to the warp and weft of wars. Diamond (1997) and Fernández-Villaverde et al. (2023) also make the point that differences in terrain topography gave rise to the early divergence in development between Europe and Asia, among other aspects. To control for the possible effect of terrain topography on military technological advancements, we construct an index of terrain ruggedness for each cell, based on the method of Nunn and Puga (2012). There is, however, a caveat that as emphasized in Chen et al. (2023), a cell's war frequency in prehistoric and early historical times was highly negatively correlated with its terrain ruggedness, so controlling for this effect will take away some of the statistical significance of our main explanatory variable—war threats faced by each region.

#### 3.2.4.3 The Coast and Rivers

Ancient civilizations emerged near rivers as both agriculture and human needed water (Boccaletti 2021). Furthermore, water routes provided by the sea and rivers offered the easiest and least costly way of transporting large volumes of goods, making commercial development more affordable in littoral and riverine regions. To adjust for this possible effect on our outcome variable, we calculate the shortest distance from each cell to the Yellow and Yangtze rivers, as well as that to the coast. Both measures of geography are exogenously determined.

#### 3.2.4.4 Longitude and Latitude

Latitude provides information on seasonal temperature variations for a region. Generally, the further north or south a region is from the equator, the greater the temperature variations during the day and throughout the year, with possible implications for military technological innovations as extreme temperatures can impact a region's development. Longitude captures a region's other environmental features, such as landforms and proximity to the eastern coast. We utilize the QGIS geospatial application to generate the longitude and latitude for each cell.

## 3.3 Empirical Analyses

As discussed earlier, the adoption of bronze technology took a long time in China and reached a mature stage in the Eastern Zhou, before giving its way to iron technology. As no war data is available prior to 770 BCE, we conduct two separate sets of panel regressions: the first set based on military grave goods and walled cities as respective proxies for war threats and for the Xia-Shang (1700–1045 BCE), the Western Zhou, and the Eastern Zhou periods, and the second based on historical wars for the Eastern Zhou and the Han periods.

Our basic regression model is as follows:

$$MiliTechAdopt_{it} = \alpha + \beta WarThreat_{it} + X_{it} + \gamma_i + \delta_t + \varepsilon_{it} \tag{3.1}$$

where $i$ denotes a grid cell, $t$ the dynastic period, and $MiliTechAdopt_{it}$ either the number of military metal grave goods, or the ratio of military to all metal grave goods, that have been excavated from cell $i$ graves for period $t$, where the metal is either bronze or iron; $WarTreat_{it}$ is the variable of war threats that cell $i$ faced in period $t$; $X_{it}$ is a vector of control variables introduced above, where, to minimize the impact of collinearity, we multiply each geographic and environmental control with the time period in the panel regressions; $\gamma_i$ for cell $i$'s fixed effect; $\delta_t$ for period fixed effect, and $\varepsilon_{it}$ for the error term, with the standard errors clustered at the cell level.

### *3.3.1 Baseline Results*

Panel A of Table 3.2 presents the ordinary least squares (OLS) panel regression results with fixed effects and for the three sample periods—the Xia-Shang, the Western Zhou, and the Eastern Zhou, from 1700 to 221 BCE—where the logarithmic value of military grave goods is the war proxy. Columns (1) and (2) show that even after the impact of the control variables is accounted for, war threats had a positive and statistically significant effect (at the 1% level) on bronze technology adoption on the battlefield: regions with a higher quantity of military grave goods exhibited a higher ratio of military bronze grave goods, demonstrating a higher likelihood to apply new technology for battles. Note that each cell has the same area size, so its number of archaeological sites that have been discovered for a given period can be treated as the cell's archaeological site density, which in turn serves as a proxy for the cell's population density (Chen et al. 2023). From column (2), the coefficient estimate for archaeological site density is negative and statistically significant, meaning that regions with higher population density (and hence better development) did not necessarily apply the bronze technology more actively for battlefield uses. War was a more dominant determinant of the demand for new technology.

This finding supports Parker's (1996) "challenge-response dynamic" narrative and our hypothesis. During the Western Zhou, there were more than 100 feudal states, but by the end of the Eastern Zhou, only seven states survived, with all the others having been violently conquered and folded into one of the seven. Clearly, between 1700 and 256 BCE, not every chiefdom and state faced the same level of war threats or fought the same number of external wars; thus, those who fought more and had to cope with frequent survival challenges adopted more aggressively the most advanced technology of the time—bronze—to get ahead of their competitors and win.

Due to some cells having zero military grave goods in certain periods, we have followed the common practice of taking the logarithmic value of 1 plus each cell's number of military grave goods (similarly for other logarithmic transformations), which may introduce artificial distortions. Additionally, as shown in Figs. 2.5–2.8 of Chapter 2, many cells do not contain any metal grave objects. To address such concerns, we consider alternative regression models—the negative binomial model (NB), the Poisson pseudo maximum likelihood model (PPML), the censored regression model (Tobit), and the OLS model—separately shown in columns (3)–(6) of Panel A of Table 3.2, where the number of military grave goods is directly used in each case without the logarithmic transformation. The resulting estimates for the military-grave-goods coefficient are all positive and statistically significant at the 1% level, suggesting that the statistical significance of the main explanatory variable is unaffected under the alternative specifications.

Although the coefficient estimates for the control variables are not reported in Table 3.2 to save space, we offer two observations. First, the coefficient on rice suitability is negative and statistically significant, while the coefficient on millet suitability remains positive regardless of the regression model adopted. Given that northern China is more suitable for growing millet while the south for rice, the difference in coefficient sign may be just capturing the north–south divide, with the north having more military bronze grave objects. Second, the coefficient on distance to rivers is negative and statistically significant in most cases, implying that regions closer to the Yellow and Yangtze rivers were more likely to adopt new military technology, perhaps as they faced more war threats due to being closer to the major rivers.

In Panel B of Table 3.2, we replace the number of military grave goods with that of walled cities as the proxy for war threats, with the understanding that city walls were built for defensive purposes: more walled cities mean the presence of higher war threats in a cell at the time (Chen et al. 2023). Columns (1) and (2) present the

**Table 3.2** Baseline panel regressions based on the 1700–256 BCE data

| | Ratio of military bronze goods to all bronze grave goods | | Number of military bronze grave goods | | | |
|---|---|---|---|---|---|---|
| | OLS | | NB | PPML | Tobit | OLS |
| | (1) | (2) | (3) | (4) | (5) | (6) |
| **Panel A: Military grave goods as war proxy** | | | | | | |
| Military grave goods (log) | 0.113*** | 0.110*** | | | | |
| | (23.29) | (21.22) | | | | |
| Military grave goods | | | 0.001*** | 0.003*** | 1.007*** | 0.872*** |
| | | | (6.81) | (6.47) | (28.54) | (5.49) |
| Archaeological sites | | −0.00*** | 0.000 | 0.000 | 0.877*** | 0.647 |
| | | (−4.58) | (0.12) | (0.08) | (5.70) | (1.40) |
| R-squared | 0.734 | 0.742 | | | | 0.571 |
| **Panel B: Walled cities as war proxy** | | | | | | |
| Walled cities (log) | 0.155*** | 0.115*** | | | | |
| | (7.50) | (5.06) | | | | |
| Walled cities | | | 0.006 | −0.057 | 17.038*** | 25.189** |
| | | | (0.20) | (−1.47) | (3.67) | (2.49) |
| R-squared | 0.511 | 0.548 | | | | 0.410 |
| **Common specifications for Panels A and B** | | | | | | |
| Observations | 3,012 | 3,012 | 705 | 705 | 3012 | 3012 |
| Controls | NO | YES | YES | YES | YES | YES |
| CELL FE | YES | YES | YES | YES | NO | YES |
| Period FE | YES | YES | YES | YES | NO | YES |

*Note* Columns (1)–(2) are based on the logarithmic value of the main explanatory variable (military grave goods, or walled cities), while columns (3)-(6) on its absolute value. Columns (1), (2), and (6) are all OLS regressions; column (3) is the negative binomial model (NB); column (4) the Poisson pseudo maximum likelihood model (PPML), and column (5) the Tobit model with random effects. Controls include rice suitability, millet suitability, terrain ruggedness, coast distance, river distance, longitude, and latitude, each multiplied with the dynastic period (i.e., the Xia-Shang, Western Zhou, and Eastern Zhou). Robust t statistics are in parentheses. ***, **, and * indicate statistical significance at the 1%, 5%, and 10%, respectively

coefficient estimates based on the logarithmic value of cities, which are positive and statistically significant at the 1% level (even after the control variables are included). When the absolute value of walled cities is used as the main explanatory variable, columns (5) and (6) also show positive and statistically significant coefficient estimates. However, those in columns (3) and (4) do not exhibit statistical significance, which has two implications. First, from the Xia-Shang to the Eastern Zhou, military grave goods may provide a more accurate measure of war threats than the number of walled cities, as also evidenced by the regression results in Panel A. Second, as more grid cells have zero-walled cities than those with zero military grave goods, the former as a proxy of war threats imposes a higher hurdle for what constitutes a war threat, so that some regions that would be considered as exhibiting no war threats according to the former may have had significant such threats as captured by the latter standard. Since grid cells with zero-walled cities are excluded from the NB and PPML models in Panel B, these regressions in columns (3) – (4) have much fewer observations than in columns (1)–(2).

Overall, Table 3.2 establishes that our hypothesis holds under both measures of war threats.

### *3.3.2 Results with Actual War Data*

As discussed earlier, by the time of the Eastern Zhou, iron technology became available across many regions (Fig. 2.8 of Chapter 2), enabling us to examine the extent to which war threats affected each region's adoption of iron and other types of metal to make weapons. From Panel A of Table 3.1, the average ratio of bronze weapons among all bronze grave goods reached its peak value of 11.5% during the Eastern Zhou but declined thereafter (to reach 2.7% during the Han and 1% during the Period of Division) as bronze was gradually replaced by iron. Panel B of Table 3.1 illustrates that the average cell-level ratio of iron weapons to all iron grave goods was 4.3% during the Eastern Zhou, reaching its peak at 8% during the Han dynasty and falling thereafter. Thus, by the Han dynasty, iron became the more important metal for making weapons.

For the two dynastic periods—the Eastern Zhou and the Han dynasties, there are data for both war and military grave goods to capture each region's war threats, which allows us to conduct the panel regressions in Table 3.3, with Panel A based on each cell's logarithmic value of foreign wars and Panel B on its logarithmic value of military grave goods (for the comparison between the two war-threat proxies). Three outcome variables are considered: each cell's ratio of military bronze grave goods to all bronze grave goods (columns (1)–(2), with the first not including controls), ratio of military to all iron grave goods (columns (3)–(4)), and ratio of military to all metal grave goods (columns (5)–(6)).

In Panel A of Table 3.3, columns (1)–(2) indicate that both before and after the effects of the controls being included, the coefficient estimate for the number of foreign wars is statistically significant and positive, supporting our claim that external war drove the demand for new technology applications. The same holds true when the outcome variable is the ratio of military to all metal grave goods in columns (5)–(6).

The results in columns (3)–(4), however, appear puzzling. When no control is included in column (3), the number of foreign wars has a positive and statistically significant (at the 1% level) effect on the adoption of iron technology for battlefield uses. But, once the effects of the controls are accounted for, the impact of war is no longer statistically significant and even changes its sign. To investigate the possible

**Table 3.3** Panel regressions on war's impact on technology adoption (770 BCE–220 CE)

| | Ratio of military bronze goods to all bronze grave goods | | Ratio of military to all iron grave goods | | Ratio of military to all bronze and iron grave goods | |
|---|---|---|---|---|---|---|
| | (1) | (2) | (3) | (4) | (5) | (6) |
| **Panel A: Number of foreign wars as proxy of war threats** | | | | | | |
| Foreign wars (log) | 0.114*** | 0.040** | 0.066*** | −0.028 | 0.113*** | 0.040** |
| | (9.75) | (2.10) | (5.75) | (−1.20) | (9.51) | (2.22) |
| R-squared | | 0.671 | | 0.637 | | 0.700 |
| **Panel B: Military grave goods as proxy of war threats** | | | | | | |
| Military grave goods (log) | 0.093*** | 0.089*** | 0.069*** | 0.055*** | 0.098*** | 0.087*** |
| | (25.54) | (12.99) | (14.79) | (6.32) | (26.71) | (11.79) |
| R-squared | | 0.770 | | 0.676 | | 0.790 |
| **Common specifications for Panels A and B** | | | | | | |
| Observations | 2008 | 2008 | 2008 | 2008 | 2008 | 2008 |
| Controls | NO | YES | NO | YES | NO | YES |
| CELL FE | NO | YES | NO | YES | NO | YES |
| Period FE | NO | YES | NO | YES | NO | YES |

*Note* In these panel regressions, the Eastern Zhou and the Han dynasty are the two dynastic periods used. For the main explanatory variable—war threats, Panels A and B each rely on a different proxy. See the Notes of Table 3.2 for explanations of the variables and symbols, as well as the Controls

reasons for this, in columns (3)–(4) of Panel B, we replace the number of foreign wars with the number of military grave goods as a proxy for war threats again and re-run the panel regressions for the two dynastic periods, in which case both coefficient estimates for the war threats are positive and statistically significant at the 1% level. To the extent that archaeologically excavated grave goods represent a less biased sampling of each region's war experience in each historical period than the written records, the military grave goods may present a more accurate picture of the spatial distribution of war threats, especially for early historical periods. Accounts of historical events for the Eastern Zhou are notoriously spotty and selective (Zhao 2015).

Another possible explanation is that the replacement of bronze with iron weapons during that time was probably not as significant as the transition from stone and bone weapons to bronze weapons. This is because, although iron weapons were sharper and easier to make than bronze weapons, they shared many similar features. By the time iron technology was brought to China, bronze weapons had been in battlefield use for more than a millennium (Mei 2000). Consequently, the marginal effect resulting from the replacement of bronze with iron weapons may have been much smaller than that brought about the earlier replacement of stone and bone by bronze weapons. In addition, iron had much wider applications than bronze. Thus, the ratio of military to all iron grave goods may not accurately capture the full extent of demand for iron technology when it represented the cutting-edge technology of the time. This topic is worth further inquiry.

### 3.3.3 *Robustness Checks*

In this subsection, we conduct a series of robustness checks. These checks will help ensure the validity of our findings. There are several exercises whose results are not reported here to save space. First, instead of panel regressions using multiple dynastic periods, we run separate cross-sectional regressions for each of the Xia-Shang, the Western Zhou, the Eastern Zhou, and the Han dynasty, with results similar to our baseline finding that war threats drove the demand for battlefield applications of new technology. Second, we replace foreign wars with each cell's total wars (external and internal conflicts), to find largely similar results as well.

In the subsections to follow, we discuss additional robustness checks.

#### 3.3.3.1 Adoption of Chariots During Subperiods of 770–221 BCE

In addition to the material used in producing weapons, we consider the extent of use of advanced weapons as another proxy of a region's demand for new technology. As mentioned earlier, bronze chariots were brought to China from Central Asia's steppes around 1200 BCE, but it was not until the Spring and Autumn period that they were extensively utilized on the battlefield (Lee 2015). Therefore, we can further investigate whether war threats were a significant driver of each region's extent of chariot adoption.

For this exercise, we construct a panel dataset by treating each of the 130 feudal states that existed in 770 BCE as the basic unit of analysis and dividing the Eastern Zhou into six subperiods: the early (770–672 BCE), middle (671–574 BCE), and late Spring and Autumn (573–476 BCE), and the early (475–391 BCE), middle (390–305 BCE), and late Warring States (304–221 BCE). Since some states were conquered by and merged with other states during each of the six subperiods, resulting in increasingly fewer states as time went by, the territorial size differs among the states of the same subperiod and for the same state across the subperiods. We thus rely on both state and time-period fixed effects to control for the impact of such heterogeneities. In total, there are 780 state subperiods. We then add together the number of foreign wars and bronze chariot fittings for each state in each given subperiod, where the chariot fittings are sourced from the archaeological excavation reports in the CADB. Furthermore, we construct a territorial-area variable for each state in each subperiod—*State area,* respectively based on the years 770, 650, 505, 403, 305, and 230 BCE, where the area of each state is calculated using QGIS and historical maps. It is assumed here that a state's territorial size is positively correlated with its foreign war threats because larger territorial reach means more exposure to threats from neighboring states. Figures 2.1, 2.7 of Chapter 2 displays the time-sequential evolution of the spatial distribution of bronze chariot fittings and foreign wars by state.

The panel regression model for the 780 state-subperiod observations is as follows:

$$Chariots_{it} = \alpha + \beta WarThreat_{it} + X_{it} + \gamma_i + \delta_t + \varepsilon_{it} \tag{3.2}$$

where $X_{it}$ is a vector of controls, including each state's rice suitability, millet suitability, terrain ruggedness, and its capital city's longitude and latitude, each multiplied by the time subperiod. Each state's rice suitability index is set to be the average of rice suitability values across all the cells within the state's territory. A state's value for millet suitability and terrain ruggedness is similarly constructed.

In Table 3.4, columns (1) and (3) include only state and subperiod fixed effects (FE) without the controls, whereas columns (2) and (4) have both the fixed effects and the controls accounted for. The coefficient estimates on foreign wars in columns (1)–(2) are positive and statistically significant at the 1% level, indicating that foreign war threats stimulated the greater demand for chariots—the new military technology, consistent with Parker's "challenge-response dynamic." The same conclusion holds when foreign war threats are proxied by each state's territorial area in columns (3)–(4), except that the coefficient is statistically significant at the 5% level in column (4).

**Table 3.4** Impact of foreign wars on chariot adoptions in the Eastern Zhou (6-subperiod panel regressions)

| | Number of bronze chariot fittings (log) | | | |
|---|---|---|---|---|
| | (1) | (2) | (3) | (4) |
| Foreign wars (log) | 0.924*** | 0.857*** | | |
| | (5.99) | (5.52) | | |
| State area | | | 0.111*** | 0.097** |
| | | | (4.22) | (2.27) |
| Observations | 780 | 780 | 780 | 780 |
| R-squared | 0.554 | 0.568 | 0.489 | 0.499 |
| Controls | NO | YES | NO | YES |
| State FE | YES | YES | YES | YES |
| Period FE | YES | YES | YES | YES |

*Note* The panel regressions are based on the 130 feudal states that existed in 770 BCE and 6 subperiods: the early (770–672 BCE), middle (671–574 BCE), and late Spring and Autumn (573–476 BCE), and the early (475–391 BCE), middle (390–305 BCE), and late Warring States (304–221 BCE). The same controls as in Tables 2 and 3 are included here. Robust t statistics are in parentheses. ***, **, and * indicate statistical significance at the 1%, 5%, and 10%, respectively

#### 3.3.3.2 Bronze Arrows During the Eastern Zhou

According to Shi (2008) and Li (2011), arrows were mostly made of stone and bone in the Neolithic period, which were gradually replaced by bronze during the Zhou dynasty. Therefore, bronze arrows represent another example of advanced military technology during the Eastern Zhou. As an additional robustness check, we use each grid-cell's ratio of bronze arrows among all arrows excavated from graves of the period, to measure the cell region's demand for and adoption of this specific advanced weapon, and conduct cross-sectional regressions based on the Eastern Zhou data in Table 3.5, where both a cell's number of foreign wars and that of walled cities are separately utilized as war-threat proxies. Columns (1)–(2) indicate that the coefficient estimates on war threats, as proxied by either one, are positive and statistically significant at the 1% level, implying that war threats increased the demand for bronze arrows. To the extent that higher population density (proxied by higher archaeological site density in a cell) indicates a higher level of development in early historical times, the coefficient for archaeological sites in both columns (1)–(2) suggests that more developed/populated regions also adopted more bronze arrows.

In columns (3)-(4), we replace the ratio of bronze arrows with the ratio of stone and bone arrows (representing outdated technologies). As a result, the coefficient estimate on war threats is either negative or statistically significant when war threats are proxied by the number of foreign wars in column (3), or statistically insignificant in column (4). In both cases, the coefficient on archaeological sites is not statistically significant. Taken together, Table 3.5 shows that foreign war threats favored new and advanced technologies but discouraged the use of outdated technologies.

**Table 3.5** Which regions adopted more bronze arrows during the Eastern Zhou

| | Ratio of bronze arrows among all arrows | | Ratio of stone and bone arrows among all arrows | |
|---|---|---|---|---|
| | (1) | (2) | (3) | (4) |
| Foreign wars | 0.147*** | | –0.016** | |
| | (4.72) | | (–2.03) | |
| Cities | | 0.180*** | | 0.008 |
| | | (5.45) | | (0.83) |
| Archaeological sites | 0.003*** | 0.002*** | 0.000 | –0.000 |
| | (4.23) | (3.65) | (1.51) | (–0.49) |
| Observations | 1,004 | 1,004 | 1,004 | 1,004 |
| R-squared | 0.418 | 0.426 | 0.054 | 0.049 |
| Controls | YES | YES | YES | YES |

*Note* These cell-level cross-sectional regressions include the same Controls as in Tables 2 and 3. Robust t statistics are in parentheses. ***, **, and * indicate statistical significance at the 1%, 5%, and 10%, respectively

**Table 3.6** Foreign war and farming applications of new technology during the Eastern Zhou

| | Ratio of farm bronze tools to all bronze grave goods | | Ratio of farm iron tools to all iron grave goods | |
|---|---|---|---|---|
| | (1) | (2) | (3) | (4) |
| Foreign wars (log) | | −0.000 | | 0.010 |
| | | (−0.18) | | (0.83) |
| Cities (log) | −0.0001 | | 0.0188 | |
| | (-0.15) | | (1.43) | |
| Archaeological sites | −0.0000 | −0.000 | 0.0005** | 0.001*** |
| | (−0.33) | (-0.36) | (2.23) | (2.73) |
| Observations | 1,004 | 1,004 | 1,004 | 1,004 |
| R-squared | 0.022 | 0.022 | 0.110 | 0.106 |
| Controls | YES | YES | YES | YES |

*Note* These cross-sectional regressions use the same Controls as in Tables 2 and 3. Robust t statistics are in parentheses. ***, **, and * indicate statistical significance at the 1%, 5%, and 10%, respectively

#### 3.3.3.3 New Technology for Agriculture?

Diamond (1997) attributes the rise of complex societies and the spread of technological advancements to the invention of agriculture as the latter triggered the demand for technology to better cultivate land for growing crops and raising domesticated animals. As a corollary of this narrative, agriculture, rather than the battlefield, would be expected to be a primary context for applications of new technology. For this reason, we repeat the preceding cell-level cross-sectional falsification exercise by using the ratio of farm bronze tools to all bronze grave goods in columns (1)–(2) of Table 3.6, as well as the ratio of farm iron tools to all iron grave goods excavated in columns (3)–(4), for the Eastern Zhou. In these cases, war threats (proxied by foreign wars and walled cities) do not have a statistically significant impact on the two outcome variables; thus, the foreign war did not stimulate more farming applications of bronze and iron technologies. This, together with our earlier results, means that foreign war threats mainly created more battlefield demand for new technology.

## 3.4 Hexi Corridor as an Instrumental Variable

For our baseline results in Table 3.2, there may be concerns about the impact of reverse causality and omitted variables. Earlier, we learned that metallurgical technology came to China from Central Asia through the Hexi corridor of the northwest (Fig. 2.3 of Chapter 2). Studies based on Eurasian experience suggest that new metal weapons such as chariots and cavalry led to more frequent and more intense wars (Turchin et al. 2013). It is thus likely that the closer a region was to the Hexi corridor, the greater the war threats it faced. For this reason, we use a cell's distance to the Hexi corridor as an instrumental variable to conduct a two-stage least squares (2SLS) regression.

In the first stage, we run a panel regression of the logarithmic value of each cell's military grave goods on its distance to the Hexi corridor (log) multiplied by the period, where the panel data cover the Xia-Shang, Western and Eastern Zhou periods. Then, in the second stage, we regress the ratio of military bronze grave goods to all bronze grave goods on the predicted value of military grave goods (log) from the first stage, with all controls included. The results are reported in Table 3.7, respectively, for the full sample and the China Proper subsample.

For the full sample, the first-stage coefficient estimate on the distance to the Hexi corridor in column (1) is negative and statistically significant; that is, regions closer to the Hexi corridor had more military grave goods, hence they faced more war threats. For the second stage in column (3), the coefficient on predicted military grave goods is positive and statistically significant at the 1% level, implying that cells with more war threats had higher demand for bronze weapons.

**Table 3.7** Panel IV results for the Pre-Qin sample (1700–256 BCE)

| | First stage | | Second stage | |
|---|---|---|---|---|
| | Military grave goods | | Ratio of bronze weapons to all bronze grave goods | |
| | Full Sample | China Proper | Full Sample | China Proper |
| | (1) | (2) | (3) | (4) |
| Hexi corridor distance * Period | −0.121*** | −0.203** | | |
| | (-3.74) | (-2.94) | | |
| Military grave goods | | | 0.111*** | 0.108** |
| | | | (2.94) | (2.97) |
| Archaeological sites | 0.003 | 0.002 | −0.000** | −0.000** |
| | (1.68) | (1.32) | (−2.81) | (−2.80) |
| Observations | 3,012 | 1,461 | 3,012 | 1,461 |
| R-squared | 0.590 | 0.610 | 0.513 | 0.489 |
| Controls | YES | YES | YES | YES |
| CELL FE | YES | YES | YES | YES |
| Period FE | YES | YES | YES | YES |
| KPF statistic | | | 14.002 | 8.669 |

*Note* Controls include rice suitability, millet suitability, river distance, longitude, and latitude. Three dynastic periods—the Xia-Shang, Western Zhou, and Eastern Zhou—are used in the two-stage OLS panel regressions. Columns (1) and (3) report the estimates based on all 1,004 grid cells on China's landmass. To check the robustness of the results, we restrict in columns (2) and (4) the sample to the grid cells within China Proper. Robust t statistics are in parentheses. ***, **, and * indicate statistical significance at the 1%, 5%, and 10%, respectively

To check the robustness of the results, we restrict the sample cells to those within China Proper, with the resulting estimates respectively reported in columns (2) and (4). In this case, the coefficient estimates are largely similar to their counterparts in columns (1) and (3), with a slight decline in the statistical significance level. The IV estimates thus support our hypothesis that higher war threats led to more adoptions of, namely higher demand for new technology. Note that the K-P F-statistic in Table 3.7 is 14.00 for the full sample and 8.67 for the China Proper, implying that the IV is acceptable. Given that many human sites and graves of early historical China remain undiscovered archaeologically, our war-threat proxy—military grave goods—is admittedly noisy, which influences the K-P F-statistic.

Caution should be applied here: our suggestive IV exercise is intended to be exploratory and not comprehensive. Though each grid cell's shortest distance to the Hexi corridor is exogenous and uncorrelated with socioeconomic development indicators during the 1700–256 BCE period,[1] what the Hexi corridor represents may not be fully exogenous as it corresponds to the route through which early metallurgical technology such as bronze spread into China. Still, the introduction of bronze was not dependent on socioeconomic development of the time, so its occurrence was a random shock and hence exogenous. Therefore, our choice of the IV is justified.

## 3.5 Concluding Remarks

There are numerous causes and explanations for why China led the world with many inventions and innovations up to the Song dynasty but lagged behind subsequently and missed the opportunity to start its own Industrial Revolution in the fifteenth century or later. In this and the previous chapter, we approach this puzzle by focusing on the war channel, through which unification led to reduced demand for new technology. Our exercise differs from Fernández-Villaverde et al. (2023) in that we follow a regression-based empirical approach to establish the negative impact of unification on the demand for technology, whereas they apply the simulation method of Turchin et al. (2013) to show the negative effect of unification on long-term institutional development.

In addition, we rely on archaeological data from excavated graves to establish at the micro-level that at least from 1700 BCE to 220 CE more foreign war threats led to increased demand for new technology; that is, the micro-level evidence supports our claim that reduced frequencies of external war due to unification reduced China's demand for new technology, which is at least partly why China was inventive up to the Song but did not convert inventions into productive or useful applications: the lack of demand was the main cause. Of course, further work is needed to fully appreciate the roles played by war and unification in China's developmental history.

[1] If we treat each cell's archaeological site density as a proxy for its development level during 1700–256 BCE, its correlation with the shortest distance to the Hexi corridor is close to zero and statistically insignificant, consistent with the exclusion restriction for an IV.

**Acknowledgements** We thank Cameron Campbell, Dongdong Li, William Guanglin Liu, Chicheng Ma, Debin Ma, Tetsuji Okazaki, Paul Seabright, Billy K. L. So, Tuan-Hwee Sng, and participants at the Area of Excellence—Quantitative History Conference 2023 at The University of Hong Kong for their comments and suggestions. Our thanks also go to Kai Chen, Ruoran Cheng, Li Duan, Qing Fang, Suwei Guo, Lei Huang, Ke Liu, Guenther Lomas, Luyao Pan, Wanda Wang, Zihe Wang, Linxu Yang, Cangyang Ye, Xiao Yu, and Xiaoming Zhang for their excellent research assistance. The work described in this paper was substantially supported by a grant from the Research Grants Council of the Hong Kong Special Administrative Region, China (Project Reference Number: AoE/B-704/22-R). Any remaining errors are ours.

## References

Bai, Ying, and James K. S. Kung. 2011. Climate Shocks and Sino-Nomadic Conflict. *The Review of Economics and Statistics* 93 (3): 970–981.

Boccaletti, Giulio. 2021. *Water: A Biography*. New York: Pantheon.

Chen, Zhiwu, and Xiaoming Zhang. 2022. Quantitative Archaeological Evidence on the Origin of the First Chinese State(s). Working Paper.

Chen, Zhiwu, Peter Turchin, and Wanda Wang. 2023. War and the Origins of Chinese Civilization. Working Paper.

China's Military History Editorial Committee. 2003. *A Chronology of Warfare in Dynastic China* (Zhongguo lidai zhanzheng nianbiao). Beijing: Jiefangjun chubanshe.

Diamond, Jared M. 1997. *Guns, Germs, and Steel: the Fates of Human Societies*. New York: W. W. Norton & Company.

Fernández-Villaverde, Jesús, Mark Koyama, Youhong Lin, and Tuan-Hwee Sng. 2023. The Fractured-Land Hypothesis. *The Quarterly Journal of Economics* 138 (2): 1173–1231.

Galor, Oded, and Ömer Özak. 2016. The Agricultural Origins of Time Preference. *The American Economic Review* 106 (10): 3064–3103.

Guo, Moruo. Ed. 1996. Atlas of Chinese History, Volume 1 (Zhongguo shigao dituji). Zhongguo ditu chubanshe.

Lee, Wayne. 2015. *Waging War: Conflict, Culture, and Innovation in World History*. New York: Oxford University Press.

Li, Gang. 2011. *The Culture Elements of Eurasian Steppes in the Bronzes of North China* (Zhongguo beifang qingtongqi de ouya caoyuan wenhua yinsu). Beijing: wenwu chubanshe.

Mei, Jianjun. 2000. *Copper and Bronze Metallurgy in Late Prehistoric Xinjiang: its Cultural Context and Relationship with Neighbouring Regions*. BAR International Series 865. Oxford: Archaeopress.

Needham, Joseph. 1954. *Science and Civilisation in China*. Cambridge: Cambridge University Press.

Nunn, Nathan, and Diego Puga. 2012. Ruggedness: The Blessing of Bad Geography in Africa. *The Review of Economics and Statistics* 94 (1): 20–36.

Parker, Geoffrey. 1996. *The Military Revolution: Military Innovation and the Rise of the West, 1500–1800*. Cambridge: Cambridge University Press.

Scott, James C. 2017. *Against the Grain: A Deep History of the Earliest States*. New Haven: Yale University Press.

Shi, Yan. 2008. *Research on Bronze Arrows in North China during the Pre-Qin Period* (Zhongguo beifang xianqin shiqi qingtongqi yanjiu). Ha'erbin: Heilongjiang daxue chubanshe.

Turchin, Peter, Thomas E. Currie, Edward A. L. Turner, and Sergey Gavrilets. 2013. War, Space, and the Evolution of Old-World Complex Societies. *Proceedings of the National Academy of Sciences* 110 (41): 16384–16389.

Vandkilde, Helle. 2016. Bronzization: The Bronze Age as Pre-Modern Globalization. *Prähistorische Zeitschrift* 91 (1): 103–223.
Xu, Hong. 2017. *Archaeological Walled Cities in Pre-Qin China* (Xianqin chengyi kaogu). Beijing: Gold Wall and Xiyuan Press.
Zhao, Dingxin. 2015. *The Confucian-Legalist State: A New Theory of Chinese History*. Oxford: Oxford University Press.

# Part II
# Rulers, Institutions and the Military

# Chapter 4
# A Quantitative History of Regicide in China

**Zhiwu Chen and Zhan Lin**

## 4.1 Introduction

Imperial China is known for its autocratic governments. But was it truly static and stagnant over several millennia, with no noticeable change until modern times, as claimed by Hegel (1956) and Elvin (1972), among others? If there were changes, how effective were they? For at least the past two centuries, these questions have captivated scholars studying Chinese history, especially its institutional development history. In imperial China, the ruler monopolized almost all the power and played a dominating role in its governance (Wei 1989; Xu and Zhu 1996; Zhou 1999), although governance reforms were introduced from dynasty to dynasty. To study the effectiveness of China's institutional development and address the above questions, this paper focuses on the history of regicide, as any positive progress in governance innovations should result in a sustained decline in the regicide rate. In the existing literature, studies of historical rulers are often based on the experience of a single emperor or emperors of a single dynasty, with only a few exceptions that cover the entire imperial period (Gong 1992; Chen 2007). In contrast, our analysis includes all the 1,948 rulers, both kings and emperors, from the entire period of 1046 BCE – 1911 CE.

In the existing Chinese historiography, especially economic-history work on the effect of state capacity, the quality of a dynasty's institutions and the value of institutional reforms are typically evaluated using narrow but quantifiable outcomes such as economic growth, population increase, and productivity gains (e.g., Broadberry

Z. Chen
Centre for Quantitative History, Faculty of Business and Economics; Hong Kong Institute for the Humanities and Social Sciences, The University of Hong Kong, Hong Kong, China
e-mail: zhiwu.chen@hku.hk

Z. Lin (✉)
Institute of Qing History, Renmin University of China, Beijing, China
e-mail: zhan.lin@ruc.edu.cn

 
Z. Chen et al. (eds.), *Quantitative History of China*, Studies in Economic History,
https://doi.org/10.1007/978-981-96-8272-0_4

et al. 2018; Qian and Sng 2022). Thus, since growth in economy and population was higher during the eighteenth century than in the nineteenth century, institutional quality and governance during the reign of Emperor Kangxi (1661–1722 CE) and Qianlong (1735–1796 CE) are considered far better, creating the era of Kangxi-Qianlong Prosperity, whereas nineteenth-century China was an empire in decline. Nevertheless, according to Chen et al. (2017), from 1660 to 1820 CE, China's homicide rate for ordinary people steadily increased and personal security deteriorated. Based on this and other similar findings (Chen 2022), economic growth and productivity cannot be used alone to conclude the quality of governance institutions and the effectiveness of a dynasty's system. We must also consider the level of personal security and other adverse outcomes caused by a dynasty's institutions (see Chen 2022 for related discussions).

The homicide data used in Chen et al. (2017) are, however, limited to 1660 to 1885 CE, based on the *Xingke Tiben* (Criminal Case Memorials). Earlier historical records on violent crimes are rare and unsystematic, if available at all. According to Eisner (2011) and Baten (2021), in the absence of reliable violence data for long historical periods, one can instead focus on regicide data to investigate the history of human violence as the full sample of past rulers is relatively easier to obtain (as opposed to that of commoners or elites) and regicide represents an extreme form of violence that is related to the level of general violence in a given society. Therefore, constructing China's quantitative history of regicide is not only of interest for its own sake but also for studying its history of institutional development.

A ruler may die naturally (due to illness or aging) or unnaturally (i.e., regicide). The ruler's life risk is a function of personal, institutional, social, and environmental factors. A regicide can bring dramatic economic, social, and political turmoil with far-reaching consequences for the country, upending existing institutional arrangements and perhaps even leading to dynastic collapse (which can be good or bad). Still, well-functioning governance institutions should yield minimal regicide risk as such unexpected shocks can upset the larger society through interruptions to the public goods provided by the government and threaten the population's livelihood. For example, using a sample of post-Second World War leaders, Jones and Olken (2005) find that a sudden leader's death affected economic growth negatively in autocratic countries but not in democracies. Given China's long tradition of autocratic rule, a reduction in regicide through institutional reforms should mean higher welfare for the larger society, as that would bring more stability and security. Thus, the regicide rate serves as a key indicator of institutional quality.

A few studies have investigated Chinese regicides in history.[1] For example, Zhu (2015) examines 261 usurpation and regicide cases from the Qin (221–206 BCE) to the Qing dynasty (1644–1911 CE), with detailed statistical analysis. His study is, however, limited to emperors who were usurped or murdered, excluding both those who were not and the kings who ruled peripheral states outside the mainstay state or

[1] For example, Zhao (2015) discusses the regicide rate of the nine main states in the Warring States period (476–221 BCE), claiming that the greater the aristocratic power, the higher the regicide rate. But his study is limited only to the Warring States with a small sample.

empire.[2] Thus, his sample is relatively small and does not present the whole picture of Chinese regicide history and institutional development. Wang (2022) also conducts a quantitative analysis of Chinese regicide cases among 282 mainstay emperors but for the historical period beginning in the Han dynasty (206 BCE-220 CE).

Our ruler sample is much broader in scope and longer in the historical period covered, encompassing not only the emperors of the mainstream dynasties featured in the *Ershiwu Shi* (Twenty-Five Histories), but also the kings of peripheral states that were folded into a Chinese empire at some point from 1046 BCE to 1911 CE, including nomadic polities (e.g., Xiongnu, ~ 215 BCE- ~ 220 CE), rebel regimes (e.g., Huangjing, 184–192 CE), exile regimes (e.g., Beiyuan, 1368–1389 CE), and polities established by peasant uprisings (e.g., Taiping Tianguo, 1851–1864 CE). Specifically, our dataset covers 1,948 rulers in 448 states or polities that existed on today's territory of China, from King Wu of Zhou (the Western Zhou, 1046–771 BCE) to the last emperor of the Qing dynasty (1644–1911 CE), Xuantong.

Following Eisner (2011), we employ two indicators to measure the rulers' violent death rate: *regicide ratio* (i.e., percentage of rulers who died unnaturally) and *regicide rate* (probability of a ruler being killed per year, expressed as the number of unnatural deaths per 100,000 ruler-years). The latter is commonly used in criminology and allows us to establish a comparable index across time and space.

Based on the full sample, we find the regicide ratio to be 35.7%, or 695 rulers to have died unnaturally, which translates into a regicide rate of 2,899.8 deaths per 100,000 ruler-years, placing Chinese rulers as one of the most dangerous occupations in human history[3] and in sharp contrast with the commoners' homicide rate in eighteenth- and nineteenth-century China of slightly less than 3 per 100,000 person-years (Chen et al. 2017). This may explain why Chinese rulers had to be much more ruthless than ordinary people, or else they would be killed first. It is also why the reduction in the ruler's life risk should be a major yardstick for evaluating the effectiveness of government institutional reforms (Chen 2022). In a society where even rulers are concerned about their safety, it is unlikely that ordinary people will be safe from violence.

In *Politics,* Aristotle remarked:

> *"[D]emocracy appears to be safer and less liable to revolution than oligarchy. For in oligarchies, there is the double danger of the oligarchs falling out among themselves and also with the people; but in democracies, there is only the danger of a quarrel with the oligarchs. ... A government that is composed of the middle class more nearly approximates democracy than oligarchy and is the safest of the imperfect forms of government."*

In a democracy, it is the electorate that decides who becomes the ruler, so that even if someone were to assassinate the sitting ruler, he or she would not gain legitimate

---

[2] The book is based on the author's 1964 master thesis.

[3] Saleh (2019) argues that being a ruler of the Roman Empire was the most dangerous occupation, as 62% of them died violently. The prevalence of violent deaths among Chinese rulers was, on average, lower than that among Roman emperors. However, some Chinese dynasties, such as the Western Yan (384–394 CE) and the Later Liang state (907–923 CE), experienced a higher rate of violent deaths, with the regicide ratio reaching even 100%.

power to rule automatically. Thus, regicide is of little value, sharply reducing the incentives for such action. However, in a centralized regime, such incentives are high as the return from being the emperor is perceived high: not only are aristocrats motivated to eliminate and replace the emperor, but also the public can be enticed to start a revolution to remove him or her. In other words, both the inner court and the broader society pose threats to an autocratic ruler.

Given Aristotle's hypothesis, the existing literature has not yet established which of the two, the inner court or the masses, poses a bigger threat to an autocratic ruler's life. Historians have predominantly focused on the role of peasant uprisings and social turmoil in ruler assassination and dynastic collapse, rather than quantitatively assessing the extent of court members killing the ruler or forcing him to commit suicide. This emphasis may give contemporary readers the impression that it was the masses who posed the main threat to the ruler's and his regime's life. But our analysis reveals that of the regicides in Chinese history, 28.4% were ministers, 20% were the ruler's relatives, 48.7% were the rulers or generals of invading peripheral polities, and only 1.4% (nine individuals) were the leaders of civilian or peasant uprisings. That is, other than external threats, almost all the internal threats to the ruler's life came from the inner court (the ruler's ministers and relatives, contributing 48.4%), with the mass uprisings and rebellions playing a negligible role. This indicates that Chinese rulers were largely successful in mitigating life risks from mass revolts, but not in coping with threats from their inner circles and foreign enemies. When restricting our sample to only mainstream emperors covered in the *Ershiwu Shi* (Twenty-Five Histories) for 221 BCE-1911 CE, we find that of all the emperor killers, 73.9% were their ministers and relatives, 24.2% the rulers or generals of invading states, and only 1.3% were mass revolt organizers. Thus, court members were even a bigger threat in the mainstream empires than the peripheral states, perhaps due to most of the offshoot polities not lasting long enough for the rulers' inner circle members to develop successful plots against the rulers.

Our findings of historical regicide patterns in China generally corroborate the experience in historical Europe and modern totalitarian nations. Among medieval European regicides, 16.1% were committed by their ministers, 17.4% by relatives, and 18.8% by external forces. The proportion of cases perpetrated by organizers of civilian uprisings was 4.9%. Similarly, Svolik (2012) analyzed a sample of 316 totalitarian leaders from 1946 to 2008 and found that 205 of them, or 64.9%, were overthrown or executed by insiders within their ruling circles.

Our regression exercise indicates that appointing a successor in advance reduced succession uncertainty, which lowered the likelihood of regicide, a finding that aligns with contemporary practice in corporate succession management (Zhang and Rajagopalan 2010). Throughout Chinese history, rulers have debated the merits of appointing a successor. It remains unclear whether Emperor Taizu of the Song dynasty (960–1279 CE), who died unexpectedly, designated his younger brother as heir or if his brother ascended to the throne through regicide. But, upon assuming power, his brother, the future Emperor Taizong, posited that the disadvantage of appointing a successor in advance lies in the disruption of power dynamics within the court, as the successor might be motivated to assassinate the emperor to seize immediate control, forcing the emperor to take precautions against such a threat.[4] Later, Emperor Zhenzong of the Song expressed similar concerns. However, their doubts and rationalization do not align with our results, because succession planning not only mitigates uncertainty but also deters potential rivals from harboring ambitions for the throne, thereby preventing violent conflicts.

We also find that the probability of regicide would be higher if the ruler had a ministerial regency upon ascending the throne at a young age. Regent ministers, typically held administrative and military power, may harbor motives to undermine and eventually kill the rulers. It is also true that shorter-duration dynasties corresponded with higher rates of regicide. With 48.4% of ruler deaths attributed to court insiders, a higher rate of regicide within a dynasty signifies lower internal governance quality, culminating in shorter dynastic lifespans. Additionally, there is a significantly positive autocorrelation in the mode of death between consecutive rulers; that is, when one ruler died unnaturally, the likelihood that the next ruler would have the same fate would be significantly higher. Our data indicate that 41.6% of the regicide cases involved the killings of two or more consecutive rulers, consistent with Eisner's (2011) observations on European kings. Moreover, the more competing polities coexisting, and the more wars, droughts, and floods, within each 50 years, the higher the regicide rate during the same period.

Using data on the deaths of 1,513 kings from 45 European kingdoms between 600 and 1800 CE, Eisner (2011) found a regicide ratio of 22%, corresponding with an average annual violent death rate of 1,547 per 100,000, both figures much lower than in historical China. This finding offers another perspective on the origins of the economic Great Divergence between the East and the West since the late eighteenth century. A closer examination illustrates that both the Chinese and European regicide rates declined from the seventh century onward, attributed to institutional innovations in both regions. However, the decline of Chinese emperors' regicide rate was more relatively gradual but marked by greater fluctuations. Globally speaking, from the eleventh century to the end of the eighteenth century, the average duration of European rulers extended due to improved governance reforms, juxtaposed with a decline in the average tenure of Islamic rulers (Blaydes and Chaney 2013). But China followed a different pattern: its ruler duration swung up and down wildly, implying that it never figured out how to institutionally apply checks and balances to ensure the peaceful transfer of power at the top.

Our study makes four contributions to the existing literature. First, we highlight the extremely high life risk faced by autocratic rulers, which worked to shape ruler behavior. This is in contrast with ruler behavior models in which the ruler's objective is to maximize his long-term fiscal income, with rebellion from the commoners acting as a constraint on his actions, an assumption that is only valid when the ruler has a relatively stable reign and encounters a minimal risk of regicide (Sng 2014; Ma and Rubin 2019). However, our finding indicates that autocratic rulers confronted a

---

[4] Patricia Ebrey. "Succession to high office: The Chinese case", In *Technology, Literacy, and the Evolution of Society: Implications of the Work of Jack Goody* edited by David Olson and Michael Cole, 49–71. Mahwah, N.J: Lawrence Erlbaum, 2006.

significantly higher life risk than assumed in existing studies. The primary life threat for such a ruler originated from members in his inner circles, rather than from the commoners.

Second, our research contributes to the state capacity literature by emphasizing the importance of ruler security and peaceful transfer of power. As defined by Bates (2020), a state comprises "a political hierarchy consisting of tax collectors to collect income, a police force, and a military to assist with security, and a judiciary to administer legal justice. This political body is led by a chief executive (sometimes referred to as "the monarch") in conjunction with a noble or parliamentary council." Existing work on state capacity largely focuses on fiscal extraction ability and the rule of law, while overlooking governance institutions at the top (Ma 2013). It can be argued that a regime with high risk to the ruler's life could hardly possess high state capacity (Wang 2022), a point especially important for studying imperial China.

Third, we offer another perspective on the Great Divergence in terms of institutions ensuring political stability or the lack thereof (Blaydes and Chaney 2013). Our analysis introduces quantitative evidence highlighting the institutional differences among Eastern, Western, and Islamic polities and their institutional performance, as viewed through the lens of regicide rate and rule duration. Lastly, we construct a quantitative history of regicide for historical China since 1046 BCE, with the most comprehensive coverage of all polities that existed in today's Chinese territory, adding to the Chinese history literature.

The remainder of the chapter is organized as follows: Sect. 4.2 offers the historical background and regicide examples. Sect. 4.3 presents descriptive statistics for data on the dynasties and rulers. Section 4.4 examines factors affecting rulers' life risk, while Sect. 4.5 investigates the temporal variations in regicide, ruler duration and perpetrator type. Section 4.6 concludes the paper.

## 4.2 Historical Background and Regicide Examples

Constructing our ruler sample for 1046 BCE-1911 CE presents us with two immediate challenges. First, what states or polities should be included in what is called "China"? For the long period under study, China was always a "work in progress," with the borders of the mainstream state or empire frequently redrawn, which means there were always competing polities that coexisted outside those territories. To address this, we use China's map of 1820 CE as a reference point and include in our sample any state that existed within that 1820 territory over any subperiod of 1046 BCE-1911 CE, which produces 448 states or polities (including the empires),[5] a significant increase compared to the 25 mainstream states documented in the official historical records, *Ershiwu Shi* (Twenty-Five Histories). For this reason, we will, for robustness checks, consider both samples: the full sample and the 25 mainstream dynasty sample.

---

[5] Following Baten (2021), we include any state that survived for more than one day and that is mentioned in the history sources.

Next, who can be treated as a "ruler"? During the formative centuries of historical China, or the Zhou dynasty (1046–221 BCE), there were no emperors but lots of kings, as there were many separate polities, each with a king, especially during the Spring and Autumn (770–476 BCE) and the Warring States period (476–221 BCE). While later eras witnessed the emergence of supposedly unified empires such as the Han (206 BCE-220 CE), the Tang (618–906 CE), the Song (960–1279 CE), and the Ming dynasty (1368–1644), all ruled by emperors, their territories were mostly smaller than that of the Qing dynasty in 1820, so they each had lingering peripheral states constantly knocking at their borders and threatening the mainstream emperor (Fairbank and Reischauer 1989). Our full sample includes all these kings and emperors of the 448 states or polities based on Baten (2021), wherein a ruler is defined as an individual who "possessed a certain degree of autonomy in high-level decision-making"[6] which gives us 1,948 rulers in total.[7]

Note that our primary source of information on the dynasties, polities, and rulers (including how they died) is the *Zhongguo Lishi Jinian Zongbiao* (Comprehensive Chronological Tables of Chinese History), on which Wilkinson (2013) commented that it is "on a huge scale and indispensable" and "puts all previous chronological tables out of business" (p. 277, p. 521). Additionally, we incorporate information from the *Ershiwu Shi* (Twenty-Five Histories) and the *Zhongguo Lishi Dituji* (*Atlas of Chinese History*). There are five rulers in our collection who ascended to the throne on two distinct occasions, in which case each ruler is treated as two separate occurrences in our sample. As in Eisner (2011), where possible, we cross-check our ruler data with other scholarly publications and in cases of discrepancies, we defer to what is in published scholarly work.

To facilitate comparison with existing work and for robustness checks, we divide the full sample into three subsamples. Subsample A has all the rulers (kings) from the pre-Qin period (1046–221 BCE), while subsample B comprises all the emperors of the mainstream empires and states from 221 BCE-1911 CE, as documented in *Twenty-Five Histories*, including the Qin, the Han, the Three Kingdoms (220–280 CE), the Jin (266–420 CE), the Sixteen Kingdoms (304–439 CE), the Northern and Southern Dynasties (420–589 CE), the Sui (589–608 CE), the Tang (618–906 CE), the Five Dynasties and Ten Kingdoms (907–960 CE), the Song (960–1279 CE), the Yuan (1279–1368 CE), the Liao (916–1125 CE), the Jin (1115–1234 CE), the Western Xia (1038–1227 CE), the Ming (1368–1644 CE), and the Qing (1644–1911 CE). This emperor sample has been widely examined in existing studies (e.g., Wang 2022). Subsample C collects all the rulers who were not emperors of any mainstream

---

[6] As a result, empresses dowagers who exercised power from behind the veil, such as Empress Dowager Cixi of the late nineteenth century, powerful ministers who assumed sovereign power but were not labeled as rulers, such as Cao Cao who "held the emperor hostage to control the warlords," Li Te of the Cheng Han state and Fu Hong of the Former Qin state are not counted as rulers.

[7] Actually, we obtained a sample of 1,962 rulers; however, 14 of them, accounting for 0.7%, had missing death information. Consequently, the actual sample of rulers utilized for our analysis has 1,948 rulers. The last emperor of the Qing dynasty, Emperor Xuantong, died in 1967.

empire from 221 BCE to 1911 CE, comprising the rulers of peripheral states (e.g., Xiongnu and Dali), exile regimes (e.g., Beiyuan and Xiliao), rebel regimes (e.g., Huangjing), and polities established by civilian uprisings (e.g., the Da Shun regime established by Li Zicheng). These rulers are seldom included in existing regicide studies, but they coexisted with and affected those in subsample B.

For example, if we only consider the emperors, the Qing Dynasty has 12 of them in subsample B. However, for the same period, subsample C has 89 rulers from 62 other regimes that coexisted, including exile regimes (e.g., Southern Ming), frontier regimes (e.g., Yarkand Khanate), rebel regimes (e.g., Wu Zhou, founded by Wu Sangui), and regimes established by uprising organizers (e.g., the Taiping Tianguo).

Note that in Chinese intellectual discourse, "emperor," or *huangdi*, means "the son of heaven": "He is Heaven's son and rules all under Heaven according to His will" (Zhou 1999, 2). Historians generally agree that Qin Shi Huang, founder of the first Chinese empire—the Qin—was China's first emperor. He was born in 259 BCE and died in 210 BCE. After unifying China at the age of 39 (221 BCE), he gave himself the title of emperor to convey his status as the empire's sole monarch and to distinguish himself from former monarchs titled "king" (wang) (Loewe and Twitchett 1986). That's why 221 BC is of special importance in Chinese history and the dividing line between our subsample A and subsamples B and C.

The first emperor killed was also from the Qin dynasty, Qin Er Shi, whose name was Huhai. His successor was killed as well.[8] After Qin Shi Huang, historical scholarship lacks consensus on which rulers can be classified as emperors. We follow *Ershiwu Shi* (Twenty-Five Histories) for our purpose. To provide more background on our regicide data, we present four cases, each representing a different type.[9]

### Case 1: Huhai of the Qin Dynasty

Qin Shi Huang, founding emperor of the Qin dynasty (221–206 BCE), declared that he would hand over the throne to his eldest son, Fusu, before his death. However, in collaboration with Chancellor Li Si, eunuch Zhao Gao falsified the imperial edict, forced Fusu to commit suicide and crowned Huhai, Qin Shi Huang's younger son.

To consolidate the usurped throne, Huhai assassinated his brothers, Meng Tian and Meng Yi (who commanded the army), beheaded 12 of his siblings, and dismembered six brothers and 10 sisters.

Since Huhai blamed Zhao Gao for the fact that the uprising army led by Chen Sheng and Wu Guang was approaching the capital, Zhao Gao began plotting a coup. Yan Le, Zhao Gao's son-in-law, led an army into the palace and forced Huhai to

[8] Sima Qian (1994), *Records of the Grand Historian: The Basic Annals of Pre-Han China* (Vol. 1), translated by Nienhauser, W. H., and published by Indiana University Press (p. 123). It should be noted that the correct reference is the eleventh year of Qin Shihuang, rather than the "fifty-first." Additionally, the translation of Chinese names in this quotation has been changed from Wade-Giles to Hanyu Pinyin.

[9] Given the wealth of historical records on emperors, the following examples exclusively involve emperors.

commit suicide in 207 BCE; Huhai died at the age of 24 and reigned for only three years.

**Case 2: Emperor Ping of the Western Han (206 BCE-9 CE)**

Having learned the lessons about the consequences of power monopolization during the reigns of preceding emperors, Liu Ao (51–7 BCE), known as the Emperor Cheng of the Han dynasty, made his mother Wang Zhengjun Empress Dowager. He also appointed his uncle Wang Feng as marshal of the state and general in chief and gave him authority over the secretariat as well as overall responsibility for state affairs. And Empress Dowager Wang's five younger half-brothers were all given the title of marquis. Both Emperor Cheng and his successor Emperor Ai (27–1 BCE) had no sons, so their nephews were made heirs. When Emperor Ai's nephew, Liu Kan, later Emperor Ping (9 BCE-6 CE), took the throne at the age of eight, Empress Dowager Wang was still alive and appointed her nephew, Wang Mang (45 BCE-23 CE), marshal of the state. With Emperor Ping as his puppet, Wang Mang seized the highest power and forbade Emperor Ping's consort kin from serving as officials in the court but kept them with some titles in the Zhongshan state, Emperor Ping's former fiefdom when he was still a prince. As Emperor Ping grew older, he became increasingly dissatisfied with Wang Mang. So, feeling insecure, Wang Mang murdered Emperor Ping and later usurped the throne, establishing the Xin dynasty (9–25 CE).

**Case 3: Emperor Taizu of Later Liang During the Five Dynasties**

Zhu Wen (852–912 CE) was a general in the Huang Chao Rebellion (874–884 CE), who later surrendered to the army of the Tang dynasty (618–906 CE), and was given the name Quanzhong, literally "full of loyalty," by Tang Emperor Xizong (862–888 CE). Subsequently, he increased his forces and prepared to usurp the throne. In 904 CE, he assassinated Tang Emperor Zhaozong (867–904 CE) and declared the 13-year-old Li Zhu (892–908 CE) as crown prince and later Emperor Ai, who was only a puppet emperor under Zhu Wen's control. Zhu Wen began to murder members of the Tang imperial clan, including Empress Dowager He, Emperor Ai's mother. Zhu forced Emperor Ai to abdicate the throne in 907 CE and murdered him in 908 CE, putting the Tang dynasty to an end.

After the usurpation, Zhu founded the Later Liang state (907–923 CE), abolished the Bureau of Military Affairs, which had been controlled by eunuchs in the Tang, and established the Office for the Veneration of Governance, filled with literati rather than eunuchs. He then made his second son, Zhu Youwen, the crown prince. After hearing the news, his third son, Zhu Yougui (886–913 CE), led his army to kill Zhu Wen. In 912 CE, Zhu Yougui declared himself Emperor and named Zhu Wen's fourth son, Zhu Youzhen (888–923 CE), governor of Kaifeng and regent of the Eastern Capital. In the following year, with the help of military commissioner Yang Shihou, Zhu Youzhen assassinated Zhu Yougui and ascended to the throne as Emperor Mo of the Later Liang.

**Case 4: Emperors Huizong and Qinzong of the Song**

Emperor Huizong (1081–1135 CE) of the Song dynasty was Emperor Shenzong's eleventh son. Because his elder brother, Emperor Zhezong (1076–1100 CE), died at the age of 24 with no living male issue, Huizong became the eighth emperor of the Song dynasty. Despite his artistic achievements, he was deemed foolish by the ruling circles. The Song was invaded by the Jin State (or, the Jurchen) in 1125 CE. Out of fear, Emperor Huizong abdicated the throne in favor of his son, Zhao Heng (1100–1161 CE), who later became Emperor Qinzong. After the Jin army retreated in 1126 CE, Huizhong fled to Zhenjiang and was taken back to Kaifeng, the capital, by Qinzong. The Jin army staged a comeback and captured Kaifeng at the end of the year. Both Huizong and Qinzong were captured and escorted to the enemy Jin State in an episode known as the Jingkang Incident.

The Jin State's ruler dubbed Emperor Huizong the "Duke of Faint Virtue" and Emperor Qinzong the "Marquis of Heavy Faint," mocking both the father and the son for their repeated fainting. Tortured by the Jin, Huizong died at Wuguocheng in the Jin State (in today's Heilongjiang) in 1135 CE, becoming the Song dynasty's first emperor to die in a foreign country. Emperor Qinzong was tortured to death in 1156 CE.

## 4.3 Data Description

In addition to the ruler data above, we collect data on wars from *Zhongguo Lidai Zhanzheng Nianbiao* (A Chronology of Wars in Dynastic China) and on droughts and floods, for which data is available only for 115 BCE - 1911 CE from Zheng et al. (2006). More details will be provided when used in analysis.

Table 4.1 provides summary statistics of the dynasties and rulers for the full sample.The duration of rule for these dynasties ranges from 0.1 years to 957 years, with an average of 62.1 years. The longest-lasting regimes were mainly from the pre-Qin period and ethnic-minority regimes in the frontier areas. For example, the Eastern Zhou dynasty lasted for 515 years, and the kingdom of Khotan lasted for nearly 1000 years. The fact that these regimes are not among the much-celebrated unified empire polities is quite telling as it signals that the unified empires must have been much more challenging to rule peacefully (unless the rulers were able to adopt well-functioning governance systems). The number of rulers in each dynasty ranges from 1 to 40, with an average of 4.3. Each dynasty's number of emperors killed ranges from 0 to 12, averaging about 1.6, implying an average regicide ratio of 56.8% by dynasty. This ratio is quite high because about 247 regimes have a single ruler, of which 70% are killed. In these regimes, the regicide ratio is 100%.

Table 4.2 presents summary statistics on the 1,948 rulers. Ruler lifetime exhibits significant variation, with the youngest life ending at two years and the oldest at 103. On average, rulers lived for 42.2 years. The average age when assuming the throne was 27.7, with the youngest being one year old and the oldest 73 years. The

**Table 4.1** Descriptive statistics by dynasty

| Variable | Obs | Mean | Std. Dev | Min | Max |
|---|---|---|---|---|---|
| Start year | 448 | 727.1 | 698.3 | –1046 | 1895 |
| End year | 448 | 789.2 | 645.5 | –771 | 1911 |
| Dynasty duration | 448 | 62.1 | 138.4 | 0.1 | 957 |
| No. of rulers | 448 | 4.3 | 6.7 | 1 | 40 |
| No. of regicides | 448 | 1.6 | 1.9 | 0 | 12 |
| Regicide ratio by dynasty | 448 | 56.8 | 42.3 | 0 | 100 |

**Table 4.2** Descriptive statistics of rulers

| Variable | Obs | Mean | Std. Dev | Min | Max |
|---|---|---|---|---|---|
| Age at death | 444 | 42.17 | 17.23 | 2 | 103 |
| Age at enthronement | 464 | 27.74 | 14.59 | 1 | 73 |
| Ruler duration | 1776 | 12.82 | 13.1 | 0.07 | 75 |
| No. of sons | 984 | 3.44 | 4.82 | 0 | 42 |
| No. of brothers | 866 | 4.71 | 5.89 | 0 | 41 |
| Appointed a successor | 1243 | 0.5 | 0.5 | 0 | 1 |
| Minister's regency | 1425 | 0.19 | 0.39 | 0 | 1 |
| Regicide ratio | 1948 | 0.357 | 0.48 | 0 | 1 |

*Notes* Three variables, Appointed a Successor, Minister's Regency and Regicide ratio, are "dummy" variables; for example, Appointed a Successor is set to 1: if the ruler appointed a successor during his/her lifetime; otherwise, it is 0. Due to certain missing information for some rulers, the number of observations differs across the variables. Among the three subsamples defined in the preceding section, subsample B, containing only the emperors, has the least missing information, whereas the other two have missing information for more rulers. Refer to Appendix A for the descriptive statistics of these three subsamples

average reign lasted for eight years, with the shortest at less than one month and the longest at 73 years. Among the 984 rulers with available data, the average number of sons was 3.4, with some having no sons and some over 40. Of the 1,243 rulers with clear records regarding whether he or she appointed a successor while alive, 50% did so. Detailed information on the initial enthronement process is available for 1,425 rulers, of whom 19% needed a minister's regency (*Guming Dachen*). Out of the 1,948 rulers, 35.7% of them died unnaturally.

### *4.3.1 Regicide Ratio and Regicide Rate*

In the literature, two indicators are used: regicide ratio (defined as the proportion of rulers who died unnaturally) and regicide rate (number of unnatural deaths per 100,000 ruler-years) (Eisner 2011). Among the 1,948 rulers in our full sample, 695 were victims of regicide, accounting for 35.7%, which translates into a regicide rate of 2,899.8 per 100,000 ruler-years, calculated as the number of unnatural deaths in the sample divided by the sum of each ruler's years of reign among all the rulers, multiplied by 100,000. Thus, the regicide rate so computed captures how many rulers would be killed for every 100,000 rulers during each reign year. For comparison, Chen et al. (2017) find that the homicide rate for ordinary people was about 3 per 100,000 person-years between 1660 and 1885 in Qing China. Thus, the death risk for Chinese rulers is nearly 1,000 times as high as for ordinary people.

In Europe, homicide rates for the– common population were typically from 20 to 50 per 100,000 person-years during the High Middle Ages and declined to the 1–10 range in the eighteenth century (Eisner 2011). Contemporary homicide rates are from 0.6 to 1.5 in Western Europe (Aebi et al. 2006), about 120 for young black men in the early 1990s United States (Blumstein 2000), and about 130 in Ciudad Juárez, Mexico, one of the most murderous cities in the world today.

### *4.3.2 Types of Murderers*

Given the high regicide rate among rulers, it is of great interest to understand the sources of threat and identify perpetrators by type. In Table 4.3, we classify the perpetrator's relationship with the ruler into two categories: internal ruling court members and external members. Internal members are further divided into relatives, ministers, and assistants (e.g., eunuchs and concubines), while external members consist of leaders of civilian uprisings and the rulers and generals of competing co-existing regimes.

**Table 4.3** Relationship between murderers and rulers

| Relation between Murderer and Ruler | China | | | | | | | | Europe | |
|---|---|---|---|---|---|---|---|---|---|---|
| | Full Sample | | Subsample A | | Subsample B | | Subsample C | | Full Sample | |
| | Freq | % | Freq | % | Freq | % | Freq | % | Freq | % |
| Co-existing regimes | 304 | 48.7 | 14 | 16.9 | 38 | 24.2 | 252 | 65.6 | 42 | 18.8 |
| Ministers | 177 | 28.4 | 28 | 33.7 | 63 | 40.1 | 86 | 22.4 | 45 | 20.1 |
| Relatives | 125 | 20 | 35 | 42.2 | 53 | 33.8 | 37 | 9.6 | 52 | 23.2 |
| Uprising Organizer | 9 | 1.4 | 3 | 3.6 | 2 | 1.3 | 4 | 1 | 11 | 4.9 |
| Others | 9 | 1.4 | 3 | 3.6 | 1 | 0.6 | 5 | 1.3 | 31 | 33 |
| Total | 624 | 100 | 83 | 100 | 157 | 100 | 384 | 100 | 224 | 100 |

*Notes* The full sample of Chinese rulers was divided into three subsamples: subsample A (kings from 1046 to 221 BCE); subsample B (emperors from 221 BCE to 1911 CE), and subsample C (rulers of peripheral and rebel regimes from 221 BCE to 1911 CE). The list of European kings is from Eisner (2011). We manually collected the information about the murderers

For the full sample in Table 4.3, 48.7% of the regicides were from external co-existing regimes, with 49.8% of them coming from within the polity. Specifically, of the perpetrators, 28.4% were internal ministers, 20% relatives, and 1.4% leaders and organizers of civilian or peasant uprisings. Thus, internal court members (the ruler's ministers and relatives) made up 48.4%,—a figure much higher than that from the civilian uprising organizers (1.4%)—and contrary to the impression generally conveyed to students by history books in Chinese classrooms that emphasize the role, and portray the importance, of the peasant class in toppling historical regimes. In total, there were only nine instances where civilian or peasant rebellions led to the ruler's death, including the killing of King Ziying (?-206 BCE) of the Qin by Xiang Yu's rebels during the Qin, of Wang Mang (Emperor of the Xin, 45 BCE-23 CE) by merchant Du Yu, and the suicide of Emperor Chongzhen (1611–1644 CE) of the Ming when Li Zicheng entered the capital city—Beijing—at the end of the Ming dynasty. This evidence also shows that between the two types of threat to an autocratic ruler's life as postulated by Aristotle, members in his inner circle within the court were much more dangerous than the public, as organizers of commoner uprisings and rebellions hardly posed real threats to the ruler's life.

The subsamples reveal variations in the patterns. For subsample A, which comprises the pre-Qin kings, 79.5% of perpetrators were from within the kingdom, with ministers accounting for 33.7%, relatives for 42.2%, the two groups which made up 75.9% of the total, and those out of civilian uprisings accounting for only 3.6%. Direct external threats to the ruler's life were lower, contributing only 16.9% of the cases, than for the full sample. This is perhaps the case due to the smaller states in pre-Qin times having shorter borders to defend than the bigger unified empires starting from the Qin. It might also be caused by the underrepresentation of actual events in pre-Qin historical records.

For subsample B, including all the mainstream emperors from the Qin to the Qing, 75.2% of murderers were from within the empire, with ministers accounting for 40.1% of the total, relatives for 33.8%, and civilian uprising organizers for only 1.3%. The emperor's inner circle was still the biggest threat, signaling the lack of proper power sharing, succession planning, and governance institutions, which resulted in the emperor having too much power that could not be peacefully transferred and was up for grabs upon, or even prior to, his death.

For subsample C, containing the non-emperor rulers for peripheral and rebel states from 221 BCE to 1911 CE, external threats from co-existing regimes (including the mainstream Chinese empire) were the key with them being responsible for perpetrating 65.6% of the regicides. Most of these ruler killings were committed by the troops and generals of the mainstream empires in subsample B. In these instances, the ruler's ministers accounted for 22.4% of the regicides, relatives for 9.6%, and civilian uprising organizers for only 1%.

To contrast China's historical experience with that of Europe, we use the European regicide data for 600–1800 CE from Eisner (2011) and decompose the perpetrators into similar categories. The results displayed in the last two columns of Table 4.3. demonstrate a similarity: the European ruler's ministers, family members, and external enemies from other states constituted the three most significant risks to the ruler's life. Of the 224 regicide cases, 18.8% were committed by external perpetrators, 20.1% by ministers, and 23.2% by relatives.

## 4.4 Factors Affecting Ruler Life Risk

Our analysis so far shows that the biggest group of regicide perpetrators consisted of people closest to the rulers, as well as foreign enemies. Next, we explore factors that influence the risk to a ruler's life. We start with Table 4.4 where, of the full sample, the unnatural-death ruler group is compared with the natural-death ruler group. Note that rulers who died naturally lived longer with an average age of 46.3 years, as opposed to 34 years for those who were victims of regicide. The natural-death rulers had an average enthronement age of 28.3 years, versus 26.6 years for the unnatural-death rulers, ascended at an average age of 26.6 years; ruled on average for 16.5 years, versus 6.6 years for the other group; had an average of 3.8 sons, versus 2.4 sons for the other group; and 4.6 brothers, versus 4.9 brothers for the unnatural-death group, suggesting slightly more competition for the latter group as they had more brothers. The data also show that 62% of natural-death rulers appointed a successor before death, compared to only 24% of those who died violently, resulting in a 38-percentage point gap, and indicating a significant impact of advance succession planning. Moreover, 16% of rulers in the former group relied on a minister's regency at the time of their ascension, whereas this figure was 25% for the latter group, suggesting that this may have been a determinant of the likelihood of regicide. Our T-test exercise confirms that except for the number of brothers, the mean difference between the two groups is statistically significant at the 1% level for all the other variables examined in Table 4.4.

**Table 4.4** Comparison between natural- and unnatural-death rulers

| Variables | Natural-death rulers | | | Unnatural-death rulers | | | p-value for Diff T-test |
|---|---|---|---|---|---|---|---|
| | Sample Size | Average | Std Dev | Sample Size | Average | Std Dev | |
| Age | 295 | 46.3 | 16.6 | 149 | 34 | 15.5 | 0.00 |
| Age at Enthronement | 308 | 28.3 | 14.8 | 156 | 26.6 | 14.1 | 0.00 |
| Ruler Duration | 1116 | 16.5 | 13.9 | 660 | 6.6 | 8.6 | 0.00 |
| No. of Sons | 729 | 3.8 | 5.2 | 255 | 2.4 | 3.4 | 0.00 |
| No. Brothers | 562 | 4.6 | 6 | 304 | 4.9 | 5.6 | 0.45 |
| Appointed a Successor | 837 | 0.62 | 0.5 | 406 | 0.24 | 0.43 | 0.00 |
| Minister's Regency | 929 | 0.16 | 0.37 | 496 | 0.25 | 0.43 | 0.00 |

War and natural disasters may have also played a role in regicide outcomes, either directly or indirectly, as such events may have generated enough distress in the larger society, providing an opportunity for a rival to act against the ruler. Due to the limitations of historical data, it is difficult for us to precisely match wars and disasters, especially those in early Chinese history, by year and with each regime. Therefore, we use 50-year intervals to examine the impact of wars and disasters within each interval on the regicide rate of that period.

Next, we examine the influence of the following factors: (1) whether the ruler appointed a successor in advance, (2) whether the ruler ascended to the throne with a minister's regency, (3) whether his predecessor died from regicide, (4) the dynasty's duration, (5) the number of external co-existing regimes, (6) the number of wars within the contemporary 50 years, and (7) the number of flood and drought events within the contemporary 50 years.

### 4.4.1 *Effect of Successor Appointment*

When a ruler appoints a successor, there are two effects: the chosen crown prince is eager to succeed, threatening the sitting ruler's life, and there is also the barrier effect that the presence of a crown prince removes succession uncertainty, reducing the ruler's life risk (Konrad and Mui 2017).

To illustrate the first effect, we can look at the example of Emperor Kangxi (1654–1722 CE) of the Qing, who appointed his one-year-old first son, Yunreng, as the crown prince when the emperor himself was only 23 years old. As Yunreng grew older, he and his father had a falling out, which resulted in the son being deposed twice and eventually imprisoned for life. That experience made Emperor Kangxi end the practice of appointing a successor for the rest of the Qing. Another example is Yang Guang, Emperor Yang of the Sui dynasty (581–618 CE), who murdered his father before being enthroned.

As for the barrier effect, when a successor is known, it shifts the life risk from the incumbent ruler to the crown prince as potential competitors will now focus on attacking the successor. For instance, Li Shimin (598–649 CE), who later became Emperor Taizong of the Tang, assassinated the crown prince and two brothers, Li Jiancheng and Li Yuanji, to gain control of the throne. In the example above, during the Qing, Kangxi's other sons who aspired to assume the throne also attacked the crown prince.

To evaluate the net impact of these two effects, we conduct various analyses in Table 4.5. Of the 1,243 rulers with clear succession information, 619 appointed a successor, with 15.5% of the incumbent rulers suffering regicide. In contrast, among the 624 rulers who did not appoint a successor, 49.7% died unnaturally. The net impact of successor appointment is evident.

**Table 4.5** Impact of successor appointment on regicide risk

| Sample type | Sample size | Appointed a successor | Mode of ruler's death | | |
|---|---|---|---|---|---|
| | | | Natural death (%) | Regicide (%) | Obs |
| All rulers | 1243 | Y | 84.5 | 15.5 | 619 |
| | | N | 50.3 | 49.7 | 624 |
| Rulers with at least one son | 794 | Y | 85.1 | 14.9 | 592 |
| | | N | 64.9 | 35.1 | 202 |
| Rulers with at least one son and in regimes that had more than three rulers | 731 | Y | 85.5 | 14.5 | 558 |
| | | N | 66.5 | 33.5 | 173 |
| Rulers with at least one son and in regimes that had more than three rulers, excluding the last ruler of each regime | 666 | Y | 85.7 | 14.3 | 517 |
| | | N | 65.1 | 34.9 | 149 |

Excluding rulers who died young and did not have the opportunity to have a son, we focus on the remaining sample of 794 rulers who had at least one son. In this sample, 592 rulers appointed a successor, and 202 did not. Among those who did appoint, 14.9% experienced regicide, while 35.1% of those who did not face the same fate.

Furthermore, we can also restrict our attention to regimes that had at least three separate rulers with at least one son. This led to a sample of 731 rulers, of which 558 rulers appointed a successor and 173 did not. The regicide ratio was 14.5% for those who appointed a successor and 33.5% for those who did not.

Finally, we remove the last ruler of each regime from the preceding sample as their reign was typically short, so they might not have had enough time to appoint a successor, which may have affected our analysis. After these removals, we are left with 666 rulers, of whom 517 appointed a successor (with a regicide ratio of 14.3%) and 149 did not (with a regicide ratio of 34.9%).

The above analysis thus confirms that the violent death risk for rulers who appointed a successor was less than half of that for those who did not. Succession planning would clearly improve the ruler's safety.

### 4.4.2 *Minister's Regency*

The presence of a minister's regency was often associated with young rulers. These ministers frequently held military and political power, making it relatively easy for

**Table 4.6** Impact of Minister's regency on regicide

| Sample type | Sample size | Minister's regency | Mode of ruler's death | | |
|---|---|---|---|---|---|
| | | | Natural (%) | Regicide (%) | No. of obs |
| Full sample | 1425 | Y | 55.1 | 44.9 | 272 |
| | | N | 67.6 | 32.4 | 1153 |
| Subsample A | 420 | Y | 76.8 | 23.2 | 69 |
| | | N | 79.2 | 20.8 | 351 |
| Subsample B | 341 | Y | 47.1 | 52.9 | 136 |
| | | N | 70.2 | 29.8 | 205 |
| Subsample C | 664 | Y | 49.3 | 50.8 | 67 |
| | | N | 59.8 | 42.2 | 597 |

*Notes* The full sample of rulers is divided into three subsamples: subsample A, which includes kings from 1046 to 221 BCE, subsample B, comprising the emperors from 221 BCE to 1911 CE, and subsample C, containing all non-emperor rulers during 221 BCE to 1911 CE

them to usurp the throne, as exemplified by Wang Mang (45 BCE-23 CE) in the late Western Han Dynasty. Table 4.6 shows that a ruler with a minister's regency during their initial ascension faced a significantly higher probability of regicide. Of the 1,425 rulers with complete information on regency, 272 were assisted by ministers, and 44.9% of them died unnaturally. In contrast, 32.4% of the other 1,153 rulers suffered regicide.

The difference between the two groups becomes even more pronounced when only the emperors in subsample B are considered. Among the 341 emperors with regency information, 136 had a minister's regency, of whom 52.9% died from regicide. In contrast, 29.8% of the other 205 emperors died unnaturally.

### 4.4.3 Regicide Continuity

We address the question of whether a ruler's fate was affected by that of his predecessors by investigating the correlation in death mode between consecutive rulers in the same regime. Our analysis reveals a significant autocorrelation in death mode, that is, when a ruler dies from regicide, there is a significant chance that his successor would die in the same way, implying that the regicide rate reflects a regime's quality of governance institutions that can be changed only through institutional reforms.

In our full sample, there are 136 instances (68 pairs) of two consecutive rulers being assassinated; for example, Qin Er Shi and King Ziying of the Qin dynasty (221–206 BCE) both died from regicide. We also find 69 instances (23 groups) of three consecutive rulers being murdered; for example, Emperor Wu (or Taizu), Prince Ying (Zhu Yougui), and Emperor Mo of the Later Liang state (907–923 CE). In total, 289 rulers were consecutively murdered, accounting for 41.6% of the 695 regicide cases.

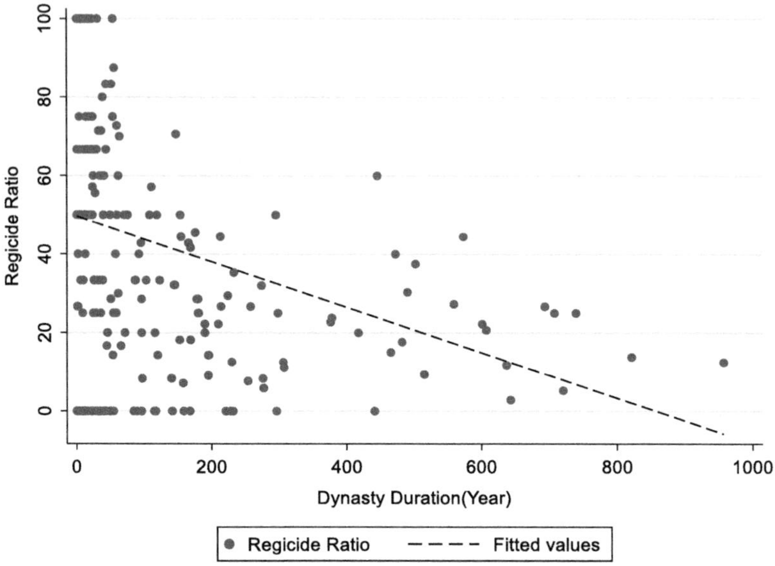


**Fig. 4.1** Correlation between dynasty duration and regicide ratio (full sample). *Notes* The regicide ratio is defined as the proportion of rulers who died unnaturally

These findings are consistent with Eisner's (2011) based on European regicide history. Thus, within each dynasty, regicide occurrences tended to cluster, reflecting the wrongs of a regime's underlying institutions.

### *4.4.4 Dynasty Duration and Regicide Ratio*

The longevity of a regime often reflects its success in governance institutions. Consequently, a longer dynasty duration should be accompanied by a lower regicide rate within that dynasty. Figure 4.1 plots the relationship between the two, where the horizontal axis represents a regime's duration and the vertical axis is its regicide ratio, showcasing a significant negative correlation, that is, longer-lasting regimes had significantly lower regicide rates.

### *4.4.5 Competing Regimes, War, and Regicide*

Invading armies from competing polities accounted for a large portion of regicide cases. In Fig. 4.2, the horizontal axis stands for the number of competing regimes that existed in the 1820 CE land of Qing China and within each 50-year interval

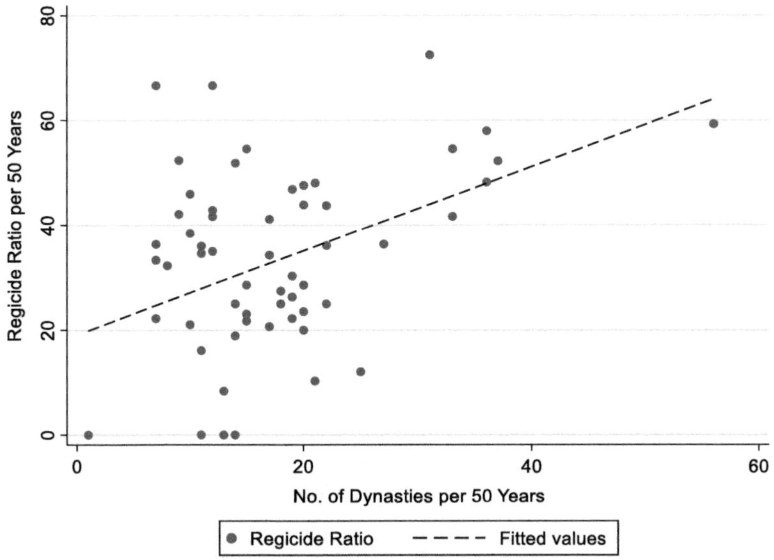


**Fig. 4.2** Relation between competing regimes and regicide ratio (full sample). *Notes* The regicide ratio for each 50-year interval is the percentage of the period's rulers who died unnaturally

while the vertical axis is the regicide ratio in the given period. It is evident from the chart that more co-existing polities meant higher regicide rates.

Similarly, Fig. 4.3 shows that more wars in a 50-year interval were associated with a higher regicide ratio.

### *4.4.6 Natural Disasters and Regicide*

Natural disasters play a significant role in triggering conflicts (Bai and Kung 2011). It is expected that natural disasters can cause much distress, economic and otherwise, in the larger society, which can translate into severe political distress in the ruler's court and lead to regicide. To examine the possible relationship between natural disasters and regicide, we select two types of disasters: drought and flood. Figures 4.4 and 4.5 respectively illustrate that over each given 50-year interval, higher numbers of drought and flood were associated with a higher regicide ratio. By combining both types of disaster into a summary indicator, Fig. 4.6 demonstrates a positive correlation between natural disasters and the regicide ratio in each period.

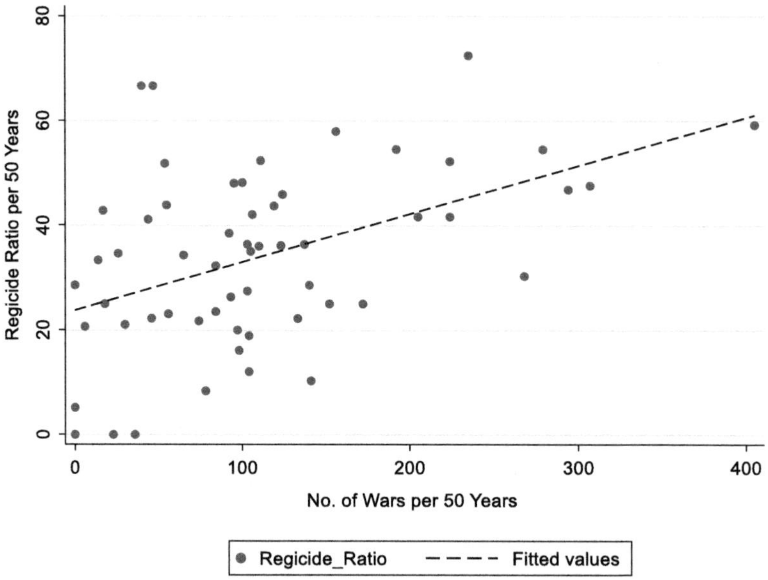


**Fig. 4.3** Relation between the number of wars and regicide ratio (full sample). *Notes* The regicide ratio for each 50-year interval is the percentage of the period's rulers who died unnaturally

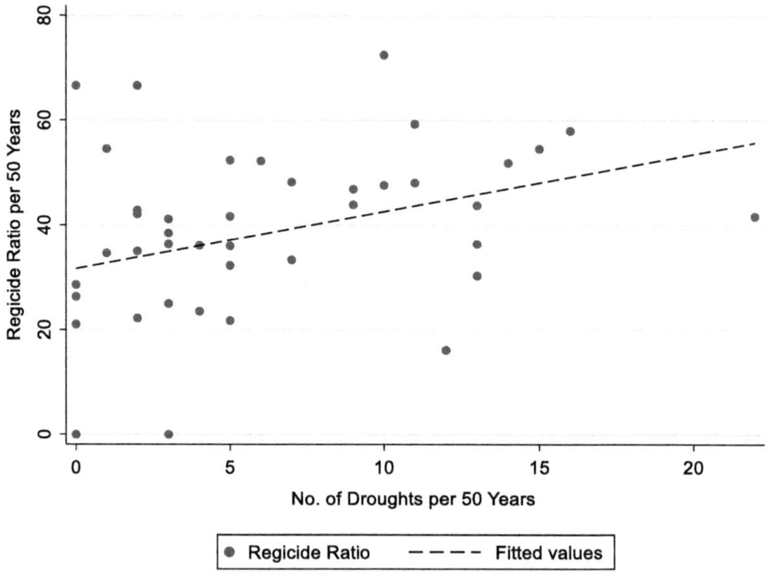


**Fig. 4.4** Correlation between drought and regicide ratio (sample after 115 BCE). *Notes* The regicide ratio for each 50-year interval is the percentage of the period's rulers who died unnaturally. Due to the availability of disaster data, the sample used here is from 115 BCE onwards

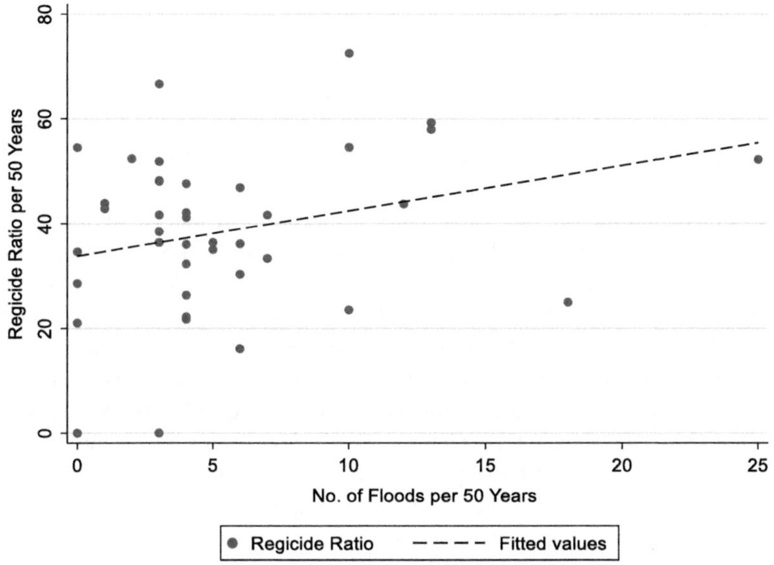


**Fig. 4.5** Correlation between flood and regicide ratio (sample after 115 BCE). *Notes* The regicide ratio for each 50-year interval is the percentage of the period's rulers who died unnaturally. Due to the availability of disaster data, the sample used here is from 115 BCE onwards

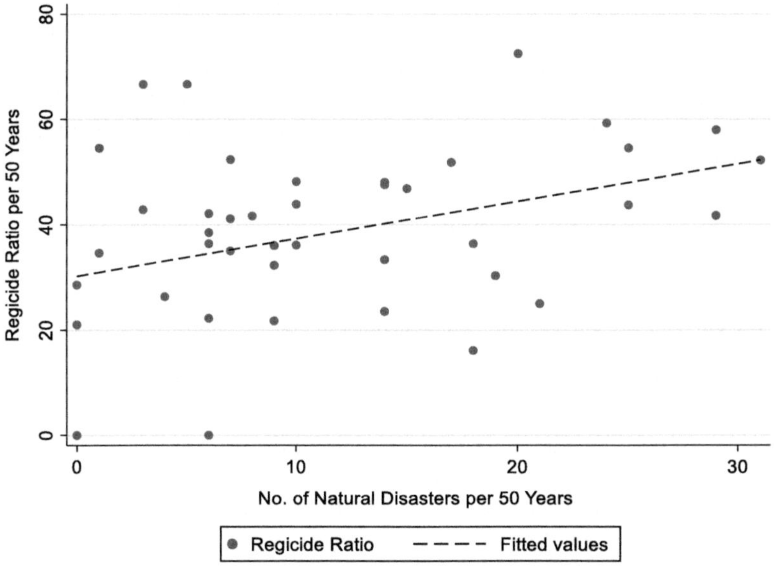


**Fig. 4.6** Correlation between natural disasters and regicide ratio (sample after 115 BCE). *Notes* The regicide ratio for each 50-year interval is the percentage of the period's rulers who died unnaturally. Natural disasters are drought and flood. Due to the availability of disaster data, the sample used here is from 115 BCE onwards

### *4.4.7 Regression Analysis*

This subsection builds upon the univariate analysis of the preceding subsections by incorporating the different factors into a multivariate regression model. Table 4.7 presents the results of a probit model in which the dependent variable takes a value of 1 if a ruler died from regicide and 0 otherwise. The primary explanatory variables include: (1) whether the ruler ever appointed a successor, with a value of 1 indicating yes and 0 indicating no; (2) whether the ruler ascended to the throne with a minister's regency, with a value of 1 representing yes and 0 otherwise; (3) the number of wars occurring in the year of the ruler's death; (4) the number of co-existing competing regimes; (5) years of dynasty duration; (6) the number of floods and droughts in the ruler' death year; (7) numbers of the ruler's sons and brothers, respectively.

The main control variables are regional and century-fixed effects. We divide China into seven regions: Northeast, East, Central, North, South, Northwest, and Southwest. For a regime and for each of these regions, its regional dummy takes a value of 1 if its capital or main territory was inside the region, and 0 otherwise.

Due to varying degrees of missing data, we organize the regression analyses according to sample size, from the largest to the smallest. In Table 4.7, successor appointment in each regression has a statistically significant (at the 1% level) and negative effect on regicide, which means that ruler succession arrangement was almost a significant institution for ensuring smooth and peaceful power transition and that efforts to add power transfer uncertainty would increase the ruler's life risk. While practical, regency arrangements for a young ruler would also put the ruler's life in danger; so, would more wars. In addition, the greater the number of competing regimes, the higher the probability of regicide.[10] The longer a regime lasted, the lower its regicide rate. Droughts and floods did not have a statistically significant impact on regicide, partly because these events were exogenous and did not reflect the quality of a regime's institutions. The numbers of the ruler's sons and brothers, respectively, did not have a statistically significant impact, as the two variables' importance is probably captured by the ruler's other variables.

## 4.5 Temporal Variation in Regicide and Ruler Duration

The analysis so far has treated all rulers as if they came from the same cross-section, regardless of era, which clearly does not take into account the effect of institutional changes during the 3,000-year sample period. Thus, this section investigates the evolution of both the regicide rate and ruler duration over time. In the presence of quality governance institutions, the regicide rate should be low and ruler duration should be long, at least prior to the advent of democracy.

[10] Owing to the high degree of correlation between the number of co-existing external regimes and the number of wars, we include the two variables in separate regressions.

**Table 4.7** Probit regression analysis of regicide

| | Depended variable: Regicide = 1, Others = 0 | | | | | | | |
|---|---|---|---|---|---|---|---|---|
| Variables | (1) | (2) | (3) | (4) | (5) | (6) | (7) | (8) |
| Appointed a successor | -1.11*** | -1.22*** | -1.26*** | -1.19*** | -1.26*** | -0.88*** | -0.57*** | -0.71*** |
| | (-11.75) | (-11.66) | (-10.05) | (-11.32) | (-9.75) | (-5.69) | (-2.92) | (-3.83) |
| Minister's regency | | 0.33*** | 0.40*** | 0.35*** | 0.47*** | 0.75*** | 0.80*** | 0.84*** |
| | | (3.09) | (3.20) | (3.16) | (3.48) | (4.37) | (3.83) | (4.09) |
| Wars | | | 0.11*** | | 0.09*** | 0.10*** | 0.13*** | 0.13*** |
| | | | (3.66) | | (2.93) | (2.60) | (2.76) | (2.99) |
| Competing regimes | | | | 0.06*** | | | | |
| | | | | (3.46) | | | | |
| Years of dynasty duration | | | | | -0.0005*** | -0.001*** | -0.001*** | -0.001** |
| | | | | | (-4.95) | (-4.20) | (-3.18) | (-2.31) |
| Floods | | | | | | 0.00 | 0.11 | -0.08 |
| | | | | | | (0.01) | (0.46) | (-0.34) |
| Droughts | | | | | | -0.03 | -0.14 | -0.13 |
| | | | | | | (-0.20) | (-0.63) | (-0.62) |
| Sons | | | | | | | -0.02 | |
| | | | | | | | (-1.29) | |
| Brothers | | | | | | | | 0.01 |
| | | | | | | | | (0.61) |

(continued)

**Table 4.7** (continued)

| | Depended variable: Regicide = 1, Others = 0 | | | | | | | |
|---|---|---|---|---|---|---|---|---|
| Variables | (1) | (2) | (3) | (4) | (5) | (6) | (7) | (8) |
| Constant | –3.68*** | –3.41*** | –1.57** | –3.61*** | –0.96 | –1.08 | –0.95 | –1.09 |
| | (–11.85) | (–9.08) | (–2.12) | (–9.33) | (–1.33) | (–1.46) | (–1.19) | (–1.39) |
| Region FE | Y | Y | Y | Y | Y | Y | Y | Y |
| Century FE | Y | Y | Y | Y | Y | Y | Y | Y |
| Observations | 1,210 | 1,000 | 700 | 1,000 | 700 | 439 | 303 | 299 |

*Notes* Robust z-statistics are in parentheses; *** means $p < 0.01$, ** $p < 0.05$, * $p < 0.1$; The coefficients in the table are not marginal effects

### 4.5.1 Long-Term Trends in Regicide

Figures 4.7 and 4.8 present the temporal evolution of the regicide rate based on the full sample and subsamples A and B combined, respectively. To focus on the long-term trends, we use a 300-year moving average.

Figure 4.7 shows that for the full sample, the regicide rate exhibits noticeable fluctuations: It was low during the pre-Qin period, gradually increasing following the Qin and Han dynasties (221 BCE-220 CE), peaked during the Three Kingdoms (220–280 CE), the Eastern and Western Jin (266–420 CE), and the Northern and Southern Dynasties (420–589 CE), then gradually declined from the late Tang onward, and rose again during the Ming (1368–1644 CE) and the Qing (1644–1911 CE). Therefore, with all the kings and emperors of states included, big and small, long- and short-lived, institutional development did not converge to a stable condition.

However, one may argue that many of the polities in the full sample existed for a short life and their rebel and even some peripheral states never amounted to much, so it is not surprising that they did not develop a workable political order, let alone well-functioning governance institutions. For this reason, Fig. 4.8 uses only subsample A and subsample B, which contain all the emperors from the mainstream dynasties covered in the *Ershiwu Shi* (Twenty-Five Histories). In this case, the regicide rate started a long-term declining trend after the middle of the Tang dynasty, with sharp declines during the second half of the Tang, then the Song and the Ming dynasties.

These changes suggest much institutional improvement in China, rather than stagnation as stated by others (e.g., Hegel 1956; Elvin 1972), since the late eighth century. This is consistent with the general view among historians that statecraft innovations introduced during the Tang and Song transition created the imperial Chinese state as we know it (e.g., Fairbank and Reischauer 1989; Wang 2022). "In more than two thousand years of feudal society, despite fluctuations in imperial power, the general trend has been the continuous strengthening of the emperor's autocratic rule. Absolute monarchy, with unlimited imperial power, has dominated history since the Qin and Han dynasties." Still, succession arrangements, the civil service examination system (*keju*) for selecting senior officials being opened to grassroots candidates since the early Song dynasty (Wang 2022), and other reforms must have been responsible for the gradually improving institutional environment, making it increasingly safer for the rulers.

Note that Figs. 4.7 and 4.8 diverge after the Song dynasty, with the regicide rate for the full sample rising thereafter in Fig. 4.7, whereas the regicide rate for subsample B continues its downward trend during the Yuan (1279–1368 CE), Ming (1368–1644 CE), and Qing (1644–1911 CE) in Fig. 4.8. This divergence is caused by the rulers of the rebel and peripheral regimes included in subsample C; especially during the Ming and Qing periods, many of these regimes were crushed by the imperial troops of the Ming and Qing, typically with their rulers executed, which exacerbated the regicide rate of these peripheral rulers.

Eisner's (2011) data cover 1,513 kings of 45 European kingdoms between 600 and 1800 CE, from which he finds a regicide ratio of 22% for European kings, implying a

**Fig. 4.7** Evolution of regicide rate (full sample). *Notes* The regicide rate line is based on a 300-year moving average. The two vertical black lines respectively stand for the establishment of the Qin dynasty in 221 BCE and of the Tang dynasty in 618 CE

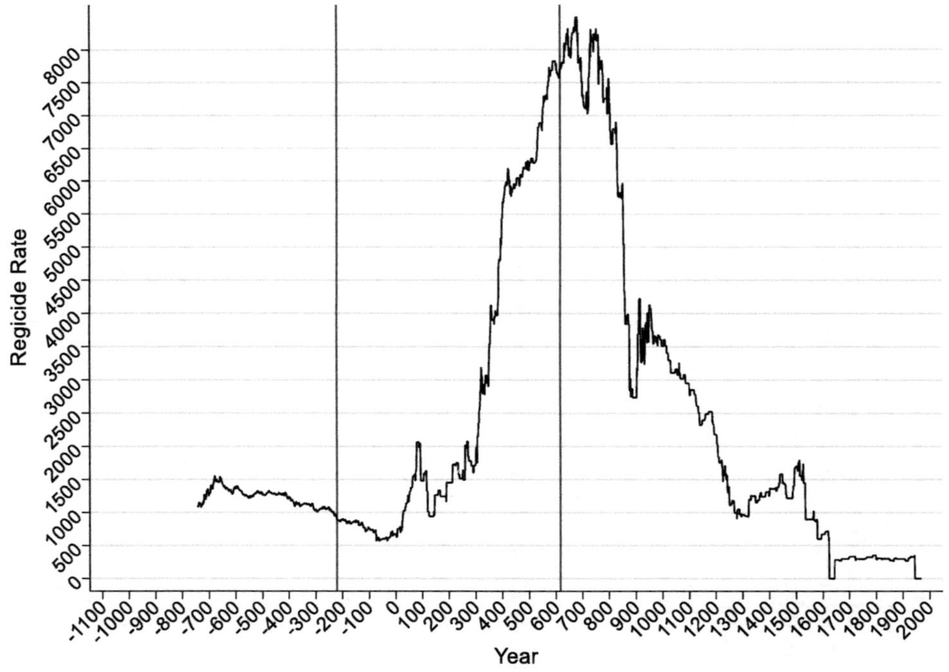


**Fig. 4.8** Evolution of regicide rate (subsamples A and B). *Notes* The regicide rate line is based on a 300-year moving average. The two vertical black lines respectively stand for the establishment of the Qin dynasty in 221 BCE and of the Tang dynasty in 618 CE. Subsample A includes kings from 1046 to 221 BCE, while subsample B all the emperors from 221 BCE to 1911 CE

regicide rate of 1,547 unnatural deaths per 100,000 ruler-years. To compare historical China with Europe, Fig. 4.9 plots the respective regicide rates of European and Chinese rulers, calculated using 100-year intervals. Clearly, from 600 to 1800 CE, the European regicide rate experienced a continuous downward trend, whereas the Chinese regicide rate was consistently higher and fluctuated.

If we limit our attention only to the Chinese emperors covered in subsample B (together with subsample A), Fig. 4.10 tells us that between 600 and 1800 CE, the regicide rate for Chinese rulers was about the same as for European kings, both following a declining trend. However, the Chinese regicide rate was far more volatile than its European counterpart, implying more unstable or unsettled institutional development in China's mainstream empires even in modern times. It begs the question: why didn't China's institutions evolve and improve, to learn from past lessons and improve ruler security? This topic is obviously beyond the scope of the present chapter.

The differences between Figs. 4.9 and 4.10 remind us that when comparing China with Europe, we need to be careful with sample selection and should apply the same standard to define rulers; otherwise, biases would occur. We provide more comparisons using different subsamples in Appendix B.

### *4.5.2 Changes in Ruler Duration Over Time*

Ruler duration is another metric for measuring the quality of a regime's governance institutions. Before elections and term limits were introduced in modern times, the higher the quality and stability of institutions, the longer the state's average ruler duration. In Table 4.4, we saw that, for natural-death cases, Chinese rulers had an average reign duration of 14.4 years, while rulers who died from regicide had a reign duration of only 7.4 years. This indicates a significant negative correlation between regicide rate and ruler duration.

Figure 4.11 plots both the 100-year and 300-year moving averages of China's ruler duration, based on the full sample. Comparing both Figs. 4.7 and 4.11, we see an inverse relation between regicide rate and ruler duration: high regicide rates were associated with low ruler reign durations, and vice versa. It is intriguing that though the Spring and Autumn (770–476 BCE) and then the Warring States period (476–221 BCE) were supposed to be the unruliest times in early Chinese history, the pre-Qin rulers experienced the lowest regicide rates and the highest ruler durations. But, as shown in Fig. 4.11, ruler duration started a sharp downward trend after the Qin unified China, which continued until the Tang dynasty's statecraft innovations encouraged the ruler duration to move upward. This finding suggests that when China was divided into many kingdoms, the incentive to murder a king was not high, making the regicide rate lower and ruler duration longer; but once the divided regimes were unified into one large empire, the emperor controlled a large territory and much more resources, raising his power to a new level; as a result, the incentive to kill the emperor and take over his throne became tremendously higher unless institutional innovations

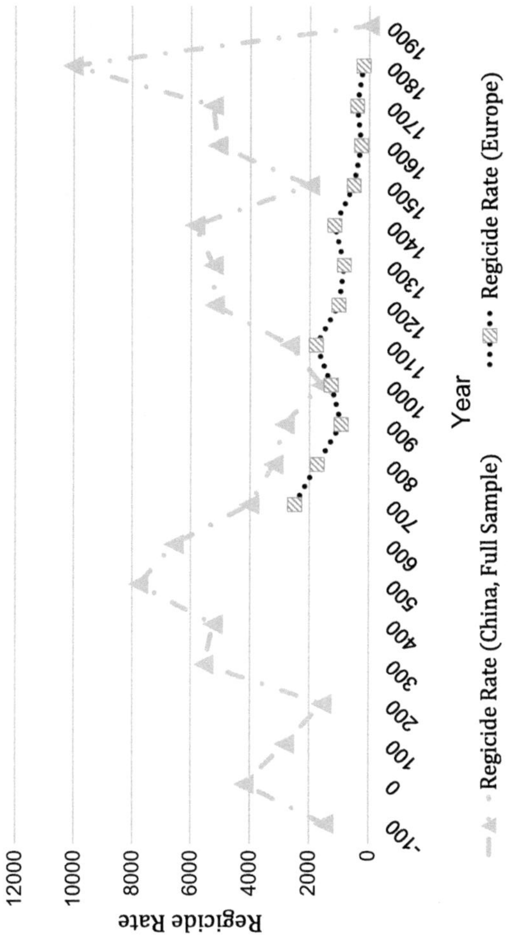


**Fig. 4.9** Regicide rate by century—comparison between China (full sample) and Europe. *Notes* Regicide rate stands for the number of regicides per 100,000 ruler-years. Data for Europe are from Eisner (2011)

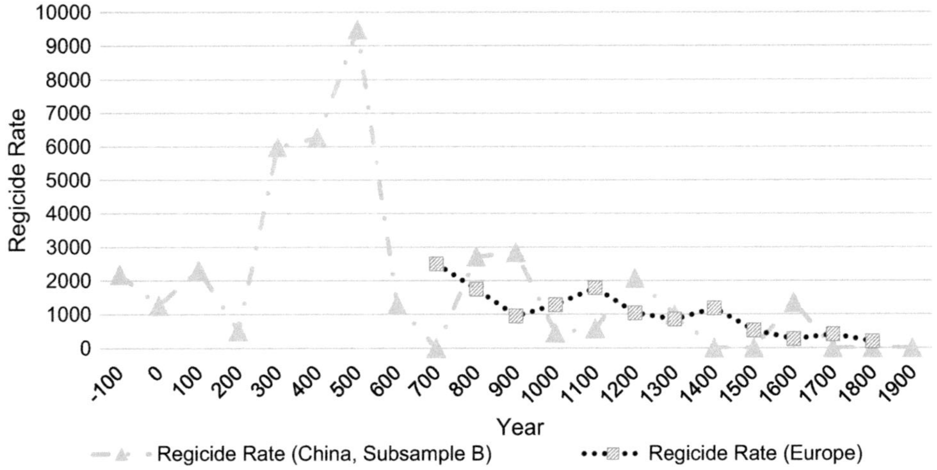


**Fig. 4.10** Regicide rate comparison between China (Subsample B) and Europe. *Notes* Regicide rate stands for the number of regicides per 100,000 ruler-years. For China, subsample B comprises all emperors from 221 BCE to 1911 CE. Data for Europe are from Eisner (2011)

were introduced to constrain such behavior; hence, regicide rates were higher and ruler durations were shorter during periods of unified empires and before statecraft development advanced. Prior to the Qin, the average ruler duration fluctuated between 17 and 25 years; however, from the Qin to the Qing Dynasty, the average ruler's reign moved between 10 and 15 years.

Once we change our focus to the mainstream states, that is, subsamples A and B, Fig. 4.12 reveals a different story than the one based on the full sample. The general pattern for the average ruler duration remains similar between Figs. 4.11 and 4.12, for the 1046 BCE-618 CE period. But, as mentioned earlier, after the Tang dynasty was founded in 618 CE, it took statecraft development to a new level, followed by further institutional innovations during the Song (960–1279 CE). Consequently, the average ruler duration reversed its long-term declining trend after the Qin and started rising from the Tang dynasty onward and thus noticeable progress in governance institutions since the Tang.

Finally, we conduct a comparative analysis of ruler durations among Chinese, European, and Islamic rulers. Again, the data are from Eisner (2011) for European kings and from Blaydes and Chaney (2013) for Islamic sultans. The overlapped period between their datasets is 600–1500 CE, so we employ our subsample B of Chinese emperors for this same period. Figure 4.13 plots the 100-year moving averages of ruler duration for the three sets of rulers. Based on Fig. 4.13, over the given period, the average ruler duration rose steadily in Europe, reflecting continuing improvement in governance institutions, whereas for Islamic societies, their average ruler duration was initially rising but, after the mid-ninth century, followed a clear downward trend partly because of the Sunni Revival. In contrast, China's average ruler duration did not just go in one direction; instead, it swung up and down, implying that though there was cumulative progress in institutional innovations, China never found a solution to the power-governance challenge.

## 4.6 Conclusion

This paper presents a quantitative analysis of Chinese regicide history from 1046 BCE to 1911 CE. Our findings reveal that Chinese rulers faced a significantly higher risk of regicide than European kings but fared better than Islamic sultans. The life risk for an autocratic ruler in historical China was determined by a host of factors, such as how much power he monopolized, whether a successor was appointed, whether he assumed the throne at a young age and received assistance from a minister or ministers, how many competing polities were surrounding the regime, how many wars and natural disasters were happening, as well as dynastic characteristics. Still, statecraft innovations since the Tang dynasty did improve the quality of governance, leading to a long-lasting downward trend for the regicide rate, and an upward trend for ruler duration—at least for the mainstream dynasties. Thus, starting with the Tang-Song transition, China did not seem to stagnate in institutional development, contrary to the claims by Hegel (1956), Elvin (1972), and Jin and Liu (2011). However, China's

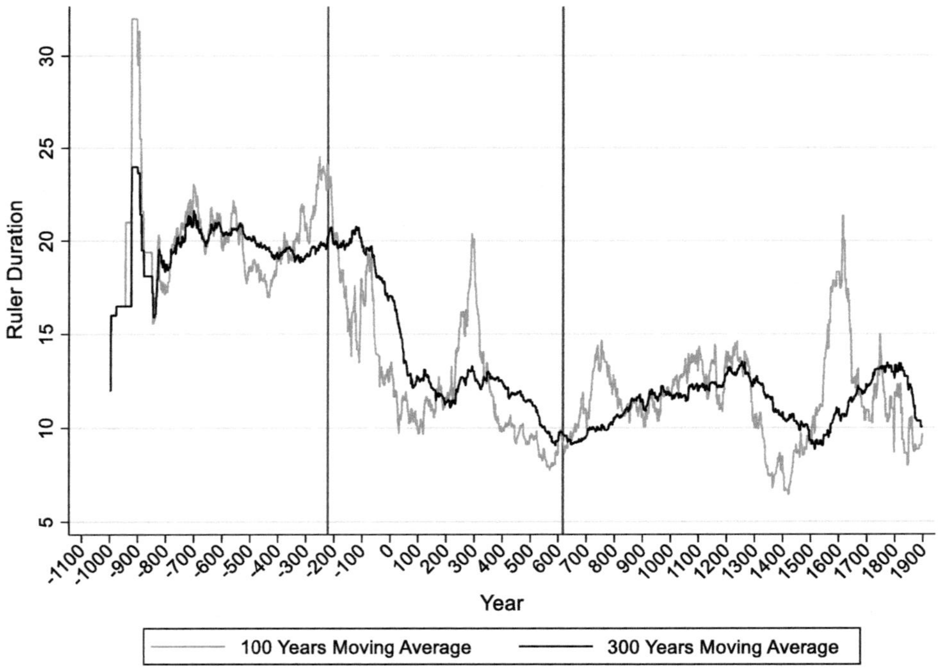


**Fig. 4.11** Moving averages of Chinese ruler duration (full sample). *Notes* The two vertical black lines respectively stand for the establishment of the Qin dynasty in 221 BCE and of the Tang dynasty in 618 CE

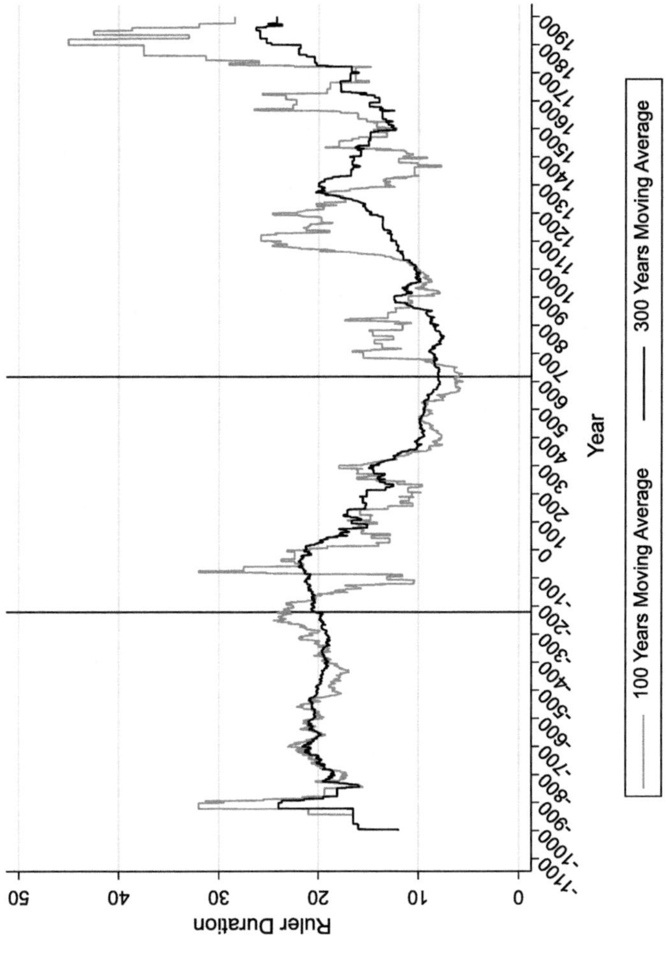


**Fig. 4.12** Moving averages of Chinese ruler duration (subsamples A and B). *Notes* The two vertical black lines respectively stand for the establishment of the Qin dynasty in 221 BCE and of the Tang dynasty in 618 CE. Subsample A includes all kings from 1046 to 221 BCE, while subsample B comprises all emperors from 221 BCE to 1911 CE

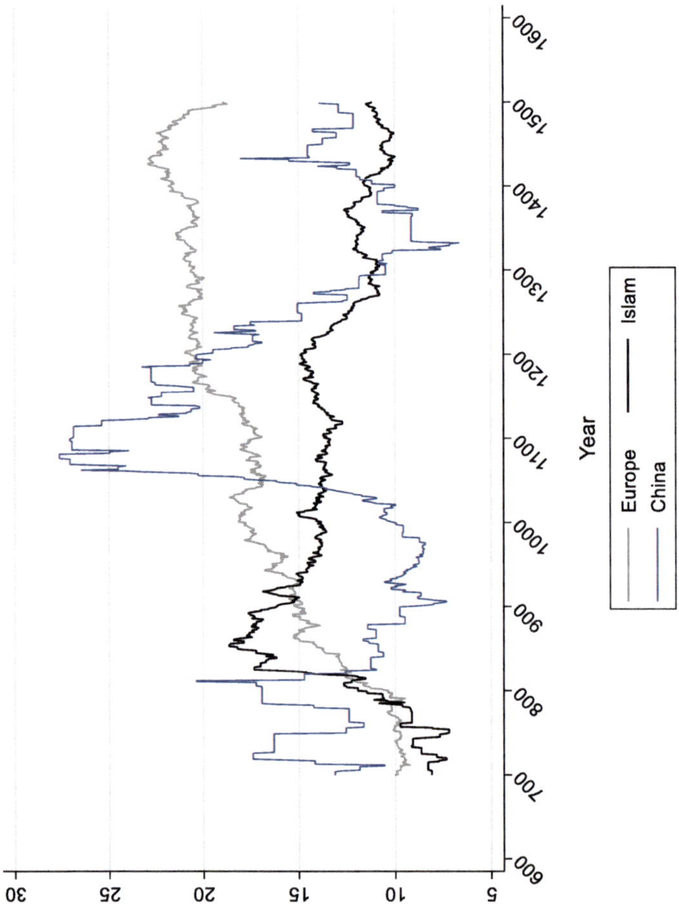


**Fig. 4.13** Ruler duration comparison among Chinese (Subsample B), European, and Islamic rulers. *Notes* The ruler duration lines are based on 100-year moving averages. For China, subsample A includes all kings from 1046 to 221 BCE, while subsample B comprises all emperors from 221 BCE to 1911 CE. Data for Europe and Islam are from Blaydes and Eric Chaney (2013)

long-term decline in regicide occurred later and at a slower and much more volatile pace than Europe's.

The existing literature on state capacity has largely focused on its impact on economic growth, rather than on such outcomes as regicide, homicide, and general violence (e.g., Broadberry et al. 2018; Qian and Sng 2022). Broadberry et al. (2018) estimate that China's real per capita gross domestic product peaked in the Northern Song (960–1126 CE) and declined thereafter, implying that whatever happened in state capacity development since then did not amount to any meaningful improvement in living standards. Figures 4.10 and 4.12 show that the regicide rate declined and ruler duration increased during the Song, Ming, and Qing dynasties (see also Figs. 4.14 and 4.15 in Appendix B). Therefore, while governance innovations in these periods may not have improved state capacity for economic development, they brought about progress in terms of institutional quality for political governance and social stability, especially for the peaceful transfer of power. Perhaps in this sense, the Ming and Qing emperors put too much emphasis on political stability and holding onto power at the expense of economic growth for the people.

## Appendix A. Summary Statistics for Subsamples

Tables 4.8–4.10 present the dynasty/regime-level statistics for the three subsamples, while Tables 4.11–4.13 display ruler-level information.

**Table 4.8** Statistics by dynasty: subsample A (kings, 1046–221 BCE)

| Variable | Obs | Mean | Std. Dev | Min | Max |
|---|---|---|---|---|---|
| Start year | 29 | –685.7 | 208.3 | –1046 | –229 |
| End year | 29 | –352.7 | 132 | –771 | –195 |
| Dynasty duration | 29 | 331.2 | 198.5 | 8 | 643 |
| No. of rulers | 29 | 17.4 | 11.3 | 1 | 36 |
| No. of regicides | 29 | 3.6 | 3.5 | 0 | 12 |
| Regicide ratio | 29 | 18.3 | 15.7 | 0 | 57.1 |

**Table 4.9** Statistics by dynasty: subsample B (emperors, 221 BCE-1911 CE)

| Variable | Obs | Mean | Std. Dev | Min | Max |
|---|---|---|---|---|---|
| Start year | 67 | 579.7 | 362.6 | –221 | 1616 |
| End year | 67 | 642 | 390 | –207 | 1911 |
| Dynasty duration | 67 | 62.9 | 69.9 | 3 | 296 |
| No. of rulers | 67 | 6.1 | 4.6 | 1 | 25 |
| No. of regicides | 67 | 2.5 | 2.3 | 0 | 12 |
| Regicide ratio | 67 | 46 | 30.8 | 0 | 100 |

**Table 4.10** Statistics by dynasty: subsample C (non-emperors, 221 BCE-1911 CE)

| Variable | Obs | Mean | Std. Dev | Min | Max |
|---|---|---|---|---|---|
| Start year | 352 | 870.8 | 634.3 | –209 | 1895 |
| End year | 352 | 911 | 610.8 | –208 | 1895 |
| Dynasty duration | 352 | 40 | 117.9 | 0.1 | 957 |
| No. of rulers | 352 | 2.9 | 5.1 | 1 | 40 |
| No. of regicides | 352 | 1.2 | 1.5 | 0 | 10 |
| Regicide ratio | 352 | 62 | 43.7 | 0 | 100 |

**Table 4.11** Statistics by ruler: subsample A (kings 1046-221BCE)

| Variable | Obs | Mean | Std. Dev | Min | Max |
|---|---|---|---|---|---|
| Birth year | 0 | | | | |
| Death year | 483 | –551.24 | 169.19 | –1043 | –221 |
| Ruler duration | 489 | 19.37 | 14.46 | 1 | 75 |
| Age | 17 | 45.29 | 19.44 | 11 | 82 |
| Age at Enthronement | 19 | 22.26 | 16.33 | 2 | 62 |
| No. of sons | 335 | 1.98 | 1.9 | 0 | 20 |
| No. of brothers | 219 | 2.58 | 2.37 | 1 | 20 |
| Minister's regency | 420 | 0.16 | 0.37 | 0 | 1 |
| Appointed a successor | 394 | 0.76 | 0.43 | 0 | 1 |
| Regicide | 506 | 0.2 | 0.4 | 0 | 1 |

**Table 4.12** Statistics by ruler: subsample B (emperors, 221 BCE-1911 CE)

| Variable | Obs | Mean | Std. Dev | Min | Max |
|---|---|---|---|---|---|
| Birth year | 320 | 701.06 | 457.17 | –259 | 1906 |
| Death year | 409 | 675.07 | 435.57 | –210 | 1967 |
| Ruler duration | 409 | 11.09 | 11.61 | 0.07 | 61 |
| Age | 321 | 41.3 | 17.64 | 2 | 89 |
| Age at enthronement | 326 | 27.37 | 14.69 | 1 | 67 |
| No. of sons | 330 | 5.99 | 7 | 0 | 42 |
| No. of brothers | 343 | 7.81 | 7.7 | 0 | 41 |
| Minister's regency | 341 | 0.4 | 0.49 | 0 | 1 |
| Appointed a successor | 380 | 0.51 | 0.5 | 0 | 1 |
| Regicide | 412 | 0.41 | 0.49 | 0 | 1 |

**Table 4.13** Statistics by rulers: subsample C (non-emperors, 221 BCE-1911 CE)

| Variable | Obs | Mean | Std. Dev | Min | Max |
|---|---|---|---|---|---|
| Birth year | 123 | 1124.95 | 497.41 | –58 | 1849 |
| Death year | 728 | 802.63 | 577.52 | –209 | 1903 |
| Ruler duration | 878 | 9.97 | 11.6 | 0.08 | 69 |
| Age | 106 | 44.33 | 15.45 | 16 | 103 |
| Age at enthronement | 119 | 29.63 | 13.83 | 7 | 73 |
| No. of sons | 319 | 2.34 | 2.66 | 0 | 20 |
| No. of brothers | 304 | 2.74 | 3.18 | 1 | 19 |
| Minister's regency | 664 | 0.1 | 0.3 | 0 | 1 |
| Appointed a successor | 469 | 0.27 | 0.44 | 0 | 1 |
| Regicide | 1030 | 0.41 | 0.49 | 0 | 1 |

## Appendix B. Evolution of Regicide Rate Over Time

Based on the full sample, Fig. 4.14 presents the 100-year moving average of regicide rate per 100,000 ruler-years, exhibiting significant volatility; during the Three Kingdoms, the North and South Dynasties, and the Qing Dynasty, the regicide rate was notably high. Figure 4.15 portrays the regicide ratio by century, displaying a similar trend to Fig. 4.14.

Figures 4.16 and 4.17 are constructed similarly to Figs. 4.14 and 4.15, except that they are based on subsamples A and subsamples B. The main difference between Figs. 4.14 and 4.16 is that for the mainstream emperors from the Tang dynasty onward, their life risk started a long-term decline because of the statecraft innovations that began in the Tang, with the regicide rate reaching its low in the Qing. Figure 4.17 shows a similar pattern as in Fig. 4.16 but based on the regicide ratio within each century, where the regicide ratio peaked during the Eastern and Western Jin dynasties as well as the Northern and Southern dynasties and reached its lowest level during the Ming and the Qing.

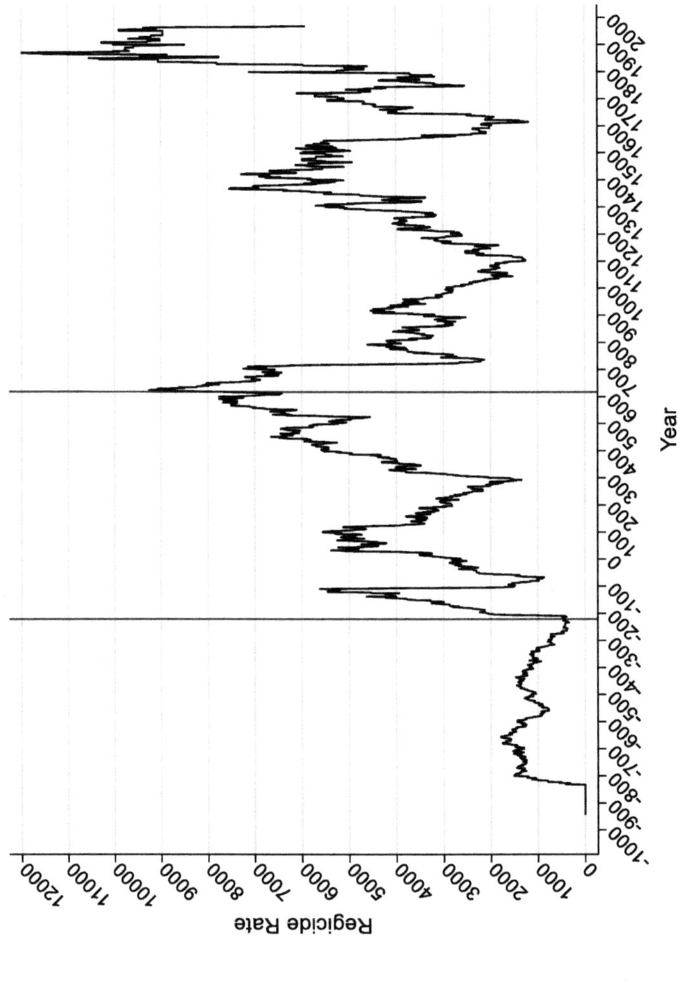


**Fig. 4.14** Regicide rate over time (Full Sample). *Notes* Regicide rate stands for the number of regicides per 100,000 ruler-years. The two vertical black lines respectively stand for the establishment of the Qin dynasty in 221 BCE and of the Tang dynasty in 618 CE

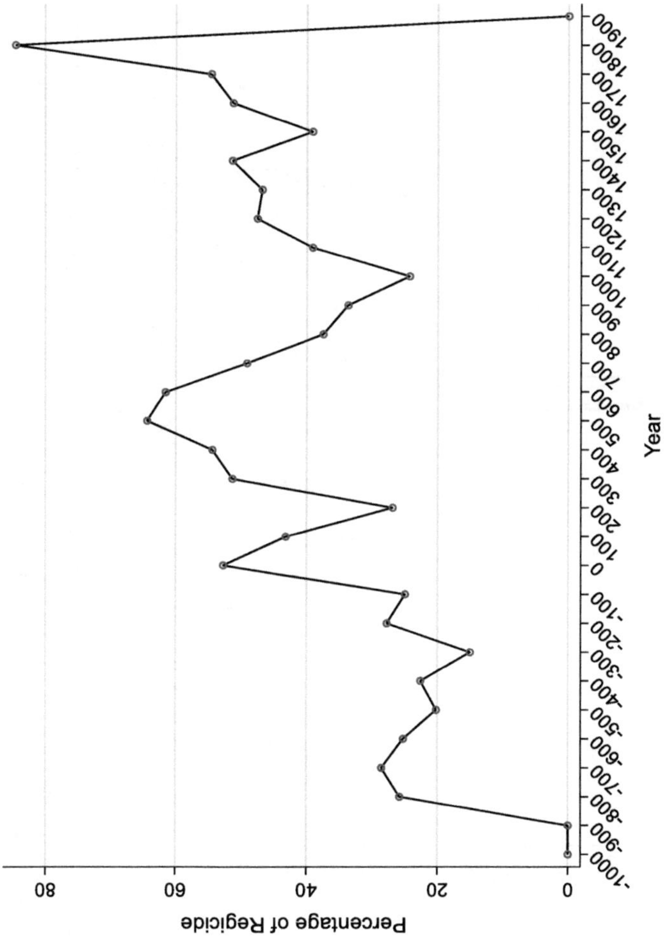


**Fig. 4.15** Regicide ratio by century (full sample)

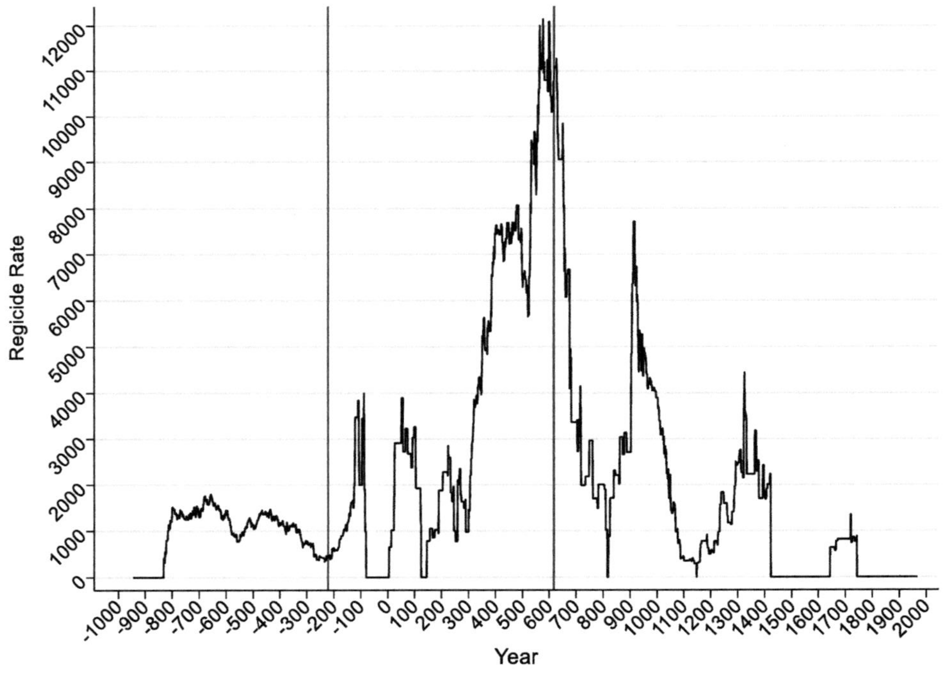


**Fig. 4.16** Regicide rate over time (subsamples A and B). *Notes* Regicide rate stands for the number of regicides per 100,000 ruler-years. The two vertical black lines, respectively, stand for the establishment of the Qin dynasty in 221 BCE and of the Tang dynasty in 618 CE. Subsample A includes all kings from 1046 to 221 BCE while subsample B comprises all emperors from 221 BCE to 1911 CE

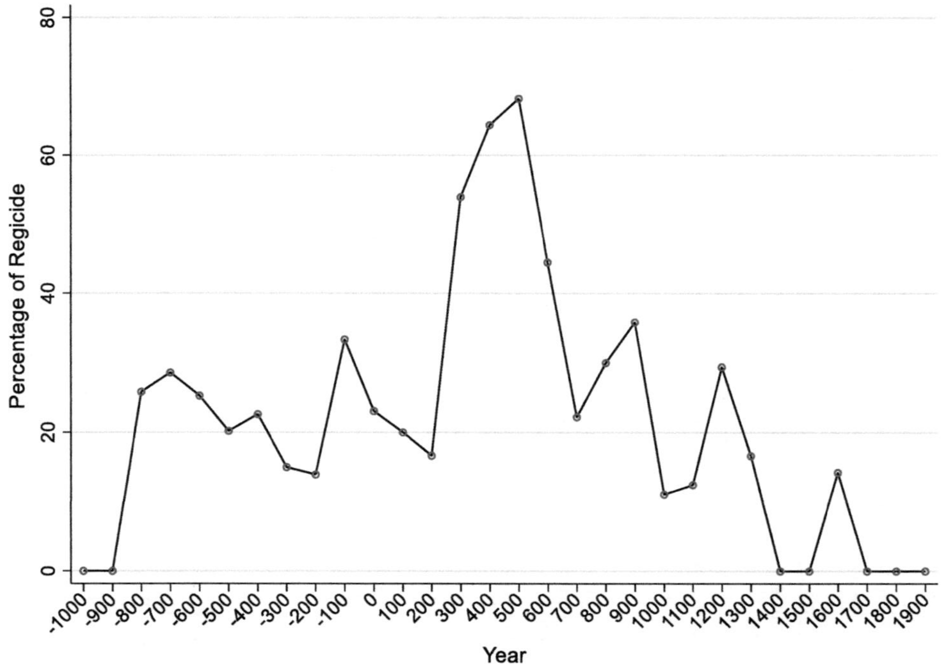


**Fig. 4.17** Regicide ratio by century (subsample A&B). *Notes* Subsample A includes all kings from 1046 to 221 BCE while subsample B comprises all emperors from 221 BCE to 1911 CE

## References

Aebi, Marcelo F., Kauko Aromaa, Bruno A. de Cavarlay, Gordon Barclay, Beata Gruszczynska, Hanns von Hofer, Vasilika Hysi, Jörg - Martin Jehle, Martin Killias, Paul Smit, and Cynthia Tavares. 2006. *European Sourcebook of Crime and Criminal Justice Statistics*. Amsterdam: Boom Juridische Uitgevers.

Aristotle. 1999. Translated by Benjamin Jowett. *Politics*. Kitchener, Ontario: Batoche Books.

Bai, Ying, and James K.S. Kung. 2011. Climate Shocks and Sino-nomadic Conflict. *The Review of Economics and Statistics* 93 (3): 970–981.

Baten, Jörg., Thomas Keywood, and Georg Wamser. 2021. Territorial State Capacity and Elite Violence from the 6th to the 19th Century. *European Journal of Political Economy* 70: 102037.

Bates, Robert H. 2020. *The Political Economy of Development*. Cambridge: Cambridge University Press.

Blaydes, Lisa, and Eric Chaney. 2013. The Feudal Revolution and Europe's Rise: Political Divergence of the Christian West and the Muslim World before 1500 CE. *American Political Science Review* 107 (01): 16–34.

Blumstein, Alfred. 2005. Disaggregating the Violence Trends. In *The Crime Drop in America,* ed. Alfred Blumstein and Joel Wallman, 13–44. Cambridge: Cambridge University Press.

Broadberry, Stephen, Hanhui Guan, and David D. Li. 2018. China, Europe, and the Great Divergence: A Study in Historical National Accounting, 980–1850. *Journal of Economic History* 78 (4): 955–1000.

Chen, Lei. 2007. Tangdai huangdi de chusheng jiwei he siwang didian kaoxi (Study on the place of birth, ascending the throne and death of emperors of Tang Dynasty). *Lishi yanjiu* (Historical Review) 5 : 118–127.

Chen, Zhiwu. 2022. *Wenming de luoji* (The Logic of Civilization). Beijing: zhongxin chubanshe.

Chen, Zhiwu, Kaixiang Peng, and Lijun Zhu. 2017. Social-economic Change and its Impact on Violence: Homicide History of Qing China. *Explorations in Economic History* 63: 8–25.

Dincecco, Mark, and Yuhua Wang. 2022. State Capacity in Historical Political Economy. Working Paper.

Ebrey, Patricia. 2006. Succession to High Office: The Chinese Case. In *Technology, Literacy, and the Evolution of Society: Implications of the Work of Jack Good*, ed. David Olson and Michael Cole, 49–71. Mahwah, N.J: Lawrence Erlbaum.

Elvin, Mark. 1972. The High-Level Equilibrium Trap: The Causes of the Decline in Traditional Chinese Textile Industries. In *Economic Organization in Chinese Society*, ed. William E. Willmott. Stanford: Stanford University Press.

Eisner, Manuel. 2011. Killing Kings: Patterns of Regicide in Europe, AD 600–1800. *British Journal of Criminology* 51 (3): 556–577.

Fairbank, John K., and Edwin O. Reischauer. 1989. *China: Tradition & Transformation*. Boston: Houghton Mifflin College Division.

Gong, Yanming. 1992. *Songdai de huangdi zhidu* (The Emperor's system in the Song dynasty). *Henan daxue xuebao (shehui kexue ban)* (Journal of Henan University (Philosophy and Social Science Edition)) 32 (1): 69–73.

Hegel, Georg W. F. 1956. Translated by J. Sibree. *The Philosophy of History*. New York: Dover Publications.

Huang, Ray. 1981. *1587, A Year of No Significance: The Ming Dynasty in Decline*. New Haven: Yale University Press.

Huang, Yasheng, and Clair Yang. 2022. A Longevity Mechanism of Chinese Absolutism. *The Journal of Politics* 84 (2): 1165–1175.

Jin, Guantao, and Liu Qingfeng. 2011. *Xingsheng Yu Weiji: Lun Zhongguo Shehui Chaowending Jiegou* (Prosperity and Crisis: on the Superstable Structure of Chinese Feudal Society). Beijing: Falv chubanshe.

Jones, Benjamin F., and Benjamin A. Olken. 2005. Do Leaders Matter? National Leadership and Growth since World War II. *The Quarterly Journal of Economics* 120 (3): 835–864.

Konrad, Kai A., and Vai-Lam. Mui. 2017. The Prince—or Better No Prince? The Strategic Value of Appointing a Successor. *Journal of Conflict Resolution* 61 (10): 2158–2182.

Loewe, Michael, and Denis C. Twitchett, eds. 1986. *The Cambridge History of China: Volume 1: The Ch'in and Han Empires, 221 BC-AD 220.* Cambridge: Cambridge University Press.

Ma, Debin. 2013. State Capacity and Great Divergence, the Case of Qing China (1644–1911). *Eurasian Geography and Economics* 54 (5–6): 484–499.

Ma, Debin, and Jared Rubin. 2019. The Paradox of Power: Principal-agent Problems and Administrative Capacity in Imperial China (and other Absolutist Regimes). *Journal of Comparative Economics* 47 (2): 277–294.

Olson, David R, and Michael Cole. 2006. *Technology, Literacy and the Evolution of Society Implications of the Work of Jack Goody.* Mahwah, N.J: Lawrence Erlbaum.

Poe, Dison H.F.. 1981. 348 Chinese Emperors: A Statistic-analytical Study of Imperial Succession. *Tsing Hua Journal of Chinese Studies* 13 : 1–2.

Qian, Jiwei and Tuan-Hwee Sng. 2022. The State in Chinese Economic History: A Survey." EAI Working Paper No. 170, National University of Singapore.

Saleh, Joseph H. 2019. Statistical Reliability Analysis for a Most Dangerous Occupation: Roman Emperor. *Palgrave Communications* 5 (1).

Sima, Qian. 1994. Translated by William H. Nienhauser. *The Grand Scribe's Records: The Basic Annals of Pre-Han China (Vol. 1).* Bloomington, Indiana: Indiana University Press.

Sng, Tuan-Hwee. 2014. Size and Dynastic Decline: The Principal-Agent Problem in Late Imperial China, 1700–1850. *Explorations in Economic History* 54: 107–127.

Sng, Tuan-Hwee, and Chiaki Moriguchi. 2014. Asia's Little Divergence: State Capacity in China and Japan before 1850. *Journal of Economic Growth* (Boston, Mass.) 19 (4) : 439–70.

Svolik, Milan W. 2012. *The Politics of Authoritarian Rule.* Cambridge: Cambridge University Press.

Tan, Qixiang. 1996. *Zhongguo Lishi Dituji* (Atlas of Chinese History). Beijing: Zhongguo ditu chubanshe.

Wang, Yuhua. 2022. *The Rise and Fall of Imperial China: The social origins of state development.* Princeton University Press.

Wei Qingyuan. 1989. *Lun Fengjian Huangquan Yu Huangwei Jicheng Wenti* (On feudal imperial power and the problem of succession to the imperial throne). In *Mingqing Shi Bianxi* (Discussion and Analysis of the History of the Ming and Qing Dynasties), Beijing: Zhongguo Shehui Kexue Chuanbanshe.

Wilkinson, Endymion. 2013. *Chinese History: A New Manual.* Cambridge, Mass.: Harvard University Asia Center.

Xu, Lianda and Ziyan Zhu. 1996. *Zhongguo Huangdi Zhidu* (The Emperor System in China), Guangzhou: Guangdong Jiaoyu Chubanshe.

Yu, Baolin. 2010. *Zhonghua Lishi Jinian Zongbiao* (General chronological table of Chinese history ). Beijing: Shehui kexue wenxian chubanshe.

Zhang, Yan, and Nandini Rajagopalan. 2010. CEO Succession Planning: Finally at the Center Stage of the Boardroom. *Business Horizons* 53 (5): 455–462.

Zhao, Dingxin. 2015. *The Confucian-Legalist State: A New Theory of Chinese History.* Oxford University Press.

Zheng, Jingyun, Wei-Chyung. Wang, Quansheng Ge, Zhimin Man, and Piyuan Zhang. 2006. Precipitation Variability and Extreme Events in Eastern China during the Past 1500 Years. *TAO : Terrestrial, Atmospheric, and Oceanic Sciences* 17 (3): 579–592.

Zhongguo Junshi Shi Bianxiezu (China's Military History Editorial Committee) Ed. 2003. *Zhongguo Lidai Zhanzheng Nianbiao* (A Chronology of Warfare in Dynastic China), 2nd ed. Beijing: Jiefangjun chubanshe.

Zhou, Liangxiao. 1999. *Huangdi yu Huangquan* (The Emperor and the Imperial Power). Shanghai: Shanhai guji chubanshe.

Zhu, Jianzhang. 2015. *Lidai Cuanshi Yanjiu* (A Study of Usurpation and Regicide through the Chinese History). Taipei: Lianhe baike dianzi chuban youxian gongsi.

**Zhiwu Chen** is Chair and Cheng Yu-Tung Professor in Finance at The University of Hong Kong (HKU). He currently serves as director of both Hong Kong Institute for the Humanities and Social Sciences (HKIHSS) and Centre for Quantitative History (CQH). His research covers finance theory, the sociology of finance, economic history, quantitative history, emerging markets, as well as China's economy and capital markets. He was a former Professor of Finance at Yale University (1999–2017) and a Special-Term Visiting Professor at Peking University and Tsinghua University. In 2013, he started the annual Summer School for Quantitative History cum International Symposium on Quantitative History at Tsinghua University and continues to organize them at Peking University with the goal of promoting quantitative research on the history of China and beyond.

**Zhan Lin** is an Associate Professor of Chinese Economic History at the Renmin University of China. He received his Ph.D. in economics from Tsinghua University in 2014. He is the author of *The Logic of Usury: The Market Mechanisms in Private Lending in the Qing Dynasty and the Republic of China*, a Chinese book. Dr. Lin serves as the associate editor of the *Qing History Journal* and on the editorial board of *Quantitative History Research*. Professor Lin is also a Co-Principal Investigator of RGC's Area of Excellence (AoE) project, Quantitative History of China. He was the winner of the 10th Golden Fleece Award for Financial Books (2022) and the 2018 Sun YeFang Economics Papers Award (the top honorary prize in China's economics).

# Chapter 5
# War Breeds Warriors: Long-Term Impacts of Historical Conflicts on Warrior Culture Formation

**Yicheng Chen, Zhiwu Chen, and Chicheng Ma**

## 5.1 Introduction

A general view among historians is that due to Confucian orthodoxy, Chinese society historically prized the civilian over the martial, or the *wen* over the *wu*, as a way to resolve disputes and conflicts (Lee 2016; Weber 1968); consequently, the Chinese people are not supposed to have any strong aspiration for martial skills or preference for a military career when young. However, this view is not supported by historical facts: young Chinese practiced *kungfu* martial arts diligently and studied hard for the military service examinations, as success in these would put them on a military career path (Fried 1952; Pearce 2008; Cosmo 2009). Moreover, there was never a shortage of inspiring military generals and war heroes in Chinese history. Panel 1 of Fig. 5.1 presents the spatial distribution of famous historical military elites from 770 BCE to 1912 CE, based on data from Shi et al. (1988).[1] This chart reveals not only many impactful historical warriors but also a highly uneven distribution across the regions, with disproportionately high number coming from northern China. Also, in China today, the stereotypical view is that people in northern regions are generally more aggressive, often preferring to settle disputes with force rather than through

[1] We compute the number of military elites that a prefecture (based on the 1820 administrative zoning) nurtured from the Spring and Autumn period to the Qing dynasty, that is, 770 BCE–1912 CE, based on the recorded birthplace of each famous military leader. The map is confined within China Proper, consisting of the 18 core provinces of Qing China.

Y. Chen (✉)
Department of Economics, Boston University, Boston, USA
e-mail: cyccool@bu.edu

Z. Chen · C. Ma
Centre for Quantitative History, Faculty of Business and Economics, The University of Hong Kong, Hong Kong, China
e-mail: zhiwu.chen@hku.hk
e-mail: macc@hku.hk

 
Z. Chen et al. (eds.), *Quantitative History of China*, Studies in Economic History,
https://doi.org/10.1007/978-981-96-8272-0_5

negotiations like southerners do (Talhelm et al. 2014; Gong et al. 2021). If this view has any merit, then it raises the question of why is there so much regional variation in warrior culture? Our goal is to answer this question by investigating the historical roots of warrior culture.

The role of culture in conflicts is widely noted (Nisbett and Cohen 1996; Brown et al. 2009; Glowacki and Wrangham 2013; Dafoe and Caughey 2016; Nawata 2020). For example, cultures that value honor, reputation, revenge, and masculinity—attributes of what is often referred to as warrior culture (Mrozek 2007; Carton and Morrell 2012; Malmin 2013)—are found to encourage individuals to resort to violence. In this paper, we investigate the reverse causality that military conflicts breed warrior culture. For this purpose, we define warrior culture as a collection of preferences and beliefs that emphasize martial skills and value force over negotiation for dispute resolution. Our goal is to examine whether and how past military conflict exposure led to warrior culture formation, to both explain the regional variation in the prevalence of warrior culture in historical China and estimate its persistent effect on the regions of today. Our primary hypothesis posits that greater historical exposure to war fostered a deeper warrior culture, evidenced by a regional population's emphasis on martial skills and higher violent crime rates.

The first part of our inquiry concentrates on the experience of the Qing dynasty (1644–1912). The Qing bureaucracy comprised three levels: provinces, prefectures and counties. Every three years, imperial civil service exams (i.e., *keju*) and military service examinations (*wuju*) were conducted, with each candidate starting at the respective county-level exam, of which the winners would take the provincial exam, of which the survivors (referred to as *juren*) would advance to take the national exam. The military exams primarily assessed physical strength and martial skills. At each level of exams, only a small fraction of candidates could succeed and advance to the next.[2] Those who passed the provincial military exams were awarded the *wujuren* degree, whereas those who succeeded in the national exam would receive the *wujinshi* degree. Utilizing data for the 257 prefectures in China Proper,[3] we demonstrate that prefectures with a higher number of military conflicts prior to the Qing dynasty had a greater number of recorded *wujuren* per million people between 1650 and 1789.[4] We select *wujuren* as the main outcome variable, capturing the degree of warrior culture presence in a region, because it represents the lowest military degree for which detailed records are available. The higher military degree, *wujinshi*, was

[2] For example, according to Zhou (2013), fewer than one-twentieth of the candidates would pass the provincial exam.

[3] Figure 5.3 compares China Proper with the Qing territory of 1820. We focus on China Proper for two reasons. First, as the traditional agrarian core of the country, China Proper was populated by the dominant Han population. Restricting attention to it helps reduce the interference of heterogeneity in culture and institutions. Second, historical archives were better created and preserved in chronicles and gazetteers by local governments in China Proper than in peripheral regions where much fewer historical documents are available.

[4] We normalize the number of *wujuren* by the length of the period covered by data. We will further explain this in Sect. 5.3.

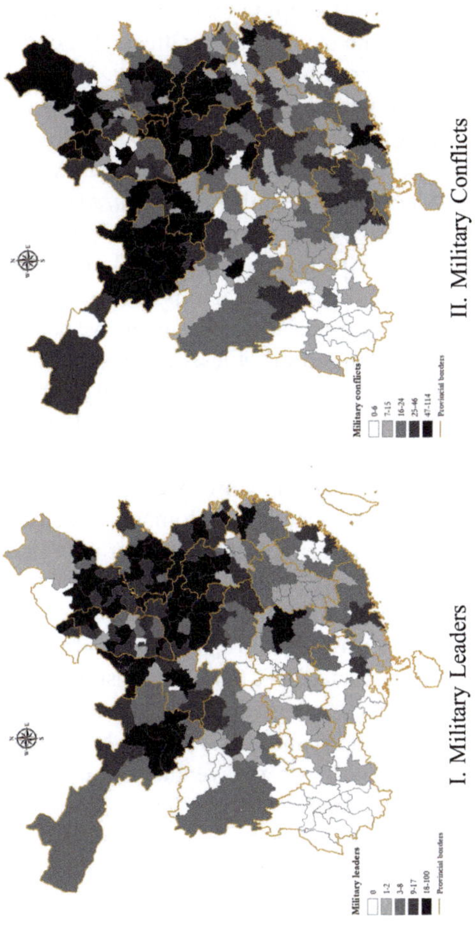


**Fig. 5.1** Spatial distribution of military leaders and conflicts from 770 BCE–1912 CE

much harder to obtain and fewer in number awarded,[5] probably requiring political connections to ultimately attain and reflecting the achievement by a much narrower spectrum of the local population. Thus, the density of *wujuren* degree holders better reflects the average level of the broader population's efforts to achieve excellence in martial skills and of their aspirations for a military career among residents. The period 1650–1789, instead of the entire Qing period, is chosen for two reasons. First, the late Qing dynasty witnessed numerous civil wars and foreign invasions that could potentially confound the effect of our main variables being studied. Also, the chaos created by the civil wars made record keeping more spotty and less reliable. Second, our *wujuren* records primarily come from local gazetteers, the compilation of which did not start during the initial years of the Qing dynasty. We select 1650–1789 to strike a balance between sample period length and data coverage.

Our analysis demonstrates a significant and positive correlation between pre-Qing military conflicts and *wujuren* density, that is, prefectures that experienced more wars from 770 BCE–1644 CE produced significantly more *wujuren* per million population, suggesting a link between past war exposure and the development of warrior culture. For example, Panel 2 of Fig. 5.1 indicates that northern China had clearly more wars than the south, which may be why the former regions have a stronger warrior culture presence. However, before drawing a causality conclusion, we need to address several issues, including concerns about omitted variables. First, we introduce province-fixed effects to account for time-invariant provincial heterogeneity, especially considering that *wujuren* quotas were allocated across provinces. Second, we control for terrain ruggedness, which can have a long-lasting impact on socioeconomic development (Chen et al. 2023; Nunn and Puga 2012). Third, we include the density of rivers, measured as the total length of rivers per square kilometer, to control for the effect of commercial development and inter-regional influence through human interactions. Fourth, considering China Proper being predominantly agrarian during the Qing time and earlier, we expect agricultural productivity to play a role on culture formation and institutions. Therefore, we control for the caloric suitability index developed by Galor and Özak (2015) to measure a region's agricultural suitability. Fifth, climate is a known factor in military conflicts (Burke et al. 2009; Miguel et al. 2011; Hsiang and Burke 2013; Baysan et al. 2018; Harari and Ferrara 2018; McGuirk and Nunn 2020), so we include controls for years with extreme weather events during the estimation period. Lastly, we consider the distance to the coastline, as this factor may determine both a region's trade potential and its residents' exposure to Western technology and culture. Even after accounting for these confounding variables, our finding on the link between historical war exposure and warrior culture formation remains robust.

To establish causality from historical wars to *wujuren* density (hence warrior culture), however, we face challenges due to potential omitted variables and the possibility that wars were more likely to occur in regions with a pre-existing warrior culture that was transmitted over time. Our strategy is to employ an instrumental

[5] For instance, our dataset consists of approximately 57,700 *wujuren* but only 5,900 *wujinshi*. Considering the lower level of recognition and smaller probability of *wujuren* being documented, the actual ratio should be even greater.

variable (IV): each prefecture's minimum distance to strategically important locations, such as passes, ferries, mountains and paths. These locations held significant military importance in pre-industrial times due to their geographic features, which in turn made wars more likely to occur there.

We indeed find a significant and negative correlation between a prefecture's distance to strategic locations (DTSL) and its number of historical wars before the Qing dynasty. Next, we examine the exclusion restriction for the IV. First, DTSL is shown to be orthogonal to most of the potentially confounding variables. Second, once historical wars are controlled for, the correlation between DTSL and *wujuren* density diminishes to non-significance, which implies that the impact of DTSL on *wujuren* density operated solely through the historical war channel. Based on this suggestive evidence for the exclusion restriction, we proceed to conduct IV estimations. Our IV results confirm a causal link from historical war exposure to *wujuren* density. Thus, in regions that experienced more wars in the past, a stronger warrior culture was likely to rise.

We interpret these findings as follows. More exposure to war violence motivated the locals to invest more in martial skills and promote warrior-friendly cultural values, as such elements were crucial for survival in a violent and disorderly environment (Carton and Morrell 2012; Gutierrez and Gallegos 2016; La Mattina 2017; Sng and Zhong 2018). In this sense, culture is just a response to challenges that a society faces. From an economic perspective, an unsafe environment makes the return from investing in warrior skills and physical strength higher. Over time, this fosters the development of a stronger warrior culture.

To further explore the hypothesis on warrior culture formation, the second part of our exercise centers on the long-term persistence of warrior culture's impact. First, we document a positive correlation between historical wars and the number of violent crime cases per million people during the Qing dynasty, suggesting that greater historical war exposure for a region nurtured a stronger local warrior culture, which incentivized the locals to invest in martial skills and resort to force for resolving disputes, at the same time nurturing a culture of violence. Second, we find a negative correlation between historical wars and the number of elementary and middle schools per million people during the Qing dynasty. Thus, as regions with more historical wars cultivated a stronger warrior culture, it should not be surprising that their children prioritized learning martial skills over book knowledge, leading to a divergence in human capital investment between regions with and those without much historical war exposure.

There may be other channels to consider. For instance, it is possible that wars were associated with economic growth, urban development, and state building (Tilly 1975; Besley and Persson 2008; Dincecco and Onorato 2016; Dincecco 2021; Chen et al. 2023), which could influenced a region's *wujuren* density. To address this concern, we estimate the correlation between historical wars and economic variables, such as population density, land tax per capita, and urbanization rate during the Qing dynasty. However, we find no statistically significant correlations. In addition, we explore the possibility that past wars facilitated state building, solidifying the social networks among state elites or strengthening individuals' preferences for careers as government officials, which could increase each region's efforts to succeed in elite cultivation beyond just *wujuren*. To investigate this, we replace our outcome variable, *wujuren* density, with each region's success rate in other types of exam degrees, namely *wujinshi*, *juren*, and *jinshi*, with the latter two being respectively the second-highest and the highest degree awarded for the imperial civil service exams. However, our IV estimations do not yield statistically significant results for *juren* and *jinshi* densities. Thus, our placebo tests show that past war exposure did not motivate locals to invest more for success in the civil service exams.

The last part of our paper provides evidence on the persistent impact of each prefecture's warrior culture in the twenty-first century. We find that prefectures with more historical wars today have more martial arts schools but fewer elementary and middle schools per million population. These results remain statistically significant even after controlling for the confounding factors described earlier and using DTSL as an IV. However, GDP per capita today is not correlated with historical wars in either the ordinary least squares (OLS) or IV estimations.

Our paper contributes to two branches of literature. Nunn (2020) provides a comprehensive review of recent research explaining cross-societal differences in culture and determinants of cultural traits. Existing studies cover various dimensions such as trust (Nunn and Wantchekon 2011; Bauer et al. 2016; Rubin and Karaja 2017; Moscona et al. 2020), individualism (Talhelm et al. 2014; Bazzi et al. 2017; Ang 2019), patience (Galor and Savitskiy 2018), supernatural beliefs (Gershman 2020), gender roles (Fernández et al. 2004; Alesina et al. 2013; Sng and Zhong 2018; Xue 2018; Teso 2019), and more. Specifically, our paper relates to a growing literature that investigates the culture of violence. For example, Grosjean (2014) found that a culture of violence was transmitted across generations of Scots-Irish immigrants in the southern United States. Cao et al. (2021) demonstrated that as herders were more prone to conflicts, they had a greater inclination to take revenge, leading to the formation of a culture of honor. Our paper contributes to this line of research by shedding new light on the historical roots of warrior culture and its implications.

We also add new insights to the literature on the impacts of violence exposure. Previous research has demonstrated that violence has adverse effects on child health and education (Akresh and de Walque 2008; Shemyakina 2011; Islam et al. 2016; Akresh et al. 2017; Li and Koulovatianos 2020), induces violent behavior (Miguel et al. 2011), undermines trust (Nunn and Wantchekon 2011; Cassar et al. 2013), but also fosters cooperation (Bellows and Miguel 2009; Bauer et al. 2016), and promotes state building and economic development (Dincecco and Prado 2012; Dincecco and Onorato 2016; Dincecco et al. 2021; Dincecco 2021). To the best of our knowledge, we are the first to isolate martial skills acquired outside formal education and estimate the heterogeneous effects of war exposure on both martial and civilian human capital.

The remainder of this paper is organized as follows. Section 5.2 provides the historical background. Data sources and variable construction are discussed in Sect. 5.3. In Sect. 5.4, we focus on the causal link between historical exposure to military conflicts and *wujuren* density in the Qing dynasty. Section 5.5 further examines the possible channels through which past war exposure affected military elite production. Section 5.6 presents evidence on the persistent impacts of warrior culture on human capital investment in the twenty-first century. Section 5.7 concludes.

## 5.2 Historical Background

### *5.2.1 Wars in the History of China*

To provide the historical context for our quantitative exercise to follow, we start with a brief overview of China's military conflicts over time and across space. Based on data from Fu et al. (2003), Fig. 5.4. illustrates how the spatial distribution of military conflicts changed over different periods.[6] At the beginning of China's recorded history, 770–221 BCE, military conflicts were concentrated in northern China (Panel 1 of Fig. 5.4), which remained largely true until the fourteenth century.

There are two reasons behind this observed pattern. First, archaeological evidence shows that up to 2000 BCE, all walled settlements, or complex societies, that represented the more advanced development of time occurred along the middle to lower basins of both the Yellow and the Yangtze rivers (Xu 2017; Chen et al. 2023), where the Yellow River is located at the center of the north while the Yangtze River at the north–south borderline. As these walled cities were the early cradles of civilizational development, the Chinese civilization is generally considered to have originated in northern China (Tong 1994). In particular, Chen et al. (2023) demonstrated that during the Neolithic and early historic times of China, war was more prevalent in the north than in the south, which caused the Chinese civilization to emerge in the north but not in the south. Given that prehistory, it is no surprise that China's economic and political centers stayed in the north from the first dynasty, the Xia dynasty (2070–1600 BCE), onward until the Tang dynasty (618–907). In contrast, southern China did not gain economic and political importance until the Tang or even the Song dynasty (960–1278) (Zheng and Chen 1984; Liu 2007). Consequently, inter-state competition, military and otherwise, had to be concentrated in the north. In addition, given the dominance in early state development by the north, the states in the north not only could mobilize resources to fight bigger and more wars but also their bureaucracies were better equipped to keep historical records, leaving behind more and better war records for later historians to use.

Second, after China was unified in 221 BCE, it was repeatedly invaded by nomadic and Semi-nomadic peoples from the Eurasian steppe (Grousset and Walford 1970; Barfield 1989; Cosmo 2002; Chaliand 2005; Sng and Zhong 2018). This was seen as an inevitable outcome of China's geography (Ko et al. 2014). During periods

[6] We employ the three dynasties that (re)unified China Proper—Qin, Sui, and Song—to divide the history of China before the Mongol conquest into four periods. After the conquest, we take the following Yuan, Ming, and Qing dynasties as the other three periods. Figure 5.4 exhibits the distribution of military conflicts in each period.

of drought, the steppe nomads facing extensive survival challenges were often compelled to invade the settled farmers in the Chinese plains for food (Lattimore 1940; Bai and Kung 2011; Ko et al. 2014; McGuirk and Nunn 2020). These circumstances produced disproportionally more wars centered in northern China. As shown in Fig. 5.4, there were numerous wars near the Great Wall or the northern border except for the Yuan and Qing dynasties, established and ruled by nomads from the steppe and Manchuria, respectively. During these two dynasties, there were few wars brought by steppe nomads.

Due to the limitations of transport technology in ancient times, geography played a crucial role in warfare. Certain locations with specific geographic features held great strategic value in war and were often the focal points of battles. "*It is obvious that in each country there are some points of exceptional importance, where a number of roads converge, where it is easy to stockpile supplies, whence one can conveniently move in several directions; in short, whose possession satisfies a number of needs and offers a number of advantages*" (Clausewitz 1989).

In Chinese history, there were many notable locations of strategic importance. One example is the Hangu Pass, which witnessed numerous battles during the Warring States (481–221 BCE) as it served as a crucial choke point that protected the state of Qin (897–221 BCE) from the armies of the eastern states.[7] These strategic locations were often referred to as "the throat of the world" by ancient Chinese military strategists, and they were frequently occupied and controlled by state troops of each dynasty (Song 2009). In Sect. 5.4, we will use these strategic locations as our instrumental variables for military conflicts.

Figures 5.1 and 5.2 together suggest a close link between the spatial distributions of both famous historical military generals and past wars as both were heavily clustered in northern China. Thus, we would expect the north, rather than the south, to develop a prominent warrior culture in historical China, a hypothesis that we will prove.

### 5.2.2 Military Service Exams in Late Imperial China

Launched in the Sui dynasty (581–618 CE), China's imperial civil service exam system, known as *keju*, was an enduring institution used to select senior bureaucrats based on merits. Initially, only sons of aristocrats were qualified to take the *keju* exams. But the Song dynasty extended eligibility to all males, regardless of family background, and fundamentally transforming Chinese society culturally, politically and economically (Ho 1962; Elman 2000; Elman 2013; Bai and Jia 2016; Chen et al. 2020; Hao et al. 2022). There also existed a parallel but lesser-known military service exam system, *wuju*, which was started by Empress Wu Zetian in 702 CE, to identify and recruit talented warriors as military leaders (Xu 1997; Cao and Cao 2010).

[7] Hangu Pass separated the upper Yellow River valley from the North China Plain. Only the state of Qin, which occupied the upper western part of the River, could fully utilize the Hangu Pass for defense.

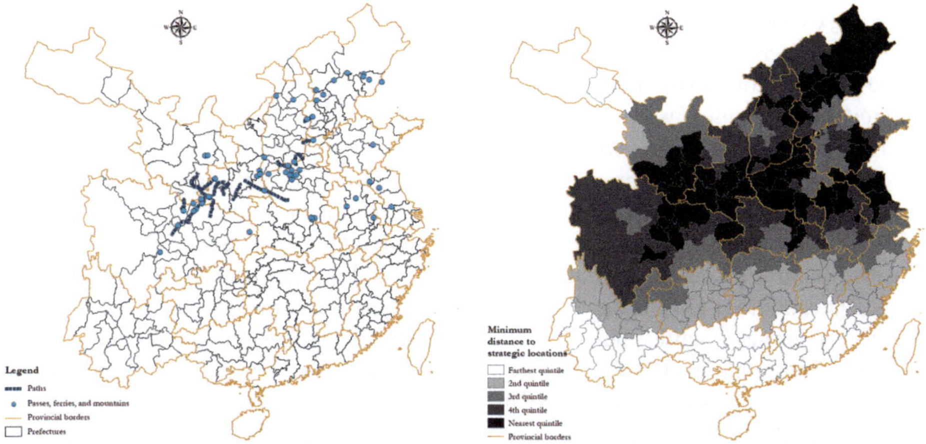


I. Strategic Locations II. Minimum Distance to Strategic Locations

**Fig. 5.2** Spatial distribution of and minimum distance to strategic locations

*Wuju* continued in subsequent dynasties. After its abolition in the Yuan dynasty (1280–1368), it was reinstated during the Ming dynasty (1368–1644) and reached the peak of its importance in the Qing dynasty. Although *wuju*'s purpose of senior warrior selection remained unchanged over time, its setting varied across dynasties. In the remainder of this paper, we focus specifically on the *wuju* system as practiced during the Qing dynasty. From 1646 to 1898, *wuju* was operating as officially and regularly as *keju*. Both the military and civil service exams had analogous structures, starting at the entry level (the prefectural exam), which encompassed a series of exams held in counties and prefectures (Chang 1955; Yan 2009), continuing to the middle level (the provincial exam), and finishing at the national level. Successful candidates would receive the qualification title of *wushengyuan* for entry-level military exam takers, *wujuren* for provincial-level exam takers, and *wujinshi* for national military exam takers. Only *wushengyuan* were eligible to enter the provincial exam and compete for the degree of *wujuren*. Finally, at the national level, *wujuren* could participate in the metropolitan and palace exams, with passers being granted the *wugongshi* and *wujinshi* degrees, respectively (Xu 1997).

The military service exams were regulated by a quota system. At the lowest level, *wushengyuan* quotas were apportioned to counties and prefectures based on their population size (Chang 1955; Xu 1997). Though a *wujuren* quota was assigned to each province, how that quota was distributed across the prefectures and counties within the province was competitively determined and not pre-assigned in any way. This practice in the Qing dynasty was essentially inherited from the preceding Ming dynasty and changed little over time (Chen et al. 2017). A province's *wujuren* quota was set to be half of its *juren* quota in the civil service exams by Kangxi Emperor in 1687 (Zhao 1927) and was only slightly increased in the late Qing dynasty (Xu 1997; Zhang et al. 2015). As for *wujinshi*, there was only an implicit quota system in the Ming dynasty based on a north–south divide in which all provinces were grouped into the northern and the southern regions so that the admitted *wujinshi* must satisfy some pre-set ratio between the north and the south. However, starting in 1712, an explicit *wujinshi* quota was allocated to each province (Xie 2009; Xu 1997). Still, as the overall number of *wujinshi* for each cohort was small, we will focus our analysis on each prefecture's *wujuren* number as our main outcome as this quantity is more representative of the broader population's martial skill achievements.

In contrast with *keju*, which emphasized candidates' knowledge of Confucian classics, *wuju* focused on examining martial knowledge and skills, comprising both indoor and outdoor skill tests. The indoor test questions were based on the *Seven Military Classics*,[8] while the outdoor part evaluated archery skills and physical strength, including arrow-shooting (both on horseback and on foot), bow-drawing, sword-swinging, and stone-lifting and throwing (Xu 1997; Zhou 2013). Some studies suggest that the outdoor tests generally carried more weight than the indoor ones in most cases (Zhou 2013).

The imperial exams had two distinct characteristics. First, both *wuju* and *keju* were open to all males who had no criminal record and whose father and grandfather were not in "restricted professions".[9] This restrictive qualification was relaxed in the mid-Qing dynasty Zhang et al. (2015). Candidates were allowed to take the exams repeatedly until they succeeded. This meant that a commoner had an opportunity to keep trying to work his way up the social ladder. Even if his ancestors had never held any official position or passed any level of the imperial exams, he was eligible to participate in the entry-level exams and, upon succeeding, qualified for the next level. For instance, it was estimated that roughly 2.5% of the male population aged between 15 and 49 in the mid-Qing dynasty registered for the prefectural civil service exam Bai and Jia (2016).

Second, the imperial exams followed a strict birthplace principle, to prevent the non-locally born from using up the local quotas. Migrants were excluded from the exams unless they satisfied the 20-year local residence requirement (Xu 1997; Zhang et al. 2015). According to the regulations, a candidate could only take the prefectural and provincial exams in his home county or prefecture and province. However, the national exams were only held in the capital, Beijing. With such strict birthplace and residence regulations, we consider each prefecture's *wujuren* density to be a good proxy for the prevalence level of warrior culture in the locality, reflecting the local population's extent of emphasis on martial skills as well as the amount resources devoted to military service exam preparations.

---

[8] The Seven Military Classics (Wujing Qishu) in ancient China were *The Art of War*, *The Methods of the Sima*, *Wuzi*, *Wei Liaozi*, *Six Secret Teachings*, *Three Strategies of Huang Shigong*, and *Questions and Replies between Tang Taizong and Li Weigong*, as canonized in the Song dynasty Loewe (1993).

[9] These professions included musician, barber, pedicurist, sedan-chair bearer, boat tracker, and so on Zhang et al. (2015).

## 5.3 Data Description

Administrative zoning changed from one dynasty to another, and even within a dynasty, making it a challenge to find a time-consistent administrative unit of analysis. To address this issue, we follow a common practice in the literature to select the Administrative prefectures determined by the Qing dynasty in 1820 as the basic unit and exclude those prefectures outside China Proper (due to their limited data availability). We also exclude the 11 prefectures with no data on *wujuren* (including Taiwan). Our remaining sample has 257 prefectures, with respect to which we convert all datasets used to maintain geographic consistency. For example, to calculate each Qing prefecture's number of elementary and middle schools in 2010, we intersect current Chinese cities with Qing prefectures, creating overlapping fragments between them. Assuming that schools within a current city were evenly distributed, for each Qing prefecture we multiply the current city's number of schools by the percentage of its territory that is in the Qing prefecture, repeat this for each city that overlaps with the given Qing prefecture, and sum the products across all such overlapping cities. This conversion procedure is applied to each variable used in this study.

### 5.3.1 *Outcome Variables*

The main outcome variable is each prefecture's level of warrior culture prevalence, proxied by its density of *wujuren* (winners of the provincial military exam) per million local population. This variable and its comparative alternative, *wujinshi* (winners of the national military exam), *juren* (winners of the provincial civil exams), and *jinshi* (winners of the national civil exam), are all constructed out of the local gazetteers completed in different years of the Qing dynasty. As mentioned earlier, there was no gazetteer compilation in the first few years, and was of lower quality during the last century, of the Qing, leading to our choice of 1650–1789 as our main period for the outcome variable. Note that if we would end the sample period earlier, we would have more prefectures covered but the sample would be shorter. Although some prefectures have local gazetteers available for post-1789 years that recorded degree-holder information, the number of prefectures covered would be too small.[10] Our chosen sample period is relatively peaceful and includes the reigns of the Kangxi, Yongzheng, and Qianlong emperors. Since our interest lies in understanding long-term determinants of warrior culture, using data from a relatively peaceful time is more appropriate as it allows us to minimize the impact of short-term transitory events (e.g., ongoing wars) on our results.

Data on *wujuren* and *wujinshi* are manually collected from 14 provincial gazetteers and 84 prefectural gazetteers of the Qing dynasty. Data on *juren* and *jinshi* are

[10] Of the 257 prefectures in our analysis, gazetteers with *wuju* data ending after 1789 were available for 218 of them. For the other 39 prefectures gazetteers with *wuju* data ending during the Qianlong Emperor (1736–1796) covered 32.

provided by Hao et al. (2022), supplemented with additional local gazetteers. Despite our best efforts, we are unable to obtain full degree-holder data coverage for all prefectures throughout the Qing dynasty, especially for the later decades, which is why we choose to concentrate on the 1650–1789 period.[11]

A second outcome variable is each prefecture's *violent crime rate*, proxying for the extent to which locals relied on violence, as opposed to peaceful negotiations, to settle disputes. Violent crime data for the Qing dynasty are provided in Chen et al. (2017), whose estimates are sourced from the *First Historical Archives of China*. During the Qing, local governments from the county level up were required to report homicide and other serious crime cases to the central government using a standardized template known as *xingke tiben*, or criminal case memorial (Chen et al. 2017). These memorials were then sent to the Grand Secretariat and upon the emperor's approval, they were transmitted to the Ministry of Justice for execution (Chang 2018). Subsequently, the Ministry of Justice compiled these cases into booklets, which have been preserved to this day (minus those that were lost or water-damaged due to roof leakage). The dataset encompasses 283,104 criminal cases that occurred between 1736 and 1897. However, our analysis only focuses on the 1736–1839 period because post-1840 China became more disorganized due to destabilizing foreign interferences and domestic rebellions, especially the Taiping Rebellion (1850–1864) (Têng and Fairbank 1954).

Besides outcomes in the Qing dynasty, we alternatively utilize each prefecture's contemporary *number of martial arts schools* as another measure of warrior culture prevalence. For this measure, two sources of data are used. The first source is Lv et al. (2003), which compiled a catalogue of 975 renowned martial arts schools in China of today, from which 954 schools' addresses are successfully matched with the respective prefectures. We refer to this variable as Famous Martial Arts Schools. Out of concerns about the representativeness of FMAS, we also employ an online source. Using fuzzy-search terms such as "martial arts school" and "martial arts club" on a map, one of China's most prominent map apps today, we find over 48,384 sites with matching names and coordinates. To ensure accuracy, we manually remove any organization that is not in martial arts education or training.[12] We refer to this variable as web-searched martial arts schools (WMAS).

---

[11] The *wuju* data for some prefectures may not cover the entire 1650–1789 period, with some starting later than 1650 and others ending earlier than 1789, leading to potential biases. To address this issue, we adjust the *wuju* data by extending a prefecture's *wuju* success rates during the years with data to years with data missing. For instance, we have data on *wujuren* and *wujinshi* from *Xuanhua Fuzhi* (*Gazetteer of Xuanhua Prefecture*), but its gazetteer series discontinued in 1757, with 32 years missing. Thus, the *wuju* data for Xuanhua Prefecture are good for 1650–1757, with a total of 108 years covered. In order to match the sample period of other prefectures, we multiply the number of *wujuren* achieved in Xuanhua Prefecture during 1650–1757 by $140/108 = 1.29$. We apply this adjustment method to all 39 prefectures with *wuju* data missing for some subsets of years. In addition, the *wuju* data for Guizhou province start in 1654, instead of 1650, and we adjust data for its prefectures similarly.

[12] For instance, from the results, there are restaurants whose names contain characters with similar meanings to "martial arts".

As a countermeasure of warrior culture, we examine each region's emphasis (or the lack thereof) on civil (as opposed to warrior) education by using its number of elementary and middle schools in 1900 and 2010, respectively.

The logic is that we should not expect past war exposure to have a positive impact on civil education; if anything, it should have a negative effect. We can also treat this as a placebo test. The school data for 1900 are obtained from *Diyici Jiaoyu Tongji Tubiao* (*The First Educational Statistical Compendium*). The contemporary school data are gathered from *Zhongguo Chengshi Tongji Nianjian* (*China City Statistical Yearbook*) of 2011.

### 5.3.2 Explanatory Variables

Our main explanatory variable of interest is each prefecture's past exposure to military conflicts, based on data from Fu et al. (2003), covering 3,746 historical wars with such information as the time and place of occurrence, duration, participating parties, and other details. Battle locations in the historical records may be under names different from their contemporary counterparts, in which case information in the dataset is relied on to make the conversion. The 30 wars from the pre-770 periods are excluded from our sample due to their unreliability, leaving 7,576 war records in our sample.[13] We then match the battle locations with the administrative prefectures of 1820 and obtain the number of wars that took place within each prefecture from 770 BCE–1912 CE.

To address potential endogeneity issues of historical wars, we need an instrumental variable, for which purpose we utilize the set of major strategic locations in the history of China as identified by Rao (2003) which studied the geographic patterns of China Proper from a military history perspective. These strategic sites are digitized by Ditushu, providing us with detailed geographic coordinates from each location. These locations encompass cities, passes, mountains, paths, rivers and ports, mostly determined by their geographic features but not so much by their socioeconomic conditions. However, we exclude rivers from our analysis since they did not hold the same military importance as other types of locations—in comparison, ferry sites played a more critical role. We also omit cities from our strategic sites as they are highly correlated with local population and economic development factors for which we separately control.

The remaining sample of strategic locations includes 14 paths, traversing through the Qin and the Taihang Mountains; 40 passes, each serving as a military fortress; 10 ferry piers; and four mountains. In particular, the Qin Mountain separates the Wei River valley from the Sichuan Basin while the Taihang Mountains isolate the Wei River valley from the North China Plain, so these paths played special roles in Chinese history as these areas are known for their dense population and as the

[13] One war might occur in several places, and each war record is defined by a unique war-location pair.

birthplaces of Chinese civilization. Figure 5.2 illustrates the spatial distribution of the strategic locations and of the minimum distance from each prefecture to the strategic locations (DTSL). Note that if a prefecture contains a strategic location, its DTSL value is 0.

### 5.3.3 Control Variables

Outcomes such as *wujuren* density, martial arts school density and elementary and middle school density are likely to be affected by economic development, besides warrior culture. For this reason, we must correct for the impact of these factors.

First, a region's commercial development can be captured by its distance to the coastline and major rivers, since water transport was the main means for commerce prior to the arrival of modern mechanized conveyances in the late-nineteenth century. To obtain these data, we use both the China Historical Geographic Information System (CHGIS) and the Harvard Worldmap ChinaX project to geolocate each coastline and major river and calculate the distances, which are employed to control for commercial development.

Second, for explaining contemporary outcomes, we control for per capita gross domestic product (GDP), for which data on prefectural population and GDP of 2019 are obtained from the county-level statistical yearbook of 2020 published by the National Bureau of Statistics. For historical outcomes, data on prefectural population are calculated from Ge (2002), which provides prefectural population estimates for various historical time points, from which we extrapolate each prefecture's population at in-between time points by assuming a constant growth rate for the years between the estimation points.

Third, geography is known to have played important roles in human socioeconomic development (Nunn 2012; Chen et al. 2023), so we need to control for this as well. Following Nunn (2012), we calculate each prefecture's terrain ruggedness based on the difference in elevation between adjacent grid cells of 90 square meters, with data from the United States Geological Survey (USGS).

Fourth, agricultural productivity should have some impact on local cultural formation. Following Galor and Ö zak (2016), we construct an agricultural suitability index, to capture a prefecture's potential agricultural crop output. Specifically, from their Caloric Suitability Indices for different crops in a given grid cell of size $5' \times 5'$ on the earth's surface, we take the average for each cell, attainable given the set of crops that are suitable for cultivation in the post-1500 years.

Fifth, to account for the effect of historical weather patterns, we obtain data from *Zhongguo Jin Wubainian Hanlao Fenbu Tuji* (*Yearly Charts of Drought and Flood in China for the Last 500 Years*), edited by the Chinese Academy of Meteorological Sciences, which provides a weather index ranging from 1–5, with a higher value representing less rainfall,[14] allowing us to calculate the number of flood years (with a weather value of 1) and that of drought years (with a value of 5) within an estimation period.

Lastly, we also control for the effect of development by using each prefecture's tax payments and urbanization ratio, with data respectively from the *Jiaqing Daqing Yitong Zhi* (*Jiaqing National Chorography of the Great Qing Dynasty*), compiled under the command of the Jiaqing Emperor, and Cao (2001). The assumption here is that more tax payments per capita and a higher urbanization ratio for a region imply better development and higher economic income per capita, which may favor certain cultural development.

### 5.3.4 Summary Statistics

Table 5.1 provides descriptive statistics for the variables. A common practice in the literature is to use a logarithmic transformation to reduce the skewness of residuals. As shown in Fig. 5.6,[15] logarithmic transformations $\ln(x)$ or $\ln(x + 1)$[16] do reduce right skewness and the resulting distributions are closer to normal. However, recent studies showed that empirical estimates based on either $\text{arsinh}(x)$ or $ln(x + 1)$ as the outcome variable can be subject to arbitrary choices regarding scaling (Chen and Roth 2022; Mullahy and Norton 2022). According to Thakral and Tô (2023), a transformation is insensitive to rescaling if and only if it is an affine function of a logarithmic or power function. Since many variables in our dataset contain zero values,[17] we decide to employ a power transformation.

In Table 5.1, our main outcome variable, *wujuren* density, has a mean of 167.79 and a standard error of 208.44. We want to find a power function that approximates the natural logarithm within the interval of ± one standard error from the mean. The advantage of such transformation is that the resulting coefficients can be approximately interpreted as elasticity. In Fig. 5.7, we plot five power functions from $x^{0.1}$ to $x^{0.5}$ as well as the natural logarithm—the red curves indicate power functions and the teal curve represents the natural logarithm. We observe that $x^{0.3}$ is the closest to the natural logarithm within the interval [0, 400]. Hence, we apply the transformation, $f(x) = x^{0.3}$, to all variables in our exercise.[18]

---

[14] The index is defined as below. 1: Continuous heavy rainfall or flood that lasted for longer than one season; 2: continuous heavy rainfall or flood that lasted shorter than one season; 3: normal weather, with no continuous heavy rain, flood, or drought; 4: occurrence of drought that lasted shorter than one season; 5: drought that lasted longer than one season.

[15] We pick column (4) of Table 4.2 as the OLS regression and column (3) of Table 4.3 as the IV regression, and we apply different transformations to all variables, presenting residuals respectively.

[16] We only apply the transformation $\ln(x + 1)$ for variables containing a zero value.

[17] The number of observations with zero values is shown in Table 4.1.

[18] We also show the estimates under other transformations in Sect. 5.3.

**Table 5.1** Summary statistics

| | Mean | SD | Min | Max | #Obs | #0 Obs |
|---|---|---|---|---|---|---|
| Military conflicts from Spring and Autumn period to Ming Dynasty (770 BCE–1643) | 20.98 | 22.94 | 0 | 111 | 257 | 17 |
| Military conflicts from Sui to Ming Dynasty (581–1643) | 10.64 | 10.32 | 0 | 75 | 257 | 21 |
| *Wujuren* per million population from 1650–1789 | 167.79 | 208.44 | 0.00 | 1995.42 | 257 | 48 |
| *Wujinshi* per million population from 1650–1789 | 16.47 | 20.90 | 0.00 | 116.54 | 257 | 17 |
| *Juren* per million population from 1650–1789 | 247.28 | 228.12 | 0.00 | 1422.61 | 257 | 38 |
| *Jinshi* per million population from 1650–1789 | 44.92 | 45.24 | 0.00 | 261.11 | 257 | 9 |
| Terrain ruggedness | 236.45 | 184.32 | 4.42 | 972.47 | 257 | 0 |
| Total length of rivers per square kilometer (km) | 51.21 | 23.23 | 0.00 | 139.66 | 257 | 1 |
| Agricultural suitability | 3647.02 | 938.60 | 0.00 | 5511.54 | 257 | 2 |
| Years with extreme weather events from 1650–1789 | 20.04 | 10.24 | 6 | 44 | 257 | 0 |
| Distance to coastline in km | 521.51 | 371.45 | 2.13 | 1914.92 | 257 | 0 |
| Minimum distance to strategic locations (km) | 243.19 | 264.13 | 0.00 | 1209.76 | 257 | 41 |
| Distance from centroid to strategic locations (km) | 315.98 | 277.53 | 1.40 | 1312.44 | 257 | 0 |
| Containing strategic locations (=1) | 0.16 | 0.37 | 0 | 1 | 257 | 216 |
| Population per square km in 2 CE | 18.58 | 31.34 | 0.00 | 177.06 | 257 | 6 |
| Intentional injuries per million population from 1736–1839 | 720.81 | 691.79 | 0.00 | 8076.61 | 257 | 13 |
| Murders per million population from 1736–1839 | 31.01 | 22.67 | 0.00 | 161.53 | 257 | 13 |

(continued)

**Table 5.1** (continued)

| | Mean | SD | Min | Max | #Obs | #0 Obs |
|---|---|---|---|---|---|---|
| Average population per square km from 1650–1789 | 81.05 | 88.52 | 0.28 | 607.83 | 257 | 0 |
| Land tax per million population in 1820 (in tael) | 75,672.83 | 70,314.23 | 0.00 | 387,416.19 | 257 | 5 |
| Urbanization rate in 1910 (%) | 7.28 | 5.92 | 0.00 | 43.20 | 257 | 3 |
| Distance to provincial capitals (km) | 196.07 | 108.05 | 4.23 | 864.82 | 257 | 0 |
| Military grave goods from Neolithic Age to Western Zhou Dynasty (8000–771 BCE) | 9.45 | 31.89 | 0 | 298 | 257 | 183 |
| Elementary and middle schools per million population in 1900 | 120.76 | 218.48 | 0.00 | 1699.35 | 257 | 2 |
| Elementary and middle schools per million population in 2010 | 349.75 | 300.98 | 50.31 | 2047.53 | 257 | 0 |
| Famous martial arts schools (FMAS) per million population in 2003 | 0.63 | 1.40 | 0.00 | 17.60 | 257 | 112 |
| Web-searched martial arts schools (WMAS) per million population in 2022 | 34.60 | 84.35 | 0.00 | 1070.11 | 257 | 3 |
| Gross domestic product per capita in 2019 (in renminbi) | 4609.77 | 3199.25 | 1168.31 | 24,766.52 | 257 | 0 |

*Notes* This table summarizes statistics. See Sect. 5.3 for data sources and details of variable construction

## 5.4 War Breeds Warriors

To investigate the impact of historical exposure to wars on local culture, we estimate the following baseline regression cross-sectionally:

$$y_i = \alpha + \beta wars_j + \gamma X_i \varepsilon_j \quad (5.1)$$

where $y_i$ is the cumulative number of *wujuren* per million population from 1650–1789 in prefecture *I*; the main independent variable, $wars_i$, is prefecture *i*'s cumulative number of military conflicts (i.e., wars) from the Spring and Autumn period to the Ming dynasty, that is 770 BCE–1643 CE; $X_i$ denotes control variables. First, we control for terrain ruggedness because it can have a lasting effect on long-term economic development (Nunn and Puga 2012; Chen et al. 2017). Similarly, river network density may also have effects on transportation and production and, hence, economic development. To allay this concern, we control for the total length of rivers per square kilometer in each prefecture. Next, we control for agricultural suitability since agricultural production can have a long-lasting impact on culture (Talhelm et al. 2014; Alesina et al. 2013). Extreme weather may increase survival pressure and lead to more violence, and therefore we control for the number of years with extreme weather from 1736–1839, where extreme weather is defined by a weather index value of either 1 or 5 under a five-grade rating system for drought and flood. Distance to the coastline may affect the local population's ability to engage in international trade and be exposed to foreign culture and Western technology, so we control for the distance from each prefecture's centroid to the coastline.

To reduce skewness we transform every variable with a power function, $f(x) = x^{0.3}$. This is because $x^{0.3}$ is relatively close to the natural logarithmic transformation within the interval [0, 400].

## *5.4.1 Baseline Results*

The baseline results are presented in the first four columns of Table 5.2. We initially estimate an OLS model by incorporating control variables gradually. In column (1), we provide a benchmark estimate where province-fixed effects are the only control. Notably, we observe a significant positive correlation at the 5% level. Subsequently, in column (2), we include more controls: terrain ruggedness and river density, which reduces the significance level slightly to the 10% level. Moving to column (3) we further control for agricultural suitability and the number of extreme weather years, resulting in the coefficient becoming significant at the 5% level once again. Finally, in column (4), we add one more control: distance to the coastline, which slightly raises the wars coefficient's significance. Henceforth, we will refer to these five controls as the baseline controls.

Overall, all estimates for the wars coefficient are consistent with our hypothesis: after controlling for the other factors, we find a significant positive correlation between historical wars prior to and *wujuren* density during the Qing dynasty. Thus, regions associated with more past wars produced more *wujuren*, implying

**Table 5.2** Correlation between historical military conflicts and *Wujuren* density, OLS estimates

| Dependent variable | | | *Wujuren* density | | | *Wujuren* |
|---|---|---|---|---|---|---|
| | OLS | OLS | OLS | OLS | Tobit | Poisson |
| | (1) | (2) | (3) | (4) | (5) | (6) |
| Military conflicts | 0.560** | 0.491* | 0.498** | 0.517** | 0.584** | 1.007** |
| | (0.254) [0.210] | (0.242) [0.202] | (0.235) [0.200] | (0.229) [0.194] | (0.254) | (0.004) |
| Terrain ruggedness | | −0.529*** (0.128) | −0.533*** (0.131) | −0.464** (0.175) | −0.478** (0.184) | 0.998*** (0.001) |
| River density | | 0.209 (0.312) | 0.242 (0.301) | 0.312 (0.339) | 0.369 (0.370) | 1.009*** (0.003) |
| Agricultural suitability | | | −0.049 (0.160) | −0.071 (0.167) | −0.064 (0.175) | 1.000* (0.000) |
| Extreme weather | | | −0.092 (0.693) | −0.025 (0.683) | −0.064 (0.702) | 1.010 (0.012) |
| Distance to coastline | | | | −0.212 (0.194) | −0.229 (0.197) | 0.999 (0.001) |
| Province-fixed effects | Yes | Yes | Yes | Yes | Yes | Yes |
| Number of observations | 257 | 257 | 257 | 257 | 257 | 257 |
| Adjusted $R^2$ | 0.148 | 0.211 | 0.206 | 0.208 | | |

*Notes* This table reports baseline estimates of the specification Eq. 5.1. The dependent variable is the cumulative number of *wujuren* per million population from 1650–1789 in the first five columns, while it is the unnormalized number of *wujuren* in the last column. The independent variable of interest is the cumulative number of military conflicts from Spring and Autumn period to Ming dynasty (770 BCE–1643). In the first five columns, all the variables are powered by 0.3. The coefficients in the last column are incidence-rate ratios (IRR). For example, if the IRR is 1.01, it implies that a one-unit increase in the independent variable is associated with a 1% increase in the dependent variable. Standard errors adjusted at the province level are presented in parentheses, whereas Conley (1999) standard errors adjusted for two-dimensional spatial autocorrelation are given in brackets. Conley standard errors are constructed by assuming a binary weight matrix: for each prefecture-pair, it contains 1 if the two prefectures were located within 250 km and 0 otherwise. We conduct this with the Stata command *acreg*. Stars indicate statistical significance with the clustered standard errors, *** $p < 0.01$, ** $p < 0.05$, and * $p < 0.1$

a stronger local emphasis on martial skills and hence a stronger warrior culture. However, it is important to exercise caution when interpreting the coefficient estimates quantitatively due to the power transformation of the variables.

## 5.4.2 Robustness Tests

The robustness of the above result is verified in several ways.

### 5.4.2.1 Spatial Autocorrelation

Recent work has cautioned about potentially spurious significance in studies on historical persistence when spatial autocorrelation is overlooked (Kelly 2019). To address this concern and account for possible correlation between error terms among adjacent prefectures, we employ the Conley (1999) standard errors adjusted for two-dimensional spatial auto-correlation, as presented in brackets in Table 5.2. We construct the Conley standard errors by assuming a binary weight matrix of the covariance of error terms among prefectures: for each pair of prefectures, it has a value of 1 if the two prefectures are located within 250 km and 0 otherwise. After controlling for spatial autocorrelation, the correlation between historical wars and *wujuren* density remains statistically significant with even lower standard errors.

Furthermore, we explore alternative weight matrices to examine different scenarios. First, we maintain a binary weight matrix but vary the threshold distance. Panel A of Table 5.9 reports the estimates using a binary weight matrix respectively with threshold distances of 50, 100, 250, 500, 750, and 1,000 km. All estimates indicate a significant correlation between historical wars and *wujuren* density at the 1% level. Additionally, we allow the weights in the matrix to linearly decrease with distance and reach 0 at the distance cut-off. The results are presented in Panel B of Table 5.9, where once again all estimates are significant at the 1% level.

### 5.4.2.2 Tobit and Poisson Estimations

Of our 257 prefectures, 17 have zero *wujuren* over the sample period, which may affect our results though these prefectures make up only 6.61% of the sample. We address this issue by estimating a Tobit model, truncating the observations with zero *wujuren*. The results are presented in column (5) of Table 5.2, and the wars coefficient remains significant at the 5% level.

Considering that *wujuren* is a discrete variable, we conduct a Poisson regression where we treat *wujuren* as the outcome variable and the estimated average population during 1650–1789 as the exposure variable. The results, shown in column (6), indicate that each additional recorded military conflict before the Qing dynasty is associated with a 0.7% increase in *wujuren*.

#### 5.4.2.3 Alternative Logarithmic and Power Transformations

To further confirm the estimates in column (4) of Table 5.2, we apply alternative transformation functions to the variables, with the results presented in Table 5.10. In the first five columns, we respectively examine power transformations ranging from $f(x) = x^{0.1}$ to $f(x) = x^{0.5}$. The statistical significance of the wars coefficient reaches its peak at $f(x) = x^{0.2}$ and then declines, though it remains above the 10% level in each case. Simultaneously, the coefficient exhibits a rising trend. Column (6) assumes a linear equation without any variable transformation. However, the coefficient estimate in this case is not statistically significant, indicating the absence of a linear correlation between historical wars and *wujuren* density. In columns (7) and (8), we explore square and cubic transformations, respectively, in which cases the coefficient of interest is not statistically significant.

#### 5.4.2.4 Unadjusted Wuju Data

Recall that for 39 prefectures that have *wuju* data missing for some subsets of years, we adjusted their data by extending their *wujuren* success rates from the years with data to years without, so that all prefectural data have the same sample period. This adjustment is justified as our regressions are cross-sectional rather than time-series based. However, to alleviate concerns regarding the impact of the adjustment method on our results, we replicate Table 5.2 using unadjusted *wujuren* data for all the prefectures, with the corresponding results displayed in Table 5.11. Columns (4) to (6) show that historical wars still have a statistically significant positive impact on *wujuren* density at the 5% level.

### *5.4.3 Instrumental Variable Strategy*

Despite controlling for several potentially confounding factors, there may still be other omitted variables that could influence the results. Furthermore, the causality underlying the statistical correlation has yet to be confirmed. There is also the concern about reverse causality, wherein military conflicts were more likely to occur in regions with a strong warrior culture presence. To address these concerns, we employ an instrumental variable: the minimum distance to strategic locations.[19]

Among famous examples of strategic locations, Hangu Pass stands out as it controlled the passage connecting the upper Yellow River valley and the North China Plain, making it a focal point for numerous battles (Rao 2003). Another example is Baoxie Road, a major pathway linking the Hanzhong Plain and the Guanzhong Plain. Due to its unique geography, Baoxie Road often served as a route for swift attacks

---

[19] The strategic locations are introduced in Sects. 2.1 and 3.2. Also, in Sect. 5.5 we provide additional evidence against the reverse causality hypothesis.

(Rao 2003). As these strategic locations were of paramount military importance in ancient times, they were frequently contested by opposing forces, leading to battles in the surrounding areas. Consequently, we consider the distance to these strategic locations (DTSL) as an instrumental variable for historical military conflicts.

Of the 257 prefectures in our sample, 41 contain at least one strategic location. For these prefectures, we assign DTSL value of 0. For the remaining prefectures, DTSL is defined as the minimum distance from a prefecture to the nearest strategic location. The distribution of DTSL is depicted in Fig. 4.2.

For robustness, we will examine two alternative additional instruments that utilize the strategic locations: distance from a prefecture's centroid to the nearest strategic location and a binary variable that takes a value of 1 if the prefecture contains at least one strategic location and 0 otherwise.

#### 5.4.3.1 Exclusion Restriction

According to Rao (2003), the strategic locations were predominantly determined by geography, suggesting their exogeneity. However, three concerns remain regarding their validity as an instrument. First, certain geographic factors may have influenced both the selection of strategic locations and *wujuren* density, thereby violating the exclusion restriction. Second, there is a possibility of endogenous selection bias, where strategic locations far from centers of development may be less likely to have been documented in historical records. Lastly, DTSL might affect *wujuren* density through channels other than historical wars.

To provide suggestive evidence regarding the IV exclusion restriction, we conduct two sets of tests. Firstly, we examine the correlation between DTSL and potential confounding variables. Panel A of Table 5.12 indicates that while DTSL is not significantly correlated with terrain ruggedness (as shown in column (1) when controlling for province-fixed effects), there is a correlation between DTSL and river density at the 10% level (as demonstrated in column (2)). We replicate the tests with other baseline control variables such as agricultural Suitability, years with extreme weather, and distance to the coastline, and the results do not indicate any significant correlation.

Next, to address the concern of endogeneity, we test whether DTSL is correlated with the population per square kilometer in 2 CE. The statistically non-significant estimate in column (6) of Table 5.12 suggests no discernible correlation. Additionally, given that locations near national borders would have a higher probability of military conflicts, we identify two classical borders (exhibited in Fig. 5.8), one from the Sui–Tang period and the other from the Northern Song dynasty (960–1126 CE). Columns (7) and (8) show no significant correlation between DTSL and the distance to either border even at the 10% level.

Overall, the DTSL is shown to be orthogonal to most of the potentially confounding variables mentioned above. In Panel D of Table 5.12, we conduct similar tests for historical military conflicts. Notably, historical military conflicts were significantly correlated with population density in 2 CE at the 5% level.

In the second part of the tests, we investigate whether DTSL influenced *wujuren* density through channels other than historical wars. As demonstrated in the first two columns of Table 5.13, the correlation between DTSL and *wujuren* density becomes statistically non-significant when the impact of historical military conflicts is controlled for, evidence supporting the exclusion claim that past wars is the channels through which DTSL affected *wujuren* density.

### 5.4.4 Instrumented Results

Next, we conduct IV estimations of Eq. 5.1, using DTSL to instrument historical wars. The results are shown in Table 5.3. In column (1), we run an OLS regression with DTSL being the independent variable. With province-fixed effects and baseline controls included, the estimate implies a negative correlation between DTSL and *wujuren* density significant at the 10% level. In column (2), we control for population density in 2 CE given that unequal development in early history might lead to selection bias of strategic locations. The estimate remains significant at the 10% level.

For the IV estimations from column (3), we include province-fixed effects and baseline control variables, where the first-stage regression coefficient implies a negative and statistically significant relation between DTSL and historical wars, which is consistent with our hypothesis. In particular, the KP-F statistic is 24.75, which suggests there is no issue of weak identification. The second-stage result indicates a positive impact of historical war exposure on *wujuren* density, significant at the 5% level. Thus, it is greater past war experience that made some regions value martial skills more than others, nurturing a stronger warrior culture. In column (4), we add population density in 2 CE as another control, and the result remains unchanged.

To further alleviate the endogeneity concern about the choice of strategic locations, we consider another research design: In the first stage, we use the distance to the strategic locations established before the Sui dynasty, to instrument military conflicts from the Sui to the Ming dynasty, from 581–1643 CE,[20] of which the predicted war value is then utilized to predict a prefecture's *wujuren* density of 1650–1789 CE in the second stage. This design is to prevent the possibility that some strategic locations became famous through nearby military conflicts caused by other confounding factors. The result in column (5) informs us that this alternative design does not affect the conclusion above.

Finally, we note that all those strategic locations are in the north, leading to two challenges. First, southern prefectures were too distant to be affected by the strategic locations, challenging the ability of DTSL to predict military conflicts in the south. Second, as shown in Fig. 5.2, DTSL for southern regions is almost just proxying for latitude, simply capturing such factors as waterfalls and temperature increasing

---

[20] We manually search on the Internet for the first time a strategic location appeared in historical documents, and we take the time as the estimated time of the strategic location's establishment. As a result, we eliminate 3 out of 68 strategic locations.

**Table 5.3** Impacts of historical military conflicts on *Wujuren* density, IV estimates

| Dependent variable | | *Wujuren* density | | | | | |
|---|---|---|---|---|---|---|---|
| | OLS | OLS | IV | IV | IV | IV | IV |
| | (1) | (2) | (3) | (4) | (5) | (6) | (7) |
| Military conflicts | | | 1.088** | 1.023** | | 1.061** | |
| | | | (0.424)<br>[0.451] | (0.440)<br>[0.458] | | (0.533)<br>[0.529] | |
| Military conflicts after Sui dynasty | | | | | 1.416**<br>(0.571) | | 1.506**<br>(0.699) |
| Population density in 2 CE | | 0.329*<br>(0.166) | | 0.277*<br>(0.153) | 0.406***<br>(0.142) | 0.032<br>(0.298) | 0.150<br>(0.285) |
| | | | | | *First stage* | | |
| Distance to strategic locations | −0.214* | −0.198* | −0.196*** | −0.194*** | | -0.185*** | |
| | (0.102)<br>[0.103] | (0.102)<br>[0.102] | (0.039) | (0.039) | | (0.041) | |
| Distance to strategic locations before Sui dynasty | | | | | −0.140*** (0.039) | | −0.131*** (0.040) |
| Province-fixed effects | Yes | Yes | Yes | Yes | Yes | Yes | Yes |
| Baseline controls | Yes | Yes | Yes | Yes | Yes | Yes | Yes |
| Number of observations | 257 | 257 | 257 | 257 | 257 | 134 | 134 |

(continued)

**Table 5.3** (continued)

| Dependent variable | | *Wujuren* density | | | | | |
|---|---|---|---|---|---|---|---|
| Adjusted $R^2$ | 0.184 | 0.190 | | | | | |
| Kleibergen-Paap Wald $F$ | | | 24.752 | 24.364 | 12.988 | 20.270 | 10.479 |

*Notes* This table reports the IV estimates of the specification Eq. 5.1. The dependent variable is the cumulative number of *wujuren* per million population from 1650–1789. The independent variables of interest are the cumulative number of military conflicts from Spring and Autumn period to Ming dynasty (770 BCE–1643) and from Sui to Ming dynasty (581–1643), respectively. The instrumental variables are the minimum distance from each prefecture to strategic locations, and to those established before Sui dynasty, respectively, measured in km. All variables are powered by 0.3. In columns (6)–(7), provinces with no strategic location are excluded. Standard errors adjusted at the province level are presented in parentheses, whereas Conley standard errors assuming a binary weight matrix with a threshold of 250 km are given in brackets. Stars indicate statistical significance with the clustered standard errors, *** $p < 0.01$, ** $p < 0.05$, and * $p < 0$

in latitude. To address these concerns, we exclude all provinces with no strategic location, leaving us with 134 prefectures in 9 provinces. Based on this subsample, we replicate the IV estimations of columns (4) and (5), with the results shown in columns (6) and (7), where the wars coefficient remains statistically significant at the 5% level discussed here, the KP-F statistic is higher than 10.

#### 5.4.4.1 Alternative Measures of Strategic Locations' Effects

We also consider two alternative measures of the strategic locations' effects. The first is the distance from a prefecture's centroid to the nearest strategic location, which we refer to as centroid DTSL. The second measure is a binary variable that adopts a value of 1 if a prefecture contains strategic locations and 0 otherwise, which is referred to as the binary indicator of strategic locations. However, Tables 5.12 and 5.13 show that these two variables do not adhere to the exclusion restriction as much as DTSL does. Nonetheless, we replicate the estimations of Table 5.3 using the two measures as iVs, respectively, and the results are shown in Tables 5.14 and 5.15, with KP-F statistics lower than 10, indicating the weak identification problem.[21]

## 5.5 Channels

Our exercise has thus far established that past exposure to more wars worked to make the locals endogenously nurture aspirations for military service, supporting our hypothesis that "war breeds warriors". This explains why regions across China experienced different degrees of success in producing military officers throughout Chinese history. This finding is also consistent with Parker (1996)'s "challenge-response dynamic", in the sense that more historical war exposure simply forced the locals to be better warriors in order to protect themselves better.

If past encounters with military conflicts indeed drive the formation of a warrior culture, we should also see such a culture manifest in other ways, for example, a stronger local preference for the use of force and violence, rather than peaceful negotiations, to resolve disputes, and the establishment of more martial arts schools to train and hone locals' martial skills. Economically speaking, the experience with more wars would make the perceived returns from investing in martial skills higher.

[21] Figure 5.9 plots the correlation between DTSL and centroid DTSL, demonstrating that the two measures diverge when DTSL is low or equal to 0. Consider a scenario where a prefecture has two strategic locations (with both distance measures low enough), one near its centroid and the other on the edge. The low KP-F statistic with centroid DTSL suggests that these two strategic locations should have similar effects on military conflicts in the prefecture.

In this section, we seek to explore these implications to add color to our discussions on warrior culture formation.

### 5.5.1 Violent Crimes

To test the hypothesis that the fostering of a warrior culture is accompanied with the locals preferring to resolve disputes through violence, we look for evidence from violent crime data from the Qing dynasty.

Toward this end, we repeat the OLS and IV estimations using as the outcome variable each prefecture's cumulative number of violent crime cases from 1736 to 1839 Chen et al. (2017), normalized by its population. As explained in Sect. 5.3, we exclude the criminal cases after 1839 as China's bureaucracy became less reliable in filing reports due to distractions by wars and rebellions starting with the Opium War (1839–1842).

Table 5.4 reports the results. For column (1), the outcome variable is the number of "intentional injuries" cases per million population from 1736 to 1839, with both province-fixed effects and baseline control variables controlled for. The coefficient of historical military conflicts is positive and statistically significant at the 1% level. Thus, the OLS regression supports our hypothesis that exposure to more wars in the past made the locals more likely to rely on force to resolve disputes.

Next, we conduct an IV regression. Since historical wars are correlated with population density of 2 CE (Table 5.12), we also include this population density as a control. The IV result for the wars coefficient in column (2) of Table 5.4 is statistically significant at the 10% level, suggesting that historical war exposure did increase a prefecture's rate of intentional injuries. Similarly, when murder rate is the outcome variable in columns (3) and (4), the coefficient for historical war exposure is also positive and statistically significant. Therefore, regions that suffered more wars in the past were more likely to develop a deeper warrior culture that emphasizes the use of violence in settling disputes.

### 5.5.2 Negative Impact on Civilian Education

Warrior culture is defined by its emphasis on martial skills and the use of force. Thus, if greater historical exposure to war breeds a stronger warrior culture, we should expect such regions to put less premium and devote fewer resources to civilian education, manifested in the form of fewer elementary and middle schools per million population. For example, between Confucian classics and martial skills, locals in such regions would value the latter more than in other regions. Thus martial human capital should have a higher premium, while book human capital should be discounted more. A testable implication is that in prefectures with more historical wars (and hence a stronger warrior culture), there was lower demand for schools offering civilian

**Table 5.4** Impacts of historical military conflicts on violent crimes and civilian education

| Dependent variable | Intentional injury rate | | Murder rate | | Elementary and middle school density | |
|---|---|---|---|---|---|---|
| | OLS | IV | OLS | IV | OLS | IV |
| | (1) | (2) | (3) | (4) | (5) | (6) |
| Military conflicts | 1.031*** | 0.969* | 0.293** | 0.308* | −0.648*** | −0.998*** |
| | (0.295)<br>[0.266] | (0.558)<br>[0.512] | (0.116)<br>[0.107] | (0.174)<br>[0.174] | (0.170)<br>[0.129] | (0.370)<br>[0.346] |
| Population density in 2 CE | | −0.025<br>(0.230) | | 0.007<br>(0.107) | | 0.243<br>(0.169) |
| Urbanization rate | | | | | −0.162<br>(0.132) | −0.042<br>(0.199) |
| Province-fixed effects | Yes | Yes | Yes | Yes | Yes | Yes |
| Baseline controls | Yes | Yes | Yes | Yes | Yes | Yes |
| Number of observations | 257 | 257 | 257 | 257 | 257 | 257 |
| Adjusted $R^2$ | 0.279 | | 0.160 | | 0.628 | |
| Kleibergen-Paap Wald $F$ | | 24.364 | | 24.364 | | 26.744 |

*Notes* This table reports the OLS and IV estimates of the specification Eq. 5.1. The dependent variable is the cumulative number of intentional injuries and murders, respectively, per million population from 1736–1839 in the first four columns, while it is the number of elementary and middle schools per million population in 1900 in the last two columns. The independent variable of interest is the cumulative number of military conflicts from Spring and Autumn period to Ming dynasty (770 BCE–1643). The instrumental variable is the minimum distance from each prefecture to strategic locations (km). All variables are powered by 0.3. Standard errors adjusted at the province level are presented in parentheses, whereas Conley standard errors assuming a binary weight matrix with a threshold of 250 km are given in brackets. Stars indicate statistical significance with the clustered standard errors, *** $p < 0.01$, ** $p < 0.05$, and * $p < 0.1$

education in such topics as Confucian classics but higher demand for martial arts schools.

For this, we estimate Eq. 5.1 with the outcome variable being each prefecture's school density toward the end of the Qing, that is, its number of elementary and middle schools per million population in 1900. While the year 1900 falls outside the primary estimation period, the waning control of the central government over the local education system during that period substantiates our approach of approximating local civilian education demand through the number of elementary and middle schools. In addition, we employ the 1910 urbanization rate as a covariate to account for local economic development, which could inconceivably impact the provision of local educational institutions.

The results are displayed in column (7) of Table 5.4, showing a statistically significant (at the 1% level) and negative effect of historical military conflicts on school density in 1900. The IV results in column (8) further confirm historical war exposure's negative impact on elementary and middle school density in 1900 (significant at the 1% level), with a KP-F statistic of 26.74.

### 5.5.3 Military Elites vs. Civilian Elites

The preceding two inquiries have corroborated the claim that war breeds warrior culture, through different manifestations, with *wujuren* density being the more tangible summary indicator of wars' effect on warrior culture formation. However, it may also be argued that if war promoted state building (Tilly 1975) and political centralization (Parker 1996), it would also make government offices more powerful and more attractive to certain people, in which sense higher *wujuren* density might not mean a stronger presence of warrior culture but instead a stronger desire to become an office holder, since a *wujuren* degree would give its winner a promising pass to power (being a senior official, military or civilian in the imperial bureaucracy). In other words, efforts to succeed in the *wuju* exams might not be motivated by warrior culture but by material incentives to become an office holder, so that *wujuren* density would not just embody a prefecture's warrior culture.

In addition, there exists another legitimate concern that a prefecture's *wujuren* density can be attributed to its proximity to centers of political influence. This proximity might afford locals access to invaluable information and social resources, or, in the context of *wujuren* and *juren*, it could reduce their transportation costs associated with participating in provincial exams, thereby contributing to their success in the imperial exams.

To address these concerns, we control for the distance between each prefecture's centroid and the nearest provincial capital. Additionally, we compare *wujuren* density with the densities of other degree holders, particularly *juren* and *jinshi* winners from the civil service exams as those who were only motivated by the prospect of holding powerful offices and their material benefits should just take the civil exams. First, we conduct OLS and IV estimations of Eq. 5.1 using *wujuren* and *wujinshi* density as the respective outcome variables. Recall that *wujinshi* is a higher and much tougher-to-obtain military degree than *wujuren*, thus not as representative of the mass martial skills as the latter. As shown in columns (1)–(4) of Table 5.5, both the OLS and IV estimates suggest positive impacts of historical wars on the densities of these two types of military elites, with the IV estimate being statistically significant at the 1% level for *wujuren* density and at the 5% level for *wujinshi* density. This confirms our reasoning that candidates in the *wuju* exams were at least partly driven by their desire to pursue a martial career triggered by their home prefecture's past war experience.

Now, let's turn to *juren* density and *jinshi* density, both from the *keju* or civil service exams. These winners were only tested on their civil knowledge and skills, rather than their martial skills. Columns (5)–(8) of Table 5.5 show the respective results for these two types of imperial degree holders, where the OLS estimates indicate a positive correlation, significant at the 5% level, between historical wars and the density for both types of degrees, but the links become statistically non-significant under the IV estimations. The OLS significance is likely due to omitted variables related to state building, as the historical wars that are predictable by the IV (hence exogenous) do not have significant explanatory power of *juren* and *jinshi* densities. The KP-F

**Table 5.5** Impacts of historical military conflicts on military and civilian elites

| Dependent variable | *Wujuren* density | | *Wujinshi* density | | *Juren* density | | *Jinshi* density | |
|---|---|---|---|---|---|---|---|---|
| | OLS | IV | OLS | IV | OLS | IV | OLS | IV |
| | (1) | (2) | (3) | (4) | (5) | (6) | (7) | (8) |
| Military conflicts | 0.450* | 1.023*** | 0.215** | 0.682** | 0.394 | 0.472 | 0.263* | 0.277 |
| | (0.216)<br>[0.172] | (0.383)<br>[0.410] | (0.102)<br>[0.105] | (0.320)<br>[0.257] | (0.246)<br>[0.192] | (0.440)<br>[0.337] | (0.139)<br>[0.123] | (0.298)<br>[0.278] |
| Distance to provincial capitals | −0.461***<br>(0.158) | −0.376***<br>(0.134) | −0.300***<br>(0.076) | −0.227***<br>(0.057) | −0.520***<br>(0.161) | −0.515***<br>(0.154) | −0.344**<br>(0.128) | −0.337***<br>(0.119) |
| Population density in 2 CE | | 0.154<br>(0.131) | | 0.161<br>(0.128) | | −0.030<br>(0.199) | | 0.043<br>(0.172) |
| Province-fixed effects | Yes | Yes | Yes | Yes | Yes | Yes | Yes | Yes |
| Baseline controls | Yes | Yes | Yes | Yes | Yes | Yes | Yes | Yes |
| Number of observations | 257 lePara> | 257 | 257 | 257 | 257 | 257 | 257 | 257 |
| Adjusted $R^2$ | 0.254 | | 0.278 | | 0.414 | | 0.449 | |
| Kleibergen-Paap Wald $F$ | | 26.984 | | 26.984 | | 26.984 | | 26.984 |

*Notes* This table reports the OLS and IV estimates of the specification Eq. 5.1. The dependent variable is the cumulative number of four types of exam degree holders, respectively, per million population from 1650–1789. The independent variable of interest is the cumulative number of military conflicts from Spring and Autumn period to Ming dynasty (770 BCE–1643). The instrumental variable is the minimum distance from each prefecture to strategic locations (km). All variables are powered by 0.3. Standard errors adjusted at the province level are presented in parentheses, whereas Conley standard errors assuming a binary weight matrix with a threshold of 250 km are given in brackets. Stars indicate statistical significance with the clustered standard errors, *** $p < 0.01$, ** $p < 0.05$, and * $p < 0.1$.

statistic is 26.98, which suggests there is no issue of weak identification. Overall, our exercise here suggests that historical war exposure did not have a significant impact on a region's success rate in the civil exams, but it did so on its performance in the military exams, consistent with our hypothesis that "war breeds warriors" but maybe not book scholars.

### *5.5.4 Economic Development*

Another potential channel through which historical wars affected *wujuren* density is economic development. Wars might promote or hinder economic development which in turn determined the affordability of human capital investment and thus the success rate in the imperial exams, military or civil. To examine this possible channel, we need a proxy for each prefecture's economic development as there were no prefectural data on GDP or other economic indices for the Qing. The first proxy is population density, as is often used (e.g., Ashraf and Galor 2011; Chen and Wang 2022). Columns (1) and (2) of Table 5.6 demonstrate no statistically significant link between a prefecture's historical military conflicts and its average population density during 1650–1789.

The second proxy is land tax per capita, with data collected from the national chorographical study compiled during the Jiaqing Emperor's reign (1760–1820). Columns (3) presents a positive effect of historical wars on land tax per capita, statistically significant at the 10% level; but this significance diminishes under the IV estimation in column (4).

Lastly, we utilize each prefecture's urbanization rate in 1910 as a proxy for economic development. In this case, as presented in columns (5) and (6) of Table 5.6, the coefficient for historical wars is significant at the 10% level under the OLS model but not so under the IV estimation. To summarize, our exercise in this subsection suggests that historical wars affected *wujuren* density not through the channel of economic development.

### *5.5.5 Pre-Existing Warrior Culture*

Lastly, we further address the possible issue of reverse causality that wars were more likely to happen in regions where there had long been a warrior culture. Of course, our IV, DTSL, is mostly exogenous and thus unlikely to coincide with the spatial distribution of warrior culture that existed at the beginning of the Eastern Zhou (770–221 BCE). In other words, the IV estimations should not be subject to the reverse causality effect. In addition, our hypothesis asserts that conflict exposure breeds warrior culture, but it does not say that warrior culture cannot reversely lead to more military conflicts. It is possible that war and warrior culture interact with

**Table 5.6** Impacts of historical military conflicts on economic development

| Dependent variable | Population density | | Land tax per capita | | Urbanization rate | |
|---|---|---|---|---|---|---|
| | OLS | IV | OLS | IV | OLS | IV |
| | (1) | (2) | (3) | (4) | (5) | (6) |
| Military conflicts | −0.002 | −0.257 | 1.679* | −0.317 | 0.099** | 0.032 |
| | (0.054)<br>[0.040] | (0.194)<br>[0.161] | (0.947)<br>[0.998] | (1.983)<br>[1.642] | (0.044)<br>[0.042] | (0.115)<br>[0.102] |
| Population density in 2 CE | | 0.316***<br>(0.114) | | 1.311<br>(0.924) | | 0.046<br>(0.076) |
| Province-fixed effects | Yes | Yes | Yes | Yes | Yes | Yes |
| Baseline controls | Yes | Yes | Yes | Yes | Yes | Yes |
| Number of observations<br>Adjusted $R^2$ | Yes<br>0.780 | Yes | Yes<br>0.571 | Yes | Yes<br>0.288 | Yes |
| Kleibergen-Paap Wald $F$ | | 24.364 | | 24.364 | | 24.364 |

*Notes* This table reports the OLS and IV estimates of the specification Eq. 5.1. The dependent variables are estimated average population per square kilometer from 1650–1789, land tax per capita in 1820 (in tael), and urbanization rate in 1910, respectively. The independent variable of interest is the cumulative number of military conflicts from Spring and Autumn period to Ming dynasty (770 BCE–1643). The instrumental variable is the minimum distance from each prefecture to strategic locations (km). All variables are powered by 0.3. Standard errors adjusted at the province level are presented in parentheses, whereas Conley standard errors assuming a binary weight matrix with a threshold of 250 km are given in brackets. Stars indicate statistical significance with the clustered standard errors, *** $p < 0.01$, ** $p < 0.05$, and * $p < 0.1$

each other, much like the claim by Tilly (1975) that "war made the state and the state made war".

Still, we can use archaeological data to proxy for the possible prevalence levels of prehistoric warrior culture in each prefecture. Chen et al. (2023) treated a region's number of military grave goods from excavated graves as a proxy for its war frequency during the Neolithic and early historic times (8000–771 BCE), with data from the China Archaeological Database (CADB) maintained at the Centre for Quantitative History (CQH) at the University of Hong Kong and based on archaeological excavation reports published no later than 2021. In total, 2,735 military grave goods are included in our sample, spanning the 8000–771 BCE period.

Since the grave goods were likely to be affected by concurrent economic development, we control for population density in 2 CE—the earliest historical regional population estimates available. Column (4) of Table 5.7 shows that a prefecture's prehistoric military grave goods predict its historical wars prior to the Qing dynasty, which is statistically significant at the 1% level. This indicates significant persistence in each region's war experience: regions with more wars during prehistoric times continued to fight more wars during historical times.

Next, each prefecture's number of military grave goods is used to predict its *wujuren* density from 1650–1789 CE, respectively, employing OLS, Tobit, and Poisson estimations as reported in columns (5)–(7) of Table 5.7. The results all reject

**Table 5.7** Tests on the hypothesis of pre-existing warrior culture

| Dependent variable | Military conflicts | *Wujuren* density | | *Wujuren* |
|---|---|---|---|---|
| | OLS (1) | OLS (2) | Tobit (3) | Poisson (4) |
| Military grave goods | 0.149*** | -0.010 | -0.002 | 0.999 |
| | (0.045)<br>[0.039] | (0.063)<br>[0.074] | (0.061) | (0.001) |
| Population density in 2 CE | 0.079<br>(0.085) | 0.388*<br>(0.191) | 0.389**<br>(0.184) | 1.005<br>(0.004) |
| Province-fixed effects | Yes | Yes | Yes | Yes |
| Baseline controls | Yes | Yes | Yes | Yes |
| Number of observations | 257 | 257 | 257 | 257 |
| Adjusted $R^2$ | 0.434 | 0.169 | | |

*Notes* This table reports the test results of the hypotheses of persistent warfare and pre-existing warrior culture. The dependent variables are the cumulative number of military conflicts from 770 BCE–1643, the cumulative number of *wujuren* per million population from 1650–1789, and the unnormalized number of *wujuren*, respectively. The independent variable of interest is the cumulative number of military grave goods from Neolithic Age to Western Zhou dynasty (8000–771 BCE). In the first three columns, all the variables are powered by 0.3. The coefficients in the last column are incidence-rate ratios (IRR). Standard errors adjusted at the province level are presented in parentheses, whereas Conley standard errors assuming a binary weight matrix with a threshold of 250 km are given in brackets. Stars indicate statistical significance with the clustered standard errors, *** $p < 0.01$, ** $p < 0.05$, and * $p < 0.1$

the hypothesis that prehistoric war exposure has predictive power of *wuju* success during the Qing. If some regions had a warrior culture before 770 BCE, it did not persist to influence these regions' performance in the military service exams during the seventeenth and eighteenth century.

## 5.6 Legacy of Warrior Culture

While the cultural impact of prehistoric war experiences may not have persisted to modern times, that of historical wars may still affect today's local culture and each local population's human capital investment across the country. In this section, we continue to distinguish between martial skills and book knowledge, respectively reflecting martial and civilian human capital. We then investigate whether historical war exposure influences the local population's investment preferences between these two.

### 5.6.1 Martial Arts Schools

Two measures of a prefecture's martial arts school density are used to capture the locals' emphasis on martial human capital investment as well as its warrior culture prevalence today. One is the FMAS, based on data from Lv et al. (2003), and the other is the web-searched martial arts schools (WMAS), which are obtained by performing a fuzzy search in 2022. To standardize the variables, we divide a prefecture's respective numbers of FMAS and WMAS by its population (in millions), to arrive at its FMAS density and WMAS density per million.

Columns (1) and (2) of Table 5.8 present the OLS and IV estimates of the effects of historical wars on FMAS density, respectively, where both estimates for the historical wars coefficient are positive and statistically significant at the 1% level. We then repeat these for WMAS density, with the results respectively reported in column (3), where the OLS estimate is also positive and significant at the 1% level, and in column (4), where the IV estimate is significant at the 10% level.

Overall, these results suggest that the warrior culture resulting from historical war exposure has persisted to this day and continues to shape the local population's investment in martial skills through martial arts schools.

### 5.6.2 Elementary and Middle Schools

As a cross-validation of the above finding, we observe a significant negative correlation between historical war exposure and contemporary elementary and middle school (EAMS) density. Specifically, column (5) of Table 5.8 reveals that regions with more historical military conflicts had fewer EAMS per million population in 2010, with the effect being statistically significant at the 1% level. The IV estimate of this effect in column (6) is also significant at the 1% level.

The above results are obtained after controlling for a host of confounding factors related to geography, climate and socioeconomic development. Still, it might be suspected that the lower EAMS density in regions with more historical wars is also due to their lower contemporary economic development caused by past military conflicts. To check this potential channel, columns (7) and (8) of Table 5.8 present both the OLS and IV estimates, indicating no statistically significant impact of historical wars on GDP per capita in 2019, rejecting the notion that economic development is driving the lower EAMS density.

Finally, there is the possibility that migration may interfere with our estimates. Beijing, Shanghai, Guangzhou and Shenzhen are the best-known megacities, collectively attracting millions of migrants from all over the country. To eliminate this possibility, we exclude the two prefectures that contain these megacities, Songjiang Fu and Guangzhou Fu, from our sample and replicate the estimations above, with the results given in Table 5.16 which are basically the same as in Table 5.8.

**Table 5.8** Impacts of historical military conflicts on contemporary human capital investment

| Dependent variable | Famous martial arts school density | | Web-searched martial arts school density | | Elementary and middle school density | | GDP per capita | |
|---|---|---|---|---|---|---|---|---|
| | OLS | IV | OLS | IV | OLS | IV | OLS | IV |
| | (1) | (2) | (3) | (4) | (5) | (6) | (7) | (8) |
| Military conflicts | 0.186*** | 0.278*** | 0.479*** | 0.512* | −0.366*** | −0.816*** | −0.124 | −0.252 |
| | (0.030)<br>[0.117] | (0.085)<br>[0.291] | (0.087)<br>[0.216] | (0.292)<br>[0.418] | (0.095)<br>[0.136] | (0.220)<br>[0.333] | (0.111)<br>[0.089] | (0.444)<br>[0.281] |
| Population density in 2 CE | | 0.049<br>(0.051) | | 0.208**<br>(0.103) | | 0.191**<br>(0.086) | | 0.431*<br>(0.256) |
| Province-fixed effects | Yes | Yes | Yes | Yes | Yes | Yes | Yes | Yes |
| Baseline controls | Yes | Yes | Yes | Yes | Yes | Yes | Yes | Yes |
| Number of observations | 257 | 257 | 257 | 257 | 257 | 257 | 257 | 257 |
| Adjusted $R^2$ | 0.377 | | 0.367 | | 0.465 | | 0.538 | |
| Kleibergen-Paap Wald $F$ | | 24.364 | | 24.364 | | 24.364 | | 24.364 |

*Notes* This table reports the OLS and IV estimates of the specification Eq. 5.1. The dependent variables are the number of famous martial arts schools per million population in 2003, the number of web-searched martial arts schools per million population in 2022, the number of elementary and middle schools per million population in 2010, and GDP per capita in 2019, respectively. The independent variable of interest is the cumulative number of military conflicts from Spring and Autumn period to Ming dynasty (770 BCE–1643). The instrumental variable is the minimum distance from each prefecture to strategic locations (km). All variables are powered by 0.3. Standard errors adjusted at the province level are presented in parentheses, whereas Conley standard errors assuming a binary weight matrix with a threshold of 250 km are given in brackets. Stars indicate statistical significance with the clustered standard errors, *** $p < 0.01$, ** $p < 0.05$, and * $p < 0.1$

Our findings in this section thus support our hypothesis. Understandably, each region's resources are limited. If its local population shares a strong warrior culture, it naturally allocates more of the limited resources to martial arts education and emphasizes martial skills, at the expense of civilian human capital investment and book knowledge. Thus, these regions end up having more martial arts schools and fewer elementary and middle schools per million population. These two types of education are competing and substitutable with one another.

## 5.7 Conclusion

Chinese history books are full of stories about famous military generals and heroes, but a careful examination of their birth origins reveals much regional concentration (Fig. 4.1); disproportionally many came from the north, as well as along the Yangtze River. This pattern is largely true even in modern times. To explain this cross-regional variation, this paper goes back to the historical roots of warrior culture formation. Our exercise treats each prefecture's success rates in the military service exams, *wuju*, in the Qing dynasty as a measure of its warrior culture prevalence and then investigates the determinants of *wujuren* density in each prefecture. Our main finding is that historical war exposure prior to the Qing had a significant impact on local warrior culture formation: the more wars a prefecture experienced during 770 BCE–1643 CE, the higher its *wujuren* density. The impact of greater past war exposure on a prefecture manifested in multiple other ways as well: it had less success in the imperial civil service exams, more violent crimes and fewer elementary and middle schools in the Qing, and more martial arts schools and fewer elementary and middle schools per million population today.

All these dimensions of evidence point to the conclusion that "war breeds warriors": in regions that experienced more wars in the past, the locals naturally adapted their behavior and selected cultural elements that put a premium on martial skills, at the expense of civil skills, as the former skills were believed to increase their probability of survival (their past war experience taught them so and made them develop such preferences). As a result, these local societies demonstrate the various aspects of warrior culture: a preference for the use of force to settle disputes, aspirations for martial skills and a military career, and hence higher demand for martial arts education and lower resources allocated to civilian human capital investment. Such a warrior culture legacy has survived to this day.

## Appendix

See (Figs. 5.3, 5.4, 5.5, 5.6, 5.7, 5.8 and 5.9). Tables (5.9, 5.10, 5.11, 5.12, 5.13, 5.14, 5.15, and 5.16).

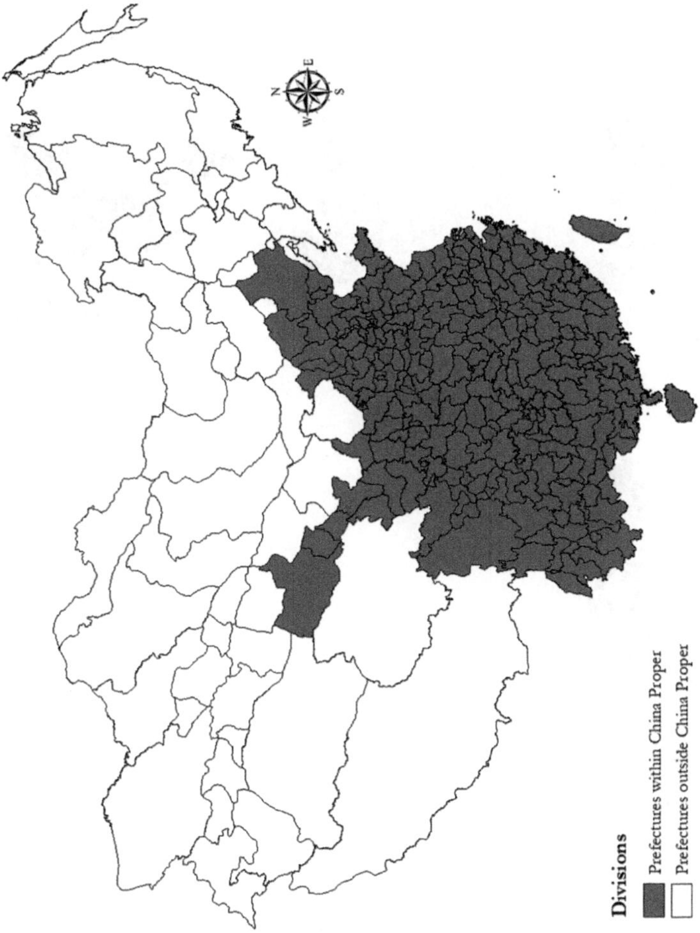


**Fig. 5.3** China Proper vs. territory of the Qing Dynasty in 1820

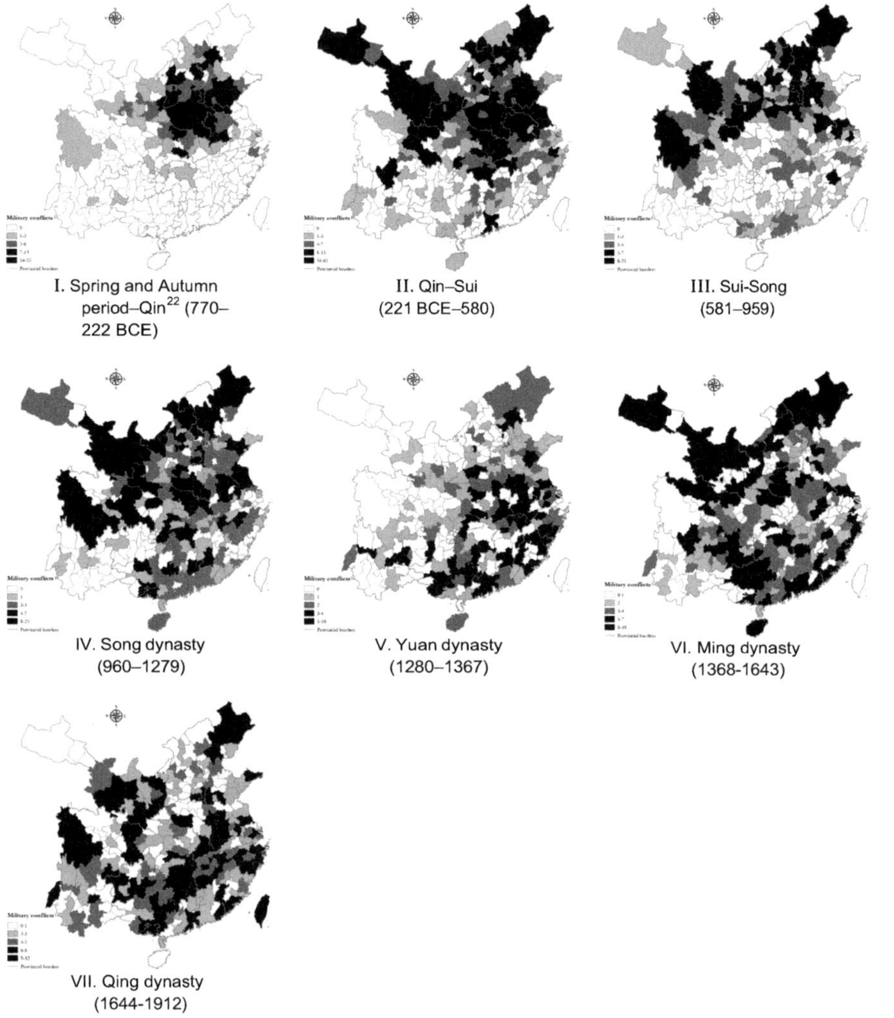


**Fig. 5.4** Spatial distribution of military conflicts in different periods

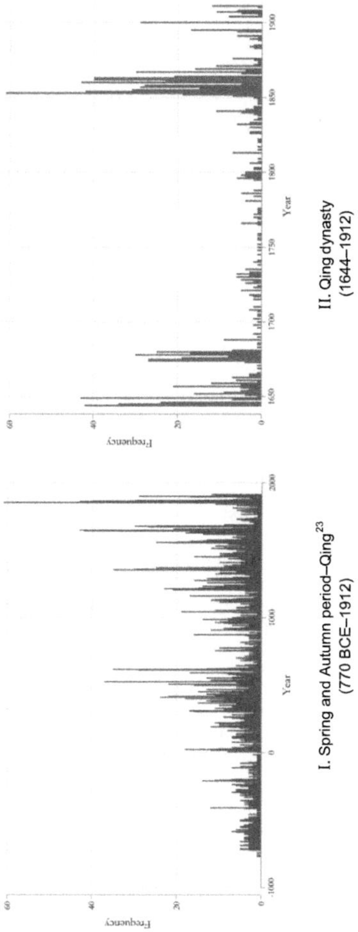


**Fig. 5.5** Time distribution of military conflicts over two periods

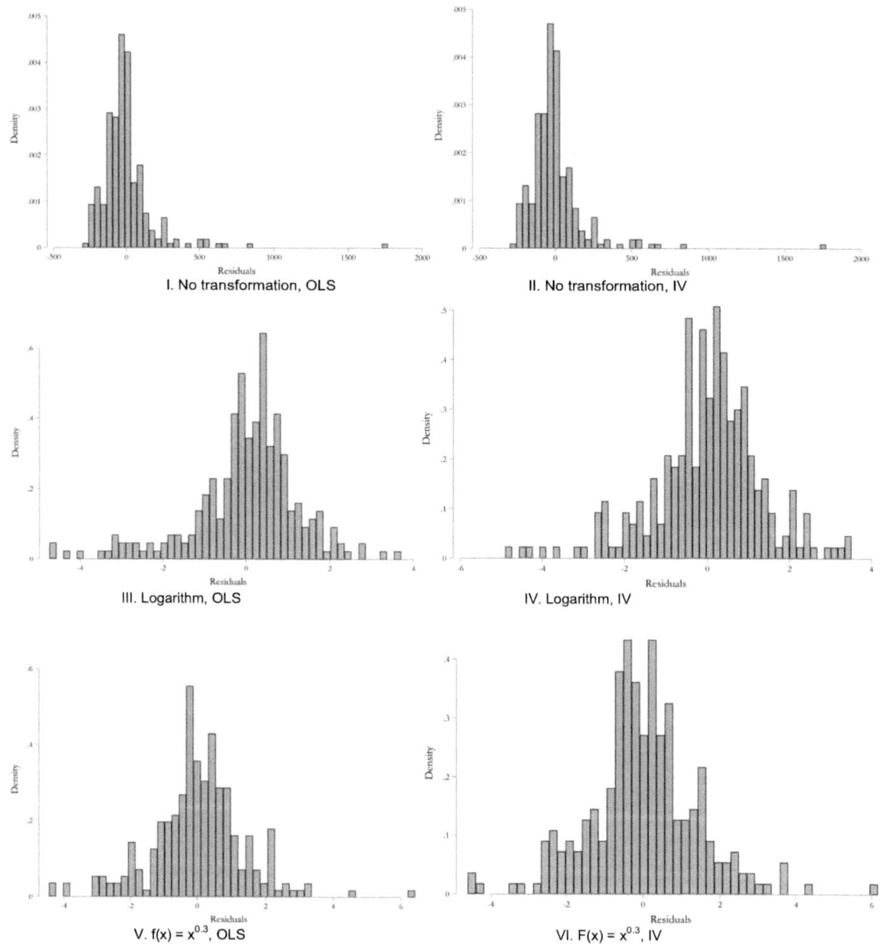


**Fig. 5.6** Distribution of residuals with *Wujuren* density being outcome[22]

[22] The residuals are from OLS and IV regressions that incorporate province-fixed effects and baseline controls. For example, the residuals in Fig. 5.6.V is corresponding to column (4) in Table 4.2.

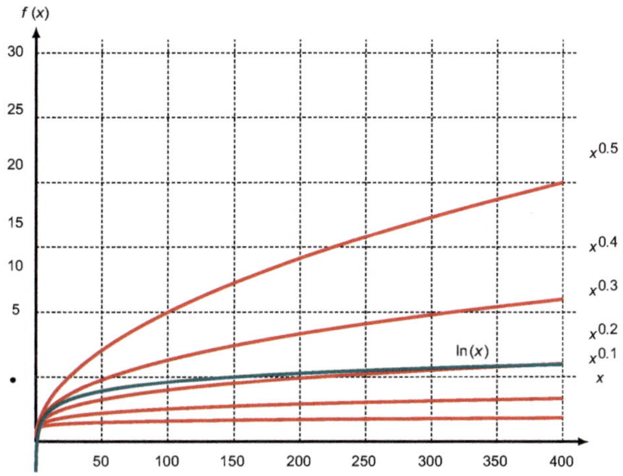


**Fig. 5.7** Comparison of power functions with natural logarithm

**Fig. 5.8** Two classic borders of Chinese dynasties

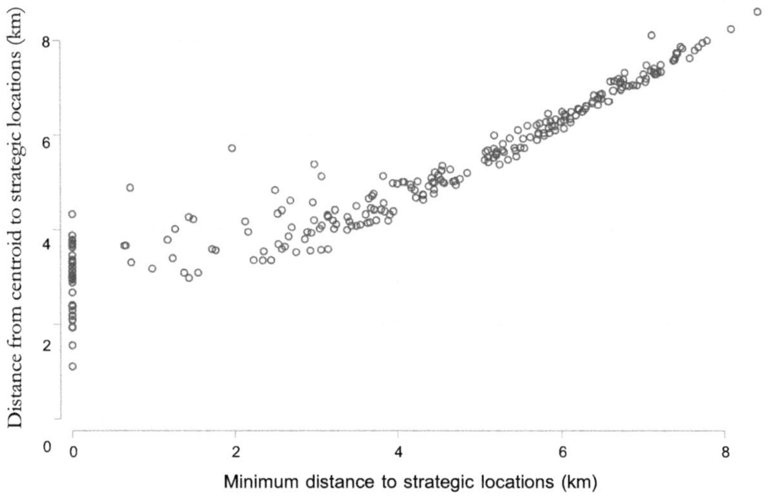


**Fig. 5.9** Correlation between two distances to strategic locations

**Table 5.9** Robustness tests with alternative Conley covariance weight matrices

| Dependent variable | *Wujuren* density | | | | | |
|---|---|---|---|---|---|---|
| | 50 km (1) | 100 km (2) | 250 km (3) | 500 km (4) | 750 km (5) | 1000 km (6) |
| *Panel A: Binary weight matrix* | | | | | | |
| Military conflicts | 0.517*** [0.148] | 0.517*** [0.144] | 0.517*** [0.194] | 0.517*** [0.186] | 0.517** [0.223] | 0.517*** [0.169] |
| Province-fixed effects | Yes | Yes | Yes | Yes | Yes | Yes |
| Baseline controls | Yes | Yes | Yes | Yes | Yes | Yes |
| Number of observations | 257 | 257 | 257 | 257 | 257 | 257 |
| $R^2$ | 0.279 | 0.279 | 0.279 | 0.279 | 0.279 | 0.279 |
| *Panel B: Linearly decreasing weight matrix* | | | | | | |
| Military conflicts | 0.517*** [0.153] | 0.517*** [0.149] | 0.517*** [0.167] | 0.517*** [0.175] | 0.517** [0.187] | 0.517*** [0.190] |
| Province-fixed effects | Yes | Yes | Yes | Yes | Yes | Yes |
| Baseline controls | Yes | Yes | Yes | Yes | Yes | Yes |
| Number of observations | 257 | 257 | 257 | 257 | 257 | 257 |
| $R^2$ | 0.279 | 0.279 | 0.279 | 0.279 | 0.279 | 0.279 |

*Notes* This table replicates the baseline estimates in column (4) of Table 5.2 using alternative weight matrices of the covariance of error terms among prefectures. Conley standard errors are given in brackets. Each column assumes a distinct threshold distance as shown at the top. In Panel A, Conley standard errors are constructed with a binary weight matrix: for each prefecture-pair, it contains 1 if the two prefectures were located within the threshold distance and 0 otherwise. Panel B adopts a weight matrix linearly decreasing with distance until reaching 0 at the distance cut-off. Stars indicate statistical significance with the Conley standard errors, *** $p < 0.01$, ** $p < 0.05$, and * $p < 0.1$

**Table 5.10** Robustness tests with alternative variable transformations

| Dependent variable | *Wujuren* density | | | | | | | | |
|---|---|---|---|---|---|---|---|---|---|
| | $f(x) = x^{0.1}$ | $f(x) = x^{0.2}$ | $f(x) = x^{0.3}$ | $f(x) = x^{0.4}$ | $f(x) = x^{0.5}$ | $f(x) = x$ | $f(x) = x^2$ | $f(x) = x^3$ | $f(x) = \ln(x)$ |
| | (1) | (2) | (3) | (4) | (5) | (6) | (7) | (8) | (9) |
| Military conflicts | 0.416** | 0.480** | 0.517** | 0.559* | 0.622* | 1.393 | 13.052 | 104.563 | 0.417** |
| | (0.185)<br>[0.157] | (0.195)<br>[0.164] | (0.229)<br>[0.194] | (0.284)<br>[0.240] | (0.354)<br>[0.298] | (0.151)<br>[0.943] | (13.783)<br>[11.290] | (133.691)<br>[110.729] | (0.165)<br>[0.145] |
| Province-fixed effects | Yes | Yes | Yes | Yes | Yes | Yes | Yes | Yes | Yes |
| Baseline controls | Yes | Yes | Yes | Yes | Yes | Yes | Yes | Yes | Yes |
| Number of observations | 257 | 257 | 257 | 257 | 257 | 257 | 257 | 257 | 257 |
| Adjusted $R^2$ | 0.198 | 0.215 | 0.208 | 0.194 | 0.177 | 0.177 | 0.034 | 0.065 | 0.214 |

*Notes* This table replicates the baseline estimates in column (4) of Table 5.2 with alternative variable transformations. All variables are transformed with the function shown at the top of each column. For the last column, the transformation function is $f(x) = \ln(x + 1)$ instead if variable $x$ contains zero observations. Standard errors adjusted at the province level are presented in parentheses, whereas Conley standard errors assuming a binary weight matrix with a threshold of 250 km are given in brackets. Stars indicate statistical significance with the clustered standard errors, *** $p < 0.01$, ** $p < 0.05$, and * $p < 0.1$

**Table 5.11** Robustness tests with unadjusted *wuju* data

| Dependent variable | *Wujuren* density | | | | | *Wujuren* |
|---|---|---|---|---|---|---|
| | OLS | OLS | OLS | OLS | Tobit | Poisson |
| | (1) | (2) | (3) | (4) | (5) | (6) |
| Military conflicts | 0.554** | 0.483* | 0.491* | 0.509** | 0.576** | 1.007** |
| | (0.254)<br>[0.210] | (0.243)<br>[0.201] | (0.235)<br>[0.199] | (0.229)<br>[0.193] | (0.254) | (0.003) |
| Province-fixed effects | Yes | Yes | Yes | Yes | Yes | Yes |
| Baseline controls | Yes | Yes | Yes | Yes | Yes | Yes |
| Number of observations | 257 | 257 | 257 | 257 | 257 | 257 |
| Adjusted | 0.149 | 0.217 | 0.212 | 0.214 | | |

*Notes* This table replicates the baseline estimates in Table 5.2 with the unadjusted *wuju* data. Standard errors adjusted at the province level are presented in parentheses, whereas Conley standard errors assuming a binary weight matrix with a threshold of 250 km are given in brackets. Stars indicate statistical significance with the clustered standard errors, *** $p < 0.01$, ** $p < 0.05$, and * $p < 0.1$

**Table 5.12** Suggestive evidence on exclusion restriction, Part A

| Dependent variable | Terrain rugged-ness | River density | Agricultural suitability | Extreme weather | Distance to coastline | Population density in 2 CE | Distance to Sui-Tang's border- line | Distance to Northern Song's border- line |
|---|---|---|---|---|---|---|---|---|
| | (1) | (2) | (3) | (4) | (5) | (6) | (7) | (8) |
| *Panel A* | | | | | | | | |
| Minimum distance to strategic locations | −0.076<br>(0.077) | −0.029*<br>(0.016) | −0.390<br>(0.253) | −0.021<br>(0.013) | −0.070<br>(0.055) | −0.060<br>(0.048) | −0.045<br>(0.062) | 0.061<br>(0.062) |
| Province-fixed effects | Yes | Yes | Yes | Yes | Yes | Yes | Yes | Yes |
| Number of observations | 257 | 257 | 257 | 257 | 257 | 257 | 257 | 257 |
| Adjusted $R^2$ | 0.710 | 0.358 | 0.457 | 0.675 | 0.853 | 0.698 | 0.759 | 0.666 |
| *Panel B* | | | | | | | | |
| Distance from centroid to strategic locations | −0.031<br>(0.125) | −0.095***<br>(0.029) | −0.872*<br>(0.434) | −0.048**<br>(0.022) | −0.125<br>(0.109) | −0.191**<br>(0.066) | −0.164<br>(0.120) | 0.127<br>(0.124) |
| Province-fixed effects | Yes | Yes | Yes | Yes | Yes | Yes | Yes | Yes |
| Number of observations | 257 | 257 | 257 | 257 | 257 | 257 | 257 | 257 |
| Adjusted $R^2$ | 0.705 | 0.378 | 0.543 | 0.680 | 0.854 | 0.716 | 0.766 | 0.667 |
| *Panel C* | | | | | | | | |
| Containing strategic locations (=1) | 0.296<br>(0.281) | 0.068<br>(0.063) | 0.999<br>(0.579) | 0.073<br>(0.049) | 0.033<br>(0.101) | 0.146<br>(0.183) | 0.047<br>(0.148) | −0.097<br>(0.263) |

(continued)

**Table 5.12** (continued)

| Dependent variable | Terrain rugged-ness | River density | Agricultural suitability | Extreme weather | Distance to coastline | Population density in 2 CE | Distance to Sui-Tang's border- line | Distance to Northern Song's border- line |
|---|---|---|---|---|---|---|---|---|
| Province-fixed effects | Yes | Yes | Yes | Yes | Yes | Yes | Yes | Yes |
| Number of observations | 257 | 257 | 257 | 257 | 257 | 257 | 257 | 257 |
| Adjusted $R^2$ | 0.709 | 0.354 | 0.392 | 0.673 | 0.850 | 0.693 | 0.757 | 0.663 |
| *Panel D* | | | | | | | | |
| Military conflicts | −0.107<br>(0.103) | 0.060<br>(0.043) | 0.162<br>(0.139) | 0.017<br>(0.019) | 0.061<br>(0.080) | 0.116**<br>(0.054) | −0.044<br>(0.059) | −0.028<br>(0.099) |
| Province-fixed effects | Yes | Yes | Yes | Yes | Yes | Yes | Yes | Yes |
| Number of observations | 257 | 257 | 257 | 257 | 257 | 257 | 257 | 257 |
| Adjusted $R^2$ | 0.707 | 0.360 | 0.357 | 0.670 | 0.851 | 0.698 | 0.757 | 0.663 |

*Notes* This table reports the results of some tests on the exclusion restriction of the instrumental variables, shown in Panels A, B, and C, respectively, and compares them with historical military conflicts under analogous tests, shown in Panel D. The dependent variables are shown at the top, where extreme weather indicates the number of years with extreme weather events from 1736–1839 CE. The distances to strategic locations in Panels A and B are measured in km, while military conflicts in Panel D indicates the cumulative number of military conflicts from Spring and Autumn period to Ming dynasty (770 BCE–1643 CE). All variables are powered by 0.3. All results are OLS estimates. Standard errors adjusted at the province level are presented in parentheses. Stars indicate statistical significance with the clustered standard errors, *** $p < 0.01$, ** $p < 0.05$, and * $p < 0.1$

**Table 5.13** Suggestive evidence on exclusion restriction, Part B

| Dependent variable | *Wujuren* density | | | | | |
|---|---|---|---|---|---|---|
| | (1) | (2) | (3) | (4) | (5) | (6) |
| Minimum distance to strategic locations | −0.214*<br>(0.102) | −0.126<br>(0.078) | | | | |
| Distance from centroid to strategic locations | | | −0.339*<br>(0.187) | −0.271<br>(0.158) | | |
| Containing strategic locations (=1) | | | | | 1.019***<br>(0.314) | 0.784***<br>(0.227) |
| Military conflicts | | 0.444**<br>(0.205) | | 0.484**<br>(0.206) | | 0.433*<br>(0.206) |
| Province-fixed effects | Yes | Yes | Yes | Yes | Yes | Yes |
| Baseline controls | Yes | Yes | Yes | Yes | Yes | Yes |
| Number of observations | 257 | 257 | 257 | 257 | 257 | 257 |
| Adjusted $R^2$ | 0.184 | 0.213 | 0.177 | 0.216 | 0.197 | 0.226 |

*Notes* This table reports the results of some tests on the exclusion restriction of the instrumental variables, the first three independent variables. The dependent variable is the cumulative number of *wujuren* per million population from 1650–1789. The distances to strategic locations in Panels A and B are measured in km, while military conflicts in Panel D indicates the cumulative number of military conflicts from Spring and Autumn period to Ming dynasty (770 BCE–1643 CE). All variables are powered by 0.3. All results are OLS estimates. Standard errors adjusted at the province level are presented in parentheses. Stars indicate statistical significance with the clustered standard errors, *** $p < 0.01$, ** $p < 0.05$, and * $p < 0.1$

**Table 5.14** IV Estimates with alternative measures of strategic locations' effects, Part A

| Dependent variable | *Wujuren* density | | | | | | |
|---|---|---|---|---|---|---|---|
| | OLS | OLS | IV | IV | IV | IV | IV |
| | (1) | (2) | (3) | (4) | (5) | (6) | (7) |
| Military conflict | | | 2.383* | 2.219 | | 1.818 | |
| | | | (1.335)<br>[1.357] | (1.395)<br>[1.409] | | (1.210)<br>[1.184] | |
| Military conflicts after Sui dynasty | | | | | 4.239<br>(3.319) | | 3.565<br>(2.578) |
| Population density in 2 CE | | 0.303*<br>(0.166) | | 0.151<br>(0.212) | 0.447<br>(0.298) | -0.170<br>(0.471) | -0.076<br>(0.582) |
| | | | | *First stage* | | | |
| Distance from centroid to strategic | 1.019*** | 0.966*** | −0.142* | −0.132* | | −0.164** | |
| locations | (0.314)<br>[0.285] | (0.317)<br>[0.289] | (0.074) | (0.069) | | (0.070) | |
| Distance from centroid to strategic | | | | | −0.074 | | −0.092 |
| locations before Sui dynasty | | | | | (0.056) | | (0.056) |
| Province-fixed effects | Yes | Yes | Yes | Yes | Yes | Yes | Yes |
| Baseline controls | Yes | Yes | Yes | Yes | Yes | Yes | Yes |
| Number of observations | 257 | 257 | 257 | 257 | 257 | 134 | 134 |
| Adjusted $R^2$ | 0.177 | 0.181 | | | | | |
| Kleibergen-Paap Wald $F$ | | | 3.720 | 3.647 | 1.739 | 5.508 | 2.655 |

*Notes* This table replicates Table 5.3 with alternative measures of strategic locations' effects: the distance from each prefecture's centroid to strategic locations, and to those established before Sui dynasty, respectively, measured in km. Standard errors adjusted at the province level are presented in parentheses, whereas Conley standard errors assuming a binary weight matrix with a threshold of 250 km are given in brackets. Stars indicate statistical significance with the clustered standard errors, *** $p < 0.01$, ** $p < 0.05$, and * $p < 0.1$

**Table 5.15** IV Estimates with alternative measures of strategic locations' effects, Part B

| Dependent variable | *Wujuren* density | | | | | | |
|---|---|---|---|---|---|---|---|
| | OLS | OLS | IV | IV | IV | IV | IV |
| | (1) | (2) | (3) | (4) | (5) | (6) | (7) |
| Military conflicts | | | 1.881*** | 1.822*** | | 2.057*** | |
| | | | (0.592)<br>[0.451] | (0.637)<br>[0.485] | | (0.777)<br>[0.525] | |
| Military conflicts after Sui dynasty | | | | | 2.901**<br>(1.135) | | 3.265**<br>(1.424) |
| Population density in 2 CE | | 0.318*<br>(0.178) | | 0.193<br>(0.198) | 0.428**<br>(0.193) | −0.233<br>(0.467) | −0.043<br>(0.498) |
| | | | *First stage* | | | | |
| Containing strategic locations (=1) | 1.019*** | 0.966*** | 0.542*** | 0.530*** | | 0.494*** | |
| | (0.314)<br>[0.285] | (0.317)<br>[0.289] | (0.168) | (0.167) | | (0.182) | |
| Containing strategic locations before Sui dynasty (=1) | | | | | 0.333**<br>(0.146) | | 0.311**<br>(0.157) |
| Province-fixed effects | Yes | Yes | Yes | Yes | Yes | Yes | Yes |
| Baseline controls | Yes | Yes | Yes | Yes | Yes | Yes | Yes |
| Number of observations | 257 | 257 | 257 | 257 | 257 | 134 | 134 |
| Adjusted $R^2$ | 0.197 | 0.202 | | | | | |
| Kleibergen-Paap Wald $F$ | | | 10.348 | 10.071 | 5.174 | 7.377 | 3.939 |

*Notes* This table replicates Table 5.3 with alternative measures of strategic locations' effects: a binary variable that equals 1 if the prefecture contained at least one strategic location and 0 otherwise, and an analogous binary indicator that considers only strategic locations established before Sui dynasty. Standard errors adjusted at the province level are presented in parentheses, whereas Conley standard errors assuming a binary weight matrix with a threshold of 250 km are given in brackets. Stars indicate statistical significance with the clustered standard errors, *** $p < 0.01$, ** $p < 0.05$, and * $p < 0.1$

**Table 5.16** Impacts of historical military conflicts on contemporary human capital investment, excluding megacities

| Dependent variable | Famous martial arts school density | | Web-searched martial arts school density | | Elementary and middle school density | | GDP per capital | |
|---|---|---|---|---|---|---|---|---|
| | OLS | IV | OLS | IV | OLS | IV | OLS | IV |
| | (1) | (2) | (3) | (4) | (5) | (6) | (7) | (8) |
| Military conflicts | 0.183*** | 0.290*** | 0.476*** | 0.641*** | −0.339*** | −0.675*** | −0.145 | −0.218 |
| | (0.029)<br>[0.026] | (0.089)<br>[0.089] | (0.072)<br>[0.072] | (0.192)<br>[0.210] | (0.096)<br>[0.091] | (0.158)<br>[0.210] | (0.104)<br>[0.090] | (0.398)<br>[0.337] |
| Population density in 2 CE | | 0.039<br>(0.054) | | 0.113<br>(0.080) | | 0.104<br>(0.099) | | 0.387<br>(0.277) |
| Province-fixed effects | Yes | Yes | Yes | Yes | Yes | Yes | Yes | Yes |
| Baseline controls | Yes | Yes | Yes | Yes | Yes | Yes | Yes | Yes |
| Number of observations | 256 | 256 | 256 | 256 | 256 | 256 | 256 | 256 |
| Adjusted $R^2$ | 0.378 | | 0.416 | | 0.520 | | 0.528 | |
| Kleibergen-Paap Wald $F$ | | 22.405 | | 22.405 | | 22.405 | | 22.405 |

*Notes* This table replicates Table 5.8 but eliminates Songjiang Fu and Guangzhou Fu. Standard errors adjusted at the province level are presented in parentheses, whereas Conley standard errors assuming a binary weight matrix with a threshold of 250 km are given in brackets. Stars indicate statistical significance with the clustered standard errors, *** $p < 0.01$, ** $p < 0.05$, and * $p < 0.1$

## References

Akresh, Richard and Damien De Walque. 2008. *Armed Conflict Aand Schooling: Evidence from the 1994 Rwandan Genocide*. The World Bank.

Akresh, Richard, Sonia Bhalotra, Marinella Leone, and Una o. Osili. 2017. First and Second Generation Impacts of the Biafran War. Working Paper 23721, National Bureau of Economic Research.

Alesina, Alberto, Paola Giuliano, and Nathan Nunn. 2013. On the Origins of Gender Roles: Women and the Plough. *Quarterly Journal of Economics* 128 (2): 469–530.

Ang, James B. 2019. Agricultural Legacy and Individualistic Culture. *Journal of Economic Growth* 24 (4): 397–425.

Ashraf, Quamrul, and Oded Galor. 2011. Dynamics and Stagnation in the Malthusian Epoch. *The American Economic Review* 101 (5): 2003–2041.

Bai, Ying, and James K. S. Kung. 2011. Climate Shocks and Sino-nomadic Conflict. *The Review of Economics and Statistics* 93 (3): 970–981.

Bai, Ying, and Rruixue Jia. 2016. Elite Recruitment and Political Stability: The Impact of the Abolition of China's Civil Service Exam. *Econometrica* 84 (2): 677–733.

Barfield, Thomas J. 1989. *The Perilous Frontier: Nomadic Empires and China*. Oxford: Basil Blackwell Inc.

Bauer, Michal, Christopher Blattman, Julie Chytilová, Joseph Henrich, Edward Miguel, and Tamar Mitts. 2016. Can War Foster Cooperation? Working Paper 22312, National Bureau of Economic Research.

Baysan, Ceren, Marshall Burke, Felipe González, Solomon Hsiang, and Edward Miguel. 2018. Economic and Non-Economic Factors in Violence: Evidence from Organized Crime, Suicides and Climate in Mexico. NBER Working Papers 24897, National Bureau of Economic Research.

Bazzi, Samuel, Martin Fiszbein, and Mesay Gebresilasse. 2017. Frontier Culture: The Roots and Persistence of "Rugged Individualism" in the United States. Working Paper 23997, National Bureau of Economic Research.

Bellows, John, and Edward Miguel. 2009. War and Local Collective Action in Sierra Leone. *Journal of Public Economics* 93 (11–12): 1144–1157.

Besley, Timothy, and Torsten Persson. 2008. Wars and State Capacity. *Journal of the European Economic Association* 6 (2/3): 522–530.

Brown, Ryan P., Lindsey L. Osterman, and Collin D. Barnes. 2009. School Violence and the Culture of Honor. *Psychological Science* 20 (11): 1400–1405 PMID: 19843260.

Burke, Marshall, Shanker Satyanath, John Dykema, and David Lobell. 2009. Warming Increases the Risk of Civil War in Africa. *Proceedings of the National Academy of Sciences of the United States of America* 106: 20670–20674.

Cao, Qingjun and Siyu Cao. 2010. *Tangchao Wuju Zhidu Ji Qi Yingxiang* [The Military Examination System in the Tang Dynasty and Its Influence]. *Sports Culture Guide*.

Cao, Shuji. 2001. *Zhongguo Renkou Shi: Diwu Juan* [Population History of China: Volume 5] Fudan University Press.

Cao, Yiming, Benjamin Enke, Armin Falk, Paola Giuliano, and Nathan Nunn. 2021. Herding, Warfare, and a Culture of Honor: Global Evidence. Working Paper 29250, National Bureau of Economic Research.

Carton, Benedict, and Robert Morrell. 2012. Zulu Masculinities, Warrior Culture and Stick Fighting: Reassessing Male Violence and Virtue in South Africa. *Journal of Southern African Studies* 38 (1): 31–53.

Cassar, Alessandra, Pauline Grosjean, and Ssam Whitt. 2013. Legacies of Violence: Trust and Market Development. *Journal of Economic Growth* 18 (3): 285–318.

Chaliand, Gerard. 2005. *Nomadic Empires: From Mongolia to the Danube*. Routledge.

Chang, Chung-Li. 1955. *The Chinese Gentry: Studies on Their Role in Nineteenth-century Chinese Society*. University of Washington Press.

Chang, Jianhua. 2018. *Qingchao Xingke Tiben Yu Xin Shixue* [Case Memorials in the Qing Dynasty and New Historiography]. *Journal of Qsinghua University [Philosophy and Social Science Edition]*, (5).

Chen, Jiafeng and Jonathan Roth. 2022. Logs with zeros? Some problems and solutions. Papers 2212.06080, arXiv.org.

Chen, Ting, James K. S. Kung, and Chicheng Ma. 2020. Long Live Keju! The Persistent Effects of China's Civil Examination System. *The Economic Journal* 130 (631): 2030–2064.

Chen, Zhiwu, Kaixiang Peng, and Lijun Zhu. 2017. Social-economic Change and Its Impact on Violence: Homicide History of Qing China. *Explorations in Economic History* 63:8–25. Special Issue: A new economic history of China.

Chen, Zhiwu, Peter Turchin, and Wanda Wang. 2023. War and the Origins of Chinese Civilization. Working paper, University of Hong Kong.

Chen, Zhiwu and Wanda Wang. 2022. Even Prehistory Never Dies: Persistent Impact of Neolithic development on Historical and Contemporary China.

Conley, Timothy. 1999. Gmm estimation with cross sectional dependence. *Journal of Econometrics* 92 (1): 1–45.

Di Cosmo, Nicola. 2002. *Ancient China and Its Enemies: The Rise of Nomadic Power in East Asian History*. Cammbridge University Press.

Di Cosmo, Nicola. 2009. *Military Culture in Imperial China*. Harvard University Press.

Dafoe, Allan, and Devin Caughey. 2016. Honor and War: Southern US Presidents and the Effects of Concern for Reputation. *World Politics* 68 (2): 341–381.

Dincecco, Mark. 2021. Warfare, Fiscal Gridlock, and State Formation During Europe's Military Revolution. *SSRN Electronic Journal*.

Dincecco, Mark, J. Fenske, A. Menon, and S. Mukherjee. 2021. Pre-Colonial Warfare and Long-Run Development in India. *The Economic Journal* 132 (643): 981–1010.

Dincecco, Mark and Massimiliano G. Onorato. 2016. Military Conflict and the Rise of Urban Europe. *Journal of Economic Growth* 21(3): 259–282.

Dincecco, Mark, and Mauricio Prado. 2012. Warfare, Fiscal Capacity, and Performance. *Journal of Economic Growth* 17 (3): 171–203.

Elman, Benjamin A. 2000. *A Cultural History of Civil Examinations in Late Imperial China*. University of California Press

Elman, Benjamin A. 2013. *Civil Examinations and Meritocracy in Late Imperial China*. Harvard University Press.

Fernández, Raquel, Alessandra Fogli, and Claudia Olivetti. 2004. Mothers and Sons: Preference Formation and Female Labor Force Dynamics. *The Quarterly Journal of Economics* 119(4):1249–1299

Fried, Morton H. 1952. Military Status in Chinese Society. *American Journal of Sociology* 57 (4): 347–357.

Fu, Zhongxia, Kerun Liu, Guangzeng Shi, Xing Zhang, Zhaolin Tian, Boshi Yang, Zhenfu Wei, Shusheng Wang, Xiukun Zhao, Gusong Zhao, Shengbi Shi, Shouquan He, Yuexuan Cao. 2003. *Zhongguo Lidai Zhanzheng Nianbiao* [Chronology of Wars in China]. People's Liberation Army Press.

Galor, Oded and Ömer Özak. 2015. Land Productivity and Economic Development: Caloric Suitability vs. Agricultural Suitability. Working Papers 2015–5, Brown University, Department of Economics.

Galor, Oded, and Ömer. Özak. 2016. The Agricultural Origins of Time Preference. *American Economic Review* 106 (10): 3064–3103.

Galor, Oded and Viacheslav Savitskiy. 2018. Climatic Roots of Loss Aversion. Working Papers 2018–1, Brown University, Department of Economics.

Ge, Jianxiong. 2002. *Zhongguo Renkou Shi: Diyi Juan [Population History of China: Volume ])*. Fudan University Press.

Gershman, Bauline. 2020. Witchcraft Beliefs as a Cultural Legacy of the Atlantic Slave Trade: Evidence from Two Continents. *European Economic Review* 122: 103362.

Glowacki, Luke, and Richard W. Wrangham. 2013. The Role of Rewards in Motivating Participation in Simple Warfare. *Human Nature* 24 (4): 444–460.

Gong, Weigang, Meng Zhu, Burak Gürel, and Tian Xie. 2021.The Lineage Theory of the Regional Variation of Individualism/Collectivism in China, *Frontiers in Psychology* 11.

Grosjean, Pauline. 2014. A History of Violence: The Culture of Honor and Homicide in the US South. *Journal of the European Economic Association* 12 (5): 1285–1316.

Grousset, Rrousset and Naomi Walford. 1970. *The Empire of the Steppes: A History of Central Asia.* New Brunswick, N.J: Rutgers University Press

Gutierrez, Italo A. and Jose V. Gallegos. 2016. *The Effect of Civil Conflict on Domestic Violence: The Case of Peru.* RAND Corporation, Santa Monica, CA

Hao, Yu, Zhengcheng Liu, Xi Weng, and Li-An Zhou. 2022. The Making of Bad Gentry: The Abolition of Keju, Local Governance, and Anti-Elite Protests, 1902–1911. *The Journal of Economic History*, pp. 1–37.

Harari, Mariaflavia and Eliana La Ferrara. 2018. Conflict, Climate, and Cells: A Disaggregated Analysis. *The Review of Economics and Statistics*, 100 (4):594–608.

Ho, Ping-ti. 1962. *The Ladder of Success in Imperial China: Aspects of Social Mobility, 1368– 1911.* New York: Columbia University Press.

Hsiang, Solomon and Marshall Burke. 2013. Quantifying the Influence of Climate on Human Conflict. *Science*, 341:1235367

Islam, Asadul, Chandarany Ouch, Russell Smyth, and Liang C. Wang. 2016. The Long-Term Effects of Civil Conflicts on Education, Earnings, and Fertility: Evidence from Cambodia. *Journal of Comparative Economics* 44 (3): 800–820.

Kelly, Morgan. 2019. The Standard Errors of Persistence. CEPR Discussion Papers 13783, C.E.P.R. Discussion Papers.

Ko, Chiu Yu, Mark Koyama, and Tuan-Hwee Sng. 2014.Unified China and Divided Europe. CEI Working Paper Series 2014–7, Center for Economic Institutions, Institute of Economic Research, Hitotsubashi University.

La Mattina, Giulia. 2017. Civil Conflict, Domestic Violence and Intra-household Bargaining in Post-genocide Rwanda. *Journal of Development Economics*, 124:168–198.

Lattimore, Owen. 1940. *Inner Asian Frontiers of China.* New York: American Geographical Society.

Lee, Wayne. E. 2016. *Waging War: Conflict, Culture, and Innovation in World History.* Oxford University Press.

Li, Jian, and Christos Koulovatianos. 2020. The Long Shadows of War in China: Battle Shocks in Early Life and Health/Wealth Accumulation. *China Economic Review* 60: 101394.

Liu, Yahe. 2007. Zhongguo Gudai Jingji Zhongxin Nanyi De Wancheng [The Completion of the Southward Shift of the Economic Center of Ancient China]. *Journal of Guangxi University for Nationalities [Philosophy and Social Science Edition].*

Loewe, Michael. 1993. *Early Chinese Texts: A Bibliographical Guide.* Number 449. Berkeley: The Society for the Study of Early China.

Lv, Weibin, Songmao Qiao, Ruiqi Zhu, Ping Li, Shixin Li, Geng Li, Houzhi Li, Pixiang Qiu, Liandeng Zhang, Haoxue Shao, Yucheng Guo, Yunfei Xia, Hangqiang Mei, Yujiu Zeng, Jinhua Huo. 2003. *Zhongguo Wushu Guanxiao Zonglan [An Overview of Chinese Martial Arts Schools].* Beijing Sport University Press.

Malmin, Mark. 2013. Warrior Culture, Spirituality, and Prayer. *Journal of Religion and Health* 52 (3): 740–758.

McGuirk, Eoin F, and Nathan Nunn. 2020 Transhumant Pastoralism, Climate Change, and Conflict in Africa. Working Paper 28243, National Bureau of Economic Research.

Miguel, Edward, Sebastián M. Saiegh, and Shanker Satyanath. 2011. Civil War Exposure and Violence. *Economics and Politics*, 23(1):59–73

Moscona, Jacob, Nathan Nunn, and James A. Robinson. 2020. Segmentary Lineage Organization and Conflict in Sub-Saharan Africa. *Econometrica* 88 (5): 1999–2036.

Mrozek, Donald J. 2007. *The Military, Sport, and Warrior Culture*, 131–154. New York Chichester, West Sussex: Columbia University Press.

Mullahy, John and Edward C. Norton. 2022. Why Transform Y? A Critical Assessment of Dependent-Variable Transformations in Regression Models for Skewed and Sometimes- Zero Outcomes. Working Paper 30735, National Bureau of Economic Research.

Nawata, Kengo. 2020. A Glorious Warrior in War: Cross-Cultural Evidence of Honor Culture, Social Rewards for Warriors, and Intergroup Conflict. *Group Processes & Intergroup Relations* 23 (4): 598–611.

Nisbett, Richard E. and Dov Cohen. 1996. *Culture of Honor: The Psychology of Violence in the South.* New directions in social psychology. Westview Press.

Nunn, Nathan. 2012. Culture and the Historical Process. Working Paper 17869, National Bureau of Economic Research.

Nunn, Nathan. 2020. *On the Causes and Consequences of Cross-Cultural Differences: An Economic Perspective.* New York: Oxford University Press.

Nunn, Nathan, and D. Puga. 2012. Ruggedness: The Blessing of Bad Geography in Africa. *The Review of Economics and Statistics* 94 (1): 20–36.

Nunn, Nathan, and L. Wantchekon. 2011. The Slave Trade and the Origins of Mistrust in Africa. *American Economic Review* 101 (7): 3221–3252.

Parker, Geoffrey. 1996. *The Military Revolution: Military Innovation and the Rise of the West, 1500–1800.* Cambridge University Press.

Pearce, Scott. 2008. The Way of the Warrior in Early Medieval China, Examined through the "Northern Yuefu." *Early Medieval China* 2008 (2): 87–113.

Rao, Shengwen. 2003. *Buju Tianxia [Layout of the World].* People's Liberation Army Press.

Rubin, Jared and Elira Karaja. 2017. The Cultural Transmission of Trust Norms: Evidence from a Lab in the Field on a Natural Experiment. Working Papers 17–08, Chapman University, Economic Science Institute.

Shemyakina, Olga. 2011. The Effect of Armed Conflict on Accumulation of Schooling: Results from Tajikistan. *Journal of Development Economics* 95 (2): 186–200.

Shi, Shanyu, Tong Bao, and Yuyi Zhang. 1988. *Zhongguo Junshi Renwu Cidian [Dictionary of Chinese Military Figures].* Science and Technology Literature Publishing House.

Sng, Tuan-Hwee and Songfa Zhong. 2018. Historical Violence and China's Missing Women.

Song, Jia. 2009. *Zhongguo Gudai Zhanzheng De Dili Shuniu [The Geographical Hub of War in Ancient China].* China Social Science Press.

Talhelm, Thomas, Xuemin Zhang, Shigehiro Oishi, Shimin Chen, Dongyuan Duan, Xuezhao Lan, and Shinobu Kitayama. 2014. Large-Scale Psychological Differences Within China Explained by Rice Versus Wheat Agriculture. *Science* 344 (6184): 603–608.

Teso, Edoardo. 2019. The Long-Term Effect of Demographic Shocks on the Evolution of Gender Roles: Evidence from the transatlantic Slave Trade. *Journal of the European Economic Association* 17 (2): 497–534.

Thakral, Neil and Linh T To^. 2023. When are estimates independent of measurement units?

Teng, Ssu-yu, and John K. Fairbank. 1954. *China's Response to the West: A Documentary Survey, 1839–1923.* Cambridge: Harvard University Press.

Tilly, Charles. 1975. *The Formation of National States in Western Europe.* Princeton University Press.

Tong, Enzheng. 1994. *Zhongguo Beifang Yu Nanfang Gudai Wenming Fazhan Guiji Zhi Yitong* [Differences and Similarities of the Development of Ancient Civilizations in North and South China]. *Social Sciences in China.*

Von Clausewitz, Carl. 1989. *On War*, 456–459. Trans. M. Howard, and P. Paret Princeton University Press.

Weber, Max. 1968. *The Religion of China: Confucianism and Taoism.* Translated by H. H. Gerth, and C. K. Yang, Free Press

Xie, Haitao. 2009. *Keju Luqu Ming'e Fenpei Zhidu Fazhan Xingcheng De Lishi* [The History of the Formation and Development of the Imperial Examination's Quota Allocation System]. *Fujian Forum [Humanities and Social Sciences]*, 1.

Xu, Hong. 2017. *Xianqin Chengyi Kaogu* [Archaeological Walled Cities in Pre-Qin China]. Beijing: Gold Wall and Xiyuan Press.
Xu, Yougen. 1997. *Wuju Zhidu Shilue* [Brief History of the Military Examination System]. Soochow University Press.
Xue, Melanie M. 2018. High-Value Work and the Rise of Women: The Cotton Revolution and Gender Equality in China. MPRA Paper 91100, University Library of Munich, Germany.
Yan, Jingping. 2009. *Qingdai Wuju Chutan* [On the Military Examination in the Qing Dynasty].
Zhang, Xiqing, Peiqi Mao and Shiyu Li. 2015. *Zhongguo Keju Zhidu Tongshi: Qingdai Juan* [General History of Chinese Imperial Examination System: Qing Dynasty]. Shanghai People's Publishing House.
Zhao, Erxun. 1927. *Qingshi Gao [The Draft History of Qing]*, vol. 108.
Zheng, Xuemeng and Yande Chen. 1984. *Zhongguo Gudai Jingji Zhongxin Nanyi De Ruogan Wenti Tantao* [On the Southward Shift of the Economic Center in Ancient China]. *Jianghai Xuekan*, (3).
Zhou, Zhenwei. 2013. *Qingdai Wukeju Zhidu Yanjiu* [A Study on the Military Examination System in the Qing Dynasty].

**Yichneg Chen** is a Ph.D. candidate in the Department of Economics at Boston University. Prior to joining the Ph.D. program, he was working in the Center for Quantitative History, The University of Hong Kong. His research interests include economic history and political economy.

**Zhiwu Chen** is Chair and Cheng Yu-Tung Professor in Finance at The University of Hong Kong (HKU). He currently serves as director of both Hong Kong Institute for the Humanities and Social Sciences (HKIHSS) and Centre for Quantitative History (CQH). His research covers finance theory, the sociology of finance, economic history, quantitative history, emerging markets, as well as China's economy and capital markets. He was a former Professor of Finance at Yale University (1999–2017) and a Special-Term Visiting Professor at Peking University and Tsinghua University. In 2013, he started the annual Summer School for Quantitative History cum International Symposium on Quantitative History at Tsinghua University and continues to organize them at Peking University, with the goal of promoting quantitative research on the history of China and beyond.

**Chicheng Ma** is Associate Professor in Economics at the Business School of the University of Hong Kong. He studies economic history and development, specializing in historical China and its contact with the West. He won the Royal Economic Society Prize for the best paper in the Economic Journal in 2020, Hong Kong University Research Output Prize in 2021, and the Economic History Association's Arthur H. Cole Prize for the best article in the *Journal of Economic History* in 2022. As Principal Investigator, Chicheng has received competitive research grants from the Hong Kong Research Grant Council and the National Natural Science Foundation of China. He serves as Associate Director of the Centre for Quantitative History and Associate Professor (by courtesy) at the Hong Kong Institute for the Humanities and Social Sciences

# Chapter 6
# Origin and Deployment of Qing Military Officers by Province, 1786–1908 CE

**Jun Chen and Cameron Campbell**

## 6.1 Introduction

We study changes from the end of the eighteenth century to the beginning of the twentieth in the allocation of Qing military officers by province for insight into changes over time in the military priorities and capabilities of the Qing state. We pay particular attention to the influence of the major conflicts and crises of the period. While the size of the military, lack of detailed records of the deployment of regular soldiers, and changes in military organization has until now made it difficult to study the overall allocation of military resources during the nineteenth century, the allocation of officers offers clues. In the nineteenth century, 8000 formally appointed military officers oversaw an army of around 800,000 regular soldiers (Chen and Campbell 2024). The numbers of officers in a location were highly correlated with the numbers of regular troops, and changes over time in the numbers of officers in a location should have been associated with changes over time in troop numbers, thus studying the geographic distribution of officers should provide insight into troop deployments and military priorities more generally.[1] Officers acted as a bridge between the Qing government and the regular soldiers, while also participating in military reforms and witnessing

[1] The Qing army was organized into units called Camps (Ying) with a fixed ratio of military officers to soldiers. For instance, in the Hunan Army system, the officer-to-soldier ratio was approximately 1:500 (Long 1990, 74–75).

J. Chen (✉)
The Institute of Qing History, Renmin University of China, Beijing, China
e-mail: 1525931996@qq.com

C. Campbell
Division of Social Science, The Hong Kong University of Science and Technology, Hong Kong, China

School of History and Culture, Central China Normal University, Wuhan, China
e-mail: camcam@ust.hk



Z. Chen et al. (eds.), *Quantitative History of China*, Studies in Economic History,
https://doi.org/10.1007/978-981-96-8272-0_6

transformations. Military officers also deserve attention because the current scholarship on the Qing state generally focuses on civil officials and largely ignores the roles of military officers, especially those with lower and mid-level ranks (Qin 2014).

Existing research on the geographic allocation of military officers in China before the twentieth century mostly covers the period before the nineteenth century. During the Tang (618–907), the number of generals appointed in the northwestern and northern regions was twice that in the southeast (Zhang 2009, 45–56).[2] The Northern Song (960–1127) and Southern Song (1127–1279) continued this focus on border defense, deploying more military officers and troops along the northwestern and northern borders (Wang 1983, 96–98).[3] By the Ming Dynasty (1368–1644), even though coastal defense began to emerge as a priority (Huang 2001, 42–57),[4] military officers remained concentrated in the north (Lai 2010, 377).[5] In the early Qing Dynasty, the northern border was still the focus of military officer deployment.[6] In the late seventeenth century, however, emphasis began to shift from land border defense in the northwest and north to a balance between land border and coastal defenses. The government began to move military officers to coastal provinces and develop naval forces.[7] There are few if any examinations of the provincial distribution of military officers in the nineteenth century, even though frequent crises would presumably have led to changes in the allocation of military resources.

We also study changes over time in the province of origin of military officers, and the relationship of province of origin to province of current post. While it is well-known that the share of officers from Hunan and to a less extent Anhui rose during the nineteenth century, especially after the Taiping Rebellion, once again most of the attention has been on well-known high-level officers who rode the coattails of

[2] Zhang (2009, 45–56) summarized four types of Military Town (*fanzhen)* in the Tang Dynasty, among which there were 17 "border-type" and 9 "southeast-type" Military Towns, with the number of "border-type" being about twice that of the "southeast-type".

[3] In the late Northern Song Dynasty, there were 17 generals in the north and only 14 generals in the southeast (Wang 1983, 96–98). In the late Southern Song Dynasty, there were 60,000 military officer and troops in the western region, and tens of thousands of troops in the northern region (Wang 1983, 195–198).

[4] Huang (2001, 42–57) found that the coastal defense of Zhejiang in the Ming Dynasty had reached a large scale. There were 65 *Bazong* (Squad Leader) and *Shaozhang* (Sentry Captain), and more than 24,000 soldiers, and more than 800 warships.

[5] Lai (2010, 377) estimated that there were 40 military officers at all levels and 39,339 soldiers in the northern military towns alone in 1602.

[6] In the early Qing Dynasty, the Qing government followed the border defense system of the Ming Dynasty. For example, in the early Kangxi (1661–1722) period, the Garrison Manchu General of Heilongjiang (*Heilongjiang Jiangjun*) was appointed to lead the defense of the region, assisted by 547 military officers from all levels of the Eight Banners (The Academy of Military Sciences of China 2005, 645).

[7] The buildup on the coast began in the seventeenth century. In 1684, the Qing government appointed several senior generals in Taiwan to lead coastal defense and allocated 10,000 Green Standard Army soldiers, of whom 8,000 were stationed in Taiwan and 2,000 in Penghu (The Academy of Military Sciences of China 2005, 688). During the Yongzheng reign (1723–1735), the Qing government expanded the Eight Banners Navy by adding over 30 military officers and more than 5,000 soldiers, and established artillery positions in coastal provinces (Pan 2020).

Zeng Guofan, and there has been less attention to changes in the origins of mid- and low-level officers. For the relationship of province of origin to province of current post, we focus on whether officers served in their home province, for evidence about the enforcement of the rule of avoidance (*huibi*) for military officers. While there are specific well-known examples of very senior military officials who served in their home provinces, previously it has not been possible to do a broader assessment of the shares of officials at different ranks serving in their home provinces.

Our primary source is a database constructed from the rosters of military officers *Zhongshu beilan* (ZSBL) that were compiled quarterly during the Qing.[8] The ZSBL is a counterpart to the quarterly *Jinshenlu* that listed civil officials, and which are the basis of the China Government Employee Dataset-Qing Jinshenlu (CGED-Q JSL) and have a somewhat similar format. Each ZSBL edition lists approximately 8,000 officers. We have transcribed 73 quarterly editions of ZSBL, creating a historical dataset that contains longitudinal information on the careers of more than 59,303 Qing military officers (Ren, Chen, Hao, Campbell, Lee 2016). Through the application of quantitative methods, including GIS, we examine changes in the spatial distribution of military officers from the mid-Qing to the late Qing providing insights into the transformation of Qing defense priorities based on big historical microdata. We also examine the relationship between the location of officers' current post and their place of origin.

Our analyses yield several important findings. First, the allocation of officers by province, and by extension troops and other resources, was unaffected by the First Opium War, and only began to change after the Taiping Rebellion, with a shift of officers toward the southeastern coastal provinces, away from the western and northwestern frontier provinces. We speculate that even though the First Opium War should have highlighted the importance of maritime defense and triggered a response, it was the influx of Hunan army officers after the Taiping Rebellion that finally disrupted traditional patterns and led to a reallocation. When we turn to province of origin, as expected we find increases in the shares of Hunan- and Anhui-origin officers. Our contribution is that we can document these increases for all military officers, not just the high-ranked officers that have been the focus of previous studies. For the rule of avoidance, we demonstrate that exceptions were not uncommon, even for high-ranked officers. They were most common in coastal provinces and in frontier. Regarding the former, naval officers needed seafaring experience, which tended to be more common in Maritime Provinces. As for the latter, we speculate that the need to deal with minority groups and difficult terrain may have favored officers with local experience.

The remainder of the paper is divided into four parts. Part 2 provides background on the organization of the military, including the ranks, and introduces the data. Part 3 presents our results on the geographical distribution of military officers. We emphasize the institutional and contextual factors that shaped the distribution. It begins with a national-level overview of the geographic distribution of military officers

[8] The practice of producing rosters of military officers began in the Ming Dynasty and continued until the end of the Qing (Shi 2021).

after the Opium War and then examines the factors underlying changes following the Taiping Rebellion. Part 4 considers another dimension of the geographic allocation of officers: the relationship between the location of an officer's post and their place of origin. In the conclusion, we discuss the implications of our findings for our understanding of the late Qing and suggest future directions.

## 6.2 Data

The ZSBL is a quarterly roster of military officers in the Qing Dynasty, listing about 8,000 high-, mid-, and low-ranking military officers in each edition.[9] These records allow for longitudinal study of the careers of military personnel, and cross-sectional study of the composition of officers in terms of location, qualifications, and other characteristics. In terms of format, the ZSBL resembles the *Jinshen Quanshu* and *Juezhi Quanlan* that listed civil officials, and which we generically refer to as *Jinshenlu* (Liu 2008). The records in the ZSBL derive from personnel files maintained by the Ministry of War (*Bingbu*), compiled by the leaders or civilian staff of various military units, detailing the personal information of officers at different ranks. These files were submitted up the chain of command to the Ministry of War, where they were synthesized into the ZSBL following a format like that of the *Jinshenlu.*

The Lee-Campbell group constructed a dataset by collecting, inputting, and integrating data from the available editions of the ZSBL. As of October 2024, the database contains 73 editions of ZSB*L*, spanning the Qianlong (1736–1795) to Guangxu (1875–1908) reigns. There are two editions from Qianlong, one from the Jiaqing period (1796–1820), 11 from Daoguang (1821–1850), four from Xianfeng (1851–1861), 11 from Tongzhi (1862–1874), and 47 from Guangxu. It contains 517,233 records of 59,303 military officers.[10] Of the total, 5% of the officers in the database are high-ranked, 25% are mid-level, and 70% are low-ranked. The availability of information on more than 56,000 mid-level and low-ranked military officers distinguishes the ZSBL as a source. Even though mid-level and low-ranked military officers accounted for most of the officers and played a crucial role, they have received little scholarly attention. Previous studies of the Qing military have focused on high-ranked officers.

The ZSBL has some limitations. First, due to the confidential nature of information about certain Eight Banners Imperial Army (*Jinlv Baqi*) military officers, there are omissions in their records. This is a minor issue since such records are rare, accounting for only 0.1% of the total. Second, the records do not include the ages of military

[9] Scholarly studies using the *ZSBL* are mostly one-off studies based on single editions. For example, Zhang Zhongli used the 1881 *ZSBL* to analyze the composition ratio of military officers' backgrounds (Zhang 2008, 98–129). Wang Yue utilized the 1784 *ZSBL* from the Nankai University Library to analyze the Manchu-Han ratio of Green Standard Army military officers (Wang 2010, 97).

[10] After analysis was completed, more editions were located and entered. These data will be included in future studies using these data.

officers and only record their final qualifications (*chushen*). These limitations are not relevant to our analysis because we do not include the Special Assignment military officers in our analysis, and do not consider ages or qualifications.[11]

In the ZSBL, the terms Jiangnan Province (*Jiangnan Sheng*) and Huguang Province (*Huguang Sheng*) were used for military officers' places of appointment. During the Kangxi reign (1661–1722), Jiangnan Province was split into Jiangsu and Anhui, but Jiangnan continued to exist as a large military region. Therefore, Jiangnan was still used as a designation for the places of appointment and places of origin of Green Standard Army military officers until 1879, when it began to appear less frequently. It did not disappear until the end of the Qing. Use of the term Huguang ceased after 1803 and was replaced by Hubei and Hunan. Our tables and figures retain the military officers from these two places of origin because without more detailed information, we cannot determine in which of the two provinces an officer was located.

Because some of our calculations distinguish officers by rank, we introduce our categorization of the original ranks recorded in the ZSBL. In the Qing, there were two types of military officers: Green Standard Army officers and Eight Banner officers. We summarize the ranks of the Green Standard Army and Eight Banners that appear in the data in Table 6.1. Positions with a total of 10 different ranks appeared in the data. We categorize officers of the first rank and the upper second rank as high rank, officers from lower second rank to upper fifth rank as middle rank, and upper sixth and seventh rank as low rank.

## 6.3 Distribution of Officers by Region and Province

Before, During, and After the First Opium War

There was little change in the allocation of military personnel during or following the First Opium War. Table 6.2 compares the percentages of officers by region and province in 1836, 1841, and 1849 in the ZSBL. Even though the First Opium War revealed serious vulnerabilities, changes were trivial. The share of officers allocated to the coastal provinces increased slightly, from 37.4% in 1836 to 38% in 1841 and 38.5% in 1849. There was a corresponding small decrease in the shares of officers allocated to the central region and the west and northeast. Even though the First Opium War had demonstrated the risk of seaborne attacks by hostile foreign powers and might reasonably have been expected to trigger a shift of resources to Guangdong and other vulnerable provinces, it does not appear to have led to any change in the allocation of officers. Given the strong correlation between numbers of officers and numbers of troops, the implication is that the distribution of troops remained the same as well.

[11] See Chen and Campbell (2024) for an analysis of qualifications.

**Table 6.1** Ranks of military officers in the green standard army and eight banners

| Rank (pinji) | Category | Green Standard Army Title [a] | Eight Banners Title [b] |
|---|---|---|---|
| *Zhengyipin* (Upper 1st Rank) | High | – | *Lingshi weinei dachen* (Grand Minister of the Imperial Household Department, Concurrently Controlling the Imperial Guardsmen) *Zhufang jiangjun* (Garrison Manchu General) |
| *Congyipin* (Lower 1st Rank) | | *Tidu* (Provincial Military Commander) | *Dutong* (Commander-in-Chief of a Banner) |
| *Zhengerpin* (Upper 2nd Rank) | | *Zongbing* (Regional Commander) | *Fu Dutong* (Vice Commander -in-chief of a Banner) |
| *Congerpin* (Lower 2nd Rank) | Middle | *Fujiang* (Regional Vice Commander) | *Sanzhi Dachen* (Grand Minister Assistant Commander of Imperial Guardsmen) |
| *Zhengsanpin* (Upper 3rd Rank) | | *Canjiang* (Assistant Regional Commander) | *Yideng Shiwei* (First Class Imperial Guardsmen) *Canling* (Regimental Commander) |
| *Congsanpin* (Lower 3rd Rank) | | *Youji* (Brigade Commander) | *Xieling* (Assistant Commandant in the Hierarchy of Provincial Bannermen) |
| *Zhengsipin* (Upper 4th Rank) | | *Dusi* (Brigade Vice Commander) | *Zuoling* (Company Commander) *Erdeng Shiwei* (Second Class Imperial Guardsmen) |
| *Zhengwupin* (Upper 5th Rank) | | *Shoubei* (Assistant Brigade Commander) | *Sandeng Shiwei* (3rd Class Imperial Guardsmen) |
| *Zhengliupin* (Upper 6th Rank) | Lower | *Qianzong* (Company Commander) | *Xiaoqixiao* (Cavalry Captain of Eight Banners) |
| *Zhengqipin* (Upper 7th Rank) | | *Bazong* (Squad Leader) | – |

[a] There are also *Waiwei Qianzong* (Additional Company Commander), *Waiwei Bazong* (Additional Squad Leader), and *Ewai Waiwei* (Additional Company Commander or Squad Leader). They are grassroots military officers of the Green Standard Army (Luo 1984, 220–223). These three types of military officers are set up outside the military officer quota of the Green Standard Army, and the military officer roster *ZSBL* does not record these three types of military officers. Therefore, the analysis in this article only discusses the formal Green Standard Army military officers of Squad Leader and above. The English translations of the titles of Green Standard Army and Eight Banners military officers in the table are from Hucker (1995). [b] Due to the complexity of the Eight Banners official system, the table only lists the most representative Eight Banner officer positions at their corresponding ranks. For detailed information on the positions and ranks of Eight Banner officers, see Du (2015)

**Table 6.2** Percentages of military officers by region and province, 1836, 1841, and 1849

| Region or Province | Winter 1836 (%) | Autumn 1841 (%) | Autumn 1849 (%) |
|---|---|---|---|
| Capital | | | |
| Jingshi[a] | 3.0 | 2.9 | 2.8 |
| Zhili | 9.0 | 9.1 | 9.3 |
| Subtotal | 12 | 12 | 12.1 |
| Coastal | | | |
| Shandong | 3.5 | 3.5 | 3.6 |
| Guangdong | 8.8 | 8.9 | 9.3 |
| Jiangnan | 8.4 | 8.6 | 8.3 |
| Zhejiang | 5.7 | 5.9 | 6.0 |
| Fujian | 7.5 | 7.5 | 7.7 |
| Guangxi | 3.5 | 3.6 | 3.6 |
| Subtotal | 37.4 | 38 | 38.5 |
| West/Northwest | | | |
| Sichuan | 6.1 | 6.0 | 6.1 |
| Guizhou | 6.8 | 6.6 | 6.7 |
| Gansu[a] | 8.7 | 8.6 | 8.3 |
| Shaanxi | 6.0 | 6.0 | 5.8 |
| Yunnan | 5.4 | 5.3 | 5.2 |
| Subtotal | 33 | 32.5 | 32.1 |
| Interior | | | |
| Shanxi | 3.9 | 3.9 | 3.8 |
| Jiangxi | 2.2 | 2.3 | 2.3 |
| Henan | 2.5 | 2.5 | 2.4 |
| Hubei | 4.0 | 3.8 | 4.0 |
| Hunan | 5.0 | 5.0 | 4.8 |
| Subtotal | 17.6 | 17.5 | 17.3 |
| Total | 100 | 100 | 100 |
| N | 6947 | 7003 | 6973 |

In Table 6.3, we present numbers of officers by rank and three key indicators to help interpret their allocations across regions and provinces in 1849: the soldier-to-officer ratio (column 2), the population-to-officer ratio (column 3), and the land area-to-officer ratio (column 4). The soldier-to-officer ratio measures military force deployment in the region. A higher ratio typically signifies a greater military presence in the form of regular soldiers and suggests a higher strategic priority for that area. Conversely, the population-to-officer and area-to-officer ratios reflect officer density. For the most part, a larger population or area per officer indicates fewer military personnel per population or land area and a correspondingly lower priority. Of course, to gain a general impression of priorities in terms of the allocation of military officers, these indicators must be considered together, since each of them is influenced by multiple factors.

In 1849, the emphasis was still on land borders and coastal regions. According to column 2 of Table 6.3, disproportionate shares of military officers and soldiers were allocated to the capital region, the six coastal provinces and five western/northwestern provinces. The capital region and the west/northwest had low ratios of population to officers (32,208:1 and 39,027:1), and so did the provinces in the coastal region except Shandong and Jiangnan. The total allocation of soldiers was even more unbalanced than the allocation of officers: these regions all had higher ratios of soldiers to officers (145:1 in the capital region, 99:1 in the coastal provinces, and 96:1 in the five western provinces). By contrast, the central region had a very high ratio of population to officers (107,612:1) and a low ratio of soldiers to officers (88:1).

Table 6.3 reveals that within these regions, Zhili, Guangdong, Fujian, and Gansu were key provinces. Zhili had a dense military presence largely because the units there were responsible for defending the capital. Zhili had the highest ratio of soldiers to officers of any province: 191:1. The capital region, of which Zhili formed the largest part, also had the lowest ratio of population to officers: 32,208:1. It also had a relatively low ratio of land area to officers: 418:1.

The Qing state's allocation of officers and soldiers to Fujian and Guangdong reflected the importance of coastal defense, control of adjacent maritime areas, and protection of maritime trade. Guangdong and its coastal neighbor Fujian also had low ratios of population to officers: 36,650:1 and 34,277:1, low ratios of land area to officers (346:1 and 296:1), and high ratios of soldiers to officers: 109:1 and 119:1. The especially high ratio of soldiers to officers reflects the presence of Green Standard Army naval forces in Guangdong and Fujian, and the need for ships' crews.

Among western and northwestern provinces, Gansu in the northwest seemed to have been the highest priority. It had a relatively high soldier-to-officer ratio of 107:1, and the Gansu/Shaanxi region of which it was part had a population-to-officer ratio of 32,784:1. Its ratio of land to officers, 730:1, was relatively high, but this reflected the sheer vastness of the region. Yunnan and Guizhou in the southwest were also the subject of particular attention. Guizhou had the lowest ratio of population to officers (18,917:1). Yunnan's ratio was also relatively low, 34,917:1. Yunnan was large and forces in Yunnan there were thinly spread: the ratio of land to officers was much higher than in Guizhou, at 1130:1 as opposed to 381:1.

The indicators in Table 6.3 suggest that interior provinces were regarded as relatively secure, in the sense of being regarded as at low risk of external incursions or internal turmoil. They had a very high ratio of population to officers: 107,612:1, and a low ratio of soldiers to officers: 88:1. Henan, Shandong, and Jiangxi provinces appear to have been regarded as the most secure, and therefore less in need of military personnel to deal with external incursions or internal disorder. They had the highest

**Table 6.3** Indices of military force composition and concentration, Autumn 1849

| | Number of Officers (High/Medium/Low Rank) (1) | Ratio of Soldiers to Officers (2) | Population to Officers Ratio (3) | Land area (km$^{2}$)) to Officer ratio (4) |
|---|---|---|---|---|
| Capital | | | | |
| Jingshi[a] | 192 (5-27-160) | 99:1 | 32208:1 | 418 |
| Zhili | 648 (10-151-487) | 191:1 | | |
| Subtotal | 840 (15-178-647) | 145:1 | 32208:1 | 418 |
| Coastal | | | | |
| Shandong | 249 (5-64-180) | 90:1 | 142912:1 | 609 |
| Guangdong | 651 (12-147-492) | 109:1 | 36650:1 | 346 |
| Jiangnan | 581 (13-151-417) | 91:1 | 141317:1 | 424 |
| Zhejiang | 421 (8-99-314) | 98:1 | 71914:1 | 239 |
| Fujian | 537 (13-114-410) | 119:1 | 34277:1 | 296 |
| Guangxi | 252(4-60-188) | 89:1 | 43500:1 | 877 |
| Subtotal | 2691(55-635-2001) | 99:1 | 78428:1 | 465 |
| West/Northwest | | | | |
| Sichuan | 424(8-109-307) | 86:1 | 69493:1 | 1442 |
| Guizhou | 465(6-96-363) | 79:1 | 18912:1 | 381 |
| Gansu[a] | 577(12-143-422) | 107:1 | 32784:1 | 730 |
| Shaanxi | 407(7-118-282) | | | |
| Yunnan | 363(9-77-277) | 110:1 | 34917:1 | 1130 |
| Subtotal | 2236(42-543-1651) | 96:1 | 39027:1 | 921 |
| Interior | | | | |
| Shanxi | 262(5-72-185) | 90:1 | 60450:1 | 752 |
| Jiangxi | 162(4-50-108) | 77:1 | 149914:1 | 1021 |
| Henan | 168(3-48-117) | 97:1 | 183161:1 | 999 |
| Hubei | 280(5-64-211) | 93:1 | 79239:1 | 655 |
| Hunan | 334(5-76-253) | 81:1 | 65296:1 | 629 |
| Subtotal | 1206 (22-310-874) | 88:1 | 107612:1 | 811 |
| Total | 6973 (134-1666-5173) | 107:1 | 64318:1 | 654 |

*Note* Includes Eight Banner and Green Standard Army officers. (1) Calculated from the ZSBL. (2) The ratio of soldiers to officers includes the numbers of soldiers from the Eight Banners and the Green Standard Army. The number of Green Standard Army soldiers is for 1849 (Wang 1985, 86) and the number of Eight Banner soldiers is from the Daoguang reign (Ming and Su 1968). (3) and (4) The population data and land area data comes from 1851 (Ge and Cao 2001, 703). [a] In the military records of the Qing dynasty, Zhili and Jingshi, along with Gansu and Shaanxi, were typically considered a single combined military region. Therefore, we have merged their data in the table

**Table 6.4** Military officers by region, 1786–1886

| Year | Coastal provinces (%) | Central provinces (%) | Capital region (%) | West/Northwest Provinces (%) |
|---|---|---|---|---|
| Spring 1786 | 39.6 | 16.2 | 11.9 | 32.3 |
| Spring 1803 | 39.3 | 17.0 | 12.5 | 31.2 |
| Fall 1841 | 38.1 | 17.5 | 12.0 | 32.4 |
| Spring 1855 | 37.3 | 16.7 | 12.6 | 33.4 |
| Winter 1869 | 42.2 | 17.4 | 12.1 | 28.4 |
| Winter 1879 | 42.7 | 16.3 | 11.0 | 29.9 |
| Winter 1886 | 43.6 | 17.3 | 12.0 | 27.2 |

*Note* (1) The six coastal provinces include Shandong, Guangdong, Jiangnan, Zhejiang, Fujian, and Guangxi. The five western provinces are Sichuan, Gansu, Shaanxi, Guizhou, and Yunnan. The Jingshi region mainly refers to Jingshi and Zhili. The inland provinces are Shanxi, Henan, Hubei, Hunan, and Jiangxi

ratio of population to officers. Each exceeded 100,000:1. They also had high ratios of land to officers, and low soldier-to-officer ratios.[12]

Before, During, and After the Taiping Rebellion

Changes in allocations across the regions took place during and after the conclusion of the Taiping Rebellion. The general trend was toward increasing shares of officers assigned to the coastal provinces, and declining shares allocated to the west and northwest. Table 6.4 compares shares of military officers across four regions before and after the Taiping Rebellion. Prior to the conflict, and in keeping with the results in Table 6.1, the distribution of military officers in coastal and western regions was relatively stable. Between 1855 and 1869, however, the share of military officers in the six eastern provinces increased by 5 percentage points, while the share in the five western provinces decreased by 5 percentage points. The shares in the central region and the capital region remained largely unchanged, indicating a gradual shift of military personnel from the western and northwestern provinces and a tilt of military resources toward the coastal provinces. A debate in the government in the 1870s over defense strategy in which Zuo Zongtang advocated for equal emphasis on both border and coastal defense appears to have had little additional effect: changes between 1869 and 1879 were small.[13]

[12] The population-to-officer ratio in Jiangnan exceeds 140,000:1, but this does not imply a lower priority for the region; rather, it reflects the region's large population. By the end of the Qianlong reign (1736–1796), the total population of Jiangnan Province was 58 million. In comparison, in 1776, the populations of Guizhou and Yunnan provinces were 5.67 million and 7.88 million, respectively. By 1851, Jiangnan's population surpassed 82 million (Ge and Cao 2001, 703).

[13] This debate was mainly divided into two factions: one advocated for abandoning coastal defense and fully focusing on border defense, while the other opposed this view. Zuo Zongtang argued that both border defense and coastal defense should not be neglected. See Zuo (1976, 1842). Despite claims of balanced importance, actual funding allocations continued to favor the defense of the northwest (Chen 2018).

Changes during the Taiping Rebellion were especially noticeable for certain provinces. Figure 6.1 presents a bar chart based on the autumn 1849, winter 1859, and winter 1869 ZSBL. Two key trends are apparent. First, consistent with Table 6.4, the number of military officers in the central region experienced a postwar rebound. As shown in Fig. 6.1, the central provinces of Jiangxi, Henan, Hubei, and Hunan experienced an increase in the numbers of military officers after the war, while other provinces had fewer officers. Jiangnan, in the eastern coastal area, was a special case: the officers in the Yangtze River Navy that was established in 1868 were assigned to Jiangnan in the ZSBL.[14] This accounted for the spike in numbers in 1869. Conversely, the southeastern coastal and western regions saw slight decreases in numbers of military officers. According to Fig. 6.1, following the Taiping Rebellion, military officer counts in Guangdong, Fujian, and Zhejiang provinces in the southeastern coastal area decreased by an average of 14%. In the western region, the number of military officers in Sichuan, Gansu, Shaanxi, Guizhou, and Yunnan provinces fell by an average of 15.4%.

## 6.4 Province of Origin

In China, place of origin has long been a consideration in the recruitment of military officers. For example, some regions—such as Shaanxi and Gansu—had a reputation for producing talented officers, which resulted in their candidates being preferred during selection. Historians of the Han Dynasty noted that the royal guard troops, namely the Yulin Army and the Qimen Army, favored selecting officers from Shaanxi and Gansu (Ban and Wang 2012, 2824). During the early Qing, 24% of lower-ranking military officers in the Green Standard Army were from Shaanxi, more than the 10% from the Eight Banners (Wang 2016, 228). Emperor Qianlong frequently remarked on the military prowess of officers from Shaanxi and Gansu and advocated for an increased number of candidates from these regions in military examinations (Zhonghua Book Company 1986, 558 Vol. 9). Additionally, the public perception during the Qing Dynasty regarded military officers and soldiers from those two regions as particularly skilled (Zhao 1980, 92).

During the Ming, the father-son inheritance of officer appointments would have contributed to making the distribution of provinces of origin more rigid. Because sons of military officers had a hereditary right to an appointment of their own (Liang 2012, 12), locations that had produced officers in the past would continue to do so in the future. Additionally, the government stipulated that the sons of high-ranking civil officials could be appointed as military officers based on their fathers' merits (Qin 2015).[15] However, the Ming government did not establish a corresponding

[14] The establishment Yangtze River Navy had its headquarters in Taiping Prefecture, Anhui Province. It was under the jurisdiction of the Jiangnan Green Standard Army.

[15] The system was not entirely hereditary. In principle, ordinary soldiers could also be appointed to low-ranked officer positions (Cao 2018).

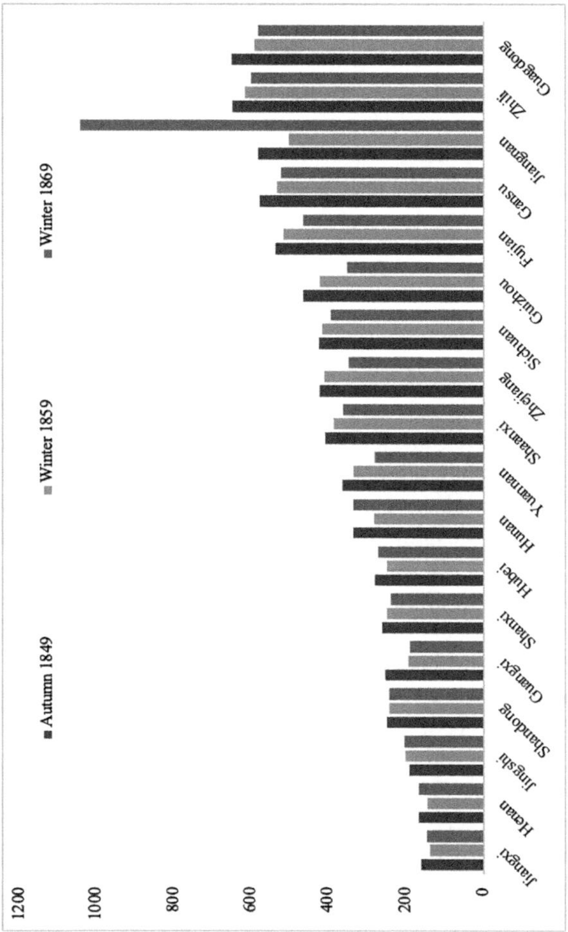


**Fig. 6.1** Numbers of military officers by province before, during, and after the Taiping Rebellion

mechanism for the elimination or retirement of officers, leading to a rapid increase in their numbers, and associated financial and administrative burdens.[16]

The Qing took a different approach to the recruitment of officers that in principle should have reduced the importance of place of origin and created possibilities for the distribution of provinces of origin to change over time. They largely eliminated the inheritance of officer appointments, limiting inheritance to appointment as a regular soldier (Luo 1984, 232). Local militia officers who had performed well could be appointed to regular positions.[17] The Qing government also introduced a rule of avoidance (*huibi*) intended to prevent high-level officers from serving in their home provinces.[18] High-level military officers, such as *Tidu* and *Zongbing*, had the authority to appoint and recommend mid- and lower-level military officers, and there was concern that they might demote or reassign qualified officers in favor of compatriots from the same province with whom they had ties (Luo 1984, 312). Mid-level officers were forbidden from serving within 500 *li* of their hometowns (Zhonghua Book Company 1991, 419 Vol 7). Low-level officers, due to salary and livelihood concerns, were permitted to serve in their place of origin. The avoidance system was intended to reduce the influence of high-level and mid-level military officers over their home regions, reduce additional non-central government appointments associated with nepotism and corruption, and centralize authority over officer organization and appointments.

Time Trends in Province of Origin

The distribution of officers by province of origin changed dramatically during the nineteenth century. This confirms that the recruitment processes introduced by the Qing to replace the hereditary appointments of the Ming created possibilities for the provincial origins of officers to change over time. Figure 6.2 presents the shares of Green Standard Army military officers from Hunan, Anhui, Jiangnan, Hubei, Shanxi, and Fujian over time. Table 6.5 summarizes changes in the provinces of origin for Green Standard Army military officers during spring 1786 and winter 1908. Figure 6.2 and Table 6.5 only consider Han Chinese officers in the Green Standard Army because the ZSBL did not record places of origin for Manchu officers who

[16] From approximately 28,000 military officers during Hongwu reign (1368–1398) (Liu 1997, 17), the number surged to over 80,000 by the Chenghua reign (1465–1487) (Zhang 1974, 5662 Vol. 19), so that there were four times as many military officers as civil officials. Although reforms were introduced in the late Ming period to reduce the number of military officers, they were still a strain exacerbating the bureaucratic management burden and financial strain, which indirectly contributed to the dynasty's downfall.

[17] Military recruitment in the Qing Dynasty was not static. At various times, the inheritance of positions as a soldier that was a legacy of the Ming co-existed with local militias and recruitment of volunteers. Militias in the Qing army first emerged around the late eighteenth century. In 1786, Fu Nai, a deputy magistrate in Hunan Province, began recruiting village militia to prevent uprisings and revolts among the Miao people. During the Taiping Rebellion, the Qing government officially recognized militias and allowed them to become widespread. Militia officers could be given regular appointments if they performed well. In 1905, the Qing, inspired by the Japanese, initiated reforms that replaced hereditary service as soldiers with recruitment of volunteers. See Robinson (2013) and Xie (2020) and Moll-Murata and Theobald (2013).

[18] See Zhonghua Book Company (1991, 419 Vol. 7).

dominated the Eight Banner Army and played an important role in the Green Standard Army. As would be expected based on common knowledge about nineteenth century China and the role of Zeng Guofan's Hunan Army, there was a spectacular increase in the share of military officers from Hunan, and a more modest increase in the numbers of officers from Anhui. The share from Hunan rose from around 2% at the end of the eighteenth century to 12–14% in the last half of the nineteenth century.

Two specific periods of increase for Hunan-origin officers were apparent. The first was after the Miao Rebellion in Hunan and Guizhou in 1795 and 1796, when the proportion from Hunan rose from 2 to 5%. The second followed the Taiping Rebellion, when the Hunan Army's outsized role in the war led to a rise in Hunan-origin officers from 4.6% before to 13.7% afterward. By autumn 1901, the number of Hunan-origin military officers in the Green Standard Army reached 1,027, surpassing the combined total of military officers from Hubei, Shanxi, Jiangsu, Jiangxi, and Henan (962), and accounting for approximately 12.5% of the total Green Standard Army personnel nationwide. Meanwhile, the share of military officers from Anhui increased after the Nian Rebellion in northern China between 1853 and 1868, with their proportion increasing from 1% after the Taiping Rebellion to 3% at the end of the Qing.

The rise of officers from Hunan and Anhui disrupted existing geographic patterns. There were corresponding reductions in the numbers of naval generals from Jiangnan, Fujian, and Zhejiang, capital generals from Zhili and Shanxi, and western and north-western generals from Gansu and Shaanxi, but there was little change in the share of officers from Guangdong. Thus, according to Fig. 6.2 and Table 6.5, the proportions of military officers from Fujian, Jiangnan, Shanxi, and Zhili declined. Specifically, the proportion of military officers from Fujian decreased from 7.6% in the late Qian-long period to 3.5% in the late Qing Dynasty, while Jiangnan's proportion fell from 7.2% to 3.6%, Shanxi's share fell from 4.3% to 2%, and Zhili's share fell from 7.2% to 6.0%. The proportion of military officers from Guangdong fluctuated between 9.2% and 9.5% in the late Qing.

Several factors played a role in the rise of the Hunan Army officers and domination of the officer ranks. There was more possibility for rapid change in the geographic origins of officers in the Qing than in the Ming. Whereas officer appointments had been hereditary during the Ming, the Qing emphasized recruitment and promotion of officers based on their ability and performance. Because officers in the Hunan Army had a decade of combat experience from their fight against the Taiping Army in Hubei, Jiangxi, Anhui, and Jiangsu, after the war wound down the Qing could transfer experienced military officers who were adept in mountain, water, siege, and breakout warfare to coastal regions. The southeastern coastal areas required more commanders, and military officers from Hunan were perceived to possess the skills necessary to excel in these roles.

The rise of Hunan Army Taiping Rebellion veterans in the military contributed to the domination of the civil bureaucracy by Hunan-origin officials. In the bureau-cracy, the distinction between civil officials and military officers was ambiguous

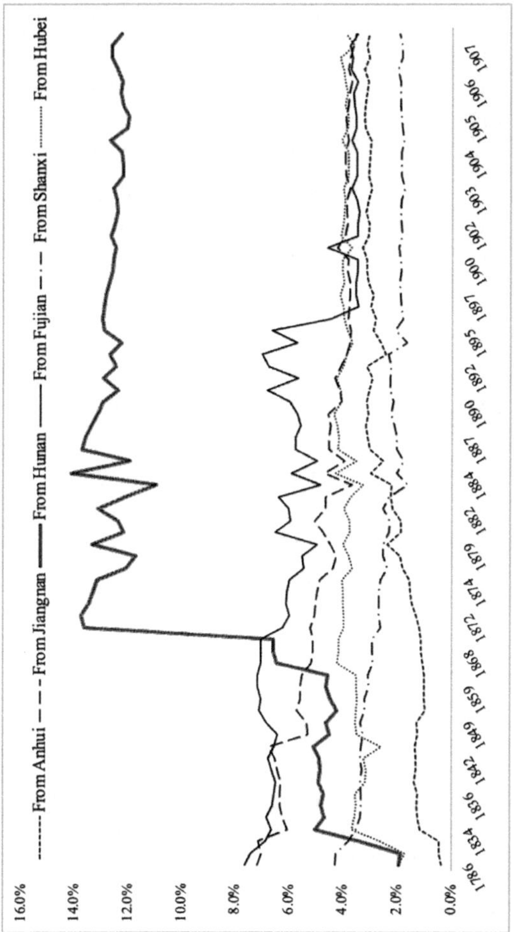


**Fig. 6.2** Province of origin of Green Standard Army military officers, 1786–1908

**Table 6.5** Province of origin of Green Standard Army military officers, Spring 1786 and Winter 1908

| Province of origin | Spring 1786% | Winter 1908% | Winter 1908–Spring 1786 |
|---|---|---|---|
| Hunan | 1.92 | 12.29 | 10.37 |
| Anhui | 0.36 | 3.05 | 2.69 |
| Hubei | 1.95 | 3.93 | 1.98 |
| Jiangsu | 0.47 | 1.61 | 1.14 |
| Yunnan | 5.35 | 6.31 | 0.96 |
| Henan | 2.14 | 2.96 | 0.82 |
| Shandong | 3.45 | 4.1 | 0.65 |
| Guangdong | 9.17 | 9.47 | 0.3 |
| Shuntian | 3.56 | 3.73 | 0.17 |
| Sichuan | 5.87 | 5.99 | 0.12 |
| Guangxi | 3.35 | 3.36 | 0.01 |
| Jiangxi | 2.18 | 2.15 | -0.03 |
| Guizhou | 6.66 | 5.93 | -0.73 |
| Zhejiang | 6.25 | 5.51 | -0.74 |
| Gansu | 9.19 | 8.19 | -1 |
| Shaanxi | 4.44 | 3.27 | -1.17 |
| Zhili | 7.24 | 6.01 | -1.23 |
| Shanxi | 4.3 | 1.95 | -2.35 |
| Jiangnan | 7.16 | 3.56 | -3.6 |
| Fujian | 7.63 | 3.5 | -4.13 |
| Xinjiang[a] | – | 0.13 | – |
| Huguang[b] | 3.69 | – | – |
| Fengtian[b] | 1.47 | – | – |
| Missing/Unknown | 2.2 | 3.0 | – |
| Total | 100% | 100% | – |
| N | 6322 | 6247 | – |

[a] Due to a change in the *ZSBL* compilation format, officers were only identified as being from Xinjiang after the summer 1893 edition. In previous editions, the same officers would have been identified as being from Gansu. [b] After the spring 1803 edition, the *ZSBL* no longer recorded officers from Huguang and Fengtian. Officers that previously were recorded as being from Huguang were recorded as being from Hubei, Hunan, or Guangxi. Officers recorded as being from Fengtian were henceforth recorded as being from Shuntian

to begin with, and cross-appointments were common.[19] Senior military officers

[19] During the Tang Dynasty, generals in key military strongholds were granted considerable administrative power, leading to an expansion of military authority that ultimately contributed to the fragmentation of the empire. To prevent a similar situation of warlordism as seen in the late Tang period, the rulers of the Song and Ming dynasties appointed senior civil officials as the highest

often transitioned into elite civilian political roles after the end of a conflict, subsequently gaining administrative power. As a result, Hunan-origin officials effectively controlled the appointment, promotion, and removal of mid- and lower-level military officers in many coastal provinces, gradually establishing a network of military power by appointing relatives, friends, fellow townsmen, and former subordinates.[20] This led to a movement of military officers closely associated with the Hunan Army and Anhui Army to the coastal provinces. Arguably, the Taiping Rebellion fundamentally undermined Qing rule because the rise of military officers from Hunan and their eventual control over appointments in the southern provinces weakened central government control.

## 6.5 Current Post and Place of Origin

Enforcement of the rule of avoidance appears to have been mostly effective, though as will be discussed below, more rigorous in some provinces than others. Table 6.6 presents the shares of high, mid-level, and low-level officers serving in their home province for more than 50,000 military officers. According to Table 6.6, the share of Han Chinese Green Standard Army military officers serving in their home province during the late Qing varied according to their rank, as it was supposed to, with high-level officers less likely to serve in their home province than lower-level officers; 12% of high officers served in their home province, versus 50% of middle-level officers, and 88% of low-level officers.

As indicated in Table 6.6, there were ten provinces that produced high-level military officers who served in their home province. Among these, the ones with higher percentages tended to be on the coast (Jiangnan, Guangdong, and Fujian) or on the frontier (Guangxi, Gansu, Yunnan). Regarding the former, the rule of avoidance was applied more leniently in the naval forces because of the need for officers with seafaring experience.[21] Regarding the latter, the rules of avoidance were also applied more leniently due to the local officers' greater proficiency in managing complex ethnic issues and their familiarity with the terrain. Guangxi and Gansu had by far the highest percentages; 50% of the high-level officers that Guangxi produced served in Guangxi, and 40% of the high-level officers that Gansu produced served in Gansu.

commanders of the military during wartime, while senior military officers were prohibited from such roles. In contrast, the Yuan Dynasty, which emphasized military power, had the opposite approach. By the Qing Dynasty, the distinction between civil officials and military officers became blurred, allowing for cross-appointments between the two. See Dai (2017).

[20] In 1866, out of the eight governors in the Qing Dynasty, six were officials or military officers from Hunan. Except for Guangxi and Shandong, Hunan officials had nearly complete control over military and political power in all coastal provinces. See Bai, Jia, and Yang (2023) for an econometric analysis of the role of networks in rise of Hunan Army veterans.

[21] In 1795, the Qing government explicitly allowed some mid-level and high-level positions in the Green Standard Navy to be filled by military officers from the same province. See Zhonghua Book Company (1991, 421 Vol. 7).

**Table 6.6** Province of origin of Green Standard Army military officers and shares serving in their home province, 1786–1911

| Province of origin | Officers from specified province | % from specified province | Percentage serving in their home province, by rank | | |
|---|---|---|---|---|---|
| | | | High (%) | Mid (%) | Low (%) |
| Guangdong | 5,074 | 9.8 | 31.60 | 67.00 | 97.20 |
| Hunan | 4,871 | 9.5 | 4.00 | 25.80 | 52.90 |
| Gansu | 4,228 | 8.2 | 40.00 | 60.20 | 77.80 |
| Fujian | 3,733 | 7.2 | 25.00 | 71.90 | 98.20 |
| Zhili | 3,484 | 6.8 | 20.00 | 33.10 | 96.80 |
| Jiangnan | 3,182 | 6.2 | 14.30 | 78.10 | 96.30 |
| Sichuan | 3,158 | 6.1 | 11.10 | 59.50 | 93.30 |
| Zhejiang | 3,071 | 6.0 | 0.00 | 68.30 | 97.60 |
| Guizhou | 3,043 | 5.9 | 0.00 | 61.60 | 97.40 |
| Yunnan | 2,634 | 5.1 | 22.20 | 78.90 | 98.20 |
| Shandong | 2,065 | 4.0 | 0.00 | 35.00 | 93.20 |
| Hubei | 1,960 | 3.8 | 0.00 | 37.60 | 91.60 |
| Guangxi | 1,805 | 3.5 | 50.00 | 61.30 | 97.90 |
| Jingshi | 1,756 | 3.4 | 0.00 | 42.70 | 58.70 |
| Shaanxi | 1,715 | 3.3 | 0.00 | 43.10 | 86.20 |
| Shanxi | 1,602 | 3.1 | 0.00 | 24.30 | 95.50 |
| Henan | 1,450 | 2.8 | 0.00 | 41.10 | 91.20 |
| Jiangxi | 1,256 | 2.4 | 0.00 | 31.60 | 89.30 |
| Anhui | 972 | 1.9 | 19.40 | 33.10 | 74.90 |
| Jiangsu | 455 | 0.9 | 0.00 | 43.20 | 78.80 |
| Total | 51,514 | 100 | 11.9 | 49.9 | 88.2 |

*Note* The data in the table represents the total number of military officers, not the number of military officers for a specific year

Notable examples include Suo Wen and Su Yuanchun, both of whom served as *Tidu* in their respective home provinces—Suo for about 14 years in Gansu, and Su for nearly 20 years in Guangxi (Wang 1987, 5018–5021).[22]

The proportion of mid-level military officers serving in their home provinces is 49.9%. The highest proportion, 79%, was in Yunnan. In coastal and frontier provinces such as Guangdong, Fujian, Jiangnan, and Guangxi, the proportion also exceeds 60%.

[22] Suo Wen, a native of Gansu, initially served as an ordinary soldier and rose through the ranks to become the Zongbing of Ningxia military town in Gansu. In 1850, he was promoted to Tidu of Gansu and gained considerable prestige in the Green Standard Army of Gansu. However, he lost his hereditary title due to his son's rebellion. See Zhonghua Book Company (1986, 643 Vol. 47) and (1986, 835 Vol. 53). Su Yuanchun, a native of Guangxi, was appointed by the Qing government to return to Guangxi as Tidu during the Sino-French War. He served in this position for twenty years until he was impeached and dismissed in 1903. See Wang (1987, 5018–5021).

These tended to be the provinces where large numbers of high-ranked officers were from their home province, once again suggesting a need for officers with a very specific set of skills. The large number of mid-level officers in their home provinces elsewhere can be attributed to the Qing government's relaxation of requirements in 1744, permitting these military officers to serve within 500 *li* of their place of origin.[23] It may also reflect that in the largest provinces, it was possible to be more than 500 *li* from place of origin and still be in the same province. This was especially the case because the distance was not measured as the crow flies, but by distance traveled along existing routes.

As expected, according to Table 6.6, the proportion of grassroots military officers serving in their home provinces is high. In some provinces, nearly all the low-level officers were from that province. In Guangdong, the ratio of lower-level military officers serving in their hometowns was 97%, while in Fujian, it was 98%. The results are not a surprise. In 1767, the Qing government had already permitted lower-level military officers to serve locally, partly to address their livelihoods and partly to ensure that patrol and inspection tasks were conducted by officers who were familiar with the terrain and customs.[24]

Trends in the percentages of officers serving in their home province were similar for low-, mid- and high-level officers from the eighteenth century until the time of the Taiping Rebellion but diverged afterward. Figure 6.3 presents the percentages of high-level, mid-level, and lower-level Green Standard Army officers serving in their home provinces over time. For all three groups, the shares of military officers serving in their home provinces rose from the late eighteenth century into the middle of the nineteenth century. The subsequent divergence reflected the different roles of the three groups, and the differing impact of policy changes. The proportion of high-level officers serving in their home provinces rose from 4% in 1786 to nearly 20% in 1872, fell to below 10% by 1881, and then rose gradually steadily afterward. The increase from the eighteenth century to the Taiping Rebellion can largely be attributed to relaxed enforcement of the rule of avoidance. Another reason is the broader applicability of the recommendation system (*Baoju Zhidu*), with local senior civil officials using their increased power to encourage the appointment of high-ranking officer candidates they recommended (Yang 2009). Such candidates often held considerable prestige within the local militias, which helped local senior civil officials consolidate control over local military power. The quick decline after the Taiping reflected the influx of Hunan-origin Taiping Rebellion veterans into the upper ranks. The subsequent gradual increase may have reflected the need for natives of coastal provinces with seafaring or other specialized experience to lead the naval forces in those areas.

---

[23] The Qing government mandated that a *Dufu* (The governor of one or two provinces) should first select military officers from other provinces. If there were no suitable candidates, they could choose military officers from their own province, provided that the distance between their place of origin and place of appointment was more than 500 li. See Zhonghua Book Company (1991, 419 Vol. 7).

[24] See Zhonghua Book Company (1991, 419 Vol. 7).

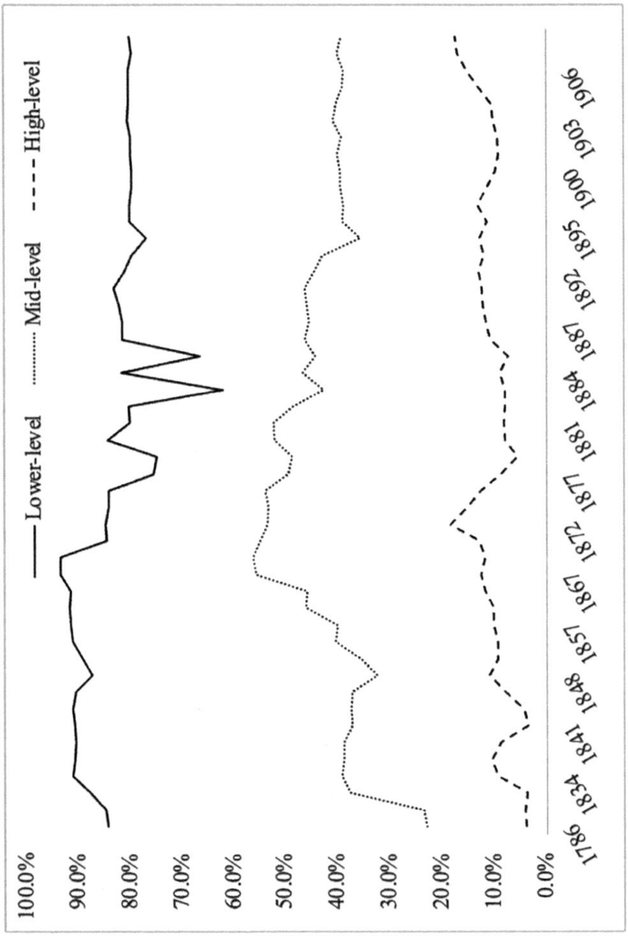


**Fig. 6.3** Percentages of high-level, mid-level, and lower-level Green Standard Army officers serving in their home provinces, over time

The percentage of mid-level officers serving in their home provinces rose from 23% in 1786 to 56% in 1868, hovered at around 50% until 1881, declined steadily until 1895, and was stable afterward. The peak between 1868 and 1881 can be attributed to the disorganization of the appointment and promotion system after the Taiping Rebellion, which gave local senior civil officials the authority to appoint mid-level officers. As a result, many local officers obtained local positions through purchase and nepotism. Later in the nineteenth century, the percentages declined to 39% because the Qing reinforced military centralization and re-emphasized the avoidance system for mid-level officers (Zhonghua Book Company 1991, 422 Vol. 7).

The proportion of lower-level officers in their home provinces increased from 85% in 1786 to 94% in 1868 then declined by approximately 9% following the Taiping Rebellion. This decline was primarily driven by a significant influx of lower-level officers from Hunan into Green Standard Army units in other provinces, disrupting local officer monopolies. By the end of the nineteenth century, the proportion stabilized around 80%, as the Green Standard Army's role shifted toward local surveillance, prompting the Qing government to select officers who were familiar with local terrain and customs to maintain order and alleviate financial burdens.

## 6.6 Conclusion

Our analysis of changes in the distributions of the current provinces and provinces of origin of military officers in the late Qing provides insights into the evolution over time for government priorities for the allocation of military resources and some possible reasons for observed changes. One important conclusion from the analysis of the current provinces of officers in the first half of the paper is that the Taiping Rebellion had a more profound impact on the geographic of officer and therefore troop and resource deployments than the First Opium War, even though the latter clearly demonstrated serious vulnerabilities in Qing naval defenses. The Taiping Rebellion disrupted traditional military deployment patterns, depleting elite forces from the Eight Banners and Green Standard Army, while facilitating the emergence of local military forces led by Hunan-origin and to some extent Anhui-origin officers. The transformation of power networks within the military by the influx of Taiping Rebellion veterans from Hunan described in the second half of the paper coincided with a change in the geographic distribution of military officers that shifted officers, troops, and presumably other resources, from border defense in the west and northwest to maritime defense on the eastern coast. In other words, even though the need to refocus on maritime defense should already have been obvious after the First Opium War, it was only when the military leadership was disrupted, and new blood injected at all levels following the Taiping Rebellion, that this apparently overdue adjustment occurred.

Another key insight is that the enforcement of the rule of avoidance weakened from the eighteenth century until the Taiping Rebellion, with increasing shares of officers serving in their home provinces, and that high-, middle-, and low-ranked officers had different trends afterward. The share of high-level officers serving in their home province fell immediately after the Taiping because of the influx of Hunan-origin Taiping Rebellion veterans into the upper ranks. The shares of mid-level officers serving in their home provinces peaked after the Taiping because local senior civil officers used their power over military appointments to select associates, then declined as the Qing began to re-centralize military authority and reassert the rule of avoidance for military officials. The numbers of low-level officers serving in their home provinces fell immediately after the Taiping Rebellion because of the influx of Hunan-origin Taiping Rebellion veterans, and then increased afterward as the Qing came to rely on the Green Standard Army as the equivalent of local police forces, tasked with maintaining local order. Accordingly, they appointed officers who were familiar with the area.

We have laid out broad trends here, and some of our explanations are speculative, but much remains to be studied and many details need to be filled in. We need more fine-grained analyses of specific provinces and regions, most clearly Guangdong, Fujian, and other coastal provinces, to better understand the sources and the implications of the reallocation of officers and presumably troops and other resources to the coastal provinces after the Taiping Rebellion. Such analyses will require integration with more traditional methods of historical research to understand how decisions at high levels translated into changes in the composition of the officer classes in those areas. Further research is needed on the Hunan Army veterans in the last half of the nineteenth century, especially with analysis of their networks, and their implications for other outcomes. The ZSBL dataset may be ideal for the application of econometric approaches to studying their networks, such as those used by Bai, Jia, and Yang (2023) to examine the rise of the Hunan Army faction. Further study of the implications of the relaxation of the rule of avoidance from the eighteenth century into the middle of the nineteenth century may also be supported by application of econometric techniques. A key question is whether the increase in the numbers of officers serving in their home provinces can be linked clearly to changes in the performance of the Green Standard Army.

This study made use of novel quantitative data and methods to shed new light on the evolution of the Qing military from the eighteenth century to the beginning of the twentieth century, especially the mid- and low-level officers. While there have been numerous studies of specific prominent military leaders, the Hunan Army faction, the rise of the militias, and important military events like the Taiping Rebellion, the Opium Wars, and various other uprisings and rebellions, there have been few aggregate studies of the composition of the officer corps that examine changes over time in their deployment and in their provincial origins, and how this composition interacted with other major historical events. We hope that going forward, the integration of quantitative analysis of the officer class as recorded in the ZSBL and more traditional approaches to historical research including archival research can transform our understanding of the late Qing military.

## 6.7 Glossary

| Pinyin | Chinese characters | English, if available |
|---|---|---|
| Baoju Zhidu | 保举制度 | Recommendation system |
| Bazong | 把總 | Squad Leader |
| Bingbu | 兵部 | Ministry of War |
| Canjiang | 參將 | Assistant Commander |
| Canling | 參領 | Regimental Commander |
| Chushen | 出身 | Qualifications |
| Congyipin | 從一品 | Lower First Rank |
| Congerpin | 從二品 | Lower Second Rank |
| Congsanpin | 從三品 | Lower Third Rank |
| Dufu | 督撫 | The governor of one or two provinces |
| Dusi | 都司 | Brigade Vice Commander |
| Dutong | 都統 | Commander-in-chief of a Banner |
| Erdeng Shiwei | 二等侍衛 | Second Class Imperial Guardsmen |
| Ewai Waiwei | 額外外委 | Additional Company Commander or Squad Leader |
| Fanzhen | 藩鎮 | Military town |
| Fudutong | 副都統 | Vice Commander-in-chief of a Banner |
| Fujiang | 副將 | Regional Vice Commander |
| Heilongjiang Jiangjun | 黑龍江將軍 | Garrison Manchu General of Heilongjiang |
| Huaijun | 淮軍 | Anhui Army |
| Huguang Sheng | 湖廣省 | Hubei and Hunan provinces |
| Hugui Miaobian | 湖貴苗變 | The Miao uprising in Hunan and Guizhou |
| Huibi | 回避 | Rule of avoidance |
| Jiangnan Sheng | 江南省 | Jiangsu and Anhui provinces |
| Jiguan Huibi Zhidu | 籍貫回避制度 | Tenure Native Parrying System |
| Jinshenlu | 縉紳錄 | Quarterly roster of Qing civil officials, JSL in the text |
| Jinlu Baqi | 禁旅八旗 | Eight Banners Imperial Army |
| Jinshen Quanshu | 縉紳全書 | Type of *Jinshenlu* |
| Juezhi Quanlan | 爵秩全覽 | Type of *Jinshenlu* |
| Li | 里 | A traditional Chinese unit of distance |

(continued)

(continued)

| Pinyin | Chinese characters | English, if available |
|---|---|---|
| Linshi Yanei Dachen | 領侍衙内大臣 | Minister of the Imperial Household Department Concurrently Controlling the Imperial Guardsmen |
| Lvying | 綠營 | Green Standard Army |
| Lvying Shuishi | 綠營水師 | Green Standard Navy |
| Nianjun Qiyi | 捻軍起義 | Nian Rebellion |
| Qianzong | 千總 | Company Commander |
| Qimen Army | 期門軍 | Gate Guardsmen |
| Sandeng Shiwei | 三等侍衛 | Third Class Imperial Guardsmen |
| Sanzhi Dachen | 散秩大臣 | Grand Minister Assistant Commander of Imperial Guardsmen |
| Shaozhang | 哨長 | Sentry Captain |
| Shoubei | 守備 | Assistant Brigade Commander |
| Tidu | 提督 | Provincial Military Commander |
| Waiwei Bazong | 外委把總 | Additional Squad Leader |
| Waiwei Qianzong | 外委千總 | Additional Company Commander |
| Xiaoqixiao | 驍騎校 | Cavalry Captain of Eight Banners |
| Yideng Shiwei | 一等侍衛 | First Class Imperial Guardsmen |
| Ying | 營 | Camps |
| Youji | 游擊 | Brigade Commander |
| Yulin Army | 羽林軍 | Palace Guard |
| Zhen | 鎮 | Military Town |
| Zhengyipin | 正一品 | Upper First Rank |
| Zhengerpin | 正二品 | Upper Second Rank |
| Zhengsanpin | 正三品 | Upper Third Rank |
| Zhengsipin | 正四品 | Upper Fourth Rank |
| Zhengwupin | 正五品 | Upper Fifth Rank |
| Zhengliupin | 正六品 | Upper Sixth Rank |
| Zhengqipin | 正七品 | Upper Seventh Rank |
| Zhongshu beilan | 中樞備覽 | Quarterly roster of Qing military officials, *ZSBL* in the text |
| Zongbing | 總兵 | Regional Commander |

**Acknowledgements** This research was supported by HK RGC Areas of Excellence AoE/B-704/22-R (Zhiwu Chen PC).

Previous versions of this paper were presented at the Area of Excellence–Quantitative History Conference 2023, held at The University of Hong Kong on October 25–26, 2023. We are grateful to the participants, discussants, and audience members for their comments and suggestions. We are also grateful to Shengbin Wei, Qin Xue, Yueran Hou, Shuaiqi Gao, and other members of the Lee-Campbell Group for their comments and suggestions.

## References

Bai, Ying, Ruixue Jia, and Jiaojiao Yang. 2023. Web of Power: How elite networks shaped war and politics in China. *The Quarterly Journal of Economics* 138 (2): 1067–1108.

Ban, Gu and Xianqian Wang. 2012. *Hanshu Buzhu* 漢書補注 (*A Supplementary Annotation to the Hanshu*), vol. 6. Shanghai: Shanghai Ancient Books Publishing House.

Cao, Xun. 2018. Mingdai zhenshu yingbing zhongde jiceng wuguan 明代鎮戍營兵中的基層武官 (The Grassroots Military Officers in the Garrison Troops of the Ming Dynasty). *Zhongguo shiyanjiu* 中國史研究 (*Journal of Chinese Historical Studies*) (1): 135–152.

Chen, Jun, and Cameron Campbell. 2024. Qinghouqi zhongxiaceng wuguan de manhanbili yu chushengoucheng 清后期中下层武官的满汉比例与出身构成 (Trends and Patterns in the Banner Affiliation and Qualifications of Low- and Mid-Level Military Officers in the Late Qing). *Lishi dangan* 歷史檔案 (*Historical Archives*) (3): 104–112.

Chen, Xiansong. 2018. Congcai zhengshi shijiao zaixi saifang yu haifang zhizheng 從財政史視角再析海防塞防之爭 (Analyzing the Coastal Defense and Frontier Defense Debate from a Financial History Perspective). *Qinghua daxue xuebao* 清華大學學報 (*Academic Journal of Tsinghua University*) (6): 132–139.

Dai, Yingcong. 2017. Qing Military Institutions and Their Effects on Government, Economy, and Society, 1640–1800. *Journal of Chinese History* (1): 329–352.

Ding, Yizhuang. 2003. *Qingdai baqi zhufang yanjiu* 清代八旗駐防研究 (*Research on the Eight Banners Garrison in the Qing Dynasty*). Shenyang: Liaoning Minzu Chubanshe.

Du, Jiaji. 2015. Qingdai baqi guanzhi yu xingzheng 清代八旗官制與行政 (*Eight Banners Officer System and Administration in the Qing Dynasty*). Beijing: China Social Science Press.

Ge, Jianxiong, ed., and Shuji Cao. 2001. *Zhongguo renkoushi* 中國人口史 (*The History of Chinese Population*), vol. 5. Shanghai: Fudan University Press.

Huang, Zhongqing. 2001. Mingdai haifang de shuizhai yu youbing明代海防的水寨與游兵 (Water Forts and Light Infantry in Ming Dynasty Coastal Defense). In *Mingshi yanjiu congkan* 明史研究叢刊 (*Collection of Ming History Research*), vol. 1, ed. Zhihe Wei. Taipei: Mingshi Yanjiu Xiaozu Kanhang.

Hucker, Charles O. 1995. *A Dictionary of Official Titles in Imperial China*. Taipei: SMC Publishing Inc.

Lai, Jiancheng. 2010. Bianzhen liangxiang: Mingdai zhonghouqi de bianfang jingfei he guojia caizheng weiji 邊鎮糧餉: 明代中後期的邊防經費和國家財政危機 (*Food and Pay in the Border Town: Border Defense Funds and National Financial Crisis in the Middle and Late Ming Dynasty, 1531–1602*). Hangzhou: Zhejiang University Press.

Liang, Zhisheng. 2012. Mingdai weisuo wuguan shixi zhidu yanjiu 明代衛所武官世襲制度研究 (*Research on the Hereditary System of Military Officers in the Ming Dynasty's Wei-Suo System*). Beijing: China Social Science Press.

Liu, Qiang. 2008. Rong lutang yu Qingdai jinsenlu zhi chuban 榮錄堂與清代搢紳錄之出版 (Ronglu Hall and the Publication of Jinshenlu in the Qing Dynasty). *Tushuguanzazhi* 圖書館雜誌 (*Library Journal*), (10): 63–68.

Liu, Xianting. 1997. *Guangyang zaiji* 廣陽雜記 (*Guangyang Essays*). Beijing: Zhonghua Book Company.

Long, Shengyun. 1990. *Xiangjun shigao* 湘軍史稿 (*History of the Xiang Army*). Chengdu: Sichuan People's Publishing House.

Luo, Ergang. 1984. *Luying bingzhi* 綠營兵志 (*The History of Green Standard Army*). Beijing: Zhonghua Book Company.

Ming, Liang, and Natai Su, eds. 1968. *Qinding zhongshu zhengkao* 欽定中樞政考 (*The Compilation of Administrative Matters of The Ministry of War in Qing Dynasty*). Taipei: Xuehai Publishing House.

Moll-Murata, Christine, and Ulrich Theobald. 2013. Military Employment in Qing Dynasty China. In *Fighting for a Living: A Comparative Study of Military Labour 1500–2000*, ed. Erik-Jan. Zürcher, 353–392. Amsterdam: Amsterdam University Press.

Pan, Honggang. 2020. Qingdai baqi shuishi yu haifang tixi 清代八旗水師與海防體系 (The Qing Dynasty Eight Banners Navy and Coastal Defense System). *Fujian luntan* 福建論壇 (*Fujian Forum*) (3): 136–144.

Qin, Bo. 2015. Mingdai wenguan yinzi wuzhi zhidu tanxi 明代文官蔭子武職制度探析 (Analysis of the System Allowing Sons of Civil Officials in the Ming Dynasty to Obtain Military Positions Due to Their Fathers' Merits). *Shixueyuekan* 史學月刊 (*Journal of Historical Science*) (11): 42–54.

Qin, Shucai. 2004. *Yunnan luying bing yanjiu* 清代雲南綠營兵研究 (*Study on Yunnan Green Standard Army Soldiers in Qing Dynasty*). Kunming: Yunnan Education Publishing House.

Ren, Yuxue, Bijia Chen, Xiaowen Hao, Cameron Campbell, and James Lee. 2016. Qingdai jinshenlu lianghua shuju kuyu guanyuan qunti yanjiu 清代縉紳錄量化數據庫與官員群體研究 (Quantitative Database of Qing Dynasty Jinshenlu and Research on Official Groups). *Qingshyanjiu* 清史研究 (*Qing History Research*) (4): 61–77.

Robinson, David R. 2013. Military Labor in China, c. 1500. In *Fighting for a Living: A Comparative Study of Military Labour 1500–2000*, ed. Erik-Jan Zürcher, 43–80. Amsterdam: Amsterdam University Press.

Shi, Peng. 2021. Guojia tushu guancang mingdai wanli ji chongzhen jinshenlu yanjiu 國家圖書館藏明代萬曆及崇禎縉紳錄研究 (Research on Ming Wanli and Chongzhen Jingshenlu in the National Library). *Wenxian* 文獻 (*Documentary Research*) (6): 116–132.

The Institute of Modern History of the Chinese Academy of Social Sciences, ed. 1978. *Xinjun bianlian yange* 新軍編練沿革 (*Evolution of the Compilation and Training of the New Army in the Late Qing Dynasty*). Beijing: Zhonghua Book Company.

The Academy of Military Sciences of China, ed. 2005. *Zhongguo junshi tongshi* 中國軍事通史 (*General History of Chinese Military Affairs*). Beijing: Military Science Publishing House.

Wang, Qingyun. 1985. *Shiqu yuji* 石渠余紀 (*Shiqu Miscellany*). Beijing: Beijing Ancient Books Publishing House.

Wang, Yue. 2010. Qingdai baqi bufang lvying wuguan wenti tanxi 清代八旗補放綠營武官問題探析 (Analysis of the Issue of Qing Dynasty Eight Banners Officers Taking Positions in the Green Standard Army). *Heilongjiang minzu congkan* 黑龍江民族叢刊 (*Heilongjiang Ethnic Studies*) (6): 93–99.

Wang, Zengyu. 1983. *Songchao bingzhi chutan* 宋朝兵制初探 (*Preliminary Exploration of Song Dynasty Military System*). Beijing: Zhonghua Book Company.

Wang, Zhiming. 2016. Qingdai zhiguan renshi yanjiu 清代職官人事研究——基於引見官員履歷檔案的考證分析 (*Research on Qing Dynasty Officials: An Analytical Study Based on the Archives of Introduced Officials*). Shanghai: Shanghai Bookstore Publishing House.

Wang, Zhonghan, ed. 1987. *Qingshi liezhuan* 清史列傳 (*Qing History Biography*), vol. 63. Beijing: Zhonghua Book Company.

Xie, Xiaohui. 2020. Funai lianbing chengfa yu zhengan bingyong de xingqi: qingdai difang junshi zhidu biange zhi zhaoshi 傅鼐練兵與鎮筸兵勇的興起: 清代地方軍事制度變革之肇始 (The Rise of Fu Nai's Troops and Village Militia in Zhengan Military Town: The Beginning of Local Military System Reforms in the Qing Dynasty). *Jindai shiyan jiu* 近代史研究 (*Modern Chinese History Studies*) (1): 4–17.

Yang, Guoqiang. 2009. Juanna baoju yu wanqing de lizhi shifan 捐納、保舉與晚清的吏治失范 (Purchasing Official Positions, Recommendations and the Breakdown of Bureaucratic Discipline in the Late Qing)." *Shehui kexue* 社會科學 (*Journal of Social Science*) (5): 130–138.

Zhang, Guogang. 2009. *Tangdai fanzhen yanjiu* 唐代藩鎮研究 (*Research on Fanzhen in the Tang Dynasty*). Beijing: China Renmin University Press.

Zhang, Tingyu. 1974. *Mingshi* 明史 (*History of Ming Dynasty*). Beijing: Zhonghua Book Company.
Zhang, Zhongli. 2008. *Zhongguo shenshi yanjiu* 中國紳士研究 (*China's Gentry*). Shanghai: Shanghai People's Publishing House.
Zhao, Erxun. 1977. *Qingshigao* 清史稿 (*Draft History of the Qing*). Beijing: Zhonghua Book Company.
Zhao, Lian. 1980. *Xiaoting zalu* 嘯亭雜錄 (*Xiaoting Miscellany*). Beijing: Zhonghua Book Company.
Zhao, Weixi. 2014. Xiangjun jituan yu xibei huimin da qiyi zhi shanhou yanjiu 湘軍集團與西北回民大起義之善後研究 (*Study on the Aftermath of Xiangjun Group and the Hui Uprising in Northwest China*). Shanghai: Shanghai Ancient Books Publishing House.
Zhong, Qi. 2011. *Huangchao suoxie lu pinhua guan suobi* 皇朝瑣屑錄•憑花館瑣筆 (*Imperial Trivia Record • Pinghua Hall Trivia*), vol. 1. Beijing: National Library of China Publishing House.
Zhonghua Book Company, ed. 1986. *Qingshilu* 清實錄 (*Factual Record of Qing Dynasty*). Beijing: Zhonghua Book Company.
Zhonghua Book Company, ed. 1991. *Guangxu qinghuidian shili* 光緒清會典事例 (*The Compilation of Administrative Matters in Qing Dynasty*). Beijing: Zhonghua Book Company.
Zuo, Zongtang. 1976. Fuchen haifang saifang ji guanwai jiaofu liangyun qingxing zhe 復陳海防塞防及關外剿撫糧運情形 (Report on Coastal Defense and Garrison Logistics). In *Zuowen xianggong quanji* 左宗棠全集 *(The Complete Works of Zuo Zongtang)*, ed. Shulin Yang. Taipei: Wemhai Publishing House.

**Jun Chen** is a Ph.D. student at Renmin University of China. He obtained his Master's degree in History from the Institute of Modern Chinese History at Central China Normal University in 2024. He was a visiting postgraduate student at The Hong Kong University of Science and Technology (HKUST) in 2023. His research interests include the social origins, career dynamics and deployment of military officers during the Qing Dynasty, as well as the political and military history of modern China. He published an article on trends and patterns in the banner affiliation and qualifications of low- and mid-level military officers in the late Qing in Lishi Dangan (Historical Archives) in 2024.

**Cameron Campbell** is Chair Professor in the Division of Social Science at The Hong Kong University of Science and Technology (HKUST). He is also a Distinguished Professor in the School of History and Culture at Central China Normal University. His research focuses on demography, stratification and inequality in historical China and in comparative perspective. For his research, he and his collaborators in the Lee-Campbell Group construct, analyze, and publicly release datasets constructed from archival and other sources. He was a Fellow of the Center for Advanced Study in the Behavioral Sciences at Stanford 2022-23, and a Guggenheim Fellow in 2004-2005. He was a Changjiang Scholar at Central China Normal University from 2017 to 2020.

# Chapter 7
# The Impact of Crises on the Careers of County Magistrates in Qing China, 1830–1912

**Cameron Campbell and Shuaiqi Gao**

## 7.1 Introduction

State capacity—the ability of a government to achieve its goals—has become a topic of interest in the study of Imperial China. Recent work has examined the role of state capacity, or lack thereof, in the Great Divergence (Pomeranz 2021) and the multiple crises of the late Qing. Weberian conceptions of state capacity emphasize the importance of a bureaucracy like the one that administered late Imperial China in which officials were ostensibly selected and promoted based on their expertise and competence (Besley et al. 2022; Weber 1922). Empirical measures of state capacity vary widely, but commonly include the ability to collect revenue, maintain a civil and military bureaucracy, and implement policies.

We suggest that a key dimension of state capacity for the Qing in the nineteenth century was its adherence or lack thereof to regulations for the review and promotion of officials. For an ostensibly Weberian bureaucracy to operate effectively and implement state policy, it had to follow its own rules for the management of personnel. Talented officials had to be rewarded, and poor performers were demoted or terminated. Recognizing the importance of a systematic approach to the management of personnel, the Qing had detailed regulations that governed performance reviews for officials, including the equivalent of "key performance indicators." Some of these

C. Campbell (✉)
Division of Social Science, The Hong Kong University of Science and Technology, Hong Kong, China

School of History and Culture, Central China Normal University, Wuhan, China
e-mail: camcam@ust.hk

S. Gao
School of History and Culture, Central China Normal University, Wuhan, China
e-mail: gsqccnu@163.com



Z. Chen et al. (eds.), *Quantitative History of China*, Studies in Economic History,
https://doi.org/10.1007/978-981-96-8272-0_7

regulations specified situations under which officials were to be terminated because their very occurrence was *prima facie* evidence of poor performance.

A common perception of the late Qing bureaucracy is that procedures for personnel management increasingly deviated from the Weberian ideal in which competence and expertise were the sole or at least key criteria for appointment and promotion. Chen et al. (2020) showed that a rising proportion of officials held purchased degrees. Zhang (2022) showed that office purchase was common. In his satirical novel *Officialdom Unmasked*, Li Boyuan (1903) depicted late Qing officials as corrupt and incompetent, with appointment and promotion dependent on bribery, flattery, patronage, and personal connections. Numerous studies document that in the late Qing, increasing numbers of officials served in an acting (*shuli*) capacity where their appointment and retention may not have been subject to the usual rules (e.g., Hu 2022; Liang 2023; Wu and Wan 2018).

To assess adherence to personnel regulations, we examine the enforcement of a rule that specified that county magistrates were to be terminated if a locust infestation originated in the area under their jurisdiction. Locust infestations are ideal for this examination because they were considered preventable, the current magistrate was responsible for prevention, their occurrence was regarded as *prima facie* evidence of neglect, and they were difficult or impossible to conceal once they were underway. Other disasters may have been regarded as impossible to prevent or, in the case of floods, the fault of other officials. In those situations, officials were assessed based on their response, and the evaluation would have been more subjective. We focus on county magistrates because personnel regulations were clear about their role in disaster prevention and response and our data on disasters that we use and which we describe below were also organized by county.

This represents a new direction in the study of state capacity in late Imperial China. To our knowledge, this is the first study to consider the state's willingness or ability to enforce a clearly defined rule relevant to bureaucratic personnel management. Previous studies relevant studies considered warfare, central government revenue, disaster relief, public good provision, the appointment of high-level bureaucrats, tax collection, and government savings (e.g., Ma 2013; Peng 2018; Yang 2022). One recent theme relevant to our analysis has been the implications of different selection processes for bureaucratic performance (Liu 2025; Liu and Zhang 2023).

We conduct a logistic regression to compare the effects of locust infestations and other disasters on the chance that a county magistrate's career would end in the current or following calendar year. The other disasters include floods, droughts, epidemics, famine, and bad harvests. If the system was operating as intended, a locust plague should have had the clearest effect on the chance of a career ending. Other disasters by themselves should have milder or no immediate effects on the chance of a career ending because they were not automatically regarded as the fault of the magistrate. A uniform adverse effect of disaster regardless of type would indicate that when any disaster occurred, the official unfortunate enough to be in charge at the time was blamed no matter what the cause was, or how they responded. A lack of effect for any disaster, even locust plagues, would indicate regulations were not being enforced.

We investigate interactions with the qualifications of the official, the characteristics of the county, and time trends. For qualifications, we compare officials with purchased and exam degrees. Officials with purchased degrees should have been easier to hold to account because they were less likely to have networks of exam classmates who could protect them if their performance was unsatisfactory (Zhang 2022). We expect effects to have been stronger in counties with a higher difficulty rating (*chong fan pi nan*) because such locations and the officials who administered them received more attention. Finally, to the extent that the capacity of the Qing state to enforce its rules declined over time, we expect the effects of disasters on careers to have declined during the nineteenth century.

Our data consists of career histories of 31,276 Qing officials who at some point between 1830 and 1911 served as county magistrates, linked to county-level records of disasters. The career histories are extracted from the China Government Employee Dataset-Qing (CGED-Q) Jinshenlu (JSL) (Chen et al. 2020). We transcribed the records of disasters from the published *Compendium of Meteorological Records in China of Three Thousand Years* (Zhang and Jiang 2005). The records in the *Compendium* were nearly all from county or prefectural gazetteers. We describe both sources in detail below. We also describe the process by which we turned the contents of the *Compendium* into the dataset we used for the analysis.

We find that infestations increased the chances that an official's career would end in the current or following year. Among other disasters, only famine increased the chances that a career would end. The effects of famine and infestation did not vary according to whether an official had an examination or a purchased degree, or the rated difficulty (*chongfan pinan*) of the county. We find no evidence of a linear decline in the effects of famine or infestation when we consider interactions with calendar year. Examination of interactions by decade suggests that before 1880, career effects of infestation were especially strong in some decades, but that after 1880, infestation no longer raised the chances that a career would end.

The remainder of the paper is divided into five sections. In the next section, we provide background. We review the role of the state and officials in preventing and responding to disasters, emphasizing the Qing. We also discuss the role of disaster response in the evaluation of officials. After that, we introduce the data we use from the CGED-Q JSL and the disaster and harvest records from the *Compendium*. We then very briefly introduce the methods for our analysis. Finally, we present and discuss our results. We conclude with an outline of our plans for further research on the influence of disasters on official careers.

## 7.2 Background

### 7.2.1 Disasters and the State in Chinese History

There is a large literature on disasters in Chinese history and state responses to them. Here, we only mention a few as a way of showcasing the range of topics that have been investigated. One of the earliest studies was Deng (1937), which provided a historical overview of the changes in policies and institutions that followed the occurrence of natural disasters. Subsequent general studies of historical disasters or relief focus on government policy, interaction of the state with local society, philanthropical organizations, and the role of local licentiates or gentry in providing relief (Leung 1997; Li and Xia 2006). Famine relief and the role of the state granary system has received particular attention (Li 2007; Will et al. 1991).

Another line of studies focuses on regional and local disasters, responses to them, and their broader impact. Examples include histories of drought relief in such regions as Shandong, Henan, and Shanxi. These rely on records in local gazetteers and focus on the role of the local government in disaster relief (Will 1990). Some studies use records left by county magistrates or provincial governors who dealt with disasters in their jurisdiction (Feng 2018; Jiang 2014). Zheng investigated the role of natural disasters in triggering local rebellions in Weixian County, Shandong (Zheng 2012). Some other studies focus on the problems and corruption of civil officials when taking advantage of the government relief policies and pointed out that this contributed to the conflicts between state and society (Zhao 2015, 2018).

### 7.2.2 Disaster Management in the Careers of Qing Officials

The state took responsibility for disaster prevention and relief and the qualifications and abilities of regional and local officials were regarded as directly related to the effectiveness of disaster relief.[1] Accordingly, success or failure in disaster management was a key performance indicator in the assessment of local officials.[2] There were rules for disaster reporting, investigation, fundraising, relief, and dealing with the aftermath. The Qing government appraised officials at every step of the disaster, and the regulations and statutes stipulated that if local officials failed to do their best, they would be punished.

County magistrates and prefectural prefects were held responsible for preventing or responding to disasters in their jurisdictions. Their performance before or during disasters was assessed in memorials and reports by the governors-general and officials who had short-term appointments overseeing responses to disaster (*Jianzhen Guan*). Magistrates and prefects who performed well during a disaster may not have been

[1] *Qing Gaozong Shilu(清高宗實錄)*. Qianlong 11, Month 2, Day 30 Juan 259, p.362.

[2] *Huangchao Jingshi Wenbian(皇朝經世文編)*. Juan 42, pp. 3660–3663.

promoted immediately but could have a favorable annotation added to their record that would increase their subsequent chances of promotion. Conversely, officials whose response to disaster was deemed inadequate or whose failure to fulfill their responsibilities was judged to have caused the disaster could be punished. Officials could be blamed for disasters even if they were no longer serving in the location where the disaster occurred. For example, if a flood occurred and investigation revealed that it was because an official who had served there previously had neglected their duties, they could be punished even if they were already serving somewhere else.

Officials could be terminated or demoted for failures including misrepresenting or covering up a disaster, embezzling funds, neglecting civilian wellbeing, procrastinating over relief efforts, and engaging in misconduct. Versions of the *Huangzheng Jiyao* compiled and edited by two Qing officials, Yao Bi and Wang Zhiyi, highlight the significance of disaster relief in local government civil officials' duties (Zhang 2010). Punishments included demotion, termination, and other sanctions. Examples of officials being punished for misconduct related to disaster response are common in the *Qing Shilu* of the Kangxi reign to the Qianlong reign. Later, during the Jiaqing and Daoguang reigns, when disasters were recorded even more frequently in local gazetteers and Veritable Records, more civil officials were also found violating the statutes.

Examples help clarify how these rules and policies were applied in practice. In 1890, the county magistrate of Jiaxing, Wang Jinyu, was charged with negligence in connection with a flood the preceding year. Specifically, he was accused of continuing to collect taxes even after the disasters had been reported to him. The prefect, Songjun, was asked to investigate. His report described Wang's response as inadequate but did not claim that he had engaged in misconduct. Wang Jinyu was nevertheless forced to retire. Higher officials could also be punished: in 1723, the provincial governor and provincial administrative commissioner of Shanxi, De-yin and Sen-tu, were found to have covered up local disasters under their jurisdiction while still collecting taxes. De-yin was demoted to a temporary and lower position at the Grand Secretariat back in the capital. Sen-tu was discharged and was given a low-level position as an escort in a cavalry camp.

The most detailed and specific regulations related to the responsibility of officials for locust prevention. The Qing regarded locusts as a threat to the food supply. If locusts were culled in timely fashion, that is before they grew wings, locust plagues could be prevented. Locust plagues were, accordingly, different from natural disasters like droughts, epidemics, or earthquakes that were difficult or impossible to prevent and to which an official could only respond. During the Qing, locust control was a primary responsibility of local officials, especially the county magistrates. If a locust plague originated in the county they administered, they were punished.[3] Their superiors and subordinates shared responsibility and could also be punished. If locusts emerged and local and prefectural officials concealed them or failed to wipe them out after they were reported but before they matured and grew wings and began to harm crops, they could be dismissed from their post. If a prefect failed to discover

[3] *Qing Shizong Shilu(清世宗實錄)*. Yongzheng 6, Month 8, Day 17, Juan 72, p. 1079.

the dereliction of duty by the magistrate, they could also be demoted.[4] For example, in 1822, Sun Yuting reported that there were locusts in Jiangnan and Jiangbei, and they did considerable damage. The locusts originated in Haizhou, and they were not extinguished right away, and officials delayed the report, hoping to conceal the problem. As a result, Liu Ling, a prefect in Haizhou, was dismissed from his post.[5]

There were also rewards for officials who were especially diligent about locust control. Qianlong stipulated in his sixteenth year that civil and military officials who eliminated locusts in time could have a commendation added to their record. In 1822, it was again stated stipulated that if civilian and military officials were able to detect and eliminate locusts in time, they could be promoted after a report by their superiors.[6] In the fifteenth year of Daoguang, Yang Xiaochun, a low-level local official in Huaining in Anhui province, died of illness resulting from his efforts in locust hunting. Locust control was supposed the responsibility of the magistrate, but to set an example and honor Yang Xiaochun, the Daoguang Emperor awarded him the title of magistrate posthumously.[7]

Officials were also responsible for flood prevention and response, but because the etiology of floods was more complex, they were not automatically blamed for disasters that occurred during their watch. Officials were held responsible for dikes constructed or maintained during their tenure in a locality, even after they no longer served in the area.[8] Thus, if a dike failed, the officials involved in its construction might be held responsible even if they had moved on, and the currently serving official might be held blameless. For example, in Xianyang in Shaanxi province in 1843, the Lijiabu embankment burst. Cheng Yimei, by then a prefect of Jingzhou Prefecture in Hubei province, was held responsible for not maintaining it properly during his time in Shaanxi. Li Tingqi of Jingzhou also was held responsible for poor supervision.[9] Even prominent officials could be caught up in an investigation. For example, in 1892 the Yongding River overflowed and seven people were dismissed from their posts, and Li Hongzhang was one of the officials held responsible.[10]

While the Qing did not have similarly detailed regulations for the handling of other types of disasters, or the consequences for officials' careers, there were requirements for disaster reporting, investigation, and relief. Officials were not only civilly liable for the handling of disasters, but also criminally liable for serious violations.[11] If a local disaster occurred during the late spring, it had to be reported before the end of the sixth lunar month. Disasters in the late summer were to be reported at the end of the ninth lunar month. If local officials concealed or lied about a disaster or treated a disaster as though it were not a disaster, they could be dismissed from their posts

[4] *Chufen Zeyao Tuli(處分則要圖例)*. Guangxu 14, Juan 4, p. 18.

[5] *Qing Xuanzong Shilu(清宣宗實錄)*. Daoguang 3, Month 8, Day 4, Juan 56, p. 997.

[6] *Da Qing Huidian Shlli(大清會典事例)*.Juan 110, pp. 6034–6047.

[7] *Qing Xuanzong Shilu(清宣宗實錄)*. Daoguangr 15, Month 8, Day 23,Juan 207,p. 157.

[8] *Chufen Zeyao Tuli(處分則要圖例)*. Guangxu 14,Juan 6, pp. 49–50.

[9] *Qing Xuanzong Shilu(清宣宗實錄)*. Daoguang 24, Month 8, Day 17,Juan 480, p. 114.

[10] *Qing Dezong Shilu(清德宗實錄)*. Guangxu 18, Intercalary Month 6, Day 4, Juan 313, p. 64.

[11] *Xu Ben and Liu Tongxun. Daqing Lvli(大清律例)*. Juan 9, pp. 551–562.

and never reappointed.[12] When it came to famines, as noted earlier, the Qing state, like its predecessors, regarded famine prevention or relief as a key responsibility, and it seems safe to assume that officials who presided over a famine could be held to account.

## 7.3 Data

### *7.3.1 Qing Officials*

For our information on the careers of Qing officials, we make use of the China Government Employee Dataset-Qing Jinshenlu (CGED-Q JSL). It provides longitudinal, individual-level data on civil officials who held formal appointments between 1760 and 1911 transcribed from surviving rosters of civil officials called *Jinshenlu* that originally were published every three months. Because this source has been described in detail elsewhere (e.g., Ren et al. 2016; Chen et al. 2020), here we only provide key details specifically relevant to the analysis. From 1820 onwards, editions are with only a few exceptions available nearly annually. For the period from 1820 to 1911, the CGED-Q JSL includes 2,929,737 records of civil offices held by 139,323 civil officials.

The CGED-Q JSL contains 358,575 records of 16,671 non-Banner (mostly Han Chinese) officials who appeared at least once as a county magistrate (*zhixian,*) between 1830 and 1911.[13] Of these, 265,661 records relate to them serving as magistrates, and the remainder from when they served in other posts. We exclude Bannermen who held posts as county magistrates because we are less confident about our linkage of them and because of the possibility that they were evaluated differently. We also exclude magistrates whose historical county names in the CGED-Q JSL could not be matched to a contemporary county name using the Harvard CH-GIS 1820 or 1911 files. This left us with 262,698 quarterly records of 13,893 officials who appeared at least once as a magistrate. Of these, 242,506 records were of themselves serving as magistrates. To align with the format of the quarterly records in the disaster and harvest data described in the next section, we collapsed these quarterly records into 94,888 annual records. We then restricted to records in editions for which the next available edition was one year or less away and excluded records from editions after 1905 because of changes in appointment and assessment, leaving 80,222 records annualized records of currently serving county magistrates.

[12] *Chufen Zeyao Tuli(處分則要圖例).* Guangxu 14, Juan 4, p. 18.

[13] In this iteration, we do not consider *zhizhou* who were the equivalent of magistrates for the county level administrative units *sanzhou.* We will add them in a later iteration.

### *7.3.2 Disaster and Harvest Data*

The *Compendium* (Zhang and Jiang 2005) is a compilation of meteorological records by Zhang De'er and Jiang Guangmei. At the time it was published, it was the most complete collection of meteorological records spanning from the twenty-third century BCE to the early twentieth century CE. The materials incorporated extend from oracle bone inscriptions to texts preserved in paper-bound books. In total, the *Compendium* drew on a total of 8228 historical texts and books. The *Compendium* is divided into four volumes. The first volume encompasses meteorological records from the twenty-third century up to the Yuan dynasty (1271–1368). The second volume contains meteorological records from the Ming dynasty (1368–1644). The third and fourth volume cover the Qing dynasty (1644–1911).

The *Compendium* compiles textual records of various weather, climate, and atmospheric phenomena. It includes at least ten types of disasters, including floods, drought, famine, locusts, and other infestations, epidemics, earthquakes, frost, wind, storm surges, fog, and hail. Among the disasters recorded in the *Compendium*, floods and drought by far were the most frequent. It details the occurrence of time and location, the scope and severity of weather-related disasters, and the post-disaster relief and exemptions. The *Compendium* also includes records related to phenology, agricultural yield variability, pest infestations, epidemics, famine, and extraordinary events, all in relation to meteorological conditions. Records sometimes also included subjective assessments of the severity of disasters, with references to events as "disaster," "catastrophe," or "the worst catastrophe in a decade/century." In other cases, records specified that an event was "not a disaster or not detrimental."

The *Compendium* mostly relies on meteorological records in local gazetteers, which account for 98.52% of all records. According to Table 7.1, most of the gazetteer records are from the gazetteers compiled during the Guangxu reign and the Republic of China periods, constituting 34.96% and 31.32% of the total, respectively. Records from other sources, including *Draft History of the Qing*, other compiled documents, and local gazetteers during the People's Republic of China, account for 1.45%. The *Compendium* did not include information from personal diaries or palace archives.

### *7.3.3 Construction of the Dataset*

The completeness of the historical meteorological records and the structure of *The Compendium* makes it suitable for transcription into a database and quantitative analysis. It is organized chronologically, with records for each year arranged by province, prefecture, and county. The records provide contemporary place names, reflecting current administrative divisions. This compilation is useful for calculating frequency and geographical distribution of various meteorological phenomena, disasters, and harvests.

**Table 7.1** Sources of the records in the *Compendium*, 1780–1909

| Source | Records(N) | Percentage |
|---|---|---|
| Gazetteers (by reign) | | |
| Qianlong | 232 | 0.62 |
| Jiaqing | 1543 | 4.11 |
| Daoguang | 4267 | 11.37 |
| Tongzhi | 4775 | 12.72 |
| Xianfeng | 581 | 1.55 |
| Guangxu | 13,120 | 34.96 |
| Xuantong | 692 | 1.84 |
| 1911–1949 | 11,756 | 31.32 |
| Draft History of the Qing Dynasty | 21 | 0.06 |
| Other | 544 | 1.45 |
| Total | 37,531 | 100.00 |

From the Compendium, we constructed records that summarized the information for a single prefecture or county in a specific year.[14] Following the original format, we created 13 variables: page number, year, sexagenary cycle, reign name, emperor's name, province, prefecture, county, season, lunar month, lunar day, original text, and source. Thus far we have entered the historical meteorological data in the *Compendium* from 1778 to 1911, that is, from the 43rd year of the Qianlong reign to the third year of the Xuantong reign in the Qing dynasty. According to Table 7.2, we have 37,531 meteorological records from 1780 to 1909. These numbers are much larger than the counts made by Deng (1937) for the Qing from 1644 to 1911.[15]

To categorize the events, we constructed a set of binary variables, each of which corresponds to the presence or absence of key characters of phrases in a county or prefecture record in a specific year. Table 7.3 summarizes these variables, and the key characters or phrases associated with them. In the original text there could be multiple expressions for the same event, and we assigned categories based on the presence of at least one of several keywords. We distinguish records according to whether they were harvest outcomes, meteorological events, or aftermath events. By aftermath events, we mean events that were not specifically meteorological but could occur subsequent to major meteorological events. The binary variables for events are not mutually exclusive, since a record might include information on a harvest, meteorological events, and aftermath events, or possibly independently.

For harvests, we distinguished between good and bad. Good harvests were indicated with terms like "bountiful" (*feng*), "harvest" (*fengshou*), "ripe" (*ren*), "great ripeness" (*daren*), "plentiful year" (*younian*), "great year" (*daoyounian*), "ripe"

[14] The *Compendium* also includes prefectural level records that we transcribed, but which we do not use here.

[15] For the 267 years of the Qing, Deng (1937) counted a total of 1121 disaster events, including 201 droughts, 192 floods, 169 earthquakes, 131 hailstorms, 97 wind disasters, 93 locust plagues, 90 famines, 74 epidemics, and 74 frost and snow disasters.

**Table 7.2** Numbers of event records in the *Compendium* by decade, 1780–1909

| Year | Records(N) |
|---|---|
| 1780–1789 | 2261 |
| 1790–1799 | 1948 |
| 1800–1809 | 2379 |
| 1810–1819 | 2506 |
| 1820–1829 | 2727 |
| 1830–1839 | 3428 |
| 1840–1849 | 2697 |
| 1850–1859 | 3491 |
| 1860–1869 | 3638 |
| 1870–1879 | 4953 |
| 1880–1889 | 2852 |
| 1890–1899 | 2486 |
| 1900–1909 | 2165 |
| Total | 37,531 |

**Table 7.3** Key characters and phrases for categories of events in the *Compendium*

| Category | Keywords |
|---|---|
| *Harvest* | |
| Good | *Feng, Fengshou, Ren, Younian, Da Younian, Daren, Shu, Dashu, Dayou, Youqiu* |
| Bad | *Qian, Suiqian, Sui Daqian, Qianshou, Boshou, Qiujian* |
| *Events* | |
| Heavy Rain | *Dayu, Baoyu, Yinyu* |
| Drought | *Han, Ganhe, Jie, Wuyu, Shaoyu, Weiyu* |
| Wind | *Feng* |
| Hail | *Bao* |
| Earthquake | *Dizhen* |
| Snow, Ice, Frost | *Xue, Bing, Dong, Shuang* |
| *Aftermath* | |
| Disease | *Wen, Yi* |
| Famine | *Ji, Huang, E, Ren Xiangshi* |
| Infestation | *Huang, Nan, Chong, Ming* |
| Flood | *Shuizai, Shuihuan, Pishui, Dashui, Hongshui, Jiao, Xiashui, Qiushui, Lao, Jue, Yi, Man, Zhang, Yan, Piaomo, Ni, Chongpi* |

(*shu*), "fruitful autumn" (*youqiu*). Bad harvests are indicated with such keywords as "scant" (*qian*), "poor year" (*suiqian*), "greatly poor year" (*suidaqian*), "poor harvest" (*qianshou*), "thin harvest" (*boshou*). Categories for meteorological events included heavy rain (*dayu, baoyu, yinyu*), drought (*gan, ganhe, jie, wuyu, shaoyu, weiyu*), wind (*feng*), hail (*bao*), earthquakes (*dizhen*) and snow, frost, or ice (*xue, bing, dong*).[16] Categories for aftermath events included disease, famine, infestation, and flood.[17]

We have yet to categorize events according to their severity or the possible culpability of officials. Most of the records are from local gazetteers, and there were no regional or national standards for making categorizations. What might have been regarded as severe at one time or place may have been regarded as routine somewhere else. While the records sometimes include additional details suggestive of the severity of events or indicated how long the event lasted, these were not consistent. Similarly, we are not yet able to separate floods solely due to extreme rain from those arising from the neglect of preventive measures such as dike maintenance. We expect that the latter would have been much more consequential for officials' careers.

A major limitation is that we only observe that an event occurred, and do not observe an official's response to it, which presumably would have been the most important for their regular assessment. The most promising event for study is infestation, since as discussed earlier, locust plagues were regarded as preventable, and for one to even occur was regarded as a failure on the part of an official, at least in the county in which it was believed to originate. While in certain locations, floods were also regarded as preventable via the upkeep of dikes and dams, there were other floods that were natural and nearly impossible to preventable, for example, as the result of extended periods of excessive rainfall. At present we can't distinguish the former from the latter. Along these lines, while some disease epidemics may have been regarded as preventable, or at least manageable, the records in the *Compendium* typically only mention the general term *wenyi* and do not specify the specific disease.

### 7.3.4 Contents of the Dataset

Floods and droughts were the most common disasters. Table 4 tabulates the disasters that we consider in our analysis by decade. According to Table 7.4, from 1780 to 1909, there were a total of 13,430 records that we categorized as floods, averaging more than 100 per year. This is a somewhat higher frequency than suggested in

---

[16] We did not create categories for events like lightning (*leidian*) or fog (*shuang*) since it is unclear whether they would have constituted disasters, as opposed to unusual events that while rare enough to be noteworthy, had little in the way of consequences.

[17] For a record to be coded as a flood, there had to be keywords suggestive of a large volume of water. These often appeared in conjunction with keywords indicating heavy rain, but not always. Sometimes heavy rain was recorded with no annotation to suggest flooding, and sometimes flooding was recorded with no annotation to indicate heavy rain.

**Table 7.4** Floods, droughts, famines, infestation, and epidemics by decade

| Year | Flood | Drought | Famine | Infestation | Epidemic |
|---|---|---|---|---|---|
| 1780–1789 | 774 | 688 | 485 | 115 | 143 |
| 1790–1799 | 733 | 284 | 220 | 74 | 41 |
| 1800–1809 | 884 | 524 | 306 | 133 | 57 |
| 1810–1819 | 841 | 690 | 448 | 74 | 104 |
| 1820–1829 | 1046 | 502 | 239 | 149 | 331 |
| 1830–1839 | 1278 | 744 | 655 | 442 | 173 |
| 1840–1849 | 1298 | 386 | 336 | 117 | 76 |
| 1850–1859 | 1133 | 618 | 399 | 776 | 152 |
| 1860–1869 | 1202 | 547 | 385 | 257 | 309 |
| 1870–1879 | 1267 | 1026 | 626 | 274 | 204 |
| 1880–1889 | 1219 | 299 | 203 | 83 | 161 |
| 1890–1899 | 965 | 440 | 306 | 202 | 176 |
| 1900–1909 | 790 | 499 | 268 | 146 | 194 |
| Total | 13,430 | 7247 | 4876 | 2842 | 2121 |

previous research (Zhang 2015).[18] There were 7247 drought events, 4876 famines, 2842 infestations, and 2121 epidemics. Numbers fluctuated greatly from one decade to the next. The decade from 1870 to 1879 included the North China Famine of 1876–1879 (*Dingwu Qihuang*) and accordingly had an especially large number of droughts and famines. The decade from 1830 to 1839 was also notable for having many records of famines. Records of floods, meanwhile, seem to have been especially common in the 1830s and 1840s. Infestation records were especially common in the 1850s and to a lesser extent the 1830s.

There is a significant variation across provinces in the number of records available. Table 7.5 tabulates events by contemporary province-level unit, as recorded in the *Compendium*. The northeastern provinces had the fewest records, followed by the northwestern provinces.[19] Xinjiang had the fewest meteorological records, with only 12 entries. Qinghai, Inner Mongolia, and Ningxia followed, with 45, 53, and 87 entries, respectively. Heilongjiang and Jilin, both border regions in the northeast and northwest, had 102 and 109 entries respectively. The provinces with the highest number of records were Shandong and Hebei, with 4,059 and 3,517 entries, respectively. Further investigation is necessary to assess how much of this variation is real, and how much reflects differences across regions in the production, level of detail, or survival of the gazetteers on which the *Compendium* relied.

[18] According to this research, over the course of the entire Qing, there were 19009 county-level flood disasters, averaging about 71 county-level occurrences per year, with large fluctuations from year to year.

[19] Regions that cannot be identified have been excluded from this analysis.

**Table 7.5** Record counts by region and contemporary province

| Region | Province | Records(N) |
|---|---|---|
| Northeast | Heilongjiang | 88 |
| | Jilin | 100 |
| | Liaoning | 282 |
| | Subtotal | 470 |
| North | Hebei | 3462 |
| | Beijing | 173 |
| | Tianjin | 213 |
| | Shanxi | 2342 |
| | Inner Mongolia | 53 |
| | Subtotal | 6243 |
| Central | Henan | 2302 |
| | Hubei | 2113 |
| | Hunan | 2141 |
| | Subtotal | 6556 |
| South | Guangdong | 2152 |
| | Guangxi | 1256 |
| | Hainan | 211 |
| | Subtotal | 3619 |
| East | Fujian | 993 |
| | Shandong | 3966 |
| | Jiangsu | 2470 |
| | Shanghai | 635 |
| | Zhejiang | 2318 |
| | Anhui | 1658 |
| | Jiangxi | 2023 |
| | Taiwan | 207 |
| | Subtotal | 14270 |
| Northwest | Xinjiang | 12 |
| | Gansu | 576 |
| | Ningxia | 85 |
| | Shaanxi | 1509 |
| | Qinghai | 44 |
| | Subtotal | 2226 |
| Southwest | Yunnan | 1209 |
| | Guizhou | 628 |
| | Sichuan | 2163 |
| | Tibet | 117 |
| | Subtotal | 4117 |

### *7.3.5 Producing the Analytic File*

We merge the information from the county-year records in the *Compendium* into the records of magistrates in the CGED-Q JSL in a series of steps. As mentioned above, we first collapse the originally quarterly CGED-Q JSL records into annual records. These include an indicator of whether an official was observed at least once as a magistrate in that year. We then match the county names originally recorded in the CGED-Q JSL to the county names in the 1820 and 1911 Harvard CH-GIS datasets. If the CGED-Q JSL county name matches to an 1820 county name in the CH-GIS, we obtain the contemporary county name from that record. In cases where there is no match to the 1820 file but there is a match to the 1911 file, we use the contemporary county name from the matched 1911 record.[20] Once we attached the contemporary county names to the records of magistrates, we matched to the records from the *Compendium* and attached the binary variables for the occurrence of events.

## 7.4 Methods

To examine the effects of infestations, famines, epidemics, droughts, and floods on the chances that an official would end their career in the current or next year, we estimate logistic regressions. Because we are interested in whether the occurrence of a disaster leads to an immediate or nearly immediate career end, the dependent variable is a constructed indicator of whether the current calendar year or the following calendar year is the last in which an official is observed in the CGED-Q JSL. To account for differences over time in models without interactions discussed below, we include categorical variables for each decade.

We account for unmeasured characteristics of the province or county with fixed effects. This addresses the possibility that a province or a county is located and characterized by especially frequent or infrequent events, which may have been related to the types of officials who were assigned there, and their career prospects. We begin with a model that includes fixed effects of province and then consider fixed effects of the county. The province fixed-effect model uses a categorical variable for province, while the models for county were estimated as conditional logits. The results for county compare magistrates serving in the same county who differed according to whether an event occurred in the specified year.

As noted above, we compare the effects of the different disasters for insight into whether career endings were related to the application of rules. We expect infestations to have had the clearest effects on career termination, since their occurrence was automatically regarded as *prima facie* evidence of duties being neglected. Famines should have had some effect since the state regarded their prevention and management as an important responsibility (Will 1990; Will et al. 1991). Floods may have had

[20] Most of the county names match to the 1820 file, but some county names that changed or were produced by the division of existing counties in the late nineteenth century match to the 1911 file.

an effect, but possibly on the careers of officials who had already moved on, since they may have been the result of neglect in earlier years. We expect droughts to have had mild or no direct effects, since officials had no control over rainfall. While some officials may have bungled their response to a drought and been terminated, we have no way of observing their management of the drought. Similarly, we doubt officials could be held directly responsible for the occurrence of an epidemic. While their management of it may have been subpar, we have no way of observing it.

We also examine whether the effects of disasters on the chance of a career ending varied over time, by whether a magistrate had an exam or purchased degree, and by the rated difficulty of the county. For this, we estimate additional models with interactions with a continuous measure of calendar year, an indicator of whether an official had an examination or purchased degree, and a count of the number of characters in the field for the county's *chongfan pinan*.[21] To the extent that the capacity of the Qing state to enforce its own personnel rules deteriorated during the nineteenth century, we expect that the effects of a disaster on the chances of a career ending would decline over time. In case the time trend is not linear, we also experiment with an alternative specification that includes a categorical variable for decade. As for the effects of qualification, we expect that purchase degree holders were more likely to be affected by disasters because they were less likely to have networks of exam classmates who could help them (Zhang 2022). We expect that a disaster in a county with a higher *chongfan pinan* rating would be more consequential for the magistrate since magistrates in those locations were subject to greater scrutiny.

## 7.5 Results

Only infestation or famine in the current year increased the chances that the current or next year would be a county magistrate's last year. Table 7.6 presents the results of the logistic regression of career termination according to type of event and harvest. In the model with fixed effects of province, an infestation increased the odds of an immediate career end by 22.8%. The strong results for infestation are consistent with the notion that infestation was regarded as preventable and that when they occurred, it was the result of negligence or incompetence, leading to termination. The effect of famine had a nearly identical effect, raising the odds of a career end by 22.9%. Such results are not a surprise: successive Chinese states, including the Qing, regarded famine management as an important responsibility (Will 1990; Will 1991). Flood, drought, and epidemics had no effects on the chance of a career ending, presumably because ascribing blame was more difficult. Droughts and epidemics were not

[21] Administrative units were categorized according to their *chong* (importance as a transportation hub), complexity (*fan*), difficulty (*nan*), and financial situation (*pi*). The total number of characters ranged between 0 and 4, in which 4 indicates that a county was complex, difficult, a transportation hub, and was a difficult place to raise taxes.

**Table 7.6** Logistic regression of career termination this or next year of county magistrates on disasters in the current year, 1830–1905

| | Province fixed effect | | County fixed effect | |
|---|---|---|---|---|
| | Coef | p-value | Coef | p-value |
| Flood | −0.057 | 0.41 | −0.026 | 0.72 |
| Drought | −0.056 | 0.50 | −0.046 | 0.60 |
| Famine | 0.206 | 0.03 | 0.230 | 0.02 |
| Infestation | 0.205 | 0.04 | 0.214 | 0.04 |
| Epidemic | −0.129 | 0.42 | −0.102 | 0.53 |
| N | 80,222 | | 79,259 | |

*Note* All models include a categorical variable for decade, but the coefficients is omitted to save space. The province model included provincial fixed effects, and the coefficients are omitted to save space

easily preventable, and floods may have been the responsibility of predecessors who neglected water course management, or officials in counties upstream.

There was no evidence from models that included interactions of disasters with linear and categorical measures of calendar year, degree qualification, or the *chongfan pinan* rating that the effects of disasters on career endings varied according to any of these. In other words, exam degree holders did not have any advantage, either because they and purchase degree holders performed similarly or were evaluated similarly. Magistrates in high *chongfan pinan* counties were not unusually sensitive to disasters, and there was no linear trend in the effects of disaster suggestive of a systematic decline in the capacity of the state to enforce regulations. When we considered interactions with decade, it was apparent that the adverse effects of infestation on the chances of a career end were high in the 1820s, the 1850s, and the 1870s, and modest in the remaining decades, but the differences are not statistically significant.

## 7.6 Conclusion

We have shown that in a situation where there was a clearly specified rule based on objective criteria for the assessment of the performance of officials for which we have relevant data, the Qing state retained the capacity to follow basic rules for personnel management. Infestations and famines that had an immediate effect on the careers of county magistrates. Both increased the chances that a career would end in the current or next year. At least for infestations, this is straightforward to explain since it is consistent with personnel regulations that made magistrates responsible for prevention of locust infestations and specified clearly that they should be punished if an infestation took place. For famines, given the importance attached by the state to their prevention and management, it appears reasonable to conclude that officials were being held to account in a similar fashion.

Lack of effect for other disasters suggests that the results for infestations and famines were not simply the result of officials being punished indiscriminately for anything untoward that happened, without regard for their actual culpability. Epidemics and droughts, which would be difficult to attribute to the actions of a magistrate, had no effect. While regulations related to floods were detailed, they could still occur even if a magistrate had been attentive to their responsibilities, or if a magistrate's predecessor had neglected their duties, and it seems reasonable to conclude that is responsible for the lack of a direct effect.

We found no evidence of systematic variation in the enforcement of the rules according to time, degree qualification, or the characteristics of the county. Regarding time, there was no suggestion of a steady downward trend in the effects of infestation or famine. Interactions with a categorical variable for decade suggest that infestations had stronger career-ending effects in the 1820s, 1850s, and 1870s, but we cannot rule out the possibility that these fluctuations were noise. For qualification, as reflected in whether an official had an exam or purchased degree, there were no apparent differences in the effects of any of the disasters. For famines and infestations, in other words, exam degree holders were not insulted by their networks. Similarly, for *chongfan pinan*, a higher rating did not seem to make officials' careers more sensitive to any of the disasters, including famine and infestation, even though officials in those counties were scrutinized more carefully.

These results contribute to the growing literature on Qing state capacity. It is distinctive in terms of its focus on low-level officials, i.e., county magistrates, and the use of performance measures, the occurrence of disasters, which in the case of infestations are objective measures of performance. Previous studies have mainly focused on higher-level bureaucrats and used broader measures of performance such as tax revenues (e.g., Ma 2013; Peng 2018; Yang 2022). We also contribute to the recent literature on selection processes and bureaucratic performance by showing that for measures like the occurrence of infestations and famines, there is no evidence that exam and purchase degree holders performed or were evaluated differently (Liu 2025; Liu and Zhang 2023).

We intend to advance research on the relationship of disasters to official careers in several directions. Most importantly, we hope to link additional spatial data on terrain, hydrology, and other characteristics to examine whether some events that seem not to have an effect overall are important in specific settings. For example, we expect that flooding may have had stronger effects on careers in riverine areas with dams and dikes that officials were responsible for maintaining, and weaker effects in areas without such infrastructure where flooding, when it occurred, was mainly the result of heavy rainfall and not regarded as preventable. We will also reverse the analysis to investigate whether disasters were more likely under certain types of officials, for example, those with purchased degrees or with fewer years of experience. We will also move the analysis up one level in the administrative hierarchy to examine prefects and consider additional administrative units including county-level *sanzhou* and prefectural-level *zhilizhou*. We believe that for ambitious young officials who have just entered the bureaucracy, especially those who seem to have little chance of advancement through the normal route, disasters or other crises provide a direct path to the center of power.

**Acknowledgements** This research was supported by HK RGC General Research Fund 16602621 (Campbell PI) and HK RGC Areas of Excellence AoE/B-704/22-R (Zhiwu Chen PC).

Previous versions of this paper were presented at the Area of Excellence–Quantitative History Conference 2023, held at The University of Hong Kong on October 25-26, 2023, the session entitled Intergenerational and Intragenerational Social Mobility Using Historical Data at the 2023 Social Science History Association meetings in Washington DC and at the 2024 American Sociological Association meetings in Montreal. We are grateful to the participants for their comments and suggestions. We are also grateful to members of the Lee-Campbell Group for their comments and suggestions.

## Glossary

| Pinyin | Characters | English (if available) |
|---|---|---|
| Bao | 雹 | Hail |
| Baoyu | 暴雨 | Heavy Rain |
| Bing | 冰 | Ice |
| Boshou | 薄收 | Harvest |
| Chong | 虫 | Infestation |
| Chongfan Pinan | 衝繁疲難 | Central, complex, finance issues, difficult |
| Chongpi | 冲圮 | Flood |
| Daren | 大稔 | Harvest |
| Dashu | 大熟 | Harvest |
| Dashui | 大水 | Flood |
| Dayou | 大有 | Harvest |
| Dayu | 大雨 | Heavy rain |
| Da Younian | 大有年 | Very good harvest |
| Dingwu Qihuang | 丁戊奇荒 | North China Famine |
| Dizhen | 地震 | Earthquake |
| Dong | 冻 | Ice |
| E | 饿 | Famine |
| Feng | 丰 | Harvest |
| Feng | 风 | Wind |
| Fengshou | 丰收 | Harvest |
| Ganhe | 干涸 | Drought |
| Han | 旱 | Drought |
| Hongshui | 洪水 | Flood |
| Huang | 荒 | Famine |
| Huang | 蝗 | Infestation |

(continued)

(continued)

| Pinyin | Characters | English (if available) |
|---|---|---|
| Jianzhen Guan | 監賑官 | Disaster relief officer |
| Ji | 饥 | Famine |
| Jiao | 蛟 | Flood |
| Jie | 竭 | Drought |
| Jue | 决 | Flood |
| Lao | 涝 | Flood |
| Leidian | 雷电 | Lightning |
| Man | 漫 | Flood |
| Ming | 螟 | Infestation |
| Nan | 蝻 | Infestation |
| Ni | 溺 | Flood |
| Piaomo | 漂没 | Flood |
| Pishui | 被水 | Flood |
| Qian | 歉 | Harvest |
| Qiujian | 秋俭 | Harvest |
| Qiushui | 秋水 | Flood |
| Ren | 稔 | Harvest |
| Ren Xiangshi | 人相食 | Famine (Resulting in cannibalism) |
| Sanzhou | 散州 | A county-level administrative unit |
| Shaoyu | 少雨 | Drought |
| Shu | 熟 | Harvest |
| Shuli | 署理 | Acting |
| Shuang | 霜 | Frost |
| Shuihuan | 水患 | Flood |
| Shuizai | 水灾 | Flood |
| Suiqian | 岁歉 | Harvest |
| Sui Daqian | 岁大歉 | Harvest |
| Weiyu | 微雨 | Drought |
| Wen | 瘟 | Disease |
| Wenyi | 瘟疫 | Disease/epidemic |
| Wuyu | 无雨 | Drought |
| Xiashui | 夏水 | Flood |
| Xue | 雪 | Snow |
| Yan | 淹 | Flood |
| Yi | 疫 | Disease |
| Yi | 溢 | Flood |
| Yinyu | 霪雨 | Heavy Rain |
| Younian | 有年 | Good Harvest |
| Zhang | 涨 | Flood |
| Zhilizhou | 直隸州 | A prefecture-level administrative unit |
| Zhizhou | 知州 | Magistrate (of a county-level unit *sanzhou*) |

## Primary Sources

| Pinyin | Characters | English (if available) |
|---|---|---|
| Chufen Zeyao Tuli | 處分則要圖例 | |
| Da Qing Huidian Shili | 大清會典事例 | |
| Da Qing Lvli | 大清律例 | Resumes of the Qing |
| Huangchao Jingshi Wen Bian | 皇朝經世文編 | |
| Huangzheng Jiyao | 荒政輯要 | |
| Qing Xuanzong Shilu | 清宣宗實錄 | Veritable Records of the Emperor Xuanzong of the Qing Dynasty |
| Qing Gaozong Shilu | 清高宗實錄 | The Veritable Records of Emperor Gaozong of the Qing Dynasty |
| Qing Shizong Shilu | 清世宗實錄 | The Veritable Records of Emperor Shizong of the Qing Dynasty |
| Qing Shilu | 清實錄 | Veritable Records |

## Referencess


Besley, Timothy, Robin Burgess, Adnan Khan, and Guo Xu. 2022. Bureaucracy and Development. *Annual Review of Economics* 14 (1): 397–424. https://doi.org/10.1146/annurev-economics-080521-011950.

Chen, Bijia, Cameron Campbell, Yuxue Ren, and James Lee. 2020. Big Data for the Study of Qing Officialdom: The China Government Employee Database-Qing (CGED-Q). *Journal of Chinese History* 4 (2): 431–460. https://doi.org/10.1017/jch.2020.15.

邓云特. 中国救荒史. 上海: 商务印书馆. 1937. [Deng, Yunte. 1937. *The History of Drought Relief in China*. Shanghai: The Commercial Press].

冯贤亮. "灾荒危机与地方社会——咸丰年间桐乡知县戴槃的活动与记述." 史学集刊, 5 (2018): 67–76. [Feng, Xianliang. 2018. Drought Crises and Local Society: The Activity and Descriptions of Tongxiang County Magistrate Dai Pan During the Reign of Xianfeng. *Collected Papers of History Studies* 5: 67–76].

胡存璐. "清代州县官署理制度研究." 史学月刊, no. 8 (2022): 54–67. [Hu, Cunlu. 2022. Research on Acting Appointments of County Magistrates in the Qing Dynasty. *Journal of Historical Science* 8: 54–67].

蒋勇军. "李星沅与晚清两江赈灾." 求索, no. 10 (2014): 157–61. [Jiang, Yongjun. 2014. Li Xingyuan and Disaster Relief in Liangjiang During the Late Qing. *Seeker* 10: 157–161].

梁其姿. 施善與教化:明清的慈善組織. 台北:聯經出版事业公司, 1997. [Leung, Angela Ki Che. 1997. *Charity and Moral Transformation: Philanthropic Organizations of the Ming and Qing periods*. Taipei: Linking Publishers].

李伯元. 官场现形记. 香港大学出版社, 2001 (1903). [Li, Boyuan. 2001 (1903). *Officialdom Unmasked*. Hong Kong University Press].

Li, Lillian M. 2007. *Fighting Famine in North China : State, Market, and Environmental Decline, 1690s–1990s*. Stanford, CA: Stanford University Press.

李文海 and 夏明方. 中国荒政全书. 北京: 北京古籍出版社, 2005 [Li, Wenhai and Xia Mingfang, Eds. 2005. *The Complete Collection of Historical Sources on China's Disaster Relief*. Beijing: Beijing Ancient Book Publishing House].

梁霄雲. "由权宜到定制:清代州县长官'署任'制度考——以四川成都府为例." 成都大学学报(社会科学版), no. 2 (2023): 90–99. https://doi.org/10.3969/j.issn.1004-342X.2023.02.007 [Liang, Xiaoyun. 2003. From Expediency to Customization- Examination of "Acting Appointment" System for Prefecture and County Magistrates in the Qing Dynasty—The Example of Chengdu Fu in Sichuan Province. *Journal of Chengdu University - Social Sciences* 2: 90–99. https://doi.org/10.3969/j.issn.1004-342X.2023.02.007].

Liu, Kevin Zhengcheng, and Xiaoming Zhang. 2023. Merit-Based Recruitment and Government Performance: Evidence from Random Assignment of Administrators. Unpublished manuscript.

Liu, Kevin Zhengcheng, and Xiaoming Zhang. 2025. Discretion, Talent Allocation, and Governance Performance: Evidence from China's Imperial Bureaucracy. *Journal of Development Economics* 172: 103391. https://doi.org/10.1016/j.jdeveco.2024.103391.

Ma, Debin. 2013. State Capacity and Great Divergence, the Case of Qing China (1644–1911). *Eurasian Geography and Economics* 54 (5–6): 484–499. https://doi.org/10.1080/15387216.2014.907530.

Peng, Peng. 2018. War, Bureaucracy, and State Capacity: Evidence from Imperial China, (November 12, version. Unpublished manuscript. Accessed at https://sites.duke.edu/statecapacity/files/2019/04/Peng-2019-War-Bureaucracy-State-Capacity-in-China.pdf.

Pomeranz, Kenneth. 2021. *The Great Divergence : China, Europe, and the Making of the Modern World Economy*. Princeton, NJ: Princeton University Press. https://doi.org/10.1515/9780691217192.

任玉雪, 陈必佳, 郝小雯, 康文林 and 李中清. "清代缙绅录量化数据库与官员群体研究." 清史研究, no. 4 (2016): 61–77 [Ren, Yuxue, Chen Bijia, Hao Xiaowen, Cameron Campbell, James Z. Lee. 2016. The Qing Jinshenlu Database: A New Source for the Study of Qing Officials. *The Qing History Journal*, 4: 61–77].

Weber, Max. 1922. *Economy and Society*. Berkeley: University of California Press.

Will, Pierre-Etienne. 1990. *Bureaucracy and Famine in Eighteenth-Century China*. Stanford, CA: Stanford University Press.

Will, Pierre-Etienne, James Z Lee, and R. Bin Wong. 1991. *Nourish the People: The State Civilian Granary System in China, 1650–1850*. Ann Arbor, MI: University of Michigan Press. https://doi.org/10.3998/mpub.19044.

吴佩林 and 万海荞."清代州县官任期'三年一任'说质疑——基于四川南部县知县的实证分析." 清华大学学报:哲学社会科学版, no. 3 (2018): 63–72 [Wu, Peilin and Wan Haiqiao. 2018. Questioning the Three-year Tenure of the County Magistrate in the Qing Dynasty-An Empirical Analysis of Magistrates in the Southern County in Sichuan. *Journal of Tsinghua University (Philosophy and Social Sciences)* 3: 63–72].

Yang, Clair. 2022. On Determinants of State Capacity: Wars, Public Goods, and Economic Shocks, February 17. https://doi.org/10.2139/ssrn.4037620.

张德二 and 蒋光美. 中国三千年气象记录总集. 凤凰出版社、江苏教育出版社, 2005. [Zhang, De'er and Jiang Guangmei. 2005. Compendium of Meteorological Records in China of Three Thousand Years. Phoenix Press and Jiangsu Educational Press.

张琨佳, 刘璐 and 苏筠. "中国清代历史水灾时空特征研究." 自然灾害学报 24, no. 4 (2015): 104–10. [Zhang, Kunjia, Liu Lu and Su Yun. 2015. Research on the Spatial and Temporary Characteristics of Floods During the Qing. *The Journal of Natural Disasters* 24 (4): 104–110].

Zhang, Lawrence. 2022. *Power for a Price : The Purchase of Official Appointments in Qing China.* Cambridge, MA: Harvard University Asia Center.

张秀红. 姚碧、汪志伊的<荒政辑要>比较研究. 硕士学位论文,安徽大学.2010 [Zhang, Xiuhong. 2010. *Comparative studies of two versions of Huangzheng jiyao edited by Yao, Bi and Wang, Zhiyi.* Master's Thesis, Anhui University].

赵晓华. "清代州县救灾机制研究——以道光二十八年仪征水灾赈济为例." 山西大学学报:哲学社会科学版 38, no. 6 (2015): 43–48 [Zhao, Xiaohua. 2015. Disaster Relief Mechanisms of Prefectures and Counties During the Qing: A Case Study of Flood Relief in Yizheng in Daoguang Year 28. *Journal of Shanxi University—Philosophy and Social Science Edition* 38 (6): 43–48].

赵晓华. "晚清州县官视野中的救灾活动——以柳堂《灾赈日记》为中心." 华南师范大学学报(社会科学版), no. 4 (2018): 178–183. [Zhao, Xiaohua. 2018. Disaster Relief Activities from the Perspective of County Officials in the Late Qing—Based on Liu Tang's Disaster Relief Diary. *Journal of South China Normal University–Social Science Edition* 4: 178–183].

郑民德. "灾荒与民变:略论道光十七年山东潍县马刚天柱教叛乱." 济南大学学报:社会科学版 22, no. 5 (2012): 52–55 [Zheng, Minde. (2012). Drought and Rebellion: Discussion on Ma Gang Tianzhujiao Rebel in Shandong Weixian County in Daoguang Year 17. *Journal of Ji'nan University—Social Science Edition 22,* 5 : 52–55].

**Cameron Campbell** is Chair Professor in the Division of Social Science at The Hong Kong University of Science and Technology (HKUST). He is also a Distinguished Professor in the School of History and Culture at Central China Normal University. His research focuses on demography, stratification, and inequality in historical China and in comparative perspective. For his research, he and his collaborators in the Lee-Campbell Group construct, analyze, and publicly release datasets constructed from archival and other sources. He was a Fellow of the Center for Advanced Study in the Behavioral Sciences at Stanford 2022–2023, and a Guggenheim Fellow in 2004–2005. He was a Changjiang Scholar at Central China Normal University from 2017 to 2020.

**Shuaiqi Gao** is a Ph.D. candidate at the School of History and Culture at Central China Normal University in Wuhan. His research areas are quantitative history and the Chinese bureaucracy. For his Ph.D. dissertation, he is applying traditional and quantitative methods to study river officials during the Qing. His papers include "The Organizational Demography of the Qing Civil Service, 1830–1911)" which was published in *Shehui Kexue Yanjiu (Social Science Research)*, co-authored with Professor Cameron Campbell. He also published "An Analysis of Rural Family Income in Northeast Hubei in 1952," in 2025 in *Da Shuju yu Zhongguo Lishi Yanjiu (Big Data and Chinese Historical Research).* He is a member of the Lee-Campbell Research Group.

# Part III
# State Capacity, Fiscal and Financial Development

# Chapter 8
# How to Finance Wars: The Crisis of Securities in Northern Song China During the 1040 s

**William Guanglin Liu and Kai Wan Kwan**

## 8.1 Introduction

In 1039 CE, the conflict between the Northern Song and the Tangut Xi Xia escalated into a large-scale war on the northwestern frontier. From 1039 to 1042, the Song armies suffered three major defeats on the battlefield: Sanchuankou, Haoshuichuan, and Dingchuan Fort. To provision the armies on the northwestern border, the Song state carried out a massive provisioning program *(ruzhong)* that enticed merchants to supply goods to the military at the frontier through vouchers redeemable in cash, tea, or salt. While the Song state suffered catastrophic defeats on the battlefield, it also underwent a financial crisis directly provoked by the war. It was not until the late 1040 s that the Song state largely overcame these crises and the domestic market regained prosperity.

This article aims to assess the state capacity of the Northern Song from a military-fiscal perspective, especially its fiscal capability of waging wars in the eleventh century. The current scholarship mainly contributes to the study of the military and political history and overwhelmingly focuses on the questions such as what policies led to the Northern Song's military defeats and the failure of the Qingli Reform (1043–45), why the Song court decided to fight against the Tanguts, whether the military

The financial supports from the RGC funds of AoE/B-704/22-R and GRF 13,604,222 enabled us to conduct this project. We presented the working paper at the conferences held at Yale and The University of Hong Kong in 2023 and received important feedback. We would also like to extend our appreciation to the two reviewers who provided valuable comments and suggestions on how to revise this paper for publication.

W. G. Liu (✉)
Lingnan University, Hong Kong, China
e-mail: guanglinliu@ln.edu.hk

K. W. Kwan
Hong Kong Shue Yan University, Hong Kong, China
e-mail: kwkwan@hksyu.edu



Z. Chen et al. (eds.), *Quantitative History of China*, Studies in Economic History,
https://doi.org/10.1007/978-981-96-8272-0_8

defeats avoidable (Li 2010; Tsang 1997), and on whom the factional struggle that had permeated Northern Song's central politics should be blamed (Qi 2009, 215–235; Fang 2001, 186–288). This policy-centered narrative, though well justified on its own grounds, has largely ignored the important connection between military mobilization and state finance as an important factor that best indicates how the Chinese state power waged that war. By drawing on both quantitative and qualitative evidence preserved in primary sources such as *Xu Zizhi tongjian changbian*, *Song shi,* and *Song huiyao jigao,* this chapter aims to provide a comprehensive framework for understanding pre-modern China's state capacity by integrating military and financial history.[1]

A cross-dynastic comparison is adopted to demonstrate the full evolution of military financing up to the mid-eleventh century. We look specifically at how the military's market-based procurement of grains started with prepayments by the state in the seventh-century Tang dynasty, then grew until it ultimately evolved into more financing by traders, often in exchange for monopoly rights on key commodities such as salt or tea toward the end of the tenth century. In the succeeding century, as war and financial headwinds increased risks at the market, the merchants won the opportunity to trade those rights, leading to a de facto securities market as well as a new administrative body to essentially regulate growing military-financial-related securities and markets.

## 8.2 The Origin and Pattern of the Provisioning Policy in the Eighth Century

Military logistics occupied a central place in the administration of imperial China, as the court deployed many soldiers across its broad territory. In the early period of the Tang dynasty (618–907 CE), transferring grain taxes to the military posts, occasionally in combination with the military-run farms and the cultivation of land by the soldiers themselves, constituted the major supply of grain to the army. When the Tang court extended its military forces into Central Asia in the seventh century, however, the shipment of grain via long-distance land transportation to the northwestern frontier became a crucial challenge. To address this issue, the Tang local administrations in the northwest, particularly in the prefectures along the Silk Road,

[1] *Song huiyao jigao*, literally Song Compendium, was the official documents originally compiled by the statemen in the Song Dynasty China (960–1279). It included a great number of decrees and edicts. The current version was a collection made available in the early nineteenth century from the Yongle Encyclopedia. Both *Xu Zizhi tongjian changbian* and *Song shi* were historical narratives about the Song dynasty. The former was published in 1182 and focused on the Northern Song period (960–1127). The latter was compiled in 1343–1345 and covered the whole history of the Song dynasty. Currently, existing literature tends to treat these two themes separately. Guo's work (Guo 1990b, 741–56, 916–34), for instance, investigates how the Song state encouraged merchant involvement in the *ruzhong* provisioning program by adjusting the salt monopoly policy and granting considerable discounts to merchants. At the same time, Wang (2003, 528–542) outlines the financial crisis that occurred in Shaanxi following the minting and circulation of iron coins in the late 1040 s.

**Table 8.1** Prices of military provisions in Dunhuang, 745 AD

| Type | Market prices (*wen* cash per *dou*) | Official procurement rates (*wen* cash per *dou*) |
|---|---|---|
| Millet | 27 | 32 |
| Wheat | 32 | 37 |
| Barley | 30 | 35 |
| Unhusked rice | 27 | 32 |
| Pea | 29 | 34 |

*Sources* Lu 2012, 124

set up granaries for purchasing the grain from farmers and merchants, in a new system of defense procurement known as "harmonious purchase".[2] Under this arrangement, the granaries acted as a lender, paying at a rate slightly above the market price in advance, up to six months, for a predetermined amount of grain such as millet, wheat, and barley. The prepayments were paid with textiles to the equivalent values. A record of a military granary discovered in modern Dunhuang indicates that most transactions involving the grain procurement were conducted at the exchange rates of 27–30 *wen* cash per *dou* (斗,a measure equivalent to about 10 L). That price was higher than the nominal market prices (see Table 8.1).

As the size of the garrisons grew, the Tang state began to recognize the increasing importance of public purchases in supplying military provisions, particularly in the capital region (Guanzhong) and at the northwestern frontier. By the mid-eighth century, the volume of grains procured through "harmonious purchases" from the private sector had surged to approximately 4.2 million *shi*, accounting for roughly 47%- of the total military supply (see Table 8.2).

As shown in Table 8.2, the grain provisions from the "harmonious purchases" were confined to the administrative districts along the Silk Road, especially from the three regions in the northwest. The purchased grain from Hexi, Shuofang, and Longyou amounted to 3412.5 *shi*, about 81% of the total. In contrast, the supplies of grain to troops in other regions, such as Pinglu and Fanyang (modern Beijing) in northeast China, Jiannan (modern Sichuan) and Lingnan (modern Guangdong and Guangxi) mostly came from both military farming and land taxes. Furthermore, credit had been rarely used in the official procurement before the tenth century. As discussed in the case of Dunhuang, the prepayment approach had been deployed when the granaries planned to purchase grain from local villagers and most transactions were often completed in small sums by short-term loans. A major step forward in the public purchase took place after the An Lushan Rebellion (755–763). As part of the salt monopoly reform, the court set up an annual provision quota of 150,000 *shi* (石)of rice (approximately 15 million liters) in 821, in exchange of which the grain-supply merchants were paid with the salt produced from the state-owned Wuchi Salt Pond at

[2] The authorities in traditional China often referred the cases of public purchases of grain for the military purposes to the term of "harmonious purchase" (*hedi*和糴). Regarding the study of "harmonious purchases" during the Tang dynasty, see Lu (2012, 90–107).

**Table 8.2** Major sources of procurement quotas in China, 742–756 AD

| Macroregion | Harmonious purchase (000 *shi*) | Percentage | Military farming (000 *shi*) | Percentage | Land tax or other sources (000 *shi*) | Percentage |
|---|---|---|---|---|---|---|
| **Inner Asia** | | | | | | |
| Beiting | 105 | 26.33% | 293.8 | 73.67% | 0 | 0 |
| Anxi | 158 | 37.57% | 261.7 | 62.43% | 0 | 0 |
| **Northwest** | | | | | | |
| Hexi | 1050 | 71.12% | 426.3 | 28.88% | 0 | 0 |
| Shuofang | 1050 | 83.57% | 206.4 | 26.43% | 0 | 0 |
| Longyou | 1312.5 | 96.92% | 41.7 | 3.08% | 0 | 0 |
| **North / Northeast** | | | | | | |
| Hedong | 525 | 47.06% | 90.6 | 8.12% | 500 | 44.82% |
| Pinglu | 0 | 0 | 678 | 100% | 0 | 0 |
| Fanyang | 0 | 0 | 828.2 | 54.19% | 700 | 45.81% |
| **Southwest** | | | | | | |
| Jiannan | 0 | 0 | 0 | 0 | 513.1 | 100% |
| **Southeast** | | | | | | |
| Lingnan | 0 | 0 | 0 | 0 | 237.8 | 100% |
| **Total** | 4200.5 | 46.79% | 2826.7 | 31.48% | 1950.9 | 21.73% |

*Note*: For the administrative districts in the Tang dynasty, Hexi is roughly located in modern western Gansu and eastern Xinjiang regions, while Shuofang and Longyou are located in modern Ningxia and eastern Gansu respectively. Hedong corresponds to modern Shanxi, while Pinglu and Fanyang correspond to the areas of modern Liaoning and Beijing areas respectively. Jiannan corresponds to modern Sichuan. Lingnan correspond to modern Guangdong and Guangxi areas
*Sources*: Li 1995, 1231–1234. The geographical locations of the above regions are based on the works of Twitchett (1979, 362–368) and Tan (1982, 34–35, 46–49, 63–66, 69–70)

Yanzhou in the Guannei circuit (Yanzhou-G) (Wang 2006a, 1911; Maruhashi 2016, 43–47), the most important center of inland salt production in the north and located near the mid-Yellow River. This salt-for-grain procurement successfully secured one-third of the total supplies.[3] A few scholars such as Wu (1994, 97–98) have speculated that this exchange could be the precursor to the *ruzhong* provisioning system as it integrated the salt monopoly into a public purchase program. However, there is also a lack of evidence indicating the use of transferable securities, typically associated with loan interest, in the public purchases conducted by the Tang court. Nor were the imperial mints able to provide enough copper coins to meet the needs for the circulation of goods.

[3] The armies stationed at the capital district and Northwest in 836 AD totaled 0.4 million and their annual grain consumption exceeded 450,000 *shi* (Li 2001, 750–751).

After the An Lushan Rebellion, monopolies in salt and tea were already adopted by the Tang court to increase state revenues and becoming more important to yearly budgetary income.[4] The merchants were allowed to pay silver, copper coins, grain, and textiles to the government in exchange for the privileged rights of selling salt and tea at a specific region for a fixed term. Yet under the circumstances of the inflation caused by the military conflicts, the merchants faced high risks in transferring and selling the monopolized goods. To boost the sales of salt, the late Tang government accepted textiles as payments at overestimated values that apparently went beyond the market prices. This practice, known as official procurement rates (*xugu,* 虛估), allowed salt merchants to purchase salt at discounted rates that were substantially lower than before (Twitchett 1970, 50–58; Wu 1997, 133–138). While this approach resulted in high nominal revenue, it also produced a significant discrepancy between the official rates and the real prices of monopolized salt and tea that led to a huge loss of state revenues (Wu 1997, 145–183; Chen and Yang 1990, 155–166). In 822, Zhang Pingshu, vice-minister of the Board of Finance, proposed the government agencies to sell salt directly to ordinary consumers rather than allow salt merchants to act as wholesalers. However, his proposal was rejected by the court on the ground that direct sales by the agencies would be even less profitable than the current arrangement (Wang 1960, 5901–5902). In short, the late Tang court began to institutionally exchange monopolized goods such as salt for grain and encouraged the merchants to cooperate with the government to maintain profits. But all these changes in monopolies and public purchases had involved little innovation of credit tools.

## 8.3 The Establishment of the Monopoly Tax Bureau at Kaifeng

The civil war continued after the collapse of the Tang dynasty in 907 and the military conflicts among the warlords escalated to an unprecedented level in the succeeding years. The two concurring trends, the monetization of the economy and the commercialization of military mobilization, laid a foundation for an emerging military-fiscal state (Liu 2015). When it came to the reunification of China by the Song dynasty in 980, the dramatic increase in the recruited professional soldiers created a heavy burden on the court. The establishment of *Quehuowu* (榷貨務), or the Monopoly Tax Bureau (MTB), at the capital city of Kaifeng led to a credit-based provisioning policy. Initially, the MTB oversaw a monopoly scheme that relied on cooperation with the merchants in the tea trade. The merchants would prepay in gold and silk to

[4] In the mid-ninth century, the Tang government also implemented the tea monopoly as a strategy to augment its revenue. This monopoly encompassed all aspects of tea production, enabling the government to levy taxes on the sales of tea. Concurrently, it imposed a prohibition on unauthorized private trading of tea, thereby ensured its complete control over the profit of tea monopoly (Twitchett, 1970, 62–65).

the MTB for tea vouchers. In return, they were allowed to transfer tea grown in the south to the north for sale (Chen 2006, 19).

After the war with the Khitan Liao at the northern border in 986, the Song court launched a defense provisioning program, a policy known as *ruzhong* (入中), *zhezhong* (折中), *or zhebo* (折博). As a means of procuring military supplies to the border troops, the merchants were incentivized to transfer grain to the northern border in exchange for economic benefits. The court soon felt necessary to link the tea monopoly scheme—which inevitably involved the cash prepayment by the tea merchants to either the official agencies in the south or the MTB at the capital—to the military provisioning program at the frontier. Upon the delivery of the military supplies, they would receive a state-issued voucher (*yin*) issued by the MTB at Kaifeng which allowed the merchant to obtain a fixed amount of salt or tea at the designated production centers corresponding to the value of the delivered food and fodder (Li 2004, 687).[5]

When it came to Emperor Zhenzong (997–1022), especially after the Northern Song signed the peace treaty with the Khitan in 1005, the military provision program gradually shifted its focus to the northwestern front to aid the Song court's fighting for control of the Silk Road. The official documents preserved during the Zhenzong reign have provided only sketchy information about the mechanism of the *ruzhong* system, especially how the central authority handled, reviewed, and reformed its policies to improve the efficiency of the military provision and minimize the state expenditure.

Essentially, the *ruzhong* program became a complicated and profit-driven process that required a huge sum of prepayments in exchange for privileges in long-distance tea trade earmarked by the vouchers. To put it simply, supervised by the MTB, this *ruzhong* program formally started from the military provision at the border and ended with the retail sale of tea at the designated districts in North China. It would take two to three years for a single merchant to complete the whole cycle, not to mention the difficulties and risks he would face. Therefore, the court allowed the merchants, who had delivered the supplies to the border, to sell the vouchers in state-authorized voucher shops at Kaifeng once they acquired them from the MTB.[6] As the vouchers were sold and re-sold at the voucher shops, the final buyers were mostly the tea and salt merchants who possessed not only a large amount of money but also rich knowledge and skills of shipping goods over long distances. In doing so, the merchants who bought the vouchers became creditors and the MTB in response became a debtor that had used vouchers as a form of credit instrument to purchase the military supplies.

The evolution of the military provisioning program gave rise to an emergence of the securities market at Kaifeng. The circulation of the vouchers was not confined

[5] According to Ma Duanlin (1245–1322), the policy of *ruzhong* began in 985 (Ma 2012, 438). However, Guo's (1990b, 719–721) research indicates that the policy was actually implemented in 986 instead of 985.

[6] For the whole process of the ruzhong program related to trade of vouchers at Kaifeng, key evidence comes from *Xu zizhi tongjian changbian* (Li 2004, 855).

**Table 8.3** Actual purchasing price of the Northern Song military provision, 1003–1005

| I. 1003 | | |
|---|---|---|
| Location | Actual price of millet per *dou* | Procurement rate of millet per *dou* |
| Zhenrongjun | 497 | 714 |
| Weizhou | ~ | 734 |
| **II.1005** | | |
| Lingzhou | 750 | 1000 ~ 2000 |

*Sources* Xu 2014, 6502–6503; Li 2004, 1335–1336

to the hands of the grain-supply merchants and the tea and salt merchants. A securities market emerged when the selling and buying of vouchers at Kaifeng attracted financiers to speculate for extra profits (Liu 2015; Li 2007). In 1005, the central authority recognized that the voucher itself had become transferable among private merchants. Its value was also negotiable as the officials said that the voucher's prices fluctuated at this market.[7]

As it was a market-based public purchase program, the court faced challenges arising from both the grain and voucher markets. Even during peacetime, the deployment of many professional soldiers at the border led to a surge in demand for military provisions. To meet these needs, the MTB offered substantial concessions to incentivize merchants in the delivery of military supplies. (Song 1979, 73–76; Golas 2015, 185–198). The increasing discrepancy between the official procurement rates and market prices of provisioning materials drove up grain prices and attracted more merchants to speculate in the provision program. In 1003, for instance, a sharp increase in the official rates of the public purchases alerted the Northern Song government (Xu 2014, 6502–6503). By 1005, official procurement rates of grain had become significantly higher than market prices, which had already risen due to increased demand (see Table 8.3).

To solve these problems, the Northern Song government implemented a "Three Items Policy" that offered to the grain and fodder merchants the exchange certificates, and a combination of cash and vouchers. After a careful examination of land transportation costs and several meetings with the merchants, the State Finance Commission redefined the exchange ratios between grain and fodder on the one hand and tea on the other hand. Meanwhile, it gave equal weights to three kinds of payments—copper coins, luxury goods such as ivory and aromatic medicines, and tea vouchers (Tuo 1977, 4484–4486). As vouchers were issued in large quantities in the preceding years, the government had struggled to honor its commitments due to the limited stocks of tea. This delay had impacted the securities market in Kaifeng, leading to

[7] A long paragraph preserved in *Xu Zizhi tongjian changbian* tells a reader that at the year of 1005 AD the State Finance Commission revised and issued the guideline in 1005 AD for the procuring military supplies after consulting with big merchants. As it describes, the vouchers had already become transferrable and their value became negotiable at the market before the year of 1005 AD, though it might have existed some years earlier.

a significant decline in both the volume of transactions and the market prices of the tea vouchers (Li 2004, 1335–1336). To issue the voucher in a much smaller quantity was a primary means of stabilizing the market prices of the vouchers. This time the MTB allowed the merchants to obtain two-thirds of the payments via both cash and ivory, and a balance between the outflow and inflow of cash out of its own reserve thus became a crucial task.

After the reform of the "Three Items Policy" was conducted in 1005, the MTB successfully obtained annually from 2 to 4 million strings (a currency unit comprising 770–1,000 cash coins bound together through holes in the center) from the tea monopoly (Li 2004, 1481–1482). In 1031, the MTB reported it would secure 1.8 million strings cash yearly out of the monopolies of the salt produced in southeast China. Later this quota increased to 4 million strings (Tuo 1977, 4440). Given the steady cash inflows, the MTB even began to redeem the vouchers from the securities market when prices fell.[8]

Providing a comprehensive assessment of the overall performance of the MTB in the eleventh century is difficult based on existing sources. For the implementation of the *ruzhong* program, the state must possess a capability to bear the risk of fluctuations in both the grain and voucher markets. Thus, the sustainability of this defense procurement program largely depended on the Song government's capability to fulfill its financial obligations to the merchants. During the three decades after the "Three Items Policy" was launched, the Northern Song and Khitan Liao remained at peace. And the defense procurement program, though still expensive, could be arranged at leisure. The MTB even found its cash inflow exceeded its outflow. Nonetheless, obtaining military supplies during wartime would turn out to be a different case. As the shortage of the monopolized goods in the governmental agencies caused delays to tea and salt merchants, the market prices of the vouchers declined and the discrepancy between the face value and the market price of the vouchers increased. Speculation occurred wildly then to drag down the prices of the vouchers, even to half of their face value. While the problem of price-gouging in military provisions caused a substantial outflow of the MTB's cash reserves, the speculation on the transferrable vouchers greatly destabilized the securities market and dealt another blow to the MTB. This is exactly what happened to Song China around 1040, which suffered a deep crisis in public finances, initially caused by the border war with Tangut Xi Xia. As shown in the following section, the poor operation of the Northern Song's military procurement program and the rampant fluctuation of the voucher prices at the securities market quickly drained the wealth of the imperial treasury and caused inflation across the country.

[8] In the Zhenzong reign, the court decided to redeem the vouchers in the years of 1014,1017 and 1021 (Xu 2014, 6790–6792;Li 2004, 1481–1482).

## 8.4 The Performance of the Securities Market During the 1040 s Crises

The longstanding rivalry between the Northern Song and the Tanguts can be traced back to the late tenth century when Li Jiqian (963–1004), the military governor of Xiazhou, refused to acknowledge the supremacy of the Song emperor. This refusal was in response to the Song court's attempt to enforce a resettlement policy on the Tangut clan within the interior regions of China in 982. Despite the Tangut's occupation of Lingzhou, the Song state pursued an appeasement policy, opting to avoid direct conflict. In 1005, both sides signed a peace treaty that formally recognized Li Deming (981–1032) as the ruler of the Tangut people. However, the political situation deteriorated when Li Yuanhao (1003–1048), the son of Li Deming, ascended to the throne. Unlike his father, who was subservient to the Northern Song, Li Yuanhao was a Tangut ruler with high-caliber military talent who aspired to lead an independent state formally recognized by the Northern Song court. He asserted control over Gansu region, capturing major cities in the Hexi Corridor, including Guazhou, Shazhou, and Suzhou. This expansion pushed his territories further westward to the northwestern border of the Song state in 1030 s. The protracted conflict between Northern Song and Tangut Xi Xia eventually escalated into full-scale war. From late 1039 to 1042, the two states engaged in at least 13 sieges and 20 battles, three of which culminated in catastrophic defeats for the Northern Song (see Table 8.4 and 8.5). In the first month of 1040, while en route to relieve the besieged city of Yanzhou in the Yongxingjun circuit (Yanzhou-Y), Song troops suffered a devastating defeat in an ambush. This led to the capture of the Song commander Liu Ping and resulted in more than 5,000 Northern Song soldiers being killed (Li 2010, 32–35, 130–131; McGrath 2009, 305–306). In the second year, the Northern Song forces were lured into an ambush at Haoshuichuan. This defeat brought the death toll to over 10,000 soldiers. Finally, in the tenth month of 1042, the battle of Dingchuan fortress ended in a massacre of the Song forces, 13 officers and 9,400 soldiers being killed (Li 2010, 132–135; Tsang 1997, 224–228).

Alongside the military setbacks, the court also had to grapple with a financial crisis, which was a direct consequence of the war. From 1041 onwards, the Northern Song government was supporting more than 200,000 professional mercenaries on the northwestern border (see Table 8.6).

The defense of the northwestern border posed an acute problem for the military provisions. In 1043, Wang Yaochen (1003–1058), Deputy Commissioner of State Finance, highlighted the fiscal burden of the court caused by the ongoing war with the Tangut. In 1038, Shaanxi's annual budgetary incomes, mostly from local tax revenues, stood at 19.78 million strings. However, after the war broke out the budgetary incomes at the discretion of the Shaanxi administration reached 33.9 million strings, a surge of nearly 72% by 1042. This increase was met by transferring revenue from the neighboring inland areas (Wang 1995, 19). Despite this increase in allocated resources, the rise in real expenditures was even more dramatic. In 1038, Shaanxi's expenditures reached approximately 15.5 million strings, but during the

**Table 8.4** Sieges between Northern Song and Xi Xia, 1040–1041

| Date (M/Y) | Location | Besieger/Défense | Outcome |
|---|---|---|---|
| 1/1040 | Jinming Fort | Xia/Song | occupied |
| 1/1040 (7 days) | Yanzhou-Y | Xia/Song | withdrawn |
| 1/1040 | Yongping Fort | Xia/Song | withdrawn |
| 1/1040 | Anyuan Fort | Xia/Song | withdrawn |
| 1/1040 | Saimen Fort | Xia/Song | occupied |
| 1/1040 | Zhenxibao | Xia/Song | withdrawn |
| 9/1040 | Sanchuan Fort | Xia/Song | withdrawn |
| 9/1040 | Baibaocheng | Song/Xia | occupied |
| 2/1041 | Liufanbao | Xia/Song | withdrawn |
| 7/1041(31 days) | Linzhou | Xia/Song | withdrawn |
| 7/1041 | Ningyuan Fort | Xia/Song | occupied |
| 7/1041 | Fuzhou-H | Xia/Song | withdrawn |
| 7/1041 | Fengzhou-H | Xia/Song | occupied |

*Sources* Li 2004, 2966–3164

**Table 8.5** Battles between Northern Song and Xi Xia, 1040–1042

| Date (M/Y) | Location | Winner |
|---|---|---|
| 11/1039 | Bao'anjun | Northern Song |
| 11/1039 | Chengping Fort | Northern Song |
| 11/1039 | Houqiao Fort | Northern Song |
| 1/1040 | Sanchuankou | Xi Xia |
| 8/1040 | Guobeiping | Northern Song |
| 9/1040 | Zhenrongjun | Northern Song |
| 9/1040 | Shizibao | Northern Song |
| 9/1040 | Bao'anjun | Xi Xia |
| 9/1040 | Zhao'an Fort | Northern Song |
| 2/1041 | Haoshuichuan | Xi Xia |
| 4/1041 | Hanqi, Xuema and Duwei forts | Northern Song |
| 9/1041 | Liulibao | Northern Song |
| 9/1041 | Longmenchuan | Northern Song |
| 4/1042 | Furonggu | Northern Song |
| 4/1042 | Anding | Northern Song |
| 5/1042 | Sansongling | Northern Song |
| 5/1042 | Tumaochuan | Northern Song |
| 10/1042 | Dingchuan Fort | Xi Xia |
| 10/1042 | Weizhou | Xi Xia |
| 10/1042 | Pengyang | Northern Song |

*Sources* Li 2004, 2944–3307

**Table 8.6** Number of professional troops on the northwestern front, 1041–1044

| | Circuits | | | | |
|---|---|---|---|---|---|
| **Year** | Fuyan | Huanqing | Jingyuan | Qinfeng | **Total** |
| 1041 | 68, 000 | 50, 000 | 70, 000 | 27, 000 | 215,000 |
| 1044 | ~ | ~ | ~ | ~ | 300,000 |

*Sources* Li 2004,0.3140–3141, 3600; Li 2010, 106–108

war with the Tangut Xi Xia, it soared to 33.6 million strings, an increase of nearly 117% (see Table 8.7).

The intensifying military conflicts between the Northern Song and Tangut Xi Xia necessitated urgent military provisions to supply the Shaanxi border. Indeed, even during times of peace, the local economy could barely sustain the garrison stationed there. In 1034, Cheng Lin (988–1056),the Commissioner of State Finance, revealed that the Shaanxi garrison forces consumed approximately 15 million *shi* yearly, but only half of that could be satisfied by the supplies of local taxes. As a result, the Song government had to import an additional 7.5 million *shi* from Kaifeng to meet the demand (Li 2004, 2675–2676; Zhang 2000, 324–325; Huang 2009, 178–180). The Northern Song government had to deploy unusual measures to wage war on the Tangut.

In 1040, just one year after the war broke out, to address the pressing wartime demand for military provisions, the Song court expanded its *ruzhong* policy to procure the necessary military supplies. Advised by the head of State Finance Commission, the court decided to sharply raise the sea salt production quota along China's south-eastern coast. The merchants who transported grain and fodder to the northwestern front would be eligible to obtain vouchers for shipping and selling salt. (Li 2004, 3072; Tuo 1977, 182; Chien 2004, 190). Two years later, this policy was further revised to procure an even greater quantity of provisions from the private sector for the garrisons in Shaanxi and Hedong. Now merchants who engaged in provisioning Shaanxi and Hedong would receive half their compensation in copper coins and half in gold and textiles at the MTB; those who preferred not to receive gold and silk were offered vouchers of tea, salt, or aromatics as alternatives (Tuo 1977, 4440; Xu 2014, 6509). Furthermore, merchants who transported other goods to the border would be

**Table 8.7** Allocated resources and actual expenditures of the major circuits in Northern Song (strings of cash)

| | Shaanxi | | Hebei | | Hedong | |
|---|---|---|---|---|---|---|
| Year | Budgetary incomes | Expenditure | Budgetary incomes | Expenditure | Budgetary incomes | Expenditure |
| 1038 | 19,780,000 | 15,510,000 | 20,140,000 | 18,230,000 | 10,380,000 | 8,590,000 |
| 1042 | 33,900,000 | 33,630,000 | 27,450,000 | 25,520,000 | 11,760,000 | 13,030,000 |

*Sources* Li 2004, 3366

compensated with salt vouchers that could be redeemed by the official agency at the Xiezhou Salt Pond (Xu 2014, 6509) (Map 8.1).

Amid the ongoing war against the Tanguts, the Song state was confronted with an unparalleled fiscal crisis that was as dire as the military defeats. Zhang Fangping (1007–1091) recounted the staggering amount of expenditure incurred following the escalation of the hostilities between Northern Song and Xi Xia:

> During the Baoyuan (1038–1039) and Kangding (1040–1041) periods, the central power of Northern Song was challenged by the Tangut. The deployment of military forces along the western border resulted in the concentration of troops and horses, which further necessitated the long-distance delivery of grain and fodder. This shipment led to a significant outflow of the vouchers, silver, cash, and textiles from the MTB's reserve, amounting to more than 10 million strings of cash annually. Since this amount exceeded the resources controlled by the State Finance Commission, immediate help [was required] from the Inner Treasury (the royal reserve at the disposal of the emperor). (Zhang 2000, 353–354)

The substantial outflow of cash from the MTB can be explained by the pressing military requirements on the northwestern border in Shaanxi. The local authorities on the border elevated the purchasing prices of military provisions to attract more merchants to supply these provisions to the border. In 1049, Bao Zheng (999–1062), Deputy Commissioner of State Finance, provided a vivid account of the state's exorbitant expenditures during the military conflict with the Tanguts:

> Since the period of Kangding (1040), those who delivered grain and fodder to the western border received vouchers that could be exchanged for copper coins, silver or textiles at the MTB. Salt produced from the Xiezhou Salt Pond would be offered in exchange for the supplies to the frontier such as feathers, sinew and horn, glue and paint, iron and charcoal, tiles and lumber. Unscrupulous merchants were tempted to collude with the corrupt officials to keep prices artificially high. A merchant could, for example, sell a pair of wooden beams at the rate of 1,000 coins of cash and could be rewarded with a large salt mat as the payment, which caused incalculable losses from the state. (Xu 2014, 6509–6510; Chien 2004, 110–111)[9]

In addition to such high official rates, which indicated the over-valuation of the procurement materials at the frontier, the payment of vouchers at hugely discounted rates also caused a great loss to the MTB. Zhang Fangping, who held the position of Commissioner of State Finance after the war, described how avidly merchants had exploited the vouchers of the Xiezhou-produced salt provided by the state's *ruzhong* provision policy to reap financial gains in the market:

> Due to the insufficient fiscal resources available in the Shaanxi circuit, the state has implemented a strategy of encouraging merchants to supply the northwestern frontier with grain and fodder. The Bureau of General Accounts pays cash and silk cloth to those merchants at a rate three times higher than the conventional one. This led to the devaluation of tea, salt, and alum [a chemical salt used in textiles and medicine]. As the profits of these commodities dissipated, the central authorities were left to swallow the cost. (Li 2004, 3895)

The devaluation of the three commodities referred to the MTB selling at hugely discounted rates. To fulfill urgent military needs, as shown in Table 8.8, the prices of

[9] For the weight of salt in Song Dynasty, 1 mat (*xi* 席) was equal to 220 *jin* (Guo 1990b, 217–218).

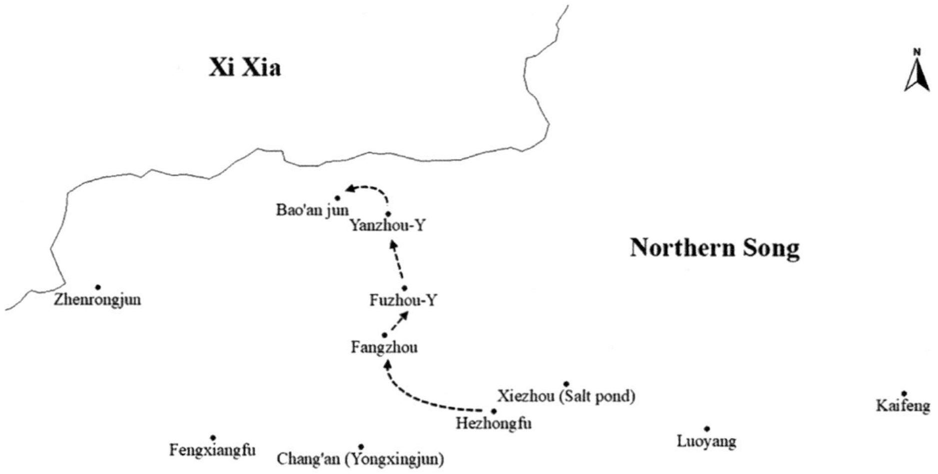


**Map 8.1** Routes of grain and fodder supplies to the northwestern frontier of Northern Song, 1040 (*Sources* Li 2004, 3613–3615; Cheng 2006,139–144)

**Table 8.8** The official rates of Xiezhou-produced salt calculated from vouchers, 1004–1042 AD

| Year | Location | *Wen* per *jin* |
|---|---|---|
| 1004 | **Most outer periphery**: Huanzhou, Qingzhou, Yanzhou-Y, Weizhou, Yuanzhou, Zhenrongjun, Bao'anjun | 12 |
| | **Secondary outer periphery**: Yizhou, Fuzhou-Y | 14 |
| | **Inner peripheral region**: Binzhou, Ningzhou, Jingzhou | 16 |
| | **Secondary inner region**: Qinzhou, Fangzhou, Danzhou, Qianzhou, Longzhou, Fengzhou-Q, Jiezhou, Chengzhou, Fengxiangfu | 18 |
| | **Secondary inner region**: Tongzhou, Huazhou, Yaozhou, Guozhou, Xiezhou, Hezhongfu,, Yongxingjun, Shanfu | 20 |
| 1026 | Huanzhou | 15.2 |
| | Zhenrongjun | 15.2 |
| | Bao'anjun | 14.5 |
| | Qingzhou, Weizhou, Yuanzhou-Y, Yanzhou-Y | 15.5 |
| 1042 | Yongxingjun, Tongzhou, Huazhou, Yaozhou, Hezhongfu, Shanfu, Guozhou, Xiezhou, Jinzhou, Jiangzhou-H, Qingchengjun | 4.55 |

*Sources* Xu 2014, 6502–3, 6788; Dai 1981, 237–238; Li 2004, 3215, 4517–4518

the Xiezhou-produced salt available through the vouchers plummeted to an unprecedented level. In the prewar time the official rates for the military procurement ranged between 12–20 *wen* cash per *jin,* depending on the shipment distance. When it came to the war, prices fell dramatically to as little as 4.55 *wen* per *jin* of salt in 1042 and it is presumed that the MTB would have had to increase the voucher supply to make up for the fall in prices.

However, the court largely failed to do so, as both production and consumption of salt and tea remained largely the same. To stabilize the market of Xiezhou-produced salt, the Song state reintroduced in 1042 a strict policy that required merchants to withdraw from the salt monopolies implemented in the hinterland prefectures close to the Xiezhou Salt Pond. Instead, both the merchants formerly involved in military provisions and the holders of salt vouchers were asked to sell their vouchers back to the state at a recalculated value.[10]

Despite of the reintroduction of officially-controlled sales along with the redemption of vouchers related to the circulation of the Xiezhou-produced salt in the Northwest, which actually constituted only a part of the state-issued vouchers, it made little difference to the securities market that had also speculated on different vouchers related to the sea salt and other goods. Following a substantial increase in the number

[10] We are unsure of how many prefectures in the north, under this policy, were defined as the highly controlled area exclusively for the official sales. The source mentioned in particular that the merchants were prohibited from the salt monopoly in Kaifeng and the eleven hinterland prefectures with both easy access to the transportation and intense density of populations. The official agents and outlets were fully in charge of the distribution and sales of Xiezhou-produced salt (Li 2004, 3215). For further information see Tuo 1977, 4417; Chien 2004, 111; Guo 1990b, 919–920.

of salt vouchers in circulation, the over-supply caused by excessive military procurement became apparent. As the salt merchants at Kaifeng found it difficult to receive the fixed amount of salt as indicated by the voucher's face value, they became reluctant to purchase further vouchers. In 1043, Fan Zhongyan observed:

> At present the MTB has merely 100 private dealers for the voucher business. Despite the deployment of the "Three Items Policy", only a small number of merchants have participated in the *ruzhong* provisioning program, supplying a meager amount of grain and fodder for military provisioning. It remains difficult for the MTB to accumulate an adequate amount of gold, silver, coins or textiles in the current year. (Fan 2004, 544)

The sluggish sales of salt vouchers, as suggested by Guo (1990b, 921), can be attributed to the shrinking of merchant-sales regions and in consequence the decreasing numbers of the consumers that the merchants were able to target, directly resulted from the reintroduction of a stricter approach to the salt monopoly in Kaifeng and the prefectures in Shaanxi regions. Although Fan Zhongyan did not provide a complete explanation for the unattractiveness of salt vouchers to merchants, he noted that increasing the amount of sea salt offered for each voucher was a solution to this problem. Xu Yuan, who was recommended by Fan Zhongyan to head the MTB in the capital, suggested that the local authorities offer even higher official rates for grain it paid to merchants, and this extra amount could be solved by issuing the vouchers for sea salt in a much larger quantity (Ouyang 2001, 476–477).

The depletion of cash reserves forced the MTB to continue excessive sales of sea salt vouchers, creating a dilemma for the Song state. On the one hand, to curb the cash outflow out of the MTB, the Song state needed to issue fewer vouchers or even halt their issuance. On the other hand, to fulfil the urgent military needs of provisioning the frontier troops, the state had little choice but to continue selling more vouchers. After the escalation of the military conflicts between Northern Song and Tangut Xi Xia, the MTB's cash outflows ballooned. In the two years of 1039 and 1040, this figure reached 10 million strings of cash. And in 1042 it was still over 6.4 million, which far exceeded the pre-war level (see Table 8.9). Xu Yuan observed that after the state reintroduced the *ruzhong* provisioning policy, the bureau lacked sufficient cash to pay the merchants. The inability of the MTB to provide adequate cash payment to merchants led to a sharp decrease in the amount of grain delivered to the front and a corresponding increase in grain prices (Ouyang 2001, 476).

Nevertheless, as the MTB officials were pressured to meet the urgent military needs by using credit tools such the tea and salt vouchers, the over-supply of vouchers tipped the balance between the inflow and outflow of cash reserves originally designed by the MTB. By 1044, the Northern Song government, eager to achieve peace and alleviate the fiscal burden incurred by the war, concluded a peace settlement with the Tangut Xi Xia. Despite this effort, the MTB continued to experience a significant cash deficit that persisted beyond the short-lived Qingli reforms. As shown in Table 8.9, the MTB's cash outflows did not come down to prewar levels. In 1046, the bureau's cash outflows totaled 4.8 million strings of cash. It was not until the following year that a decline in the cash disbursement was observed, dropping to 2.76 million strings.

**Table 8.9** Cash inflows and outflows of the MTB, 1028–1047 (000 strings)

| Year | **Inflow** | | | **Outflow** |
|---|---|---|---|---|
| | Tea vouchers | Xiezhou salt vouchers | Sea salt vouchers | |
| 1015 | > 2,000 | | | |
| 1022 | Jiangnan:570 | Jingxi: 230 | 1,140 | |
| 1028 | | | 1,803 | 1,544 |
| 1038 | | | | ≈10,000 |
| 1039 | | | | ≈10,000 |
| 1040 | | | | ≈10,000 |
| 1042 | | | | 6,470 |
| 1046 | | | | 4,800 |
| 1047 | 1,190 | | | 2,760 |

*Sources* Xu 2014, 6797–6798;Zhang 2000, 353–354; Li 2004, 4517–4518; Guo 1990a, 96–102

Since the Song state was incapable of completely addressing the excessive cash expenditure of the MTB during wartime, it resorted to increasing the money supply by minting iron and copper coins. At the suggestion of the reform officials, low-intrinsic-value "ten cash iron coin" and "ten cash copper coin" (*dangshi daqian* 當十大錢) began to be circulated in Shaanxi in substantial quantities from the early 1040 s onward. In 1040, the Song state began to mint "ten cash copper coins" and iron coins in Jiangnan and transported them to Shaanxi to meet a shortage (Xu 2014, 6214). These new coins' intrinsic value was considerably lower than their face value. A ten cash large coin, for instance, had an intrinsic value of only 30% of its nominal value, equivalent to the value of three normal copper coins (Li 2004, 3954–3955). Officials such as Ding Du (990–1053) opposed the circulation of these coins out of concern that it would not only debase the currency and encourage large-scale manufacture of counterfeit coins but also inflate the prices of grain and fodder on the border (Li 2004, 3071–3072; Wang 2003, 532–533).

Despite such concerns, the Song state continued to increase the money supply by minting coins in low intrinsic values in the 1040 s. In the autumn of 1041, the State Finance Commission ordered prefectures with iron ore mines in Hedong circuit such as Jinzhou and Zezhou to produce "large iron coins" in support of the Song state's military expenditure in Shaanxi (Li 2004, 3173; Wang 2003, 534). In the winter of the same year, a huge number of iron coins, totaling 3 million strings of cash at face value, were manufactured at the imperial mints located in Jiangzhou, Raozhou, and Chizhou prefectures of South China for "military costs on Shaanxi border" (Li 2004, 3196; Wang 2003, 535). Even after the peace treaty was signed in the autumn of 1044, the court still faced the burden of cash outflows and ordered the production of the ten cash copper coins, by the total of 110,000 and amounting to the aggregate value of 1.1 million strings of normal copper coins at the face value, were cast at the imperial mints in South China in order to stabilize the money supply (see Table 8.10).

**Table 8.10** Amount of minted coins in Northern Song China, 1041–1045 (strings)

| Year | Location of minting | large iron coins | Small iron coins | Large copper coins |
|---|---|---|---|---|
| 1041 | Jinzhou | 288,000 | 114,500 | ~ |
| | Zezhou | 160,000 | 4,000 | ~ |
| | *Jiang-Rao-Chi* | 3,000,000 in total* | | ~ |
| 1045 | Jiangnan C | ~ | ~ | 110,000 |

*Sources* Hino 1983, 380–383
* The sum of the iron coins produced at the imperial mints in the Jiangzhou-J, Raozhou, and Chizhou prefectures was 3,000,000

The circulation of depreciated metal coins had significant repercussions for the Song state. In 1043, Fan Zhongyan, one of the most influential figures of the Qingli reforms, acknowledged that the casting of iron coins, which was intended to help finance the military expenditure in Shaanxi and Hedong, resulted in significant illegal casting (Li 2004, 3459–3460). Due to the persistent heavy expenditure on the border defense, the Song state continued to issue ten cash iron coins. However, the circulation of these metal coins was followed by sustained inflation in Shaanxi throughout the decade. To combat inflation, iron coins were withdrawn from circulation in Shaanxi from 1045 onwards. In 1048, to stabilize prices, the Song state devalued the large-nominal-value iron and copper coins by 70%, making them equivalent to only three normal copper coins (Li 2004, 3955; Wang 2003, 535–536).

A complete recovery of the voucher market took much longer years after the war had ended. To aid the defense procurement at the border in Hebei, the Song state implemented in 1048 the "Four Items Policy", which was intended as an improvement over the "Three Items Policy" that had been conducted preceding the war. However, inflation continued unabated, and the MTB could not maintain a reasonable ratio between the procurement rates of grain and that of the vouchers. "A hundred and eight *jin* of salt that previously sold at 100,000 cash were now rated at 60,000 cash only" (Tuo 1977, 4440; Chien 2004, 191). The persistent presence of the official rates of salt and tea vouchers at a heavily discounted level had significant impacts on the securities market. The MTB issued more vouchers at discounted rates, causing a sharp decline of the voucher values in the securities market. The financial officials noted with alarm that once the "Four Items Policy" was implemented, a supplier of provisioning goods would sell aromatic medicine at the price of 500–600 coins of cash per *jin*, merely one-seventh of the market prices previously paid, to the local administration. The vouchers paid to the supplier were already overwhelmingly discounted. When the salt and tea merchants bought these vouchers at Kaifeng from the market, they too asked for an extremely high discount rates, leading to a rampant speculation on an ever-low price of the vouchers. According to *Song Shi*, a voucher that guarantee a pack of tea originally worth about 100 strings cash was then resold at the value of 3 strings. The State Finance Commission was forced to negotiate with the financiers to solve the embarrassing problem. Anyone who held the voucher currently valued at 3 strings, once paying additional 44 strings cash, were immediately granted with tea worth 100 strings by the government. To stabilize the price of salt vouchers, the Song court, on the recommendation of Fan Xiang (Xiezhou Salt Monopoly Commissioner), decided to allow the provisioning merchants to use cash at the frontier in exchange for the vouchers of Xiezhou-produced salt. (Li 2004, 3970–3971; Guo 1990b, 921–925). Later, the court sometimes turned to purchase grain by cash to reduce its reliance of military procurement on vouchers. But this would certainly lead to a stagnation of the voucher market until the coming of the far-reaching financial, trade and legal reforms brought about by the New Policies introduced in 1069.

## 8.5 Conclusion

This paper aims to explore the close relationship between the market-based military mobilization and the rise of securities market at Kaifeng at the dawn of the eleventh century. It starts from a cross-dynastic comparison of public purchases between the Tang and Northern Song dynasties. As the Tang Empire expanded greatly, its territories in the seventh century, a public procurement scheme was deployed to supply the soldiers stationed along the Silk Road. After the An Lushan Rebellion, the internal fights within China Proper led to the emergence of a market-based military mobilization. Nonetheless, it was not until the reunification of the Northern Song dynasty that the central authorities in China began to systematically exploit monetized resources to sustain the large number of professional soldiers under its direct control. Around 1005 the Song court created a complicated system to supply the armies at the frontier. This system comprised three parts: a public purchase program known as *ruzhong* for providing food and fodder, a monopoly in tea and salt for receiving cash payments from the merchants in wholesale business and a special commercial administration known as the MTB for handling the receiving and paying of cash and which was responsible for issuing and supervising the vouchers as a credit tool. By paying attention to the functioning of both the *ruzhong* method and the role that the MTB played at the securities market at Kaifeng, we find the prewar financial apparatus had worked smoothly in linking the military procurement with the monopolies in salt and tea. In the three decades between 1005 and 1039 the MTB successfully maintained a subtle balance between the inflows and outflows of cash and redeemed the vouchers from the hands of private merchants to stabilize the securities market.

However, throughout the 1040 s, the Song state struggled with financial crises stemming from military defeats on the northwestern border. The official rates of the supplies purchased at the border soared to incentivize the merchants to provide what the military needed. The problem of price-gouging in transactions of military supplies caused enormous cash outflows from the MTB. While the shortage of hard currencies worsened, speculation in vouchers almost undermined the securities market. The circulation of depreciated metal coins, which were originally designed by the reformists to relieve the shortage of hard currencies as payment means, escalated into a national crisis that sparked hyperinflation. Faced with military setbacks and a financial crisis, the court decided to sign a peace treaty with the Tanguts. It would be decades before the Song authorities restored financial order and curbed inflation.

## Appendix Pinyin spelling for the place names in traditional Chinese character

Anding 安定
Anyuan Fort 安遠寨
Anxi 安西
Baibaocheng 白豹城
Bao'anjun 保安軍
Beiting 北庭
Binzhou 邠州
Chengping Fort 承平寨
Chengzhou 成州
Chizhou 池州
Danzhou 丹州
Dingchuan Fort 定川寨
Duwei Fort 都嵬寨
Fanyang 范陽
Fangzhou 坊州
Fengxiangfu 鳳翔府
Fengzhou of Hedong Circuit (Fengzhou-H) 豐州
Fengzhou of Qinfeng Circuit (Fengzhou-Q) 鳳州
Furonggu 芙蓉谷
Fuyan 鄜延
Fuzhou of Hedong Circuit (Fuzhou-H) 府州
Fuzhou of Yongxingjun Circuit (Fuzhou-Y) 鄜州
Guazhou 瓜州
Guobeiping 郭北平
Guozhou 虢州
Haoshuichuan 好水川
Hanqi Fort 漢乞寨
Hedong 河東
Hedong Circuit (modern Shanxi) 河東路
Hezhongfu 河中府
Hexi 河西
Houqiao Fort 後橋寨
Huazhou 華州
Huanqing 環慶
Huanzhou 環州

Jiangzhou of Hedong Circuit (Jiangzhou-H) 絳州
Jiangzhou of Jiangnandong Circuit (Jiangzhou-J) 江州
Jiannan 劍南
Jiezhou 階州
Jingyuan 涇原
Jingzhou 涇州
Jinming Fort 金明寨
Jinzhou 晉州
Kaifeng 開封
Lingnan 嶺南
Lingzhou 靈州
Linzhou 麟州
Liufanbao 劉璠堡
Liulibao 琉璃堡
Longmenchuan 龍門川
Longyou 隴右
Longzhou 隴州
Ningyuan Fort 寧遠寨
Ningzhou 寧州
Pengyang 彭陽
Pinglu 平盧
Qianzhou 乾州
Qinfeng Circuit (modern Shaanxi) 秦鳳
Qingchengjun 慶成軍
Qingzhou 慶州
Qinzhou 秦州
Raozhou 饒州
Saimen Fort 塞門寨
Sanchuan Fort 三川寨
Sanchuankou 三川口
Sansongling 三松嶺
Shaanxi 陝西
Shanfu 陝府
Shazhou 沙州
Shizibao 師子堡
Shuofang 朔方
Suzhou 肅州
Tongzhou 同州
Tumaochuan 兔毛川
Weizhou 渭州
Wuchi 烏池
Xiazhou 夏州
Xiezhou 解州
Xuema Fort 薛馬寨

Yanzhou of Guannei Circuit during Tang Dynasty, or Yanzhou-G 鹽州. It was situated in the modern Dingbian county in northern Shaanxi.

Yanzhou of Yongxingjun Circuit (Yanzhou-Y) 延州
Yaozhou 耀州
Yizhou 儀州
Yongping Fort 永平寨
Yongxingjun 永興軍
Yuanzhou 原州
Zezhou 澤州
Zhao'an Fort 招安寨
Zhenxibao 鎮西堡
Zhenrongjun 鎮戎軍

## References


Chen, Jun. 2006. *Huangchao biannian gangmu beiyao* [Chronologically Arranged Complete Essentials in Outline and Detail of the August Courts]. Beijing: Zhonghua shuju.

Chen, Yande and Yang Quan. 1990. *Tangdai yanzheng* [The Salt Administration During the Tang Dynasty]. Xi'an: Sanqin chubanshe.

Cheng, Long. 2006. *Bei Song xibei zhanqu liangshi buji dili* [Geography of the Food Supplies on the Northwestern Border in the Northern Song]. Beijing: Shehui kexue wenxian chubanshe.

Chien, Cecilia L. F. 2004. *Salt and State: An Annotated Translation of the Songshi Salt Monopoly.* Ann Arbor: Center for Chinese Studies, University of Michigan Press.

Dai, Yixuan. 1981. *Songdai yanchao zhidu yanjiu* [The System of Salt Vouchers During the Song Dynasty]. Beijing: Zhonghua shuju.

Fan, Zhongyan. 2004. *Fan Zhongyan quanji* [Collected Works of Fan Zhongyan], ed. Fan Nengjun, vol. 1. Nanjing: Fenghuang chubanshe.

Fang, Jian. 2001. *Fan Zhongyan pingzhuan* [Fan Zhongyan: A Critical Biography]. Nanjing: Nanjing daxue chubanshe.

Guo, Zhengzhong. 1990a. *Songyan guankui* [A Glimpse of the Salt During the Song Dynasty]. Taiyuan: Shanxi jingji chubanshe.

Guo, Zhengzhong. 1990b. *Songdai yanye jingjishi* [An Economic History of the Salt Industry During the Song Period]. Beijing: Renmin chubanshe.

Golas, Peter J. 2015. The Sung Fiscal Administration. In *The Cambridge History of China, vol.5, part 2: Sung China, 960–1279*, ed. John W. Chaffee, and Denis Twitchett. Cambridge: Cambridge University Press.

Hino, Kaisaburō. 1983. *Sōdai no kahei to kin'yū (jyō)* [The history of currency and finance of Song Dynasty]. In *Tōyō shigaku ronshū* [Collected works of Hino Kaisaburō on the history of East Asia], vol 7. Tokyo: Sanichi shobō.

Huang, Chunyan. 2009. *Bei Song xibei yanbian de ruzhong* [Ruzhong Provisioning Operation on the Northwestern Border of Northern Song], *Tang Song zhengzhi jingji shi lungao* [Collection of the Works on Political and Economic History of Tang and Song Dynasties], 178–189. Lanzhou: Gansu renmin chubanshe.

Li, Huarui. 2010. *Song Xia guanxi shi* [A History of Song–Tangut Relations]. Beijing: Zhongguo renmin daxue chubanshe.

Li, Jinxiu. 1995. *Tangdai caizheng shigao* [Research Manuscript of Tang Dynasty's Financial History], vol.1. Beijing: Beijing daxue chubanshe.

Li, Jinxiu. 2001. *Tangdai caizheng shigao* [Research Manuscript of Tang Dynasty's Financial History], vol.2. Beijing: Beijing daxue chubanshe.
Li, Tao. 2004. *Xu zizhitongjian changbian* [The Long Draft Continuation of the Comprehensive Mirror That Aids Administration]. Beijing: Zhonghua shuju.
Li, Xiao. 2007. *Songchao zhengfu goumai zhidu yanjiu* [Studies of the System of the Song Government Procurement]. Shanghai: Shanghai renmin chubanshe.
Liu, William G. L. 2015. The Making of a Fiscal State in Song China, 960–1279. *Economic History Review* 68 (1): 48–78.
Lu, Xiangqian. 2012. *Tangdai Zhengzhi jingjishi zonglun: Ganlu zhi bian yanjiu ji qita* [The History of Politics and Economy in Tang Dynasty: Research on Ganlu Incident and Others]. Beijing: Shangwu yinshuguan.
Ma, Duanlin. 2012. *Wenxian tongkao* [Comprehensive Studies of Historical Documents]. Beijing: Zhonghua shuju.
McGrath, Michael. 2009. *The Reigns of Jen-tsung (1022–1063) and Ying-tsung (1063–1067).* In *The Cambridge History of China, vol. 5, part 1: The Sung Dynasty and Its Precursors, 907–1279,* ed Denis Twitchett and Paul J. Smith. Cambridge: Cambridge University Press.
Maruhashi, Mitsuhiro. 2016. Tōdai Kōhan no Hokuhen Keizai saikō [Rethinking the Economy of the Northern Frontier Region During the Second Half of the Tang Dynasty]. *Ajia Shigaku Ronshū* (Studies in Asian History) 10: 43–61.
Ouyang, Xiu. 2001. *Jushi ji* [Collected Works of the Retired Scholar]. In *Ouyang Xiu quanji* [Collected Works of Ouyang Xiu], ed Li Yi'an. Beijing: Zhonghua shuju.
Qi, Xia. 2009. *Qi Xia quanji* [Complete Works of Qi Xia], vol.9. Baoding: Hebei daxue chubanshe.
Song, Xi. 1979. Bei Song shangren de ruzhong bianliang [Deliveries of grain to the borders by merchants during the Northern Song period]. In *Songshi yanjiu luncong* [Collection of Song History Studies]. Taipei: Huagang chuban youxian gongsi.
Tsang, Shui-lung. 1997. *Violence and Strategy in Flux, 960–1104 A.D.*" PhD diss., The University of Arizona.
Twitchett, Denis. 1970. *Financial Administration under the T'ang Dynasty.* Cambridge: Cambridge University Press.
Twitchett, Denis. 1979. "Hsüan-tsung (reign 712–56)". In *The Cambridge History of China, vol.3, part 1: Sui and T'ang China, 589–906*, ed. Denis Twitchett, Cambridge: Cambridge University Press.
Tan, Qixing. 1982. *Zhongguo lishi dituji* [The Historical Atlas of China], vol. 5. Beijing: Zhongguo ditu chubanshe.
Tuo Tuo. 1977. *Song shi* [History of Song Dynasty]. Beijing: Zhonghua shuju.
Wang, Pu. 2006a. *Tang huiyao* [Institutional History of the Tang Dynasty]. Shanghai: Shanghai guiji chubanshe.
Wang, Qinruo. 1960. *Cefu yuangui* [Grand Tortoise in the Imperial Treasury of Archive]. Beijing: Zhonghua shuju.
Wang, Shengduo. 1995. *Liang Song caizheng shi* [A Fiscal History of the Song Dynasty]. Beijing: Shehui kexue chubanshe.
Wang, Shengduo. 2003. *Liang Song huobi shi* (A Monetary History of the Song Dynasty). Beijing: Shehui kexue chubanshe.
Wang, Zengyu. 2006b. Songchao de hedi liangcao [The Harmonious Purchase of Fodder and Provisions during the Song Dynasty], *Zizhu bian* [Collection of Trifle Things] Baoding: Hebei daxue chubanshe.
Wu, Liyu. 1994. *Shiyan de huobi zuoyong yu zhebozhi de fazhan——jianlun chaoyinzhi de qiyuan* [The Monetary Role of Salt and the Development of the *Zhebo* System: A Discussion on the Origin of the Voucher System]. *Zhongguo jingjishi yanjiu* [Researches In Chinese Economic History] 4: 94–102.
Wu, Liyu. 1997. *Sui-Tang Wudai de yanye* [The History of Salt Industry During the Sui-Tang and Five Dynasties period]. In *Zhongguo yanye shi: gudai bian* [History of Salt Industry in China: Ancient China], ed. Guo Zhengzhong, 79–237. Beijing: Renmin chubanshe.

Xu, Song. 2014. *Song huiyao jigao* (The Recovered Draft of the Collected Essential Documents of Song). Shanghai: Shanghai guji chubanshe.

Zhang, Fangping. 2000. *Zhang Fangping ji* (Collected Works of Zhang Fangping). Zhengzhou: Zhongzhou guji chubanshe.

**William Guanglin Liu** is a Professor of Chinese History at Lingnan University, Hong Kong. His research focuses on the political economy and economic change of pre-modern China from the tenth to the sixteenth century, Chinese military history, Neo-Confucianism and the market economy in historical perspective. He received his BA and MA from Peking University, Ph.D. from Harvard University. His publications include The Chinese Market Economy, 1000-1500 (Albany: SUNY Press, 2015), "The Making of a Fiscal State in Song China, 960-1279' in *Economic History Review* (2015), "Market integration in China, AD 960-1644", in A History of Market Performance from Ancient Babylonia to the Modern World (Routledge 2014).

**Kai Wan Kwan** is an Assistant Professor in Department of History at Hong Kong Shue Yan University. His research mainly focuses on the military and fiscal history of middle-period China from the seventh to the twelfth centuries. He received his BA and MPhil from Lingnan University and The Hong Kong University of Science and Technology respectively and his Ph.D. from Peking University. His publications include, "Beyond and Behind the Wall: Siege Warfare of Sui-Tang China, AD.600–900," in *The Routledge Handbook of Medieval Military Strategy*, ed. John D. Hosler and Daniel P. Franke: London and New York: Routledge, 2025. *Chinese Siege Warfare during late Tang and the Five Dynasties and Ten States Period*, Taipei: Wanjuanlou, 2021 (In Chinese). "Warfare and the Fiscal State During the Tang-Song Transition," *Research in Chinese Economic History*, 2 (2021): 39–56. (co-authored with William Guanglin Liu in Chinese). "On the Commercial Taxes from Late Tang to the Five Dynasties and Ten States Period" *Journal of Chinese Social and Economic History*, 1 (2021): 10–18 (In Chinese).

# Chapter 9
# Fiscal Revenue in Ming and Qing China (1368–1911 CE): A Quantification

**Hanhui Guan, Debin Ma, and Runzhuo Zhai**

Since Joseph Schumpeter's seminal essay, there have been a large literature that attempted to understand the rise of fiscal state marked by a shift from a system based on resources derived from the king's domain to one where the state became involved in providing funds through taxation. This has generated a large theoretical literature (Acemoglu 2005; Besley and Persson 2008, 2011; Koyama and Johnson 2017) as well as empirical works (Dincecco 2009, 2015; Karaman and Pamuk 2010). The issue of fiscal and state capacity naturally looms large is the study of Imperial China marked by the world's first bureaucracy (Liu 2005; Sng 2014; Ma 2014; Ma and Rubin 2019; von Glahn 2020) and retains the central focus of attention for our volume (see Chaps. 6–8, and 10 in this volume).

Given that carefully constructed data series form the foundation for any analysis on this topic, our paper represents the first systematic attempt to build a half-millennium series of Chinese imperial fiscal revenue in total, per capita, nominal, and real terms. We further break down the data into categories of direct versus indirect taxes, taxes in-kind and in cash. We provide estimates for each dynasty with detailed categories also discuss the case of extra-legal surge and corvée labor that are not well captured in our estimates of official central government revenue. The five hundred years of series thus reconstructed allow us to make a direct comparison with England, which emerged as

H. Guan
School of Economics, Peking University, Beijing, China

D. Ma
School of Economics, Fudan University, Shanghai, China

R. Zhai (✉)
School of Agricultural Economics and Rural Development, Renmin University of China, Beijing, China

Institute of Agrarian History, Renmin University of China, Beijing, China
e-mail: runzhuo.zhai@ruc.edu.cn



Z. Chen et al. (eds.), *Quantitative History of China*, Studies in Economic History,
https://doi.org/10.1007/978-981-96-8272-0_9

the world's first modern fiscal state from the late seventeen century. Converted into comparable measures, our estimates reveal the divergence in fiscal and state capacity between England and China had clearly emerged by the seventeenth century and only widened further afterwards.

In some sense, this chapter picks up where Chap. 8 by Liu and Kwan in this volume ended. There, they highlight the rise and fall of a fiscal state in the era before our study, the Song dynasty. The fascinating fiscal and financial innovation in Song dynasty which as they Liu and Kwan showed, originated in the fragmented era of late Tang dynasty had largely faded or abandoned in the increasingly unitary states of Ming and Qing dynasties. Indeed, following the demise of Song and Yuan dynasty, the Chinese path toward a fiscal state were largely reversed, retrogressing into a traditional agrarian structure by the Ming and Qing dynasties (von Glahn 2020). The institutional mechanism behind this reversal—the move toward land tax and away from fiscal and financial innovation—are explored in Chap. 10 (Hao and Liu) and Chap. 11 (Diao, Hu and Ma) in this volume. Indeed, as seen in Chaps. 10 and 11, the problems of political institution and lack of credible commitment that had haunted the Song became dominant by the Ming and Qing dynasties.

Although there have already been estimates of Chinese fiscal revenue in the literature, our series are the most systematic and continuous, meticulously reconstructed from the bottom up and based on a large number of primary sources such as *Ming shilu* (Veritable Records of the Ming Dynasty, 明实录), *Qing shilu* (Veritable Records of the Qing Dynasty, 清实录), *Qingchao wenxian tongkao* (Comprehensive examination of the literature of the Qing Dynasty, 清朝文献通考) and other material. We offer a detailed data appendix at the end of our chapter on primary sources and methodology. This chapter is divided into three sections. Section 9.1 provides a historical narrative of the imperial Chinese fiscal system. Section 9.2 presents our estimates, and Sect. 9.3 presents an international comparison.

## 9.1 Fiscal Regime in Imperial China

Chinese imperial taxation is fundamentally founded on state control of various categories of resources. The first item on this list is human resources, which can be divided into the tangible poll tax (人头税) and the non-tangible corvée labor (徭役). The second source of fiscal extraction is on land, which is literally translated as "land rent" (田租) or "tribute" (赋) but usually referred to by the modern term of land tax. This formed the most important source of tax revenue through several dynasties. Registering households and population (编户齐民) and surveying land was the top priority, and in some cases formed the legitimacy of every new dynastic ruler. Even though population and land were two independent items in these surveys, the technical difficulty of measuring land acreage in pre-modern times often meant much of the so-called land acreage data were obtained by some form of self-assessment (自实) (Chao 1986;Ho 1959, 1995). In that sense, the Chinese land tax had always been based on household level, making it closer to a form of poll tax.[1]

The Twice-Year Tax reform of 780 CE, introduced by Yang Yan (杨炎), started a major transition from the poll tax toward a form of household-based land property tax. But it was only at the beginning of the Ming era that the Twice-Year Tax formed the core of a pure land-based tax system. Poll tax based on individuals and households then turned up mainly as corvée labor (徭役). By the time of the One Whip Law (一条鞭法) reform that simplified fiscal laws in the sixteenth century, even corvée labor was slowly being monetized into silver payment added as a surcharge on land tax. Finally, this process progressed further through the "converting poll to acreage (摊丁入亩)" tax reform implemented by the Qing in the seventeenth and eighteenth centuries that finally completed more than a millennium of transition toward a pure form of land or agricultural tax or rent.

Outside land-poll taxes, Imperial China extracted revenue on other resources under its control or management. The first main type is tax on products under some form of governmental monopoly such as salt, tea, liquor, and natural resources. Unlike agricultural taxes that had to be collected from scattered areas across the vast empire, mines, whether for salt or other minerals, were geographically concentrated or circumscribed. Various dynasties often resort to governmental monopoly (禁榷) and state management for revenue extraction. Overtime, however, inefficiency in state management often gave way to the entry of private capital and commercial management that would yield tax revenue remitted to the state.

Commercial taxes include those levied on domestic and overseas trade, stamp duties, and license fees. Domestic trade was carried out by both migrant (行商) and indigenous merchants (坐商). Taxes on migrant merchants were levied by various trade stations along trade routes. Taxes on indigenous merchants were based on trading centers and towns. After the Song, however, the imperial government mostly focused on taxing the migrating merchants as tax stations along trading routes were vastly reduced and concentrated in several large trading towns during the Yuan, Ming, and Qing dynasties, a far cry from the several hundred tax collection stations during the Northern Song. A large recovery occurred with the introduction of the *likin* (厘金)—a tax used to raise militia—after the mid-nineteenth century as a response to the fiscal pressure stemming from the Taiping Rebellion. Similarly, taxes on foreign trade became important after the mid-nineteenth century after the founding of the Chinese Maritime Customs Service as a result of China's forced opening to global trade and Western imperialism. Before that, taxes on foreign trade during the Ming and Qing

[1] For example, during the Northern and Southern Dynasties and the early Sui and Tang dynasties, the system of "equal distribution of land 均田" was designed irrespective of whether or not people actually occupied a legal amount of land, but rather to tax them according to that set amount of land (Ho 1995: 18).

and the so-called taxes on the thirteen *cohong* merchants, who had a monopoly on foreign trade during the Qing, had always been limited.

There are various taxes sometimes specific to different periods or dynasties in the form of confiscation, donations, sale of official titles or positions and license fees on Buddhists, Daoists, and other communities. Seigniorage was another source of revenue throughout the millennium, during which the government minted copper cash and issued paper money. However, seigniorage from minting of copper cash is negligible due to the high cost of producing low-denomination currency (Wang 2003, 253–266). There are seigniorage profits from paper money, but they were only in large circulation during the Ming and very early Qing (Peng 2015, 597–603). We summarize the main categories of imperial fiscal revenue for the Ming and Qing in Table 9.1.

**Table 9.1** Chinese fiscal revenue categories

Panel A: The general picture

| Corvée labor | Land-poll taxes | Industry | Commerce | Others |
|---|---|---|---|---|
| Regular projects: military, transport, grassroots governance, royal artisans, etc. Temporary projects: military, transport, water works, royal works, etc | Land tax and poll tax | Salt, wine, vinegar, tea, mining (silver, gold, copper and others) | Commerce, sales, tariff, transaction and others | Penalties, government title trafficking, donation, interest, sovereign tax, royalty business etc |

Panel B: Ming and Qing (1368–1911)

| Dynasty | Population-land taxes | Industry: Excise (monopolization) | Industry: Mining revenue | Commerce and others |
|---|---|---|---|---|
| Ming Dynasty (1368–1644) | Twice-Year Tax (plus a poll tax after the One Whip Law) | Salt, tea | Gold, silver, copper, Iron, lead, tin, etc | Domestic circulation tax, customs and miscellaneous tax (杂税) |
| Early Qing Dynasty (1644–1840) | Twice-Year Tax and poll tax (地丁银) | Salt, tea | Gold, silver, copper, Iron, lead, tin, etc | Domestic circulation tax, customs and miscellaneous tax (杂税), donations and Keju titles selling |
| Late Qing Dynasty (1840–1911) | Twice-Year Tax and poll tax (地丁银) | Salt, tea, opium, etc | Gold, silver, copper, Iron, lead, tin, etc | Domestic circulation tax (old and *likin*), customs under Chinese and foreign jurisdiction, miscellaneous tax (杂税), donations and Keju titles selling |

*Sources* Zheng (1994), Huang (2015), Liu (2015), Chen and Shi (2000), Zhang and Zhou (2015), and Chen and Cai (2013a, 2013b)

One consequence of taxation through the governmental control of resources is that there is not a unified central fiscal system. For example, although the so-called Ministry of Finance (户部), which administered, transferred, and audited the land-poll tax through its information gathered on national population and land comes closest to a modern treasury, it did not have control over all revenue extracted from resources. Often each of the six ministries had its own source of income and revenue extracted from resources under their respective control and collected separately. Largely outside the purview of the Ministry of Finance, for example, ministries of Works (工部) or Army (兵部) would extract revenue independently (Hartwell 1988; Li 2019).

Above this structure stood the Imperial palace finance that in principle was independent from the state finances and the finance ministry. Over time, the palace finance (内帑 or 内务府) did become increasingly detached from the state revenue (Qi 2009). It derived income from imperial estates, loans, and government-owned enterprises such as silk weaving. Under the Qing, the palace finance had achieved a greater degree of business complexity and operational maturity than previous generations, such as monopolizing ginseng sales in Northeast China and the Jiangning silk weaving operation in Nanjing.

Another important feature is that under a highly centralized political system, there is no autonomous local fiscal budget or system, as all local governments are in principle dispatched by the central government. Tax collection by local governments is essentially assigned by the central government to its agencies. They need to manage and collect taxes in the areas under their jurisdiction according to the requirements of the central government and transfer most of the revenue to the center. The local government can retain part of it for themselves to cover administrative expenses. In other words, Imperial China did not have a local fiscal system in the modern sense. However, due to the information asymmetry of the central government—and many other reasons—the administrative expenditures legally reserved for local governments often could not meet the daily operations of local governments. That has led to the so-called "corruption income" in various guises, some of which were actually for bridging the gap in legitimate administrative expenses (Zhou 2019).

It is notable that historical records on these forms of corruption at the local level are relatively muted before the large-scale fiscal conversion of corvée labor service into monetary revenue during the mid-Ming dynasty in the sixteenth century. In essence, corvée is similar to a poll tax but it is managed and extracted locally. Apart from some services required by the central government such as craftsmen and large-scale infrastructure projects, most corvée services mainly serve local governments, including administrative tasks. Whether it is Wang Anshi's corvée exemption law (1071) in the Song dynasty or Zhang Juzheng (张居正)'s Single Whip Law (1581) in the Ming, they all aimed at converting corvée labor into hired labor and eventually into monetized tax revenue that would become accessible to the central government (Liang 1936; Hu 2012b; Zhao and Ding 2013).

In other words, as long as the corvée system existed and formed the legitimate resource of local governance, local governments had much less incentive to acquire the non-statutory or "corruption income". Corvée service is difficult to centralize and inefficient to administer, which made it a relatively secure and useful source of local tax, despite the inefficiency itself becoming a huge burden on individual households and the overall economy. This also means that the conversion of corvée service into a monetary amount accessible to the central government, coupled with the absence of any statutory provision for local governance, inadvertently led to the hollowing out of local revenue, driving local governments to seek more "corruption income".

One case in point is the well-studied Yongzheng (雍正) fiscal reform during the 1720s and 1730s. After a rule mandating land tax payments to be paid in silver ingots from the late Ming, an extra-legal conversion surcharge called *huohao* (火耗)—was imposed by local authorities. Yongzheng's attempt to legitimize the previously hidden huohao into a form of official revenue known as *Yanglian silver* (养廉银) is lauded as the hallmark of rational fiscal reform. Unfortunately, once these surcharges became widely known, their payment was taken over by the central government under the subsequent Qianlong (乾隆) reign (1735–1796), pushing the local administration to seek new sources of "corruption income" (Hao and Liu 2020; Zelin 1984; Ma and Rubin 2019; Hao and Liu in this volume).

## 9.2 Half a Millennium of Chinese Central Fiscal Revenue

### *9.2.1 Reconstructing Ming and Qing Fiscal Revenue*

The fiscal revenue structure of the Ming dynasty followed the Yuan and can still be divided into agricultural tax and indirect tax. Agricultural tax was a mix of land and poll taxes that covered almost all the registered population. Indirect tax was the revenue from industry and commerce that mainly comes from non-agricultural activities. It is noteworthy that the Twice-Year Tax as the agricultural tax in the Ming dynasty had been firmly established, while the poll tax of previous dynasties had been gradually abolished. In other words, the mix of land and poll taxes in the Ming dynasty are closer to the land tax in normal sense. The taxes that levied on households or headcounts in previous dynasties had been completely transformed into corvée labor. It should be noted that the corvée, despite its large scale, had already begun to be paid in silver at a very early stage at the local level on a spontaneous basis, a trend that was not formalized into law until Zhang Juzheng's rule as prime minister, known as the Single Whip Law. Local gazetteers from the Wanli Period usually contain an item called *dingyin* (丁银), which is the tax item generated after the transformation of corvée and is actually equivalent to a type of poll tax. In the Qing dynasty, *didingyin* (地丁银) was the general name of sum of the land tax and poll tax.

Indirect tax came from industry and commerce, mainly taxes on salt, tea, mining, and miscellaneous goods and services. Actually, the indirect tax in this period still followed the previous principle, but many items like commercial, wine and vinegar, fisheries, and transaction taxes (such as on deeds) were included in the miscellaneous tax, and the proportion was very small compared with the Song and Yuan. Other revenues that had a relatively large impact also included paper money issued in the early Ming dynasty. As for other items, we do not calculate them such as penalties due to the limited data and the small impact. We present the estimation procedures and data sources in Appendix A.

The Hongwu (洪武) reign (1368–1398) by the founding emperor Zhu Yuanzhang (朱元璋) started the Ming dynasty at a high level of fiscal revenue, as seen in Fig. 9.1. The vigorous and notoriously brutal founding emperor conducted one of the most comprehensive population and land censuses in 1393 that laid the foundation for fiscal extraction. Fiscal revenue as shown in Fig. 9.1 since then was on a downward trend, with a visible decline during the Yongle (永乐) reign (1403–1424). But it was during the Xuande (宣德) (1426–1435) and Zhengtong (正统) reigns (1436–1449) that saw the biggest drop in land tax, owing to the decline of the military farms and collapse of the paper money due to over-issuance. That led to a reduction in taxes on commerce and mining sectors often collected in paper money. This era of rapid fiscal decline corresponded to weakening military capacity that led to the 1449 Tumu Crisis (土木堡之变)—a Ming-Mongol border conflict—which saw the capture of the Ming emperor Zhu Qizhen by Esen (也先), the Mongol ruler. Fiscal revenue began to recover during the Chenghua (成化) (1465–1487) and Hongzhi (弘治) reigns (1488–1505). Fiscal expansion began from 1581 when Zhang Juzheng embarked on one of the most important fiscal reforms, as mentioned earlier. Political and military crises triggered a massive fiscal extraction (三饷加派) which may have in turn exacerbated the crises and hastened the fall of the Ming. Overall, the entire Ming fiscal structure was locked into land tax, there was a "physiocratic" structure that became far removed from those of mercantilist Song and Yuan dynasties.

Figure 9.2 shows three broad phases of Qing fiscal revenue. The first phase runs from the founding of the Qing in the 1640s to about the 1760s when the fiscal structure and the concept of fiscal quotas—largely inherited from the Ming—were dominated by agricultural tax. The second phase goes from the 1760s until the 1840s. Although not fundamentally different from the land-tax-based first phase, this second phase does see a slow creeping of other forms of taxation, such as excise, and from the early nineteenth century, the sale of governmental titles and forced donations from elites and merchants. These partially compensated for the periodic shortfalls between received revenue and the designated land-tax quota. These shortfalls had emerged from the end of nineteenth century during the Qianlong reign (1736–1795) and progressively worsened toward the Jiaqing (嘉庆) (1796–1820) and Daoguang (道光) reigns (1821–1850) (Chen and Cai 2013b; Ni 2013; Shi and Xu 2008). As is well-known, the third phase starts from the mid-nineteenth century that saw the rise of new commercial taxes in the name of *likin* and Maritime Customs tariffs, both of which were a response to the need to repress the massive Taiping Rebellion and the Qing's forced opening to Western imperialism.

The first two phases followed the fiscal system of the middle and late Ming dynasty, which was composed of the land-poll tax (dominated by *didingyin*, the Twice-Year Tax and corvée labor revenue), indirect tax revenues from industry and commerce (dominated by salt taxes, tariffs, and miscellaneous taxes) and other revenues (dominated by the sale of official Civil Examination degree titles 捐纳 and

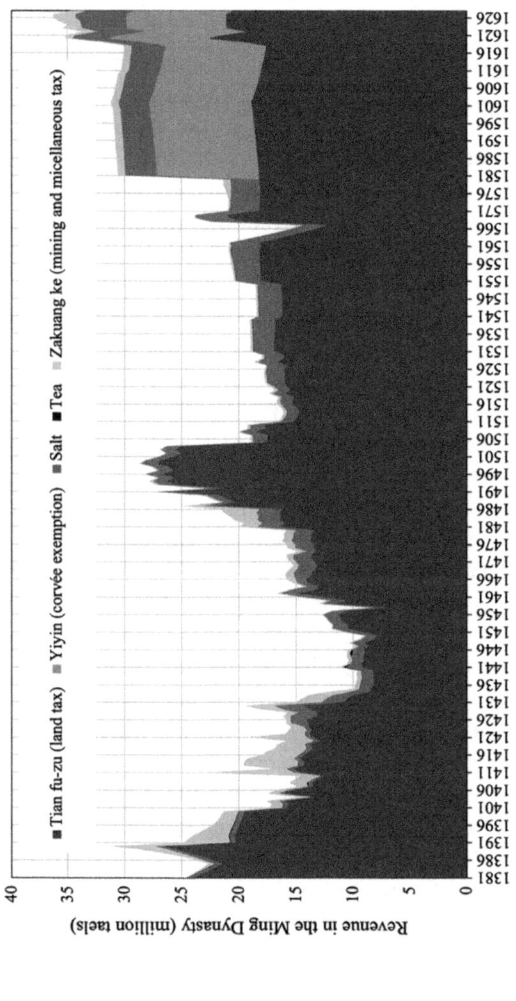


**Fig. 9.1** Central government revenue in the Ming Dynasty: categories and amounts, 1381–1626 (in silver taels) (*Sources* see the text)

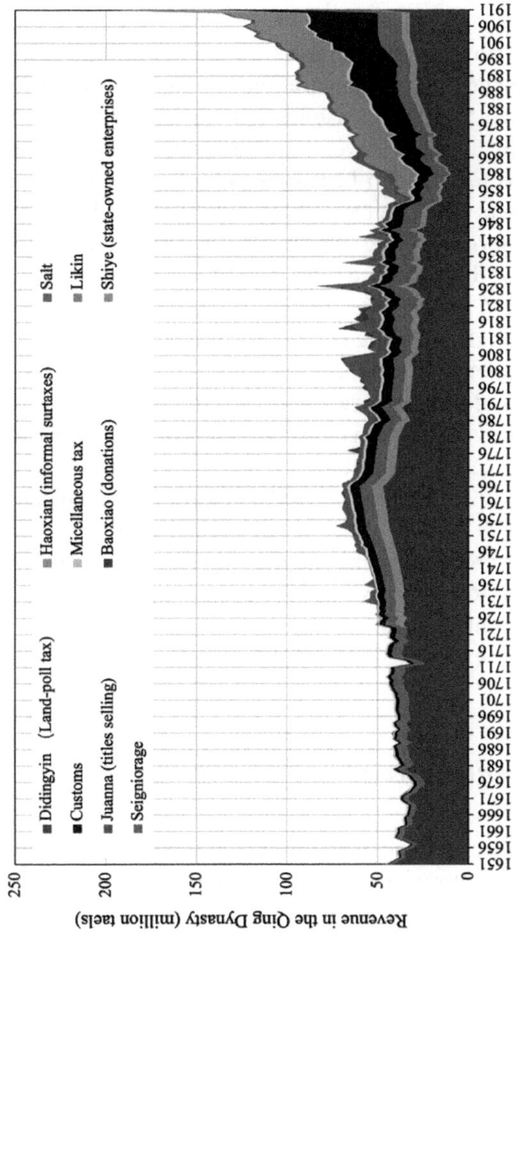


**Fig. 9.2** Central government revenue in the Qing Dynasty: categories and amounts, 1651–1911 (in silver taels) (*Sources* see the text)

donations 报效). Another distinctive feature of the Qing fiscal system was that some unusual revenues in previous dynasties such as the sale of titles and donations became increasingly important. The customary sale of titles even remained at about 3 million taels for a long time (Ni 2017a: 59), and rose to 5–10% of the total fiscal revenue at certain points. Besides, the donations from merchants also played an important role. The salt merchants provided money to fund the military, water works, and other projects, which greatly eased the financial difficulties in some periods (Ni 2017a: 60).

In the late Qing dynasty, apart from the original fiscal system, there appeared two new sources of revenue. Foreign tariffs were a major innovation in this period. By establishing a modern tax administration system and employing professional managers, the so-called Maritime Customs system, managed by non-Chinese officers, greatly improved the tariff revenue in this period (Ni 2017b). Another new source of revenue was *likin* which became similar to a local commercial tax. Due to the political and fiscal pressure caused by Taiping Rebellion and other uprisings, the central government of the Qing dynasty had to delegate its fiscal power to local governments and allow them to raise their own funds (Deng 2021). This is probably the first time in Chinese history after the late Tang dynasty that local governments were separated so strongly from the central government in terms of fiscal power. In addition, in the late nineteenth century, as China entered the world market system, many different sources of revenues were generally developed, such as the seigniorage profit from the temporary restoration of paper money in the Taiping Rebellion period, the establishment of state-owned enterprises in the Westernization Movement (洋务企业), the emergence of foreign debt, bonds, and modern financial markets, or the Copper Coin Reform (铜元改革) in the late nineteenth and early twentieth centuries. These "new" sources of revenue increased the total revenue of the Qing governments (both central and local) to a large extent. However, many of these revenue categories were not included in central fiscal system, so they are not added in our calculation. We mainly focus on new changes in tariff, *likin*, and modern enterprises.

### 9.2.2 Fiscal Revenue: Trend and Structure

Figure 9.3 plots the entire revenue of Ming and Qing Imperial central governments in terms of silver taels and units of rice. Figure 9.4 plots the series of population and rice prices under our study. We standardize all revenue into silver tael units, as taxation denoted in silver became dominant from the middle of the Ming dynasty (sixteenth century) although copper cash, paper money, or in-kind payment co-existed (Li 2017). Figure 9.3 reveals the striking feature that imperial China's central revenue remained largely below 50 million taels across the two dynasties until about the mid-nineteenth century. This long run of stability reflected the rise of what China historians called the frozen fiscal quota of 40 million silver taels especially after the founding of the Ming dynasty (Ho 1959; Huang 1974).

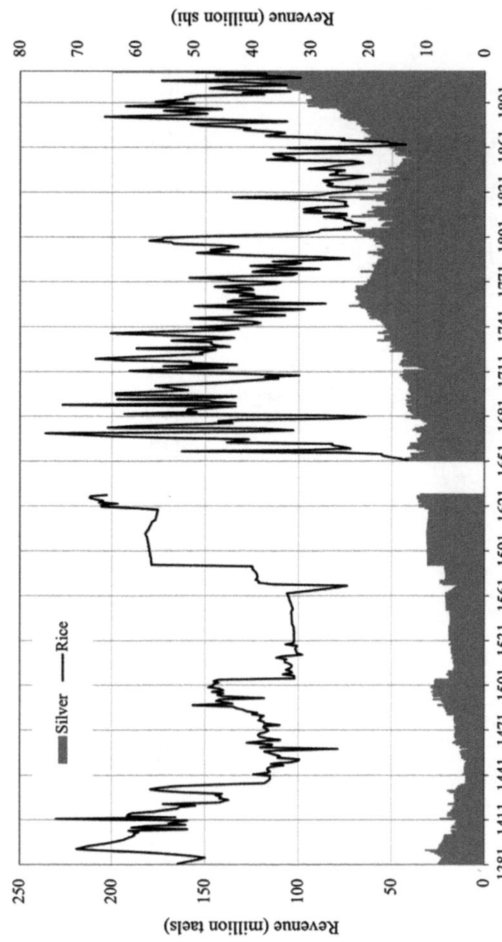


**Fig. 9.3** Central government revenue of China, 1381–1911 (left axis in silver taels and right axis in rice shi) (*Sources* and *Notes* Fiscal revenue data are from this paper. Rice price data for Ming are from Xinwei Peng (2015). The rice price index for Qing is from Kaixiang Peng (2006). The missing values are filled in using log-linear interpolation)

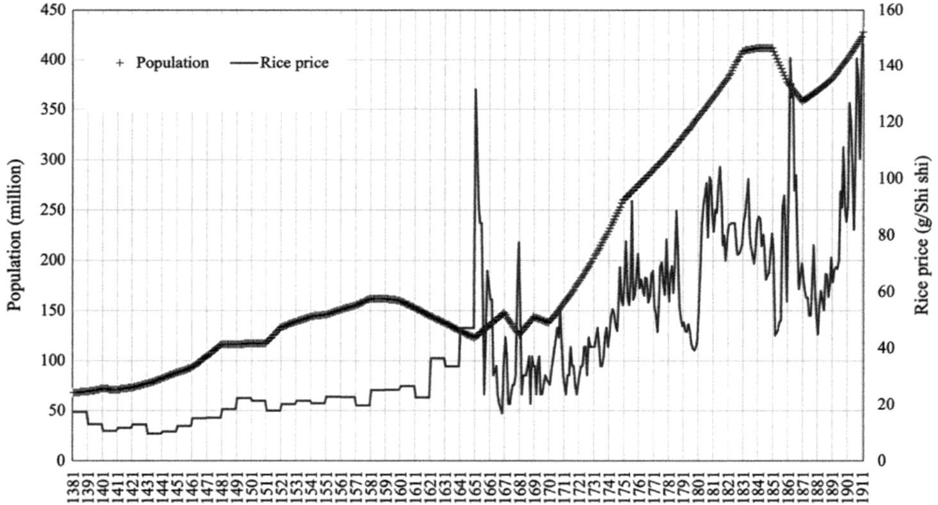


**Fig. 9.4** Population (millions) and rice price (grams of silver/ *shi* of husked rice) in China, 997–1911 BCE (*Sources* and *Notes* Population data before 1850 are taken from Broadberry et al. (2018) and Maddison (1998). Population data after 1850 are from Zhai and Lou (2022). Rice price data for Ming are from Xinwei Peng (2015). Qing's data are from Kaixiang Peng (2006). The missing values are filled in using log-linear interpolation.)

Figure 9.4 presents the population data and rice price for Ming and Qing dynasties. Figure 9.5 shows our silver fiscal revenue converted into real terms using rice price as a deflator. Even though rice price alone as a deflator is not ideal, it gives good approximation, given the predominant share of grain/rice in Chinese agriculture and the overall Chinese economy. The half a millennium of fiscal revenue now converted into units of rice as displayed remained largely trendless throughout the Ming and Qing dynasties. Among the important fiscal reforms during Ming and Qing is the Zhang Juzheng's reform (1581), which led to visible rises in fiscal revenue, whereas the effect of the Yongzheng (雍正) reforms during the Qing such as the Haoxian guigong (耗羡归公) of 1724 and the Tanding rumu (摊丁入亩) of 1729 were less pronounced.[2] The first reform focused on converting and monetizing corvée labor into central government revenue, possibly at the expense of local revenue. It is interesting to note that the Yongzheng reforms did raise fiscal revenue in silver terms, leading to the well-known peak surplus in silver reserve during the Qianlong era (Ma 2014). However, this nominal effect disappeared in real terms as shown in Fig. 9.3 owing to rising grain prices during the eighteenth century. To certain degree, the Yongzheng fiscal reform legalized previously extra-legal charges in tax collection that had been part of the local government resources. Its policy of converting polls tax into land tax (摊丁入亩) was largely a continuation and extension of the One Whip Law tax reform initiated during the Ming. Figure 9.5 presents the fiscal revenue in per capita terms.

We now organize our long-term estimates into several substantive categories. Figure 9.6 presents the category of land-poll taxes which broadly correspond to what we refer as direct taxes, against the category of indirect taxes defined by excise or levies on monopoly commodities and commerce. During the Ming, especially in the early part of the dynasty, displayed an extreme dependence on land taxes, possibly due to Zhu Yuanzhang's draconian policy of control and the rise of a type of command economy (Hu 2012a). The Qing largely inherited the agricultural-tax-based fiscal structure but reveal greater flexibility despite the nominal quota. With rising population, the per capita land tax burden began to decline.

Compared to England and Europe in general, imperial China derived a relatively small share of seigniorage revenue, partly due to the high cost of minting low-value copper cash. As shown Table 9.3, seigniorage profits remained low in the Northern Song, at only about 2% of total revenue, despite the massive quantities of copper cash produced, some of which even circulated beyond the Chinese territories and continued their use throughout the Ming and Qing dynasties (Liu 2011). This is in sharp contrast to early Ming, whose issuance of Daming Baochao (大明宝钞) banknotes sharply devalued within a few decades. Between 1376 and 1413, the Daming Baochao paper money lost 98.8% of its value. One important reason is the early Ming's failure to redeem the paper money or accept it as tax payment. Given such rapid loss in value and subsequent disappearance of the Ming paper money, the Ming ended up with negligible seigniorage revenue (Peng 2015: 494). Ming

[2] The study by Yuhua Wang documents a total of 57 major fiscal reforms during 221 BC–1911 AD with 30 of them occurring after 960AD. See Wang (2022), Appendix 2.

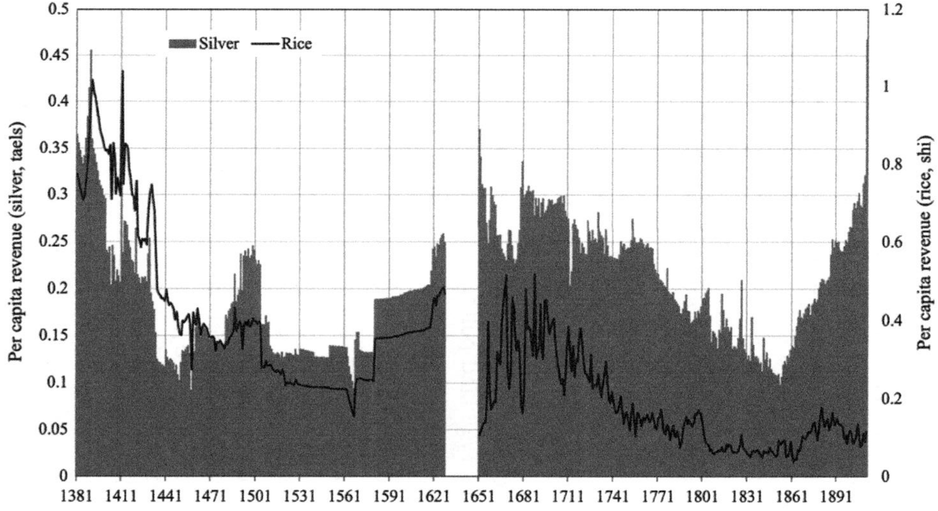


**Fig. 9.5** Per capita central government revenue, 1381–1911 (left axis in silver taels and right axis in rice *shi*) (*Sources* and *Notes* Fiscal revenue data are from this paper. Rice price data for Ming are from Xinwei Peng (2015). Qing's data are from Kaixiang Peng (2006). The missing values are filled in using log-linear interpolation. Population data before 1850 are taken from Broadberry et al. (2018) and Maddison (1998). Population data after 1850 are from Zhai and Lou (2022))

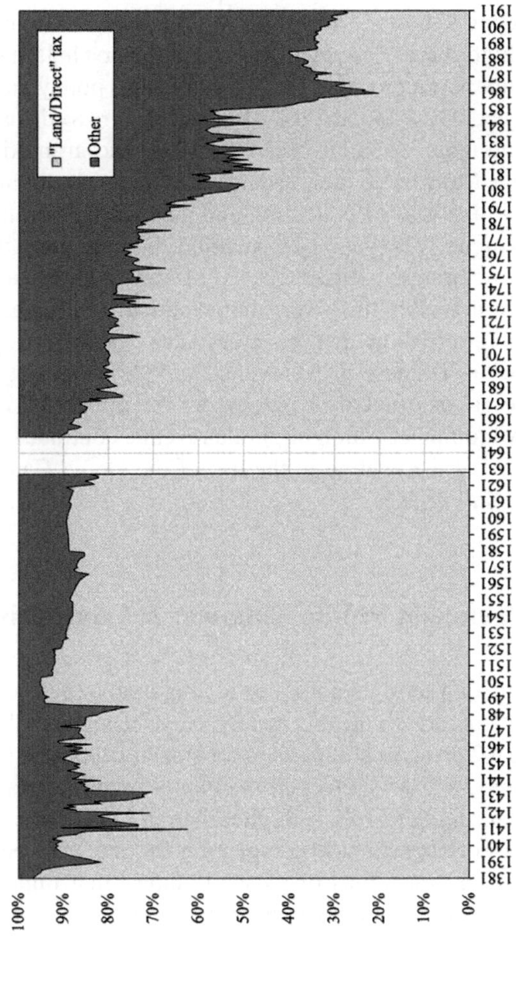


**Fig. 9.6** Share of land (direct) and other (indirect) taxes, 1381–1911 (*Sources* and *Notes* See the paper)

also issued a small amount of copper cash, but they generated so little seigniorage that we set overall Ming seigniorage revenue to zero. For Qing paper in the early period and debased copper cash from the mid-nineteenth century, we set the overall seigniorage revenue at 0.45% of total revenue, as summarized in Table 9.3. This is in sharp contrast to the nearly 20% seigniorage profits in sixteenth century England (O'Brien and Hunt 1993).

Due to data limitations, we are only able to provide a qualitative account of the monetization of Ming fiscal revenue. Figure 9.7 presents tax revenue in-kind and in money for the entire Qing dynasty. The trend toward monetization of fiscal revenue was starting from the high share of payment in-kind in the first half of the Ming. This is consistent with qualitative records that Zhu Yuanzhuang's policy turned China into nearly a barter-based economy. Indeed, the Ming revenue records used the in-kind goods as its accounting units. A barter-based economy and an in-kind dominance fiscal revenue during the Ming led to the constant conversion of units among different goods and excessively high cost of collecting and paying taxes on the society as a whole within a vast empire. The year 1436 marked the beginning of a process to convert all units into a government-stipulated silver standard known as *Jinhua Silver* (金花银). The conversion toward this silver unit eventually culminated in the well-known One Whip Law reform more than a century later. These have opened the path toward a "silverization" of Chinese fiscal revenue and the increasing conversion of corvée labor into land tax as officially begun under the reform by Zhang Juzheng in 1581. The trend toward monetization of public revenue continued throughout the Qing, especially following the decline in the use of the Grand Canal for shipping tribute grain, as shown in Fig. 9.7.

## 9.3 Great Divergence in Public Finance: A Comparison

We are able to put our long-term estimates in a comparative perspective. First, let us compare our main outcome with the widely cited benchmark based study by William G. Liu. Table 9.2 presents comparison for state revenue and land tax against the benchmark used by Liu (2005). Overall, the two estimates are fairly consistent, although our estimate for Qing in 1685 is higher than in Liu (2005).

Table 9.3 now presents benchmark comparison of total and per capita fiscal revenue across Eurasia in grams/tons of silver. It shows that imperial China had the largest total fiscal revenue in nominal silver terms until the nineteenth century when rapidly advancing Britain and France began to overtake China. In per capita terms, China's fiscal revenue was one of the lowest in the world from the seventeenth century. China fell even further behind England that at the time of defeat during the mid-nineteenth century Opium War, when its per capita fiscal revenue was a mere 2% of Britain's.

Figures 9.8 and 9.9 plot the long-term fiscal revenue for China and England in terms of total and per capita fiscal revenue in silver. Figure 9.10 adds a series for shares of gross domestic product (GDP) with due recognition that GDP estimates

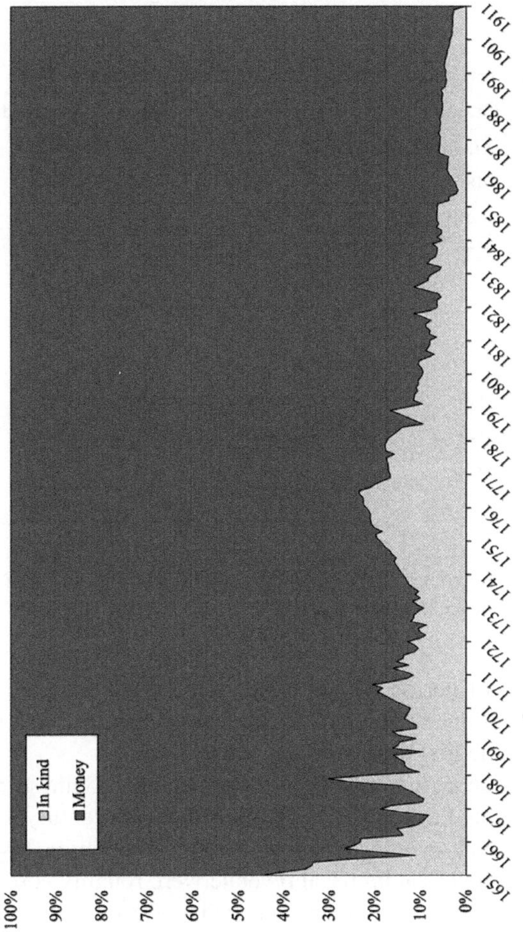


**Fig. 9.7** Share of fiscal revenues in-kind and in money, 1651–1911 (*Sources* and *Notes* See the paper)

**Table 9.2** Comparisons with William G. Liu's estimates

| | State revenues (Shi of rice) | | Land tax share (%) | |
|---|---|---|---|---|
| | Our estimates | W. Liu | Our estimates | W. Liu |
| Ming (1407) | 51.28 | 47.66 | 91 | 96 |
| Ming (1577) | 39.52 | 42.19 | 86 | 88 |
| Qing (1685) | 50.91 | 38.04 | 80 | 82 |
| Qing (1776) | 32.38 | 36.62 | 73 | 75 |

**Table 9.3** Chinese central revenue: in comparison with major Eurasian regimes

| | China | Ottoman | Russia | France | Spain | England | Dutch R |
|---|---|---|---|---|---|---|---|
| *Panel A. Aggregate revenue (tons of silver)* | | | | | | | |
| 1650–99 | 1419 | 248 | | 851 | 243 | 239 | |
| 1700–1749 | 1809 | 294 | 155 | 932 | 312 | 632 | 310 |
| 1750–99 | 2313 | 263 | 492 | 1612 | 618 | 1370 | 350 |
| 1800–1849 | 2121 | | | | | 6156 | |
| 1850–99 | 2589 | | | | | 10,941 | |
| *Panel B. Per capita revenue (grams of silver)* | | | | | | | |
| 1650–99 | 10.4 | 11.8 | | 46.0 | 35.8 | 45.1 | 13.6 |
| 1700–1749 | 9.4 | 15.5 | 6.4 | 46.6 | 41.6 | 93.5 | 24.1 |
| 1750–99 | 7.8 | 12.9 | 21 | 66.4 | 63.1 | 158.4 | 22.8 |
| 1800–1849 | 5.5 | | | | | 303.8 | |
| 1850–99 | 6.8 | | | | | 344.1 | |

*Sources* Chinese fiscal and population data, see the text, Broadberry et al. (2018), and Maddison (1998). Other countries' data, see Brandt et al. (2014)

for such a long stretch of period remain controversial. We compare with England as it has the longest continuous series of fiscal revenue that also saw a fundamental transformation toward the first modern fiscal state.

Figure 9.8 shows a sharp contrast between a stagnant Chinese revenue series against continuously rising English series. By the nineteenth century, England finally overtook China despite having only about a tenth of the population. Figure 9.9 shows that Chinese and English per capita fiscal revenue were roughly comparable before the seventeen century. But with England advancing steadily, its per capita fiscal revenue afterwards began to decisively break away from China's. By the first half of the eighteenth century, English fiscal revenue in the wake of the Glorious Revolution of 1688 was more than ten times that of China's. Given the relatively higher per capita GDP in the United Kingdom, Fig. 9.10 shows that English series for fiscal revenue as a share of GDP only overtook China in the second half of the seventeenth century, but then subsequently rose versus a downward trend in China whose the per capita fiscal burden stood at a mere 4% or below and dropped further to below 2%

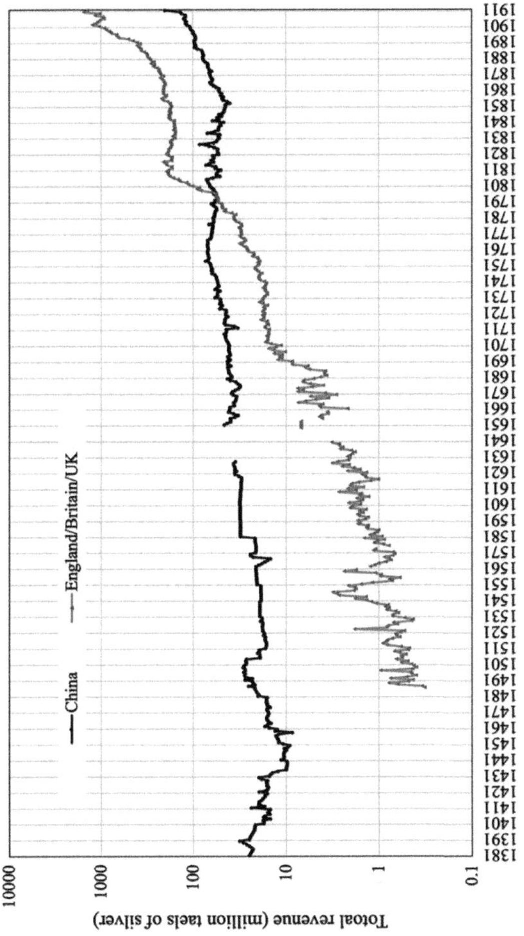


**Fig. 9.8** Chinese central government revenue: in comparison with England/Britain/UK 1381–1911 (in silver taels) (*Sources* and *Notes* Fiscal revenue data are from this paper. British data are taken from "A millennium of macroeconomic data for the UK, version 3.1" by the Bank of England (2018) (https://fred.stlouisfed.org/categories/33839#). Silver-GBP exchange rate data are from GPIH database (https://gpih.ucdavis.edu/Datafilelist.htm))

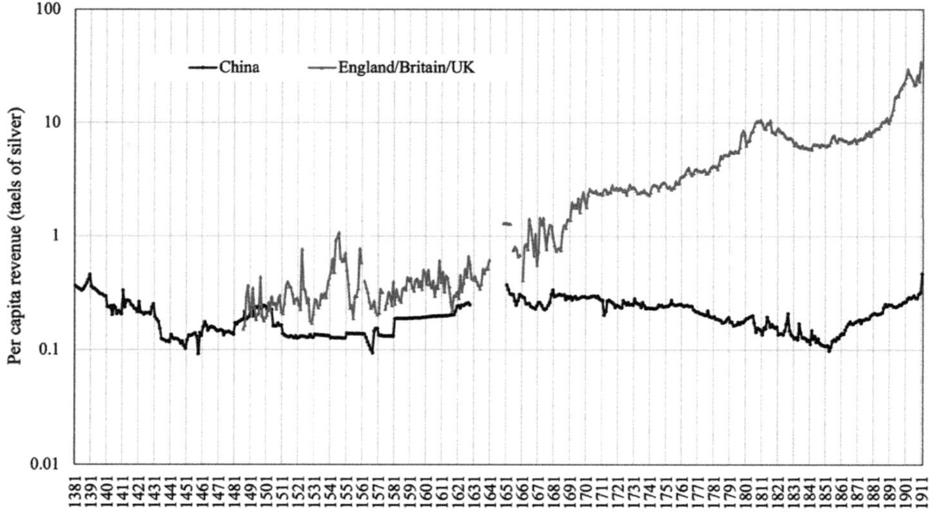


**Fig. 9.9** Chinese central government revenue per capita: in comparison with England/Britain/UK 1381–1911 (in silver taels) (*Sources* and *Notes* Fiscal revenue data are from this paper. British fiscal and population data are taken from "A millennium of macroeconomic data for the UK, version 3.1" by the Bank of England (2018) (https://fred.stlouisfed.org/categories/33839#). Silver-GBP exchange rate data are from GPIH database (https://gpih.ucdavis.edu/Datafilelist.htm))

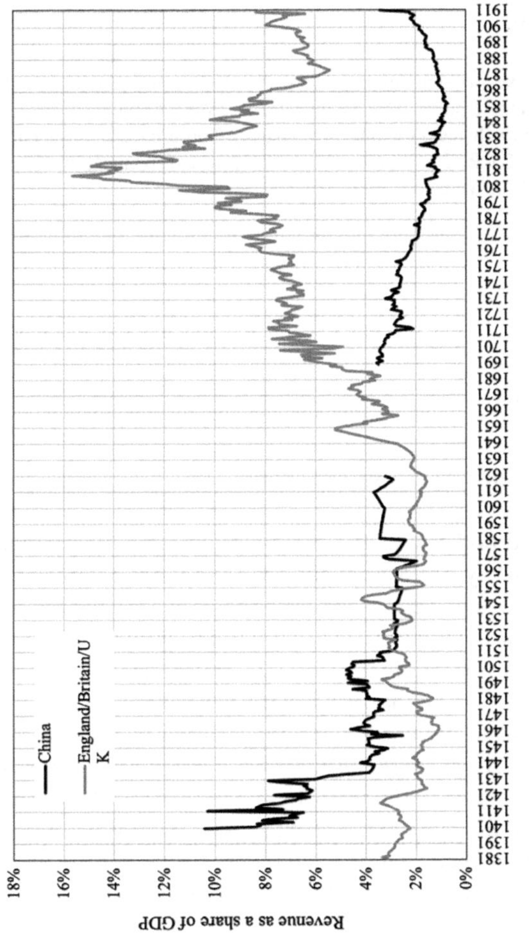


**Fig. 9.10** Chinese central government revenue as a share of GDP: in comparison with England/Britain/UK 1381–1911 (in percent) (*Sources* and *Notes* Fiscal revenue data are from this paper. Chinese GDP data from 1368–1840 are derived from Broadberry, Guan, and Li (2021). GDP data from 1840–1911 comes from Ma and de Jong (2019). British data are taken from "A millennium of macroeconomic data for the UK, version 3.1" by the Bank of England (2018) (https://fred.stlouisfed.org/categories/33839#))

of GDP by the Qing. Furthermore, structure of taxation had evolved in completely opposite direction with England increasingly leaning toward indirect or commercial taxation coupled with fiscal and financial innovation whereas China in Ming and Qing increasingly locked into an agrarian based low-tax regime. The shadow of fiscal and financial innovation experimented in Tang and Song dynasties as captured in Chap. 8 by Liu and Kwan had long faded. Hence, the divergence in fiscal and financial capacity between England and China had emerged in the seventeen century, fully one hundred years before the rise of the Industrial Revolution in England (see also Ma and Rubin 2019).

**Acknowledgements** We acknowledge funding from the AoE grant centered in the Centre for Quantitative History at The University of Hong Kong (HKU). We acknowledge comments from the participants of the Area of Excellence—Quantitative History Conference 2023 at The University of Hong Kong, held on October 25–26 2023, particularly the comments from Zhiwu Chen, Tuan-hwee Sng and William Guanglin Liu. All errors are our own.

## Data Appendices

### *The Ming Dynasty**

#### The Land-Poll Taxes (The "Agricultural" Tax)

Compared with the land-poll tax of the previous dynasties, the structure of this revenue in the Ming dynasty was very clear, with the main components being the Twice-Year Tax, farm rent, and the revenue from the *juntun* (军屯) military encampments. In terms of records, compared to the fragmentary splicing of multiple sources in the previous dynasties, the original records of the Ming dynasty are also very complete due to the survival of the *Ming shilu* (Veritable Records of the Ming Dynasty, 明实录). We have obtained direct tax records of 144 years from 1381 to 1626 in *Ming shilu leizuan: jingji shiliao juan* (Veritable Records of the Ming dynasty Compiled by Category: Volume of Economic Historical Materials 明实录类纂: 经济史料卷) (Li and Yang 1993: 429–515). Specifically, before 1464, the raw records did not differentiate between rice and wheat for the Twice-Year Tax, while after 1464, rice and wheat were documented separately. Therefore, we segment the data before 1464 by the ratio of rice and wheat after 1464. In addition to rice and wheat, we also calculate value of items like cloth, silk, cotton, paper money, and others. Except for the Twice-Year Tax, we calculate the size of *Tuntian zili* (屯田子粒), which was grain produced by frontier military garrisons. Revenue from items like waterborne transport of grain (漕运) was also calculated. It should be noted that the tax deduction and exemption recorded in *Ming shilu* is also included in our calculation. Besides, the extra-legal revenue (三饷加派) that started from the 47th year of Wanli (1619) is also added in our consideration (Liang 2008: 529).

It should be noted in particular that the records in *Ming shilu* used physical items as accounting units, but the phenomenon of converting physical items into money existed throughout most of the Ming dynasty. Even in the late Ming dynasty, almost all revenues were collected and received in silver. However, silver was not legal tender at that time. During most of the Ming dynasty, the official units of fiscal account were the physical items that had been determined in the Hongwu period. Therefore we need to use price data to convert all physical items recorded in *Ming shilu* into silver. The official conversion price was not based on the market price in many cases. So the prices we use are mainly based on the time series data of rice price provided by Peng Xinwei. The official conversion ratios given in *Ming huidian* (Collected Statutes of the Ming Dynasty 明会典) and *Wanli kuaijilu* (Accounting Records in the Period of Wanli, 万历会计录) are use as the relative value of different physical items (Wan and Xu 2015). Peng's rice price data are the result of about 400 observations in different areas of the country documented in *Ming shilu*. Since most of these observations are official conversion data, it is reasonable to use them to reflect changes in official conversion price. To some extent, that is why the rice price data provided by Peng were once criticized by Hu Tieqiu and others for not reflecting market price changes (Hu 2016; Qiu 2018: Appendix 6). Prices of gold, silver, copper, and paper money (*Baochao*宝钞) are taken from Peng Xinwei (2015: 468–482).

**Revenues from Industry and Commerce (The "Indirect" Tax)**

Revenue from salt, tea, mining, and miscellaneous taxes are also taken from *Ming shilu*. The data coverage time is consistent with the agricultural tax, and the calculation of converting different physical items into silver is still referred to the above method.

**Seigniorage and Others**

As in the Song dynasty, currency during the Ming dynasty was mainly paper money and copper coins. But unfortunately, there was no accurate data on the amount of currency in circulation in that period. Compared with the Song dynasty, the mintage size in the Ming dynasty was very small. The indiscriminate issuance of paper money under the *Daming Baochao* system in the early Ming dynasty led to a collapse in the credibility of the paper money system. The banknotes were eventually unable to be recognized by the market, as was the case in the Yuan dynasty, during which paper money maintained its status as legal tender for almost a century. The amount of copper coins minted in the Ming dynasty was much smaller than that in other dynasties (Peng 2015: 468–482), thus making the mintage size in the whole Ming dynasty considerably small. We can generally believe that since paper money was still widely circulated in the market with an increasing inflating trend during the

Hongwu (洪武) and Yongle (永乐) periods, the seigniorage revenue at that time may exceed the 8% of the Yuan dynasty. While in the subsequent period, it might be much lower than the 3% of the Northern Song dynasty. Therefore, we can assume that before the period of Xuande (宣德), the seigniorage revenue in the Ming dynasty might be roughly 10% of the total direct/agricultural tax and indirect tax. However, the seigniorage profit in subsequent years might be negligible. As for other items, we do not add them in our calculation due to the lack of data and their limited impact.

## *The Qing Dynasty*

### The Land-Poll Taxes ("Agricultural" Tax)

Compared with previous dynasties, fiscal data in the Qing dynasty are of higher quality. The cross checks of different historical publications and archives enables us to clearly figure out the true meaning of each record. The quality of data in the Qing dynasty is obviously higher than the vague fiscal entries documented in literature of previous dynasties. However, there is still no unified document including all the revenue records in the Qing dynasty. Therefore, we still need to search a large number of different materials to obtain a continuous fiscal revenue series.

The land-poll taxes (direct/agricultural tax) in the Qing dynasty mainly consisted of *didingyin* (Twice-Year Tax and poll tax) and physical revenues like grain and fodder. There are detailed annual data of "*Diding qianliang*" (revenue of Twice-Year Tax and poll tax (地丁钱银) from 1651 to 1734 in *Qing shilu* (Veritable Records of the Qing Dynasty 清实录) (Department of History, Nankai University 1959, 9–35). We tend to think that this data can reflect the actual tax received. According to Chen Feng's (2013b, 213–228) discussion on the records of salt tax in *Qing shilu*, the data in the early Qing dynasty are reliable. However, Chen believes that after the Revolt of the Three Feudatories (三藩之乱), the salt tax data recorded in *Qing shilu* were only "frozen quota" (原额), not reflecting the real salt revenue received, which should have shown a decreasing pattern. Actually, in this period, the revenue of twice-a-year tax and poll tax did also show a certain trend in the "frozen figures", which means the data in this period probably could not reflect the real situation. However, unlike salt tax, agricultural taxes like *didingyin* strictly abide by the "quota system". As the Qing government's fiscal situation improved in the late seventeenth and early eighteenth centuries (Shi 2009), large-scale failures to fulfill revenue quotas–such as those seen in the nineteenth century–were relatively rare. Therefore, we believe that even if the data after the Revolt of the Three Feudatories documented in *Qing shilu* were not actual levies, they should not be too far from the actual amount received, and therefore could be used. After 1734, *Qing shilu* no longer recorded the revenue of the Twice-Year Tax and poll tax, so we refer to the data of 1753 and 1766 recorded in *Qingchao wenxian tongkao* (Comprehensive examination of the literature of Qing

Dynasty, 清朝文献通考) and *Qingshi gao* (Draft history of the Qing, 清史稿).[3] Since then there have been a number of figures from a variety of sources, but most of them are not actual levies but merely a planned quota. After the middle of the eighteenth century, the planned quota could not always be met, so that the adoption of these planned figures would be biased. Therefore, as for the following data, we mainly refer to Ni Yuping's research. Specifically, we use the annual data of actual tax received from 1821 to 1850 (Ni 2013: 95–96). The annual data from 1851 to 1874 come from Ni's collection from most of the provinces in China (Ni 2017a: 109). It is important to note that Ni considered the size of the total provincial revenues to be roughly 1.3 times the size of the revenues from the provinces he obtained data from (Ni 2017a: 110). Therefore, Ni's original figures can be multiplied by 1.3 to get the annual total *didingyin* revenues data for the period. The data from 1885 to 1894 are sourced from *Guangxu kuaiji biao* (Accounting Table in the Period of Guangxu, 光绪会计表) (Liang 2008, 574). The data in 1903 are sourced from *Zhongguo caizheng lungang* (Chinese Fiscal Theses, 中国财政论纲) (Liang 2008, 576–577). The data in 1911 are taken from the budget data from the Ministry of Finance (度支部) adopted by Yeh-chien Wang (2008, 97) in estimating the total fiscal size at the time. It should be noted that for this data of 1911, we do not use Wang's estimates but just adopt the ministry's budget data. This is because the interest of our study is the fiscal revenue held by the central government, so the unreported revenues or additional revenues of the local governments are beyond this paper's scope. In addition, since 1911 was the time when the fiscal clean-up was initially completed at the end of the Qing dynasty, here it essentially amounted to a fiscal reform, i.e., the central government obtained more legitimate fiscal revenues for a short time. Therefore we initially set 1911 as the time point after the fiscal reform, while for the situation before 1911 we still adopt the size of the agricultural tax in 1903. In this way, the agricultural tax will record a jump in 1911 to reflect the effect of the central government's fiscal reform.

In conclusion, we totally obtain 153 samples of *didingyin* data from 1651 to 1911, which can basically cover the situations in most of the Qing dynasty. Considering the "frozen figure/quota" attribute of d*idingyin*, we derive the data of missing years by linear interpolation.

Except for *didingyin*, the in-kind revenues of grain and fodder also need special attention. The data of in-kind revenues before 1766 have the same data source as that of *didingyin*, while after that, we cannot find reliable and continuous data until the data of revenues in-kind that had been converted to silver in 1885. Therefore, our methods are as follows: (1) We first convert the in-kind revenues before 1766 into silver. The price data come from Kaixiang Peng, Xinwei Peng and *Wanli kuanji lu*.[4] It is worth mentioning that the in-kind revenues during the Qing dynasty included rice, wheat, and beans, but we do not know the proportion of each item. However,

[3] Data of 1753 are from in Liang (2008: 547–548, 580–582) and data of 1766 from Shi and Xu (2008: 49). Fodder data come from Liang (2008: 550).

[4] Peng (2006: Appendix 5), Peng (2015: 630), Wan and Xu (2015: 667–668). Specifically, we take the data of 1751–1760 from Peng (2015) as the benchmark and use the annual rice price index from Peng (2006) to get the level value of the annual rice price for China average. The price of each bundle of fodder is set as 7.7% of the price for each *shi* of rice.

given that in-kind revenues were mainly rice-based, we have roughly calculated all in-kind revenues on the basis of rice. While this may result in overestimation, we believe that such an error would not have a major impact. (2) After obtaining the number of silver converted from in-kind revenues before 1766, we can link this series with the data after 1885. Generally speaking, considering the "frozen fiscal system", using linear interpolation will not cause much bias. However, since 1766–1885 spans the severe mid-nineteenth century national war, this may overestimate the size of in-kind revenues during this period. Therefore, we use the volatility information of silver revenues of the Qing Cabinet Treasury (内阁大库) (Shi 2009), taking the silver revenues before and after the war obtained here as the benchmarks, and then interpolate to get the size of the silver price series of the in-kind revenues, a total of 99 figures. For the data of other missing years, we make the linear interpolation.

## Revenues from Industry and Commerce (The "Indirect" Taxes)

The revenues from industry and commerce in the Qing dynasty were mainly composed of salt tax, *likin,* and miscellaneous taxes. As mentioned above, the annual data of salt tax from 1651 to 1734 are completely documented in *Qing shilu*. However, according to the investigation of Chen, only the data before 1674 can reflect the real tax received. The data after 1674 was divorced from the real situation. Therefore, for the data after 1674, we refer to the studies of Chen and others: (1) For the data of 1675–1735 and 1811–1850, we use Chen's revisions (2013b: 213–228). (2) For other years, the data of 1753, 1800, 1873, 1885–1894 and 1900–1911 come from different studies, such as *Qingshi gao* (清史稿), *Shiqu yuji* (Records in the Royal Library, 石渠余记), *Hubu xianban geyao jielue* (户部先办各要节略), *Guangxu kuaiji lu* (Accounting Records in the Period of Guangxu, 光绪会计录), *Zhongguo caizheng lungang* (中国财政论纲) and *Qingchao xu wenxian tongkao* (Continuation to "Comprehensive Examination of the Literature" of the Qing, 清朝续文献通考) (Deng 1998: 93–94).

As for the tariff data, we refer to Yuping Ni's study (2017b). The data of 1652, 1682, and 1692 that Ni did not provide are taken from Yibing Deng (2008, 419). The earliest study about the amount of *likin* after 1853 are from Yudong Luo (2010), and this data were later revised by Yumin Zhou (2011). Therefore, here we use the data from Zhou.

The miscellaneous tax includes many items but the total amount was not large. Therefore, in the study of fiscal history of the Qing dynasty, the items of the miscellaneous tax are generally calculated together. We found a total of 20 figures about the miscellaneous tax. Among them, the raw data of 1652, 1685, 1725, 1753, 1776, 1812, and 1841 come from Benfang He (1987). But these figures seem too small, so we use the larger ones of 1753 and 1776 provided by Chen Feng as the benchmark (Chen 2013a: 368–369), and make interpolations with volatility information from He to get the revised results of the seven years above. The data of 1885–1894 come from *Guangxu kuaiji lu* (Liang 2008: 574). The data of 1903–1911 are derived from the reports and the budget of the Ministry of Finance 户部/度支部 (Wang 2008: 97).

We set 1903–1910 to the case of 1903 so that the 1911 data reflect the results after the fiscal clean-up.

### Seigniorage and Others

Other revenues also include seigniorage, sales of official titles, donations, etc. The first is seigniorage revenue. The legal tender in the Qing dynasty were copper coins and paper money during some periods. However, like previous dynasties, copper coins did not make much profit in most of the time, and paper money was soon withdrawn from circulation due to lack of credibility. According to the research of Liu and Ni, seigniorage profit in the early Qing dynasty and Taiping Rebellion may be positive. Specifically, from 1645 to 1656, the seigniorage profit was considerable and we adopt the data of Liu (1966). However, there is no data before 1652, so we set the situation as 100 thousand taels according to the average size during this period. The data of 1654 is missing, so we use the average of the two years before and after to derive it. Our result shows that in the early Qing dynasty, seigniorage profit might only be 0.3% of the total direct/agricultural tax and indirect tax. For the seigniorage profit from 1853 to 1861, we use the estimates from Ni, which is about 6 million taels per year (Ni 2017a: 270), nearly 15% of the sum of direct/agricultural tax and indirect tax.

Data for official titles come from *Zhongguo lijin shi* (The History of Likin in China, 中国厘金史) (Luo 2010: 8–9), but these are not all the official titles-sales revenues. According to Luo, titles revenues received by the Ministry of Revenue accounted for 53.4% of the total titles sales (Luo 2010: 6–7). Therefore, we use this ratio and combine with the titles-sales revenues recorded in the Ministry of Revenue to estimate the total amount of titles sales from 1724 to 1853. Data after the Xianfeng (咸丰) period are not available. We use the silver revenue series of the Ministry of Revenue to estimate the titles-selling revenues of the whole country. During the period from Jiaqing (嘉庆) to Xianfeng (咸丰), the titles-selling revenues in the whole country accounted for about 82.5% of the revenues of the Ministry of Revenue. If this proportion remained stable, combining the revenue information of the Ministry of Revenue, we can get the estimates of official titles-selling revenues after 1853. Government title trafficking was not common in the period from Kangxi (康熙) to Qianlong (乾隆), so only the years with clear records of official titles-selling items are selected in our calculation. And the quota in the early Yongzheng (雍正) period is used as a substitute when data are missing.

Donations can be divided as donations from salt merchants and donations from new enterprises in the late Qing dynasty. The data of donations from salt merchants were calculated by Chen (2013b, 294–300) and Jiang (2021). The data of donations from new enterprises from 1884–1911 come from Zhu (1997). Those donations mainly came from China Merchants Steam Navigation Company (轮船招商局), Mohe Gold Mine (漠河金矿), and the Telegraph Office (电报局). It is clear that these data did not cover all the donations but combined with the studies of Chen and

Cai (2013b, 373–385), we believe that such an underestimate will not have a large impact.

# References

## *Primary Historical Sources*

*Guangxu kuaiji biao* (Accounting Table in the Period of Guangxu). 2007. Beijing: Beijing Yanshan Press.

*Guangxu kuaiji lu* (Accounting Records in the Period of Guangxu). 2007. Beijing: Beijing Yanshan Press.

*Ming huidian* (Collected Statutes of the Ming Dynasty, compiled by Shen Shixing). 1989. Beijing: Zhonghua Publishing Company.

*Ming shilu* (Veritable Records of the Ming Dynasty). 1962. Taipei: Academia Sinica Institute of History and Philology.

*Qing shilu* (Veritable Records of the Qing Dynasty). 2008. Beijing: Zhonghua Publishing Company.

*Qingchao wenxian tongkao* (Comprehensive examination of the literature of the Qing Dynasty). 1936. Beijing: The Commercial Press.

*Qingchao xu wenxian tongkao* (Continuation to "Comprehensive Examination of the Literature" of the Qing). 1936. Beijing: The Commercial Press.

*Qingshi gao* (Draft History of the Qing, compiled by Zhao Erxun). 1976. Beijing: Zhonghua Publishing Company.

*Shiqu yuji* (Records in the Royal Library by Wang Qinyun). 1985. Beijing: Beijing Ancient Books Publishing House.

*Wanli kuaijilu* (Accounting Records in the Period of Wanli). 1987. Beijing: Catalogs & Documentations Publishing House.

## *Secondary Sources*

Acemoglu, Daron. 2005. Politics and Economics in Weak and Strong States. *Journal of Monetary Economics* 52 (7): 1199–1226.

Besley, Timothy, and Torsten Persson. 2008. Wars and State Capacity. *Journal of the European Economic Association* 6 (2–3): 522–530.

Besley, Timothy, and Torsten Persson. 2011. The Logic of Political Violence. *The Quarterly Journal of Economics* 126 (3): 1411–1445.

Brandt, Loren, Debin Ma, and Thomas G. Rawski. 2014. From Divergence to Convergence: Reevaluating the History Behind China's Economic Boom. *The Journal of Economic Literature* 52 (1): 45–123.

Broadberry, Stephen, Hanhui Guan, and David Daokui Li. 2018. China, Europe, and the Great Divergence: A Study in Historical National Accounting, 980–1850. *The Journal of Economic History* 78 (4): 955–1000.

Chao, Kang. 1986. *Man and Land in Chinese History: An Economic Analysis*. Stanford, CA: Stanford University Press.

Chen, Feng. 2013a. *Qingdai caizhengzhengce yu huobizhengce yanjiu* [Research on Fiscal and Monetary Policies in the Qing Dynasty]. Wuhan: Wuhan University Press.

Chen, Feng. 2013b. *Qingdai yanzheng yu yanshui* [Salt Policy and Salt Tax in the Qing Dynasty]. Wuhan: Wuhan University Press.

Chen, Feng, and Cai Guobin. 2013a. *Zhongguo caizheng tongshi: Qingdai caizhengshi shang* [General History of Chinese Finance: Fiscal History in the Qing, Vol. 1]. Changsha: Hunan People's Publishing House.
Chen, Feng, and Cai Guobin. 2013b. *Zhongguo caizheng tongshi: Qingdai caizhengshi xia* [General History of Chinese Finance: Fiscal History in the Qing, Vol. 2]. Changsha: Hunan People's Publishing House.
Chen, Gaohua, and Weimin Shi. 2000. Zhongguo jingji tongshi: Yuandai jingji juan [A Comprehensive Economic History of China: Yuan Dynasty Volume]. Beijing: Economic Daily Press.
Deng, Zhaohui. 1998. *Wanqing caizheng yu Zhongguo jindaihua* [Finance in the Late Qing Dynasty and Modernization of China]. Chengdu: Sichuan People's Publishing House.
Deng, Yibing. 2008. *Qingdai qianqi guanshui zhidu yanjiu* [A Study on the Tariff System in the Early Qing]. Beijing: Beijing Yanshan Press.
Deng, Hanzhi. 2021. *A History of Decentralization: Fiscal Transitions in Late Imperial China, 1850–1911*. Doctoral Dissertation, London School of Economics and Political Science.
Department of History, Nankai University. 1959. *Qing shilu jingji ziliao jiyao* [Collection of Economic Data from Veritable Records of the Qing Dynasty]. Beijing: Zhonghua Publishing Press.
Dincecco, Mark. 2009. Fiscal Centralization, Limited Government, and Public Revenues in Europe, 1650–1913. *Journal of Economic History* 69: 48–103, 2009.
Dincecco, Mark. 2015. The Rise of Effective States in Europe. *The Journal of Economic History* 75: 901–918.
Hartwell, Robert. 1988. The Imperial Treasures: Finance and Power in Song China. *Bulletin of Sung and Yuan Studies* 20: 18–69.
Hao, Yu, and Liu Kevin Zhengcheng. 2020. Taxation, Fiscal Capacity, and Credible Commitment in Eighteenth-century China: The Effects of the Formalization and Centralization of Informal Surtaxes. *The Economic History Review* 73 (4): 914–939.
He, Benfang. 1987. Qingdai shangshui zhidu chuyi [Arguments on the Commercial Tax System in the Qing Dynasty]. *Social Science Research* 1: 53–62.
Ho, Ping-ti. 1959. *Studies on the Population of China, 1368–1953*. Cambridge, MA: Harvard University Press.
Ho, Ping-ti. 1995. *Zhongguo lidai tudi shuzi kaoshi* [Verification of Land Figure in Chinese History]. New Taipei: Linking Publishing Company.
Huang, Chunyan. 2015. Zhongguo caizheng tongshi: Song Liao Xixia Jin Yuan caizhengshi shang ce [General History of Chinese Finance: Fiscal History in the Song, Liao, Western Xia, Jin, and Yuan, Vol. 1]. Changsha: Hunan People's Publishing House.
Hu, Tieqiu. 2012a. Mingdai 'Zhongyi' tizhi de xingcheng [The Formation of "Heavy Corvée" System in the Ming Dynasty]. *Social Sciences* 6: 134–146.
Hu, Tieqiu. 2012b. Mingdai guanfeng goucheng biandong yu junyaofa de qidong [The Changes in the Composition of Official Salaries and the Enforcement of Junyao Law in the Ming Dynasty]. *Journal of Historical Science* 11: 22–42.
Hu, Tieqiu. 2016. *Mingdai mi (liang) jia wenti yanjiu* (Research on Rice (Grain) Price in the Ming Dynasty). Unpublished.
Huang, Ray. 1974. *Taxation and Governmental Finance in Sixteenth-Century Ming China*, vol. 4. Cambridge: Cambridge University Press.
Karaman, Kivanci, and Sevket Pamuk. 2010. "Ottoman State Finances in Comparative European Perspective, 1500–1914", with Şevket Pamuk, *The Journal of Economic History* 70: 593–629.
Koyama, Mark, and Noel D. Johnson. 2017. States and Economic Growth: Capacity and Constraints. *Explorations in Economic History* 4: 1–20.
Jiang, Xiaocheng. 2021. Qing Qianjia liangchao yanshang juanshu shue xinkao [A New Study on the Donation Amount of Salt Merchants during the Qianlong-Jiaqing Reigns]. *Researches in Chinese Economic History* 4: 76–92.

Li, Bozhong. 2017. *Huoqiang yu zhangbu: zaoqi jingji quanqiuhua shidai de Zhongguo yu dongya shijie* [Guns and Books of Accounts: China and the East Asian World in the Early Era of Economic Globalization]. Beijing: SDX Joint Publishing Company.

Li, Yiqiong. 2019. Ming Jiajing jian shanggong wuliao zheyin yu gongbu baiyin caizheng de jianli [Material Tax Paid in Silver, Jieshen Storehouse and the Financial Practices of the Ministry of Works in the Jiajing Period of the Ming Dynasty]. *Journal of Xiamen University (Philosophy and Social Science)* 2: 133–141.

Li, Guoxiang, and Chang Yang. 1993. *Ming shilu leizuan: Jingji shiliaojuan* [Veritable Records of the Ming Dynasty Compiled by Category: Volume of Economic Historical Materials]. Wuhan: Wuhan Publishing House.

Liang, Fangzhong. 1952. Mingdai yitiaobianfa nianbiao [A Chronology of the One Whip Law in the Ming Dynasty]. *Lingnan Journal of Chinese Studies* 12 (1): 15–50.

Liang, Fangzhong. 2004. *Liang Fangzhong wenji* (Collected Works of Liang Fangzhong, compiled by Liu Zhiwei), containing: "Yi tiao bian fa" (The One Whip Law). *Research Collection of Modern Chinese Economic History* 4 (1) (1936). Guangzhou: Sun Yat-sen University Press.

Liang, Fangzhong. 2008. *Zhongguo lidai hukou, tiandi, tianfu tongji* [Statistics of Household Registration, Farmland and Land Tax in Chinese History]. Beijing: Zhonghua Publishing Press.

Lin, Wei. 1990. Mingdai chaoguan shuishou de bianhua yu shangpin liutong [The Changes in Chaoguan Taxation and Commodity Circulation]. *Journal of Graduate School of Chinese Academy of Social Sciences* 8: 67–73.

Liu, Cuirong. 1966. *Shunzhi Kangxi nianjian de caizheng pingheng wenti (1644–1722)* [The Issue of Fiscal Balance in the Period from Shunzhi to Kangxi, 1644–1722]. Master's Degree Dissertation, National Taiwan University.

Liu, William Guanglin. 2005. *Wrestling for Power: The State and Economy in Later Imperial China, 1000–1700*. Doctoral Dissertation, Harvard University.

Liu, William Guanglin. 2011. Yinjinqianchu yu Mingdai huobi liutong tizhi [Counterfeiting and the Circulation of Money in the Ming Dynasty]. *Journal of Hebei University (Philosophy and Social Science)* 2: 24–32.

Liu, William Guanglin. 2015. The Making of a Fiscal State in Song China, 960–1279. *The Economic History Review* 68 (1): 48–78.

Luo, Yudong. 2010. *Zhongguo lijinshi* [The History of Likin in China]. Beijing: The Commercial Press.

Ma, Debin. 2014. State Capacity and Great Divergence, the Case of Qing China (1644–1911). *Eurasian Geography and Economics* 54 (5–6): 484–499.

Ma, Debin, and Jared Rubin. 2019. The Paradox of Power: Principle-agent Problems and Administrative Capacity in Imperial China (and other Absolutist Regimes) (co-authored with Jared Rubin). *Journal of Comparative Economics* 47 (2): 277–294.

Maddison, Angus. 1998. *Chinese Economic Performance in the Long Run*. Paris: Organization for Economic Co-operation and Development.

Ni, Yuping. 2013. *Qingchao Jiadao caizheng yu shehui* [Finance and Society in the Period from Jiaqing to Daoguang of the Qing Dynasty]. Beijing: The Commercial Press.

Ni, Yuping. 2017a. *Cong guojiacaizheng dao caizhengguojia: Qingchao Xiantong nianjian de caizheng yu shehui* [From State Finance to Fiscal State: Finance and Society during the Period of Xiantong in the Qing Dynasty]. Beijing: Science Press.

Ni, Yuping. 2017b. *Qingdai guanshui: 1644–1911* [Customs Duties in the Qing Dynasty: 1644–1911]. Beijing: Science Press.

O'Brien, Patrick K., and Philip A. Hunt. 1993. The Rise of A Fiscal State in England, 1485–1815. *Historical Research* 66 (160): 129–176.

Peng, Kaixiang. 2006. *Qingdai yilai de liangjia: Lishixue de jieshi yu zaijieshi* [Grain Price since the Qing Dynasty: Historical Interpretation and Reinterpretation]. Shanghai: Shanghai People's Publishing House.

Peng, Xinwei. 2015. *Zhongguo huobishi* [Chinese Monetary History]. Shanghai: Shanghai People's Publishing House.

Qi, Meiqin. 2009. *Qingdai neiwufu* [Imperial Household Department of the Qing]. Shenyang: Liaoning Nationalities Publishing House.
Qiu, Yongzhi. 2018. *The Landing of "Silver Age: Monetary Silverlization and the Formation of the Structure of Silver Circulation with Copper Coins in Ming Dynasty."* Beijing: Social Sciences Academic Press.
Shi, Zhihong. 2009. *Qingdai hubu yinku shouzhi he kucun tongji* [Revenue, Expenditure and Inventory Statistics of the Silver Treasury of the Ministry of Revenue in the Qing Dynasty]. Fuzhou: Fujian People's Publishing House.
Shi, Zhihong, and Yi Xu. 2008. *Wanqing de caizheng: 1851–1894* [Finance in the Late Qing Dynasty: 1851–1894]. Shanghai: Shanghai University of Finance and Economics Press.
Sng, Tuan-Hwee. 2014. Size and dynastic decline: The principal-agent problem in late imperial China, 1700–1850. *Explorations in Economic History* 54: 107–127.
Von Glahn, Richard. 2020. Modalities of the Fiscal State in Imperial China. *Journal of Chinese History* 4 (1), 1–29.
Wan, Ming, and Yingkai Xu. 2015. *Mingdai <Wanli kuaijilu> zhengli yu yanjiu* [Collation and Research of 'Accounting Records in the Period of Wanli' in the Ming Dynasty]. Beijing: China Social Sciences Press.
Wang, Shengduo. 2003. Liang Song huobi shi, shang ce [Monetary History of the Two Song Dynasties, Vol. 1]. Beijing: Social Sciences Academic Press
Wang, Yeh-chien. 2008. *Qingdai tianfu chulun: 1750–1911* [Arguments on Land Tax in the Qing Dynasty: 1750–1911]. Beijing: People's Publishing House.
Wang, Yuhua. 2022. *The Rise and Fall of Imperial China: The Social Origins of State Development.* Princeton: Princeton University Press.
Wu, Chengming. 1996. *Shichang, jindaihua, jingjishilun* [Market, Modernization and Economic History]. Kunming: Yunnan University Press.
Xu, Dixin, and Chengming Wu (eds.). 1985. *Zhongguo zibenzhuyi fazhanshi diyijuan* [History of Chinese Capitalism, Vol. 1]. Beijing: People's Publishing House.
Zelin, Madeleine. 1984. *The Magistrate's Tael: Rationalizing Fiscal Reform in Eighteenth-Century Ch'ing China.* California: University of California Press.
Zhai, Runzhuo, and Zhaohui Lou. 2022. Chinese Agricultural Output and TFP: 1661–2019. *Economics Letters* 213: 110415.
Zhang, Jianmin, and Rong Zhou. 2015. *Zhongguo caizheng tongshi: mingdai caizheng shi* [General History of Chinese Finance: Fiscal History in the Ming]. Changsha: Hunan People's Publishing House.
Zhao, Yi, and Liang Ding. 2013. Cong yin, lichai de bianqian kan Mingdai Junyaofa de yanhua lujing [The Evolution Path of the Junyao Law in the Ming Dynasty from the Perspective of Taxes levied in Silver and Corvée: A Case Study of Zhejiang Region]. *Social Science Journal* 4: 108–119.
Zheng, Xuemeng. 1994. *Zhongguo fuyi zhifu shi* [History of Fiscal System in China]. Xiamen: Xiamen University Press.
Zhou, Jian. 2019. *Weizheng zhi gong: Qingdai tianfu yu guojia caizheng (1730–1911)* [Tax Payment to Maintain the National Economy: Land Tax and State Finance in the Qing Dynasty, 1730–1911]. Beijing: Beijing Normal University Press.
Zhou, Yumin. 2011. Wanqing lijin linian quanguo zongshouru de zaiguji [A Recalculation of the Total Annual Likin's Revenue during the Late Qing]. *The Qing History Journal* 3: 1–24.
Zhu, Yingui. 1997. Lun wanqing Zhongguo xinshi gongshang qiye dui Qingchao zhengfu de baoxiao [Study on Donations to Governments from New Industrial and Commercial Enterprises during the Late Qing]. *Researches in Chinese Economic History* 4: 73–86.

**Hanhui Guan** is an Associate Professor in School of Economics, Peking University. He received his BA and MA from Wuhan University and Central China Normal University, and major in history. He got his PhD from Zhejiang University in international economics. He once was a Post-doctoral Research Fellow in Quantitative Economics in School of Economics and Management of Tsinghua University. His research focuses on Chinese Economic History, Economic Growth and Development, and International Economics. He has published some papers in leading journals such as *Journal of Economic History* and *Economic History Review*. He once was a Steering Committee member and Organizer of the 2th Asia Historical Economics Conference which was held in Tsinghua University in October 2010, and he also was a Program Committee member and Organizer of the 3th and the 4th International Symposium on Quantitative History held in School of Economics of Peking University in 2015 and 2016.

**Debin Ma** is a Professor of Economics at Fudan University, Shanghai China and a Quondam Fellow at All Souls College, Oxford University. His main expertise is on the long-term economic growth of East Asia, especially China. His research interests include global history; the international comparison of living standards; institutions, legal traditions, and ideology; human capital and productivity; and the economic history of the silk industry. He has published widely on Asian and comparative economic history and is the co-editor of the *Cambridge Economic History of China*.

**Runzhuo Zhai** is an Assistant Professor in School of Agricultural Economics and Rural Development, Renmin University of China and a Research Fellow in Institute of Agrarian History, Renmin University of China. He obtained his DPhil degree from the University of Oxford in 2023. His research interests focus on historical economic growth, including the measurement and analysis of economic growth. Recently, he has been dedicated to measuring China's historical GDP, TFP, population, fiscal size and technology development on a millennium scale, both at the national and regional levels. His doctoral dissertation Toward the Great Divergence: Economic Growth in the Yangzi Delta, 1393–1953 was awarded the Asia-Pacific Prize in Economic History in 2024, which recognizes the best doctoral dissertation in Asia-Pacific economic history field.

# Chapter 10
# Why Did Qing China Fail to Establish Fiscal Federalism Between the Central and Local Governments?

**Yu Hao and Kevin Zhengcheng Liu**

## 10.1 Introduction

The ability to tax and provide public goods is essential for economic and political development (Besley and Persson 2013; Acemoglu and Robinson 2019). Fiscal capacity concerns not only how to raise taxes but also how to organize revenues and spending among different layers of government. In these respects, imperial China in the Qing Dynasty (1644–1911) stood in stark contrast to the rise of fiscal prowess accompanied by the emergence of a modern centralized fiscal state (Yun-Casalilla et al. 2012). Economic historians now agree that the premodern Chinese state was much weaker in fiscal capacity than its European counterparts (e.g., O'Brien 2012; Brandt 2014; Vries 2015; Lamouroux and von Glahn 2022).[1] Meanwhile, the intergovernment fiscal arrangement was characterized by a "dual-track fiscal system" in which a formal system with a central budget of legal revenues and spending coexisted with an informal local fiscal system financed by miscellaneous extralegal taxes without any oversight. Such fragmented local tax administration also impeded resource mobilization and the building of fiscal capacity.

[1] In the early eighteenth century, the annual tax burden per capita was equivalent to only two days' wages for an unskilled worker. Per capita revenues (measured by grams of silver) of the leading European states (France, Spain, England, and Dutch Republic) were 6–22 times comparable figures for Qing China ( Brandt et al. 2014).

Y. Hao
School of Economics, Peking University, Beijing, China
e-mail: maxhao1003@pku.edu.cn

K. Z. Liu (✉)
School of Economics, Zhejiang University, Hangzhou, China
e-mail: kevin.liu@zju.edu.cn



Z. Chen et al. (eds.), *Quantitative History of China*, Studies in Economic History,
https://doi.org/10.1007/978-981-96-8272-0_10

Why was the Qing state unable to establish a stable and rationalized fiscal federalism governing the relationship between vertical levels of government?[2] Why did the dual-track fiscal system persist despite its obvious flaws? What hindered the building of fiscal capacity in premodern China? As demonstrated in the necessary conditions of federalism by Weingast (2009), federalism requires institutionalized allocation of authority, meaning that "decentralization must not be under the discretionary or unilateral control of the national government. ... Instead, a set of institutions must exist that prevents the national government from altering or undoing aspects of subnational autonomy".[3] A federal system is prone to fail because officials at each level are always tempted to encroach on the powers and revenues of the other. Fiscal federalism is self-enforcing only if governments at all layers of the hierarchy, especially the higher levels, have incentives to honor the rules (Weingast, 2014). Therefore, federalism is about the problem of power and commitment. However, as we will discuss in this chapter, in an autocratic empire with a centralized bureaucratic rule like Qing China, the arbitrary and unconstrained power of the central (and upper-level) governments lack commitment because it would naturally be apt to violate the fiscal discipline and compromise the lower levels' autonomy.

Through a review of history and our empirical research on fiscal reforms in the Qing Dynasty, the goal of this chapter is to shed light on these questions and highlight the commitment problem between different levels of government. Due to the lack of formal institutions to constrain the opportunistic behavior of higher-level (or central) governments encroaching on the lower levels—"*can't keep hands tied*," the higher levels often resorted to extracting lower-level revenues and pushing down spending responsibilities to the lower levels. If the higher levels cannot commit to refraining from such encroachment, local governments had to rely on levying informal and illegal surcharges to make up for the fiscal gap and finance local expenditures. As a result, higher-level governments could only tacitly acquiesce in the prevalence of subordinate off-budget revenues and the inevitable corruption stemming from it—"*keep eyes blind*". In a word, the central (and upper-level) governments *keep eyes blind because they can't keep their hands tied.*

---

[2] Fiscal federalism refers to the arrangement of fiscal responsibilities between different levels of government. It involves the allocation of revenue, expenditure responsibilities, and intergovernmental transfers.

[3] Weingast (2009) lists five conditions for fiscal federalism: (1) hierarchy; (2) subnational autonomy; (3) common market; (4) hard budget constraints; and (5) institutionalized authority. The final condition provides the glue of the federal system. An ideal type of federalism, what he called *market-preserving federalism*, satisfies all five conditions (Weingast 1995).

## 10.2 The "Dual-track Fiscal System" as an Institutional Equilibrium

Throughout most of the Qing Dynasty, a highly centralized formal fiscal system coexisted with a highly decentralized and fragmented informal fiscal system (Zelin 1984; Iwai 2004). We refer to such a hybrid practice of public finance as a "dual-track fiscal system". Under the "formal track," the collection and spending of formal land taxes were subject to strict budget management by the central government.[4] The vast majority of them were remitted to the central government, and only a small portion was earmarked for local expenditures. One striking feature of the formal system was its rigid revenue quota inherited from its Ming Dynasty predecessors (1368–1644), resulting in a nearly fixed revenue level despite the increasing population and administrative demands (Wang 1973). These revenues were far from sufficient to cover local government administrative and functioning expenses, let alone expenditures for public goods such as local water conservancy, roads, disaster relief, granaries, and schools (Ch'u 1962). Under the "informal track," county (the lowest level) governments were tacitly allowed to levy extralegal taxes beyond the formal taxes to meet their expenditures. Meanwhile, counties also pay customary fees (*lougui*) sourced from extralegal taxes to their superiors to meet the financial needs of upper levels of government. This informal system led to rampant corruption. Due to its opaque nature, a large amount of these informal revenues ended up in the private pockets of government officials and grassroots agents (Zelin 1984).[5] In short, under the dual-track fiscal system, the behavior of local officials was more akin to tax farmers than tax agents (Zhou 2016). The fiscal relationship between the central and local governments was a "blindfolded decentralization". Most local tax-raising operated without any form of budget oversight.

To some extent, the "dual-track fiscal system" balanced the tension between centralized political authority and effective governance. On the one hand, compared with early modern Europe, a relatively peaceful geopolitical environment lowered the demand for fiscal extraction capacity and finance techniques, which also implies that domestic peace and people's livelihood are the sources of political legitimacy (Rosenthal and Wong 2011). The central government's control over formal taxes (and the bureaucratic organization underlying it) ensured domestic political stability and supported the provision of large-scale public goods, especially large-scale water projects, food storage, and relief delivery. On the other hand, the local government's flexible operation of the informal fiscal system adapted to the governance of a vast empire with diverse geography, climate, and economic conditions (Zhou 2022).

---

[4] The most important revenue source was land tax (*didinyin*). They were collected according to revenue quotas assigned to each county (around 30 million taels of silver in total). Central land tax constituted three-quarters of the formal revenues of the crown.

[5] On the detailed description on how county governments collected informal taxes, distributed private returns, and paid customary fees to superiors, also see Qiu's (2021) vivid analysis based on a diary of county administrator in the late nineteenth century.

Over significant periods of the Qing Dynasty, the regime and its ruling elites adhered to the ideological notion of "light taxes and undemanding corvée" (*qingyao bofu*). The Qing state also stuck to the principle of original quotas for the formal taxes, and almost froze the total amount of formal land tax burden at a low level.[6] From a positive perspective, they were the commitments of benevolent rule by the Manchu rulers, reflecting the historical lesson they learned from the previous dynasty—"high taxation triggering the Ming collapse" (Zhang 2023). From a negative perspective, they were necessary choices of the central government to alleviate the burden on the people and maintain social stability, given that the central government cannot effectively monitor local governments (Ma and Rubin 2019). It was not until the late nineteenth century that the "dual-track fiscal system" became unable to increase fiscal extraction and cope with domestic and foreign challenges, hindering the transformation of late Qing China towards a modern fiscal state (He 2013).

However, the dual-track fiscal system was obviously an imperfect and undesirable arrangement. First, since provincial officials are highly dependent on the customary fees paid by their subordinates, it was not surprising that they naturally connived in their subordinates' corruption. If the central government could not supervise local and grassroots officials through provincial governors, centralized authority tended to be eroded de facto. Second, under informal fiscal systems, local officials often embezzled funds allocated by the central government for other purposes or reserved for the national treasury, resulting in deficits in the formal revenues. They could also falsely report or exaggerate natural disasters and crop failure, claim that the people cannot pay taxes, and force the central government to regularly exempt tax payments. The extralegal informal taxes were first used for routine administrative expenditures at the provincial and local levels, and then shared by agents at all levels for their private benefits. As a result, the availability of funds for non-routine expenditures at all levels of government was chronically insufficient.

Therefore, throughout the Qing Dynasty, diligent rulers continuously promoted *fiscal rationalization reforms*, attempting to formalize and standardize local government informal taxes, transferring them from off-budget to in-budget funds, and establishing top-down supervision of local public finance. Their policy goals are letting "superior officials be free from extortion, local governments be free from encroachment, and people be free from the heavy tax burden".[7] However, historical accounts and empirical research indicate that these reforms ended in failure in the long run: the dual-track fiscal system disappeared temporarily in the short run but then reemerged in the long run. Every time the reform formalized the informal local taxes and brought them under the budget oversight of higher-level governments, those higher levels had a greater opportunity to encroach on these revenues, and they ultimately did so. Such vertical encroachment would squeeze local public finance and impair local

[6] This was best manifested by Emperor Kangxi's famous announcement of permanently freezing the head tax quotas ("*yongbu jiafu*") in 1712, which was formally merged into the land tax in the following 10–20 years. By 1772, the Qing state further formally stopped the land and household surveys.

[7] "上官无勒索之弊，州县无科派之端，小民无重征之累", quoted from Meng (2006, 229).

state capacity. As response, local government opted to charge new extra-legal levies, manipulate disaster reporting, and even embezzle formal central taxes.

In another word, the dual-track fiscal system formed an *institutional equilibrium* in Qing China. Reforms trying to deviate the status from the equilibrium were likely to fail, and the inter-government relationship would return to the dual-track system. In the remainder of this chapter, we will review the history and relevant empirical research to explain the underlying mechanisms and provide an institutional explanation that the dual-track fiscal system was an inevitable outcome of the commitment problem.

## 10.3 The First Cycle of Fiscal Decentralization: 1644–1850

Following the Shunzhi period (1644–1661), local governments began to levy extralegal taxes under various names. Among them, the *huohao* (or *haoxian*) land surcharges accounted for the largest portion. By the end of the Kangxi period (1661–1722), the scale of these extralegal taxes expanded and imposed a heavy burden on taxpayers. On the other hand, the operation of local informal fiscal systems led to deficits in formal fiscal revenue and compromised the effectiveness of bureaucratic supervision below the provincial level. After the Yongzheng Emperor (1722–1735) ascended to the throne, the *huohao* fiscal reforms (*huohao guigong*) were gradually rolled out across the country (Zelin 1984; Chen 2009). By establishing a fixed surcharge rate, additional taxes were formalized and (partially) included in the provincial fiscal budget management. About half of these taxes were shared by the province to cover regular and irregular expenses. The remainder was retained by county government fees for local spending (*yanglianyin*).

In the ruler's view, on the one hand, this reform could increase provincial fiscal revenue, thereby improving the provision of public goods. On the other hand, it could reduce the burden on taxpayers. In Hao and Liu (2020), we examine the impacts of this reform using the gradual implementation feature across provinces and data from 1710 to 1760 at the prefecture level. We find that the reform increased the frequency of famine relief. The reform's impact was greater when areas faced exceptional disasters, and in prefectures that had difficulties with collecting taxes, suggesting that the reform facilitated spatial redistribution of financial resources and strengthened the government's capacity to cope with disaster risks. Following this was a significant increase in both the frequency and expenditure of disaster relief actions. As shown in Table 10.1, from 1723 to 1735, the frequency of famine relief by the local governments rose to 5.5 operations per year, and 346,500 taels were spent annually. During 1736–1760, these figures increased to 19.5 operations per year and 1.35 million taels.

In the middle of the eighteenth century after the landmarked *huohao* fiscal reform, the Qing state (in principle) had established a "quasi-fiscal federalism" system with a division of revenue sources and expenditure responsibilities among the central,

**Table 10.1** Annual frequency and expenditure on disaster relief (in thousand taels of silver)

| | Central government | | Local governments | |
|---|---|---|---|---|
| | Frequency | Expenditure | Frequency | Expenditure |
| 1690–1722 | 0.63 | 166.4 | 1.53 | 103.2 |
| 1723–1735 | 1.31 | 344.6 | 5.50 | 346.5 |
| 1736–1760 | 3.92 | 1033.2 | 19.52 | 1352.7 |

*Data source* Authors' estimation based on *The Veritable Records of Qing* (*Qingshilu*)

provincial, and county governments. Table 10.2 briefly summarizes the tax categories, and their corresponding revenues shared among different layers of government. However, the sustainability of the reform's benefits depends on whether the central government can keep its promise not to interfere with provincial fiscal autonomy and whether the provinces can keep their promises not to extract counties' revenues. In other words, all higher levels of government must refrain from encroaching on the power and revenues of the lower levels (Weingast 2014). Yet, after the Qianlong Emperor (1735–1795) ascended the throne, the central government began to interfere with the expenditure of provincial public funds, and even transfer them across regions. Hao and Liu (2020) use palace memorials (*zouzhe*) from the First Historical Archives of China to collect cases in which *huohao* surtaxes were to be transferred to another province or to the central government according to the central command. We find that these incidents were associated with a decline in disaster relief frequency in the province affected.

**Table 10.2** Fiscal revenue division among central, provincial, and county governments in the middle eighteenth century (figure in millions of silver taels)

| | | Central | Province | County |
|---|---|---|---|---|
| Formal land taxes | Silver land taxes (*didinyin*) | 23 | 3[a] | 3[a] |
| | Grain tributes (*caoliang*) | 6[b] | | |
| | Salt taxes | 5.7 | | |
| Non-land taxes | Commercial taxes | 5.4 | | |
| | Regular contributions | 3 | | |
| | Other miscellaneous incomes | 0.6 | | |
| Formal Land surtaxes | Provincial public funds | | 1.7 | |
| | Provincial government fees | | 0.6 | |
| | County government fees | | | 2.2 |

*Data sources* Wang (1973), Ni (2013), and authors' construction based on *The Charter of Land Surtax* (*Haoxian Zhangcheng*)

[a]less than 20% of the formal land tax revenues were retained at the local level. These revenues, however, were earmarked for several fixed-amount expenditures such as officials' salaries, soldier's pay, and courier station fees. None of these revenues could be used for local spending (e.g., clerks' pay) or local public goods without permissions from the central government

[b]4.6 million *shi* ($\approx$ 6 million silver taels)

The late eighteenth century witnessed a gradual centralization of local land surtaxes, which turned out to undermine the quasi-federalism system established after the *huohao* fiscal reform. In the beginning, provinces had full autonomy over the expenditures of these public funds. After the announcement of the *Charter of Land Surtax* in 1750, provincial public funds were also subject to direct budgetary management by the central government. Regarding the lowest level, county governments self-collected and self-spent the county fees from land surtaxes. In 1785, a new policy further centralized the administration of the county government fees (collected from land surtaxes) to the formal oversight of provincial governments. Under the new system, all land surtax revenues were *directly remitted* to the provincial treasuries, which then provided *transfers* from these revenues to counties. As a result, counties were deprived of their full autonomy in decentralized tax collection. An *implicit commitment* in the new arrangement was that provinces should fully provide the transfer payments to the counties. However, as land surtax revenues were under their formal administration and were physically shipped to the provincial treasuries, this made it easier for provinces to encroach on the counties' revenue. Such top-down encroachment would squeeze counties' fiscal stance and hence impair their administrative capacity, and even force them to embezzle central revenues.

In Hao and Liu (2023), we empirically examine the impacts of the 1785 policy. Employing a difference-in-differences estimation, we use the amount of county government fees (*zhouxian yanglianyin*) earmarked for each county as the measure of exposure to the reform. We extract records for tax deficits (i.e., shortfall from the required revenue target) from the Ministry of Finance Archives. This enables us to construct a dataset of fiscal performance at the county-year level for the first time. Figure 10.1 plots the average deficit ratio for any central taxes (i.e., central land tax or grain tribute) by counties above and below the median of county fees in 5-year bins. The deficit ratio in both groups remained at a low level of 3% before 1785. However, after the centralization reform, the tax deficit ratio surged sharply to 12% for counties with higher county fees, and the gap between the two groups persisted. The point estimate shows that a doubling of county fees led to an increase in the likelihood of central tax deficits by 9.4 percentage points after the centralization.

Why did a fiscal centralization policy aiming at enhancing monitoring lead to more tax deficits? Empirical evidence and historical accounts point to the provincial encroachment on county revenues—a failed commitment. Based on the text data from correspondence that senior local officials sent to the crown (*zouzhe*), Hao and Liu (2023) find a substantial increase in the number of provincial government reports on diverting and withholding county surtax revenues after 1785, a direct indication of top-down encroach. In addition, the effects on tax deficits are stronger in places with a higher frequency of provincial extraction.

After 1800, as the central government's fiscal surplus was exhausted in suppressing the White Lotus Rebellion, it began to apportion many central expenditures to the provincial government, such as river works, coastal defense projects, and military spending. The provinces' encroachment on county revenues became more common. Chenglie Tang, a county administrator in Zhejiang province in the

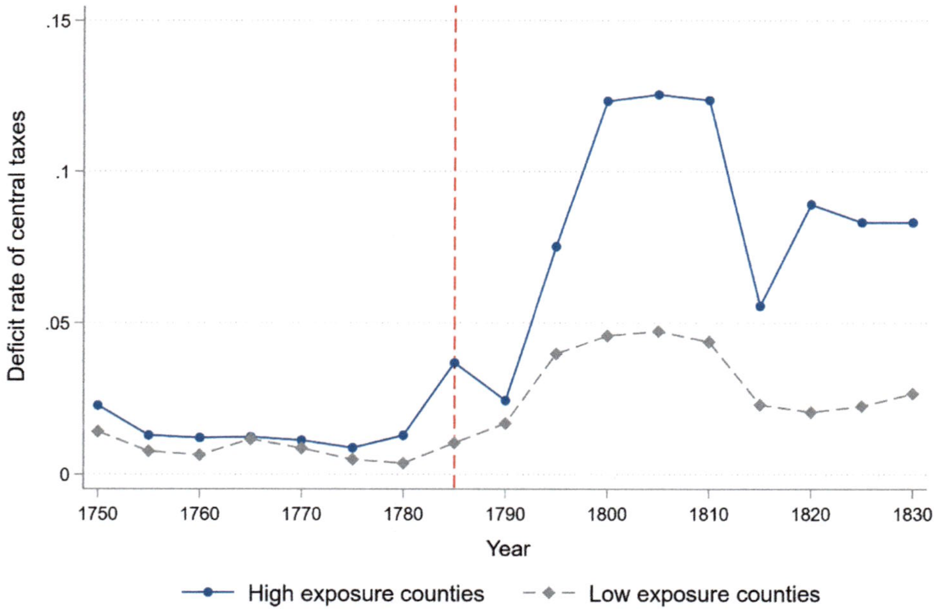


**Fig. 10.1** Average deficit ratio of central tax by exposure to the centralization (*Data source* Authors' construction based on *Ministry of Finance Archives* (*Huke tiben*))

1850s, described that "the robbery by the provincial treasury is even more ruthless than bandits".[8] Consequently, county governments had no choice but to make up by levying more extralegal taxes on local people, leading to the resurgence of informal fiscal systems (Zhou 2020).[9] This is also consistent with our quantitative evidence of the increasing cases of local governments charging extralegal levies after centralization (Hao and Liu 2023).

## 10.4 The Second Cycle of Fiscal Decentralization: 1850–1911

After 1860, following the Taiping Rebellion and foreign wars, new fiscal rationalization reforms were implemented in various regions, re-establishing fiscal decentralization between central and local governments. Now the central government acquired a large amount of new maritime customs in addition to the original formal land taxes. The temporary internal tariffs (*lijin*) levied during the wars soon became formal tax categories, and a relatively stable arrangement of revenue sharing was established between the central and local governments. Provincial governments shared 70% of the reported revenues, providing a substantial amount of funds for the establishment of new modern armies, reconstruction of coastal defenses, and the creation of state-owned modern enterprises. The central and local governments also began to raise foreign loans with tax revenues as collateral. They gradually replaced the dwindling title selling and contributions and became an important source for financing temporary expenditures.

On the other hand, to curb the rampant extralegal informal taxes and improve funding for local governments' routine expenditures, some provincial governors initiated the "second *huohao* fiscal reform," allowing county governments to levy a new surtax above formal land taxes, called "money-grain surplus (*qiancao yingyu*)," adjusted with silver and grain prices. This provided legitimate and stable revenues for county governments to cover their office expenses and public services (Zhou 2020). Notably, in this round of reforms, policymakers began to divide central, provincial, and local fiscal revenues according to different tax categories collected by separate agencies, which resembled the structure of modern fiscal federalism.

However, after the defeat in the First Sino-Japanese War (1894–1895) and the Boxer Rebellion (1899–1901), the central government apportioned a significant fiscal burden to local governments to pay enormous war reparations and repay foreign debt. The central government not only centralized most of the reported internal tariff (*lijin*) revenues but also began extracting the county's new surtax mentioned above. In the meantime, the Qing state started the ambitious New Policy *(xinzheng)* reform, promoted local autonomy, and established modern police forces and schools,

---

[8] "司计者之攘夺, 甚于剧盗", quoted from Zhou (2012a).

[9] See Zhou (2012b, 147–148) for contemporary observations by scholars and officials that the prevalence of extra-legal levies and custom fees (re)emerged during the mid-Qianlong period.

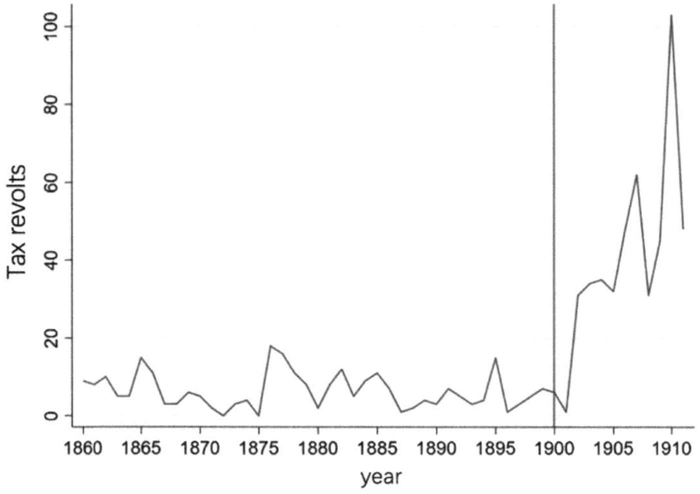


**Fig. 10.2** Frequency of tax revolts: 1860–1911 (*Data source* Authors' construction based on *The Veritable Records of Qing* (*Qingshilu*))

but pushed down most all expenditure responsibilities to local governments. As a result, local governments had to levy new informal taxes and fees to cope with various expense burdens. Greater tax burdens were evident in the surge of tax revolts following the Boxer Rebellion (Fig. 10.2).

Using the prefectural-level panel data of the whole country from 1860 to 1911, Hao and Bangshuo (2023) find that after the Boxer Rebellion, regions with a greater formal tax quota had a greater tax burden shifted from the central government and thus imposed greater extralegal levies to maintain local governance, resulting in more tax revolts. To test the mechanisms of downward burden shifting, the authors collected local tax data from the *Fiscal Investigation Book of Henan province* (河南财政说明书) towards the end of the Qing Dynasty. Using county-level cross-sectional data of Henan, they show that the amount of shifted burden from 1898 to 1911 was set in proportion of the formal land tax quota. In turn, counties with greater formal land tax quota imposed greater extralegal levies for the functioning of county government (*guifei* 规费). As a placebo test, there was no such link between land tax quota and extralegal levies that were earmarked for public good provisions.

Table 10.3 sketches out the evolution of revenue sources among different levels of government, before and after the two rounds of major fiscal rationalization reform in the Qing Dynasty. It can be seen that both reforms in the Qing Dynasty led to temporary federalism in the short run but ended up with the central government recentralizing newly established local revenues and the return of the informal dual-track fiscal system.

**Table 10.3** The evolution of revenue division among different levels of government in the Qing Dynasty

| | Before 1720s | 1730s–1785 | 1785–1850s | 1850s–1895 | 1895–1911 |
|---|---|---|---|---|---|
| Central | Formal land taxes, non-land taxes, donations | Formal land taxes, non-land taxes, donations | Formal land taxes, non-land taxes, donations **grabbing provincial revenues** | Formal land taxes, non-land taxes, donations maritime customs, internal tariffs (30%) | Formal land taxes, non-land taxes, donations maritime customs, internal tariffs (80%), **grabbing land surtaxes** |
| Province | Informal surtaxes | land surtaxes (Prov. public funds and gov't fees) | Prov. public funds and gov't fees, **grabbing county revenues** | internal tariffs (70%) internal tariff surtaxes [a] | internal tariffs (20%), internal tariff surtaxes [a], **grabbing land surtaxes** |
| County | Informal surtaxes | land surtaxes (County gov't fees) | **New informal surtaxes** | land surtaxes (Money-grain surplus) | **New informal surtaxes** |
| Status | *Dual-track fiscal system* | *Fiscal federalism* | *Dual-track fiscal system* | *Fiscal federalism* | *Dual-track fiscal system* |

[a] internal tariff (*lijin*) surtaxes denote the unreported revenues that were retained at the local level. It was estimated to be 100%–150% of the reported internal tariff revenues

## 10.5 Concluding Thoughts

By revisiting the history of inter-government relations and fiscal rationalization reforms in the Qing Dynasty, we argue that the commitment problem between higher and lower levels of government (*can't keep hands tied*), was the important institutional reason for the "dual-track fiscal system". Research on the origin and development of fiscal capacity in early modern Europe emphasizes the crucial role of constitutionalism and representative government in solving the commitment problem of rulers with society. Representation gave taxpayers a say over the state's fiscal actions, reducing tax collection costs for rulers (Levi 1988; Dincecco 2009; Becker et al. 2020; Cox and Dincecco 2021). The institutional arrangement limiting the ruler's discretion can also be a commitment device when the ruler incurred public debt from creditors (North and Weingast 1989; Stasavage 2011). In imperial China, where any minimal form of representative system was absent, the commitment problem *within* the government hindered the development of fiscal capacity.

As Ma and Rubin (2019) model, for an unconstrained ruler (central government), establishing fiscal federalism (or rational fiscal decentralization) is an incredible commitment, as it would allow the ruler (central government) arbitrary predation on officials' (local governments) legitimate income. If local officials cannot obtain any illegal income but must fulfill various responsibilities and costly tasks, they have to pay out of their own pockets. Rationally expecting this, officials would not initially accept the central government's appointment. In other words, the agent's participation constraint is not satisfied. Therefore, the acquiescence of local illegal incomes is itself a commitment, as it enables officials to fulfill their tasks even when their legitimate income is insufficient. An insight of this model is that the information asymmetry is endogenous to the credible commitment problem: to satisfy the agent's participation constraint, the principal (ruler) must reduce the ability to monitor the agent—*keep my eyes blind because I can't keep my hands tied.*

In the long run, the dual-track fiscal system usually leads to weakened control of the ruler over the bureaucracy, erosion of central tax revenues, insufficient provision of local public goods, and social unrest. They would eventually trigger a new round of fiscal rationalization reforms. Therefore, the fiscal relation between the central and local governments is always in a state of fluctuation and cyclical shocks between centralization and decentralization. To break this cycle and establish stable federalism, it is necessary to establish institutional constraints and the rule of law to limit the arbitrary and discretionary power of the central government and the ruler herself. But this would also mean touching the foundation of autocratic rule. The fiscal system always intertwines with the underlying political institution. As Edmund Burke said two centuries ago, "the revenue of the state is the state".

**Acknowledgements** We thank funding support from the Yonyou Foundation (Business Great Wall Project: 2021Z01).

## References

Acemoglu, Daron, and James A. Robinson. 2019. *The Narrow Corridor: States, Societies, and the Fate of Liberty*. New York: Penguin.

Becker, Sascha O., Andreas Ferrara, Eric Melander, and Luigi Pascali. 2020. Wars, Taxation and Representation: Evidence from Five Centuries of German History. Centre for Economic Policy Research Discussion Paper, DP15601.

Besley, Timothy and Torsten Persson. 2013. Taxation and Development. In *Handbook of Public Economics*, vol. 5, 51–110. Elsevier.

Brandt, Loren, Debin Ma, and Thomas G. Rawski. 2014. From Divergence to Convergence: Reevaluating the History Behind China's Economic Boom. *Journal of Economic Literature* 52 (1): 45–123.

Chen, Feng. 2009. *Lun Haoxian Guigong* (On the Haoxian to the Public). *Qinghua daxue xuebao* (*Journal of Tsinghua University*) 3: 17–38.

Ch'u, T'ung-tsu. 1962. *Local Government in China under the Ch'ing*. Cambridge and London: Harvard University East Asia Center.

Cox, Gary W., and Mark Dincecco. 2021. The Budgetary Origins of Fiscal-Military Prowess. *Journal of Politics* 83 (3): 851–866.

Dincecco, Mark. 2009. Fiscal Centralization, Limited Government, and Public Revenues in Europe, 1650–1913. *Journal of Economic History* 69 (1): 48–103.

Hao, Yu, and Kevin Zhengcheng Liu. 2020. Taxation, Fiscal Capacity, and Credible Commitment in Eighteenth-Century China: The Effects of the Formalization and Centralization of Informal Surtaxes. *Economic History Review* 73 (4): 914–939.

Hao, Yu, and Kevin Zhengcheng Liu. 2023. Top-down Monitoring or Top-Down Encroachment? How Centralization Undermined Fiscal Capacity in China. Working Paper.

Hao, Yu, and Bangshuo Xue. 2023. *Fenquan debenkui* [The Collapse of Tax-sharing: The Impacts of Shifting Tax Burden on Extralegal Levies and Tax Revolts in the Last Decades of Qing Dynasty]. *Jingjikexue* (*Economic Science*) 3: 225–240.

He, Wenkai. 2013. *Paths toward the Modern Fiscal State: England, Japan, and China.* Cambridge, MA: Harvard University Press.

Iwai, Shigeki. 2004. *Zhongguo jindai caizhengshi yanjiu* [A Study on Early Modern Fiscal History of China]. Beijing: Shehuikexuewenxian chubanshe (Translated from Japanese).

Lamouroux, Christian, and Richard von Glahn. 2022. Public Finance. In *The Cambridge Economic History of China*, eds. Debin Ma and Richard von Glahn, 340–380. Cambridge: Cambridge University Press.

Levi, Margaret. 1988. *Of Rule and Revenue.* Berkeley: University of California Press.

Ma, Debin, and Jared Rubin. 2019. The Paradox of Power: Principal-Agent Problems and Administrative Capacity in Imperial China (and Other Absolutist Regimes). *Journal of Comparative Economics* 47 (2): 277–294.

Meng, Sen. 2006. *Qingshi jiangyi (Lecture Notes on the Qing history).* Beijing: Zhonghua shuju.

North, Douglass C., and Barry R. Weingast. 1989. Constitutions and Commitment: The Evolution of Institutions Governing Public Choice in Seventeenth-Century England. *Journal of Economic History* 49 (4): 803.

Ni, Yuping. 2013. *Qingchao Jia-Dao caizheng yu shehui [Public Finance and Society in Jiaqing and Daoguang Periods of the Qing Dynasty].* Beijing: The Commercial Press.

O'Brien, Patrick K. 2012. Fiscal and Financial Preconditions for the Formation of Developmental States in the West and the East from the Conquest of Ceuta (1415) to the Opium War (1839). *Journal of World History* 23 (3): 513–553.

Qiu, Jie. 2021. *Wanqing guanchang jingxiang* [A mirror of the late Qing officialdom]. Beijing: Social Science Academic Press.

Rosenthal, Jean-Laurent, and R. Bin Wong. 2011. *Before and Beyond Divergence: The Politics of Economic Change in China and Europe.* Cambridge: Harvard University Press.

Stasavage, David. 2011. *States of Credit: Size, Power, and the Development of European Polities.* NJ: Princeton University Press.

Vries, Peer. 2015. *State, Economy, and the Great Divergence: Great Britain and China, 1680s–1850s.* London: Bloomsbury Academic.

Wang, Yeh-Chien. 1973. *Land Taxation in Imperial China, 1750–1911.* Cambridge, MA: Harvard University Press.

Weingast, Barry R. 1995. The Economic Role of Political Institutions: Market-Preserving Federalism and Economic Development. *The Journal of Law, Economics, and Organization* 11 (1): 1–31.

Weingast, Barry R. 2009. Second Generation Fiscal Federalism: The Implications of Fiscal Incentives. *Journal of Urban Economics* 65 (3): 279–293.

Weingast, Barry R. 2014. Second Generation Fiscal Federalism: Political Aspects of Decentralization and Economic Development. *World Development* 53: 14–25.

Yun-Casalilla, Bartolomé, Patrick K. O'Brien, and Francisco Comín Comín, eds. 2012. The Rise of Fiscal States: A Global History, 1500–1914. Cambridge and New York: Cambridge University Press.

Zelin, Madeleine. 1984. *The Magistrate's Tael: Rationalizing Fiscal Reform in Eighteenth-century Ch'ing China.* Berkeley: University of California Press.

Zhang, Taisu. 2023. *The Ideological Foundations of Qing Taxation: Belief Systems, Politics, and Institutions.* Cambridge: Cambridge University Press.

Zhou, Jian, 2012a. Qingdaicaizheng zhong de tanjuan [Withholding local revenues in public finance in Qing dynasty]. *Zhongguo jingjishi yanjiu [Researches in Chinese Economic History]* 3: 156–155.

Zhou, Jian, 2012b. Lougui yu qingjiadaozhiji de difangcaizheng [Lougui and Local Government Finance in the Early Nineteenth Century: Seen in the Lougui Investigation of 1820]. *Bulletin of the Institute of Modern History, Academia Sinica* 75: 115–158.

Zhou, Li-An. 2016. The Administrative Subcontract: Significance, Relevance and Implications for Intergovernmental Relations in China. *Chinese Journal of Sociology* 2 (1): 34–74.

Zhou, Jian, 2020. *Weizheng Zhigong: Qingdai Tianfu yu Guojia Caizheng* [Tax for the state: land tax in Qing dynasty and state's public finance, 1730–1911]. Beijing: Bejing Normal University Press.

Zhou, Xueguang. 2022. *The Logic of Governance in China: An Organizational Approach.* Cambridge: Cambridge University Press.

**Yu Hao** is an Associate Professor in School of Economics at Peking University, China. His research focuses on economic history, development economics, and political economy. He received his B.A. from Peking University, M.A. from UC San Diego, and Ph.D. from UC Davis. His work has been published in journals including *Journal of Economic History*, *Economic History Review*, and *Explorations in Economic History*.

**Kevin Zhengcheng Liu** is a ZJU Young Professor (Assistant Professor) in School of Economics at Zhejiang University, China. His research fields are political economy, public economics, and economic history. He received his B.A. from Peking University, M.Phil. from The Hong Kong University of Science and Technology (HKUST), and Ph.D. from The University of Hong Kong. His work has been published in journals including *Journal of Development Economics*, *Journal of Economic History*, *Journal of Economic Behavior and Organization*, and *Economic History Review*.

# Chapter 11
# The Rise and Fall of Shanxi Banks in Historical China: A Political Economy Explanation

**Wentian Diao, Jinyan Hu, and Chicheng Ma**

## 11.1 Introduction

China in the nineteenth century saw the rise of Shanxi banks in the absence of legal and technological support. From the 1820s, Shanxi banks developed an extensive remittance network that connected most, if not all, of China's provinces and larger cities. More than 400 branches were opened across the country out of their headquarters in Shanxi Province (Huang 2002). By the mid-nineteenth century, Shanxi banks dominated China's market for commercial remittances and government fiscal transfers.

The success of Shanxi banks questions the conventional wisdom on the importance of legal institutions and financial technologies in financial development (e.g., La Porta et al. 1997, 1998; Lin et al. 2021), given that both the laws of finance and modern financial technologies were not introduced in China until the late nineteenth

We thank Zhiwu Chen, James Kai-sing Kung, Chen Lin, Haoming Liu, Debin Ma, Tuan Hwee Sng, Hui Ren Tan, and seminar participants at the NUS Econ SIG brownbag, the Area of Excellence–Quantitative History Conference 2023 at HKU, and the 10th Annual Symposium on Quantitative History for helpful comments and suggestions.

W. Diao (✉)
School of Economics, Shanghai University of Finance and Economics, Shanghai, China
e-mail: diaowentian@mail.shufe.edu.cn

J. Hu
School of Economics, Shandong University, Jinan, China

School of Economics, Qingdao University, Qingdao, China
e-mail: hwx@sdu.edu.cn

C. Ma
Centre for Quantitative History, Faculty of Business and Economics, The University of Hong Kong, Hong Kong, China
e-mail: macc@hku.hk



Z. Chen et al. (eds.), *Quantitative History of China*, Studies in Economic History,
https://doi.org/10.1007/978-981-96-8272-0_11

to the early twentieth century. Instead, historical anecdotes suggest that Shanxi banks maintained a close connection with governments, engaging actively in government deposits and tax remittances (Wang 2021). The importance of political connections for Shanxi banks is further manifested in their rapid decline after the Qing dynasty collapsed in 1911 (Fig. 11.1). These facts imply the value of political capital in substituting the missing legal institutions for financial development in a traditional economy. In this chapter, we provide a preliminary quantitative assessment of the role of political connections in the rise and fall of Shanxi banks, drawing upon a panel data set across the 18 provinces in the Qing proper area between 1823 and 1927.

We measure the development of Shanxi banks by looking at the expansion of their branch network across provinces. We located bank branches and estimated their periods of existence based on Huang (2002), *Shanxi piaohao shiliao* (Historical Documents of Shanxi Banks). To measure the political connections of Shanxi banks, we make use of their hometown ties with Shanxi officials, i.e., provincial-level governors who were born in Shanxi but appointed in other provinces. If a province was governed by a Shanxi official, we assume that Shanxi banks would have political connections and thus open more branches in this province. Given that provincial governors were assigned directly by the emperors based on non-financial considerations, the establishment of political connections to Shanxi banks in each province should be less likely to be confounded by other provincial correlates of financial development. Nevertheless, we control for population size, financial needs (trade

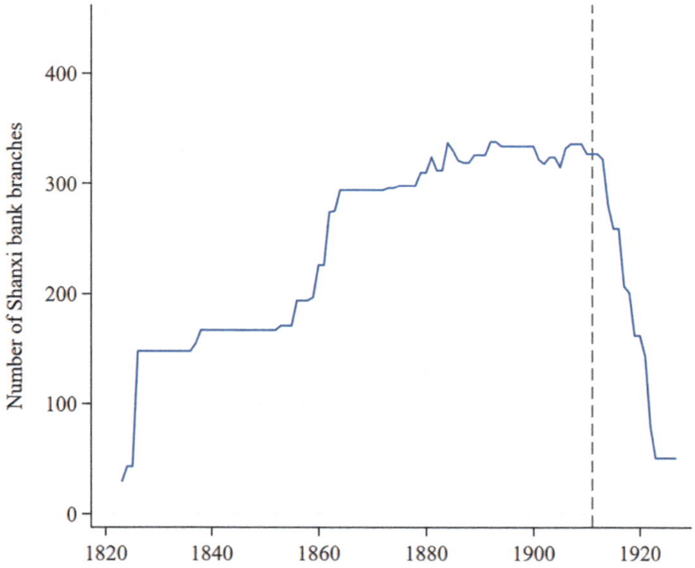


**Fig. 11.1** The Rise and Fall of Shanxi Banks (*piaohao*), 1823–1927 (*Note* The figure shows the total number of Shanxi bank branches in China in each year from 1823 to 1927. See Table 11.1 for data sources)

revenue and industrial firms), duration of treaty ports, number of railway stations and telegraph offices, and the number of civil conflicts to rule out their confounding effects on the number of Shanxi bank branches. Thanks to the panel data setting, we are able to rule out the effects of the time-invariant provincial factors (such as geography and culture) and the effects of the common shocks and trends, using the provincial and time fixed effects, respectively.

Our regression estimations show that Shanxi banks opened significantly more branches in provinces governed by Shanxi officials. On average, a province with Shanxi officials would have nearly two more bank branches than a province without such political connections in each 5- or 10-year period. The effect of Shanxi officials is robust to the effects of other provincial characteristics and alternative sample periods. Moreover, we employ the number of foreign bank branches as a placebo and find it is not correlated with the distribution of Shanxi officials. This suggests that we are estimating the political connection effect of Shanxi officials rather than the confounding effect of local financial development.

However, the political capital of Shanxi banks became a curse after the Qing dynasty came to an end in 1911. Shanxi banks declined from 1912 and almost vanished in the 1930s, despite the development of modern legal systems, technologies, and financial markets in this period. Shanxi banks did not take advantage of the momentum of China's financial modernization, but instead were trapped in the old political ties, losing the support of political elites in the new republican regime. We document this political resource curse by showing the negative impact of previous Shanxi officials on the number of Shanxi bank branches after 1911. Shanxi lost its status as a financial center in China and was replaced by Shanghai, which was able to take advantage of updated laws and other modern forces (Ma 2019; Levine et al. 2023).

So far, our results indicate the positive relationship between Shanxi bank development, on the one hand, and political connections with Shanxi officials, on the other. The puzzling rise and fall of Shanxi banks have prompted considerable studies on the rationale, but most are analytical with scant quantitative evidence (e.g., Chen 1937; Kong 1984; Cheng 2003; Liu et al. 2005; Zhang 2007; Yan 2012; Wei 2017; Qiao 2017; Zhou and Zeng 2020; Wang 2021). Our findings also illuminate the importance of traditional institutions and cultures in the vicissitude of Chinese native banks. Likewise, Wu (2016, 2024) also found that the traditional management rules, including the town-based recruitment, contributed to the early success of Shanxi banks but later inhibited their development when they faced competition from modern banking institutions.

In a broader sense, our study speaks to the literature on the determinants of historical financial development, in particular the roles of informal institutions such as kinship and solidarity groups (e.g., Chen et al. 2022; Santarosa 2015; Stulz and Williamson 2003; D'Acunto et al. 2019; Drelichman and Voth 2011). Our study also contributes fresh historical evidence to the literature on how political connections affected finance (e.g., Fisman 2001; Faccio 2006; Ferguson and Voth 2008; Akcigit et al. 2023; O'Brien and Palma 2023).

The rest of the chapter is organized as follows. Section 11.2 introduces the history of Shanxi banks and their political connections. Section 11.3 describes the data and variables. The empirical results are reported in Sect. 11.4. Section 11.5 concludes the paper.

## 11.2 Historical Background

Before Western-style modern banks were introduced to China in the late nineteenth century, China's financial sector was dominated by two types of native banks, Shanxi banks (*piaohao*) and money or silver houses (*qianzhuang* or *yinhao*) (Cheng 2003). Shanxi banks were named after their place of origin, Shanxi province in northern China. Unlike the money houses that mainly operated small credit businesses in local areas, Shanxi banks maintained a nationwide branch network to manage inter-regional silver transfers.[1] Moreover, Shanxi banks also provided other financial services, ranging from commercial deposits and loans to government tax revenue, among others. For instance, half of the tax revenue levied by the imperial court from provinces was remitted through Shanxi banks in the 1870s (Huang 2004, 243).

The origin of Shanxi banks remains unclear, but their golden age came in the nineteenth century. After the first known Shanxi bank (*Ri Sheng Chang*) was established in 1823, the number of banks increased steadily and reached 28 by 1884. These banks ran a total of 338 branches in 17 provinces, covering the entire proper area of the empire (Fig. 11.2). The growth and expansion of Shanxi banks coincide with the increasing financial demand in nineteenth-century China. Financial demand was primarily driven by the following forces. The first pertains to the flourishing long-distance trade from the late eighteenth century. Second, the Taiping Rebellion (1851–1864) created a unique momentum for Shanxi banks to undertake government remittance businesses. As the rebellion blocked transport routes between the imperial capital of Peking and the southern provinces, the governments turned to rely on Shanxi banks' remittance networks to transfer tax revenues. This business continued after the rebellion was suppressed. Third, more financial needs came from the government's Self-strengthening Movement (1861–1895) and in particular, industrial and military development, after Qing China was defeated by Britain in the Arrow War (1856–1860).

Please update this image to attachment Figure1.png with better resolution.Given the increasing demands for capital and inter-regional money transfers, Shanxi banks gained impetus to expand their branch network. However, establishing and maintaining a new branch in a remote place were costly and risky in an agrarian society that lacked market integration and inter-regional communications, let alone the missing

[1] The average initial capital size of Shanxi banks during 1823–1912 was 147,529 silver *liang* (Huang 2002, 638–665), nearly three times the average capital size of native banks (52,000 silver *liang*) (Zheng 1981, 116).

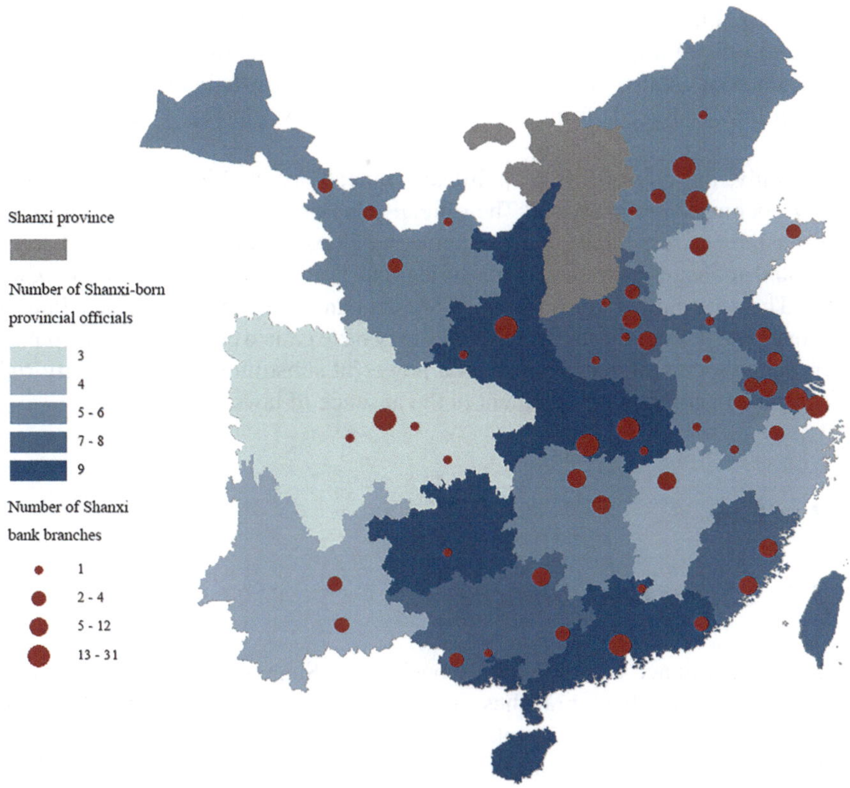


**Fig. 11.2** Shanxi Officials and Shanxi Banks in the 18 Province of China Proper, 1823–1911 (*Note* The figure shows the provincial distribution of the number of Shanxi-born provincial officials and the prefectural distribution of the number of Shanxi bank branches between 1823 and 1911. Provincial officials (positions) include the governor-general (*zongdu*), provincial governor (*xunfu*), surveillance commissioner (*anchashi*), administration commissioner (*buzhengshi*), and education commissioner (*xuezheng*). There are 17 sample provinces in China Proper based on the Qing Dynasty administration in 1911 (CHGIS, version 6). See Table 11.1 for data sources.)

legal protections and financial regulations at the time. Instead, in a centralized bureaucracy such as Qing China, an effective way to secure financial interests would be seeking protection and help from the mandarins. And hometown favoritism was usually a popular (and reliable) form of political connections cultivated by Shanxi bankers. Kang Shaoyong (1770–1834), for example, was born in Shanxi and served as the provincial governor of Hunan from 1825 to 1830 (Wei 1977). During his tenure, Shanxi banks opened 12 new branches in Hunan based on their hometown ties with Kang. After Kang left Hunan, the expansion of Shanxi bank branches stagnated until another fellow Shanxi native, Bai Enyou, was appointed as Hunan education officer from 1861 to 1863. During Bai's relatively short tenure, Shanxi banks opened six new branches in Hunan. Thereafter, no Shanxi officials were assigned to Hunan provincial government and, accordingly, Shanxi banks did not open any new branches there.

By contrast, Fujian province in southeastern coastal China had only one Shanxi provincial official throughout the nineteenth century. Accordingly, Fujian had only 12 branches of Shanxi banks by the 1880s, fewer than half of Hunan's, despite its rising financial needs from trade and industrial development (Wei 1977; Huang 2002).

Certainly, the pay-offs from political connections for Shanxi banks were not merely opening more branches. The officials also provided the banks with government businesses, especially the remittances of taxes, military funds, and foreign loans, and managing provincial treasuries and issuing government bonds (Cheng 2003). The government funds provided Shanxi banks with large and stable liquidity. Moreover, the politically connected banks may have gained credibility and reputation when the government was deemed as a powerful substitute for the property rights protection and contract enforcement in the absence of laws.

## 11.3 Data

### *11.3.1 Shanxi Bank Branches*

Given that remittance was the primary business of Shanxi banks, we use the spatial expansion of Shanxi bank branches to measure banking development. Specifically, we use the number of Shanxi bank branches in each province in each time interval (five or ten years) as our dependent variable. The data are obtained from the *Shanxi piaohao shiliao* (Historical Documents of Shanxi Banks) edited by Huang (2002). These documents provide the most systematic records of each Shanxi bank's name, branch locations, existing period, and other characteristics. Not all branches have an explicitly known date of establishment or closure. To this end, we estimate their establishment and closure, according to those of their head offices, based on the fact that most Shanxi banks promptly established their branches and rarely closed them in order to operate long-distance remittances.[2] Moreover, our 5- and 10-year time units can also attenuate the measurement errors in the time of branch establishment. Figure 11.2 shows the geography of Shanxi bank branches between 1823 and 1911.

### *11.3.2 Political Connections*

We measure the political connections of Shanxi banks based on their hometown relationship with provincial officials. Specifically, we use the tenures of officials who were born in Shanxi province but served in other provincial governments in

[2] In other words, branch network was the lifeline of Shanxi banks. Shanxi banks rarely closed branches unless they could not survive big shocks. Historical records show that most branches were not closed until the Xinhai Revolution in 1911 (Huang 2002).

each period as the measure. Of course, hometown favoritism was just one specific form of political connections, but it should be among the most stable and, more importantly, observable connections. The provincial officials refer to those holding the following positions in the provincial government: governor-general (*zongdu*), provincial governor (*xunfu*), surveillance commissioner (*anchashi*), administration commissioner (*buzhengshi*), and education commissioner (*xuezheng*). We use provincial-level officials because they were the most powerful local officials who had decision power to grant government businesses (especially tax revenue) to Shanxi banks. Moreover, provincial officials were directly appointed by the emperors and thus orthogonal to other provincial correlates of banking development. In Qing China, the appointment of provincial officials was primarily based on political rather than financial concerns, considering the candidates' ability, reputation, integrity, and experience, among other factors. However, the appointments of prefects and county magistrates below the provincial level could be subject to local factors and merchants' lobbies and hence are subject to the feedback effect of Shanxi bank development.

The data of Shanxi officials are obtained from Wei's (1977) *Offices and Personnel in the Late Ch'ing Period*, which lists the biographies of all provincial officials from 1796 to 1911. Figure 11.2 also shows the distribution of Shanxi officials across the sample provinces. Similar to the distribution of Shanxi bank branches, there are obviously regional variations in the number of Shanxi officials. To intuitively show the relationship between Shanxi officials and Shanxi banks, we simply divide all provinces into two groups based on the sample mean of the number of Shanxi officials per province between 1823 and 1911, and compare the two groups in terms of the number of Shanxi bank branches per province per year. As shown in Fig. 11.3, there are more bank branches in provinces with more Shanxi officials before 1911. To substantiate this relationship, we introduce the following provincial confounding factors and control for them in estimating the Shanxi official effect.

### *11.3.3 Control Variables*

First and foremost is the potential financial need in each province, particularly the financial services that Shanxi banks could provide. If a province had little market demand for Shanxi banking, Shanxi bankers would not invest in this region even if the region was governed by Shanxi officials. We employ two proxies for financial demand at the provincial level. One is inter-regional trade, measured by the customs revenue (*likin,* measured in silver *liang*) from domestic trade. The other is the number of newly established industrial firms. From the 1860s, the Qing elites began to industrialize the economy following the Western models, and these modern and large-scale establishments created unprecedented demands for capital and inter-regional finance (Zhang 2007).

In addition, we control for the overall economic prosperity in each province, using the population size as the proxy in the absence of statistics on income. The population data are obtained from Cao (2000), and we interpolated for years of missing data.

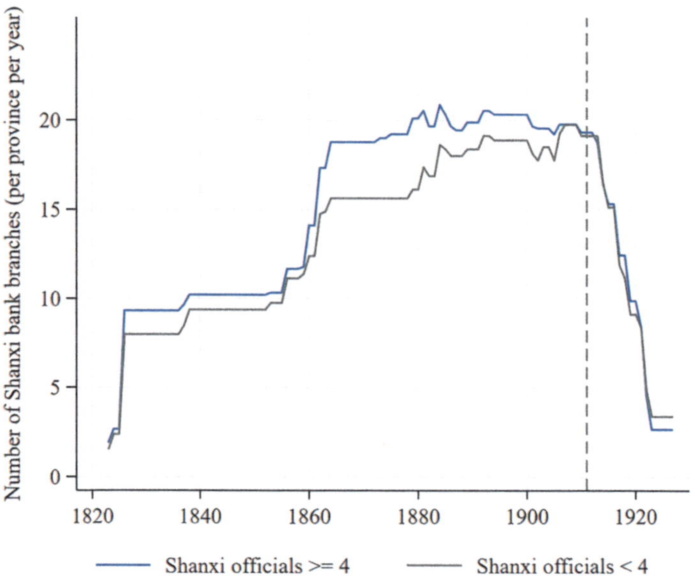


**Fig. 11.3** The Rise and Fall of Shanxi Banks by Political Connections, 1823–1927 (*Note* This figure compares the number of Shanxi bank branches (per province per year) between two groups of provinces with high and low political connections, respectively. The high and low political connections are divided by the sample median (4) of the total number of Shanxi officials appointed in each province between 1823 and 1911. See Table 11.1 for data sources)

Another critical economic factor is the treaty ports that channeled foreign trade and economic forces to inland China after 1842. While their effects on Chinese native financial sectors remain unclear, we control for the duration of treaty ports in each province to capture their possible effects on Shanxi banks.

The inter-regional financial services of Shanxi banks relied on transportation and communications infrastructures. For this reason, we control the number of railway stations and the number of telegraph offices. The data are obtained from Lin et al. (2021). No doubt financial development relies on a peaceful social environment. This is especially true for Shanxi banks that operated cross-regional silver transfers. However, late nineteenth-century China was accompanied with wars and social unrest. To account for the effect of social unrest, we control for the number of civil conflicts occurring in each province in each period based on the records in Zhongguo junshishi bianxiezu (1985). The descriptive statistics of the key variables are summarized in Table 11.1.

**Table 11.1** Data sources and descriptive statistics

| Variables | Source | N | Mean | S.D | Min | Max |
|---|---|---|---|---|---|---|
| *Province data each 5-year, 1823–1911* | | | | | | |
| Number of Shanxi bank branches | Huang (2002) | 306 | 14.971 | 13.458 | 0 | 61 |
| Tax remittance (in 10,000 silver *liang*) | Huang (2002) | 306 | 67.228 | 179.520 | 0 | 1,462.295 |
| Shanxi officials (dummy) | Wei (1977) | 306 | 0.239 | 0.427 | 0 | 1 |
| Shanxi officials (tenures) | Wei (1977) | 306 | 0.585 | 1.270 | 0 | 6 |
| Trade revenue (10,000 silver *liang*) | Luo (1970) & Yang et al. (1931) | 306 | 488.515 | 1,038.792 | 0 | 8,000 |
| Number of industrial firms | Du (1991) | 306 | 3.477 | 11.466 | 0 | 122 |
| Population (in 1,000, logged) | Cao (2000) | 306 | 9.914 | 0.490 | 8.549 | 10.735 |
| Treaty port duration | Yan (1955) | 306 | 11.980 | 18.560 | 0 | 70 |
| Number of railway stations | Ma et al. (1983) | 306 | 0.330 | 1.270 | 0 | 10 |
| Number of telegraph stations | Zhang (1931) | 306 | 4.340 | 8.938 | 0 | 33 |
| Number of civil conflicts | Zhongguo junshishi bianxiezu (1985) | 306 | 1.768 | 4.298 | 0 | 31 |
| Number of foreign bank branches | Hong (1993) | 306 | 1.379 | 2.832 | 0 | 16 |
| *Province data each 5-year, 1912–1927* | | | | | | |
| Number of Shanxi bank branches | Huang (2002) | 68 | 9.779 | 11.802 | 0 | 57 |
| Shanxi officials (1823–1911) | Wei (1977) | 68 | 4.176 | 2.246 | 1 | 8 |
| Customs revenue (in 10,000 silver *liang*) | Yang et al. (1931) | 68 | 1,044.241 | 2,171.674 | 0 | 14,000 |
| Number of industrial firms | Du (1991) | 68 | 29.397 | 55.147 | 0 | 294 |
| Population (1911, in 1,000, logged) | Cao (2000) | 68 | 9.941 | 0.532 | 8.852 | 10.735 |

(continued)

**Table 11.1** (continued)

| Variables | Source | N | Mean | S.D | Min | Max |
|---|---|---|---|---|---|---|
| Treaty port duration | Yan (1955) | 68 | 46.574 | 28.068 | 0 | 86 |
| Number of modern bank branches | Du (1991) | 68 | 1.809 | 3.387 | 0 | 21 |
| Revolution sequence | Li (2011) | 68 | 6.706 | 5.395 | 0 | 16 |

## 11.4 Empirical Results

### *11.4.1 The Rise of Shanxi Banks, 1823–1911*

To test the effect of political connections on the development of Shanxi banks, we regress the distribution of Shanxi bank branches on the distribution of Shanxi officials across the 17 provinces in each five- or ten-year, based on the following specification:

$$Banks_{i,t} = \alpha + \beta ShanxiOfficials_{i,t} + \gamma X_{i,t} + u_i + \lambda_t + \epsilon_{i,t} \qquad (11.1)$$

To provide a benchmark, we first use the binary measure of $ShanxiOfficials_{i,t}$, i.e., whether a province had Shanxi officials in a given period, to test the differential development of Shanxi bank branches between the provinces with Shanxi officials and those without. Then, we examine the intensive margin of Shanxi officials' impact using the total years of tenures of Shanxi officials who served in each province in each five- or ten-year time bin. $X_{i,t-1}$ is a vector of time-varying provincial factors introduced in Sect. 11.3.3. The time-invariant provincial characteristics are fixed by $u_i$, and the effects of common shocks and trends are fixed out by the time effects, $\lambda_t$. $\epsilon_{i,t}$ is the error term.

Panel A of Table 11.2 compares provinces where there were Shanxi officials to provinces where there were no officials in terms of the number of Shanxi bank branches. On average, a province governed by Shanxi officials has 1.5 more bank branches each five-year than a province without Shanxi officials (column 1). This difference is statistically significant, accounting for 10% of the sample mean of the number of bank branches (about 15 per province per five-year). The decadal data produce very similar results as the five-year's (column 2). For robustness, we also use annual data that substantially enlarge the sample size and find the effect of Shanxi officials robust (column 3). In column 4, we drop the observations after 1861 to rule out the effects of a series of critical junctures that followed, in particular the chaos after the Taiping Rebellion, the dynasty's self-strengthening efforts, and the penetration of Western forces, among others. In other words, we examine Shanxi bank expansion in a relatively homogenous and traditional economy before the 1860s. The effect of Shanxi officials on Shanxi banks remains robust.

**Table 11.2** Shanxi officials and the rise of Shanxi banks, 1823–1911

| | (1) | (2) | (3) | (4) | (5) | (6) |
|---|---|---|---|---|---|---|
| | Number of Shanxi bank branches | Number of Shanxi bank branches | Number of Shanxi bank branches | Number of Shanxi bank branches 1823–1861 | Number of foreign bank branches | Number of Shanxi bank branches |
| | 5-year | Decadal | Yearly | 5-year | 5-year | 5-year |
| Panel A | | | | | | |
| Shanxi officials (dummy) | 1.521** | 1.734* | 1.078*** | 0.921*** | 0.288 | 1.335* |
| | (0.703) | (0.983) | (0.379) | (0.299) | (0.206) | (0.695) |
| Tax remittance | | | | | | −0.005 |
| | | | | | | (0.071) |
| Shanxi officials (dummy) × Tax remittance | | | | | | 0.019* |
| | | | | | | (0.011) |
| Panel B | | | | | | |
| Shanxi officials (tenures) | 0.482** | 0.455** | 0.884*** | 0.191** | 0.078 | 0.388* |
| | (0.223) | (0.189) | (0.321) | (0.087) | (0.070) | (0.220) |
| Tax remittance | | | | | | −0.007 |
| | | | | | | (0.071) |
| Shanxi officials (tenures) × Tax remittance | | | | | | 0.008 |
| | | | | | | (0.005) |
| Controls | Y | Y | Y | Y | Y | Y |
| Controls × Tax remittance | | | | | | Y |
| Provincial FE | Y | Y | Y | Y | Y | Y |
| Time FE | Y | Y | Y | Y | Y | Y |
| Observations | 306 | 153 | 1,513 | 136 | 306 | 306 |

(continued)

**Table 11.2** (continued)

| | (1) | (2) | (3) | (4) | (5) | (6) |
|---|---|---|---|---|---|---|
| Adjusted R-squared | 0.906 | 0.908 | 0.901 | 0.958 | 0.786 | 0.909 |
| Number of provinces | 17 | 17 | 17 | 17 | 17 | 17 |

*Note* All columns report the OLS estimates. Both panels include the same set of controls, which include trade revenue (domestic trade revenue (*Likin*) and customs revenue), number of industrial firms, population size, treaty port duration, number of railway stations, number of telegraph stations, and number of civil conflicts. Robust standard errors are in parentheses. ***, **, * indicate significance at 1%, 5%, and 10% levels. See the text and Table 11.1 for variable definitions and data sources

To further document that the effect of Shanxi officials comes from their political connections with Shanxi banks, we employ foreign bank development in each province as a placebo. Foreign bank development in China had little to do with Shanxi officials but was also driven by the local financial environment. We measure foreign bank development using the number of foreign bank branches in each province in each five years from 1823 to 1911 based on the data of Hong (1993, 147–167). We find that the distribution of Shanxi officials does not have an effect on the distribution of foreign banks in China (Table 11.2, column 5).

Next, we examine how Shanxi officials helped develop Shanxi banks. Given the data availability, we focus on examining the role of government businesses. We interact the Shanxi official dummy with the volume of tax revenue remitted by Shanxi banks from each province. The data on tax revenue remittances are digitized from the records in Huang (2002, 128–131, 239–246). The results in Table 11.2, column 6 show that the effect of Shanxi officials on bank branches is significantly greater in provinces where Shanxi banks operate more government tax remittances. This suggests that government business was an important channel by which political connections promoted Shanxi banking development.

In Panel B of Table 11.2, we replicate Panel A but use the tenures of Shanxi officials (person-years) to measure the strength of political connections. The effect of Shanxi officials on Shanxi banks remains significant and positive. An additional year of the tenure of Shanxi officials is associated with a nearly 0.5 increase in the number of Shanxi bank branches in every five- or ten-year period (columns 1 and 2). This translates to a 3.3% increase when evaluated by the sample mean of bank branches. This effect becomes greater when Shanxi banks take more government businesses of tax remittance. Likewise, the tenures of Shanxi officials also do not have an effect on the distribution of foreign bank branches.

### *11.4.2 The Fall of Shanxi Banks after 1911*

The collapse of the Qing dynasty in 1911 provides another setting to examine the effect of political connections on Shanxi banks. The Xinhai Revolution in 1911 overthrew the Qing regime and thus deprived the powers of old elites. Political connections on which Shanxi banks had relied for nearly a century disappeared abruptly. More than that, the foregoing connection with the Qing government even became a "curse" for Shanxi banks after 1911, since the new Republican elites favored modern financial institutions over the traditional silver regime. Despite their endeavors in cultivating connections with the new Republican officials, Shanxi bankers found it difficult to win the trust of these political elites in a new institutional environment (Lin 2013). In the winter of 1913, 14 Shanxi banks collectively appealed to the new government for financial support but were declined. The next year, six representatives of Shanxi banks visited the Minister of Finance for bailouts but were refused (Hall 1921). Even the modernizing reform of Shanxi banks was not appreciated. In 1916, Shanxi banks planned to merge into the new Shanxi Remittance Industrial Banks but again failed to obtain the startup loan (five million silver *liang*) from the American banking syndicate because the Beiyang government refused to underwrite it (Wu 2016).

Accordingly, Shanxi banks could not operate government businesses and financial support, let alone their nationwide remittances because of the divisions caused by warlords. The number of Shanxi banks declined sharply, from 327 branches in 1912 to 207 in 1917, a 37% drop in five years, and had basically vanished by the 1930s (Huang 2002, 638–663). To examine the political resource curse of Shanxi banks around the Qing collapse in 1911, we regress the number of Shanxi bank branches in each province from 1892 (during the heyday of Shanxi banking) to 1927 (the end of the Beiyang regime) on the interaction terms of the post-1911 time dummy and the total number of Shanxi officials in each province between 1823 and 1911. By doing so we examine the extent to which the previous political capital of Shanxi banks affected their branch network decline after the political capital was gone. The regression is specified as below:

$$Bank_{i,t} = \beta(\sum_{t=1823}^{1911} ShanxiOfficials_i) \times Post1911_t + \theta X_{i,t} + u_i + \lambda_t + \epsilon_{i,t} \quad (11.2)$$

where $Bank_{it}$ refers to the number of Shanxi bank branches in province $i$ and period $t$. Given the short sample period for the decline analysis (1892–1927), we organize the data on an annual or five-year basis. Our key explanatory variable is the sum of the number of Shanxi officials in each province between 1823 and 1911; and we interact it with a time dummy that equals one for the post-Qing dynasty period (1912–1927) and zero otherwise. $X_{i,t}$ refers to a set of provincial controls; these include trade revenue, number of industrial firms, and treaty port duration. Given the missing population figures between 1911 and 1927, we control for the interaction terms between the population size in 1911 and the time dummies. Doing so attenuates the possible confounding effect of the initial population or economic conditions on Shanxi officials and Shanxi banks. Moreover, we control for the timing of provincial independence during the Xinhai Revolution to account for the possible effect of the Revolution on Shanxi banks. We assume that provinces declaring independence earlier would experience more conflicts and chaos that disrupt financial development. To quantify the independence timing, we simply assign higher integer values to provinces that declared independence earlier and zero for provinces that did not declare independence. As in Eq. 11.1, we control for the province and time effects, denoted by $u_i$ and $\lambda_t$, respectively.

Table 11.3 reports the results. In columns (1) and (2), we examine the full sample period from 1892 to 1927, whereas in columns (3) and (4) we narrow the period to 1907–1915 to mitigate the impacts of other shocks, most notably the First Sino-Japanese War, the Boxer Uprising, and the end of the imperial examination system before 1907 and the Warlords' unrest after 1915. Moreover, columns 1–3 examine the level effect, using the number of Shanxi bank branches as the outcome variable. In column (4), we use the first difference in the number of Shanxi bank branches between the current and the previous year to measure the decline rate. Doing so attenuates the concern that the greater decline of bank branches is just the result of their higher stock before 1911. The results show that provinces governed by Shanxi officials before 1911 saw more (and faster) closures of Shanxi bank branches after 1911. This implies a possible political resource curse of Shanxi banks upon the end of the dynastic rule. The heavy reliance on government connections turned out to be negatively affecting the banking development after the connections were gone.

The decline of Shanxi banking after 1911 could also have been shaped by other political and economic factors. What we can test here is that the old political capital across provinces independently affected the decline of Shanxi banking rather than being confounded by other alternative mechanisms. For example, the decline of Shanxi banks may also be due to their failure to adopt modern financial technology, especially telecommunications, and thus lost the competitive edge with modern banks. However, Shanxi banks employed telegraphic services for remittances when the technology was introduced to China in the 1880s (Huang 2004). It is also vague to attribute the failure of Shanxi banks to their conservativeness since they attempted to seek modernization and cooperation with modern banks after 1911. The development of modern (Western-style) banks in the early twentieth century may crowd out Shanxi banks. However, modern banks do not mitigate the significant effect of Shanxi officials as shown in columns 2–4 of Table 11.3.

## 11.5 Concluding Remarks

We provide suggestive evidence of the importance of political connections in shaping the rise of Shanxi banks in the nineteenth century and their decline after 1911. The inter-regional finance of Shanxi banks relied on local officials' support in regions outside Shanxi. Such support was primarily built on the hometown ties between

**Table 11.3** Shanxi officials and the decline of Shanxi banks, 1892–1927

| | (1) | (2) | (3) | (4) |
|---|---|---|---|---|
| | Number of Shanxi bank branches | Number of Shanxi bank branches | Number of Shanxi bank branches | Number of Shanxi bank branches (first difference) |
| | 5-year | 5-year | Yearly, 1907–1915 | Yearly, 1907–1915 |
| Shanxi officials (1823–1911) × Post1911 | −0.946* | −1.121** | −0.420** | −0.170* |
| | (0.561) | (0.556) | (0.179) | (0.091) |
| Number of modern bank branches | | Y | Y | Y |
| Controls | Y | Y | Y | Y |
| Provincial FE | Y | Y | Y | Y |
| Time FE | Y | Y | Y | Y |
| Observations | 136 | 136 | 153 | 153 |
| Adjusted R-squared | 0.860 | 0.866 | 0.984 | 0.389 |
| Number of provinces | 17 | 17 | 17 | 17 |

*Note* Controls include the trade revenue (customs revenue), number of industrial firms, population size (1911), treaty port duration, and the sequence of independence during the Xinhai Revolution that overthrew the Qing dynasty. Robust standard errors are in parentheses. ***, **, * indicate significance at 1%, 5%, and 10% levels. See the text and Table 11.1 for variable definitions and data sources

Shanxi banks and their fellow officials from Shanxi province. Thanks to the centralized personnel control of the Qing dynasty, Shanxi officials were directly appointed by the emperors to different provinces, which created an exogenous regional variation of political connections to Shanxi banks. Making use of this variation, we find that provinces governed by Shanxi officials developed more Shanxi bank branches from 1823 to 1911.

The importance of political connections for Shanxi banks is further gleaned from the sharp decline of the banks after their political capital was removed after the 1911 revolution. In provinces where Shanxi officials could aid Shanxi banks to set up more branches in the Qing dynasty, Shanxi banks also experienced greater decline in the new Republican era from 1912 to 1927. Political connections with the dynastic rule resulted in a reversal of fortune upon the dynastic collapse in 1911. After that, modern banks dominated China's financial market; Shanghai replaced Shanxi to be the new financial center.

## References

Akcigit, Ufuk, Salomé Baslandze, and Francesca Lotti. 2023. Connecting to Power: Political Connections, Innovation, and Firm Dynamics. *Econometrica* 91 (2): 529–564.

Cao, Shuji. 2000. *Zhongguo renkou shi: Qing shiqi (Population History of China: Qing Dynasty).* Shanghai: Fudan daxue chubanshe.

Chen, Qitian. 1937. *Shanxi piaozhuang kaolve (Investigation of the Shanxi Piaohao).* Shanghai: Shangwu yinshu guan.

Chen, Zhiwu, Chicheng Ma, and Andrew Sinclair. 2022. Banking on the Confucian Clan: Why China Developed Financial Markets So Late? *The Economic Journal* 132 (644): 1378–1413.

Cheng, Linsun. 2003. *Banking in Modern China: Entrepreneurs, Professional Managers, and the Development of Chinese Banks, 1897–1937*. Cambridge: Cambridge University Press.

CHGIS. 2016. Fairbank Center for Chinese Studies of Harvard University and the Center for Historical Geographical Studies at Fudan University. Vers. 6. Accessed December 2024. https://dataverse.harvard.edu/dataverse/chgis_v6.

D'Acunto, Francesco, Marcel Prokopczuk, and Michael Weber. 2019. Historical Antisemitism, Ethnic Specialization, and Financial Development. *The Review of Economic Studies* 86 (3): 1170–1206.

Drelichman, Mauricio, and Hans-Joachim Voth. 2011. Lending to the Borrower from Hell: Debt and Default in the Age of Philip II. *The Economic Journal* 121 (557): 1205–1227.

Du, Xuncheng. 1991. *Minzu zibenzhuyi yu jiuzhongguo zhengfu (National Capitalism and Old China Government).* Shanghai: Shanghai shehui kexueyuan chubanshe.

Faccio, Mara. 2006. Politically Connected Firms. *The American Economic Review* 96 (1): 369–386.

Ferguson, Thomas, and Hans-Joachim Voth. 2008. Betting on Hitler: The Value of Political Connections in Nazi Germany. *The Quarterly Journal of Economics* 123 (1): 101–137.

Fisman, Raymond. 2001. Estimating the Value of Political Connections. *The American Economic Review* 94 (1): 1095–1102.

Hall, Ray Ovid. 1921. *The Chinese National Banks, From their Founding to the Moratorium.* New York: Columbia University Press.

Hong, Jiaguan. 1993. *Zhongguo jinrong shi (Chinese Financial History).* Chengdu: Xinan caijing daxue chubanshe.

Huang, Jianhui. 2004. *Shanxi piaohao shi (The History of Shanxi Piaohao).* Taiyuan: Shanxi jingji chubanshe.

Huang, Jianhui, ed. 2002. *Shanxi piaohao shiliao (Historical Documents of Shanxi Piaohao).* Taiyuan: Shanxi jingji chubanshe.

Kong, Xiangyi. 1984. Shanxi piaohao yu qingzhengfu de goujie (The Collusion between the Piaohao and the Qing Government). *Zhongguo Shehui Jingjishi Yanjiu* 3: 1–12.

La Porta, Florencio Lopez-de-Silanes. Rafael, Andrei Shleifer, and Robert W. Vishny. 1998. Law and Finance. *Journal of Political Economy* 106 (6): 1113–1155.

La Porta, Florencio Lopez-de-Silanes Rafael, Andrei Shleifer, and Robert W. Vishny. 1997. Legal Determinants of External Finance. *The Journal of Finance* 52 (3): 1131–1150.

Levine, Ross, Chen Lin, Chicheng Ma, and Yuchen Xu. 2023. The Legal Origins of Financial Development: Evidence from the Shanghai Concessions. *The Journal of Finance* 78 (6): 3423–3464.

Li, Xin. 2011. *Zhonghuaminguo shi dashiji (Chronology of Major Events in the History of the Republic of China).* Beijing: Zhonghua Book Company.

Lin, Chen, Chicheng Ma, Yuchen Sun, and Yuchen Xu. 2021. The Telegraph and Modern Banking Development, 1881–1936. *Journal of Financial Economics* 141 (2): 730–749.

Lin, Chih-hung. 2013. *Minguo nai diguoye: zhengzhi wenhua zhuanxing xia de qing yimin (Republic as the Enemy State: Qing Loyalists in the Context of Political and Cultural Transformation).* Beijing: Zhonghua Book Company.

Liu, Jiansheng, Pengsheng Liu, and Hongzhong Yan. 2005. *Mingqing jinshang zhidu bianqian yanjiu (Institutional Change of the Shanxi Merchants in the Ming and Qing periods).* Taiyuan: Shanxi renmin chubanshe.

Luo, Yudong. 1970. *Zhongguo lijin shi (The History of Commercial Tax in China).* Taipei: Xuehai chubanshe.

Ma, Debin. 2019. Financial Revolution in Republican China During 1900–37: A Survey and a New Interpretation. *Australian Economic History Review* 59 (3): 242–262.

Ma, Liqian, Yizhi Lu, and Kaiji Wang. 1983. *Zhongguo tielu jianzhu biannian jianshi: 1881–1981 (The Simple Chronicles of Railway in China: 1881–1981).* Beijing: Zhongguo tiedao chubanshe.

O'Brien, Patrick K., and Nuno Palma. 2023. Not an Ordinary Bank but a Great Engine of State: The Bank of England and the British Economy, 1694–1844. *The Economic History Review* 76 (1): 305–329.

Qiao, Zhijian. 2017. "The Rise of Shanxi Merchants: Empire, Institutions, and Social Change in Qing China, 1688–1850." *Stanford University Dissertation Repository.* Accessed December 2024. https://purl.stanford.edu/bg803zm7823/version/1.

Santarosa, Veronica Aoki. 2015. Financing Long-Distance Trade: The Joint Liability Rule and Bills of Exchange in Eighteenth-Century France. *Journal of Economic History* 75 (3): 690–719.

Stulz, M. René., and Rohan Williamson. 2003. Culture, Openness, and Finance. *Journal of Financial Economics* 70 (3): 313–349.

Wang, Luman. 2021. *Chinese Hinterland Capitalism and Shanxi Piaohao: Banking, State, and Family, 1720–1910.* New York: Routledge.

Wei, Hsiu-mei. 1977. *Offices and Personnel in The Late Ch'ing Period: Metropolitan Officials and High Officials in Provinces and Dependencies, 1796–1911.* Taipei: Institute of Modern History, Academia Sinica.

Wei, Juxian. 2017. *Shanxi piaohao shi (The History of Shanxi Piaohao).* Taiyuan: Sanjin chubanshe.

Wu, Meng. 2024. Governance Structure, Organizational Form, and Business Performance: A Study of the Shanxi Piaohao (Banks), 1820s–1930s. *Business History* 1–27. https://doi.org/10.1080/00076791.2024.2409436.

Wu, Meng. 2016. Traditions and Innovations: An Exploration of the Governance Structure, Business Strategy and Historical Development of the Chinese Shanxi Piaohao, 1820s to 1930s. *London School of Economics and Political Science Dissertation Repository.* https://etheses.lse.ac.uk/3415/.

Yan, Hongzhong. 2012. *Zhongguo de huobi jinrong tixi (1600–1949): Jiyu jingji yunxing yu jingji jindaihua de yanjiu (Monetary and Financial Systems of China from 1600 to 1949: A Study on Economic Performance and Modernization).* Beijing: Zhongguo renmin daxue chubanshe.

Yan, Zhongpin. 1955. *Zhongguo jindai jingjishi tongji ziliaoxuanji (Selection of Statistics on Economic History of Modern China).* Beijing: Kexue chubanshe.

Yang, Duanliu, Houpei Hou, and Others. 1931. *Liushiwu nian lai zhongguo guoji maoyi tongji (Statistics of China's Foreign Trade during the Last Sixty-five Years).* Nanjing: National Research Institute of Social Sciences, Academia Sinica.

Zhang, Guohui. 2007. *Wanqing qianzhuang he piaohao yanjiu (Research on Qianzhuang and Piaohao in the Late Qing Dynasty).* Beijing: Shehui kexue wenxian chubanshe.

Zhang, Xincheng. 1931. *Zhongguo xiandai jiaotong shi (The History of Modern Transportation in China).* Shanghai: Shanghai shudian.

Zheng, Yifang. 1981. *Shanghai qianzhuang (1843–1937): Zhongguo chuantong jinrongye de tuibian (Shanghai Native Banks (1843–1937): The Transformation of China's Traditional Financial Industry).* Taipei: Academia Sinica.

Zhongguo junshishi bianxiezu. 1985. *Zhongguo junshishi fujuan (The Appendix of The Military History of China).* Beijing: Jiefangjun chubanshe.

Zhou, Jianbo, and Jiang Zeng. 2020. Yinhang, piaohao xingti yu qingmo minchu jinrong biange (The Rise and Fall of Banks and Piaohao and Financial Reforms in Late Qing and Early Republican China). *Social Sciences in China* (8): 178–203, 208.

**Wentian Diao** is an Assistant Professor in the School of Economics at Shanghai University of Finance and Economics. Her current research focuses on the economic impact of informal institutions and cultural norms (e.g., elite groups, militia, and religions). Before joining SUFE, she obtained her Ph.D. in Economics from the National University of Singapore and her M.Phil. in Social Science from The Hong Kong University of Science and Technology.

**Jinyan Hu** is a Professor in the School of Economics in Shandong University and currently serving as Party Secretary at Qingdao University. He earned his Ph.D. in Economics from Shandong University and completed postdoctoral research at Fudan University. His research focuses on informal finance, inclusive finance, rural finance, financial investment, capital markets, and monetary and financial theory and policy. He has successively presided over a number of key research projects funded by the National Natural Science Foundation of China and the National Social Science Fund of China. He published works in peer-reviewed journals such as *Journal of Comparative Economics*, *Journal of Banking and Finance*, and *International Review of Finance.*

**Chicheng Ma** is an Associate Professor in Economics at the HKU Business School of The University of Hong Kong. He studies economic history and development, specializing in historical China and its contact with the West. He won the Royal Economic Society Prize for the best paper in the *Economic Journal* in 2020, Hong Kong University Research Output Prize in 2021, and the Economic History Association's Arthur H. Cole Prize for the best article in the *Journal of Economic History* in 2022. As Principal Investigator, Chicheng has received competitive research grants from the Hong Kong Research Grant Council and the National Natural Science Foundation of China. He serves as an Associate Director of the Centre for Quantitative History and Associate Professor (by courtesy) at the Hong Kong Institute for the Humanities and Social Sciences.

# Part IV
# Religion and Agricultural Development

# Chapter 12
# Protestantism and Agricultural Development in China

**Ying Bai and Xiaoyu Bian**

## 12.1 Introduction

Inspired by Max Weber's classic work, "The Protestant Ethic and the Spirit of Capitalism," social scientists have devoted significant attention to examining the influence of Protestantism on economic prosperity. Throughout this exploration, scholars have come to understand that the impact of Protestantism on economic development extends beyond Protestant ethics and operates through various other channels.[1] For instance, Bai and Kung (2015) discovered that the diffusion of Protestantism played a role in stimulating economic prosperity in China from 1840 to 1920. They found that 90% of this effect was attributed to the dissemination of valuable Western knowledge. Specifically, the establishment of modern schools and hospitals facilitated China's urbanization and industrialization. However, considering that 80–90% of the total population in China at that time resided in rural areas and were engaged in agriculture, it is important to explore the influence of Protestantism on the rural and agricultural sectors of China.

Similar to their efforts in the urban sector, Protestant missionaries also endeavored to disseminate knowledge in the rural sector, which had the potential to benefit agricultural development. During the nineteenth century, when Protestant missionaries first arrived in China, their primary focus was to spread the Gospel through medical and educational missions, establishing Protestant hospitals and schools throughout

[1] The possible channels include moral codes (e.g., Lipset and Lenz 2000), a country's openness (La Porta et al. 1998), religious beliefs (e.g., McCleary and Barro 2003; Barro 2004), social networks (e.g., Glaeser and Sacerdote 2008) and human capital (e.g., Becker and Woessmann 2009, 2010; Gallego and Woodberry 2010; Woodberry 2012).

Y. Bai · X. Bian (✉)
Department of Economics, The Chinese University of Hong Kong, Hong Kong, China
e-mail: xiaoyubianhk@gmail.com

Y. Bai
e-mail: ybai@cuhk.edu.hk



Z. Chen et al. (eds.), *Quantitative History of China*, Studies in Economic History,
https://doi.org/10.1007/978-981-96-8272-0_12

the country. By the early twentieth century, however, only a small number of Chinese individuals had converted to Protestantism, prompting missionaries to seek new, more practical avenues. In the 1910s and 1920s, the concept of "agricultural missions" gained prominence (Stross 1986; Cheng 2018). Missionaries saw this as an opportunity for Protestantism to make a tangible impact on agricultural production in China. The hope was that by enhancing agricultural productivity, which directly affected the majority of the Chinese population (approximately 85% engaged in farming at the time), farmers would embrace the Protestant faith with gratitude. Consequently, Protestant missionaries became a medium for spreading Western agricultural knowledge, to a certain extent.

Since then, various agricultural technologies have been introduced into China through these missionaries. By the 1920s, Western agriculture had already advanced in terms of chemical fertilizers and machine operation, while Chinese agriculture still relied on organic fertilizers and intensive labor input. Consequently, it is reasonable to expect that missionaries may have had a positive effect on the development of China's agriculture.

However, the impact of specific agricultural technology is largely determined by agricultural characteristics and local conditions, such as environment, endowments, and socioeconomic factors, and hence varies across regions. As the "inappropriate technology hypothesis" suggests, customizing technology to local conditions hinders its diffusion and productivity benefits in other contexts (Stewart 2016; Basu and Weil 1998; Acemoglu and Zilibotti 2001). In other words, new technologies are attached to specific conditions and characteristics of production (Griliches 1957; Atkinson and Stiglitz 1969). To take an agricultural example, genetically modified corn varieties designed to be toxic specifically to corn rootworms are less effective against other pests, such as the maize stalk borer, a pest endemic to sub-Saharan Africa that is estimated to destroy 10% of Kenyan corn every year (Bessin 2019; Campagne et al. 2017). Moscona and Sastry (2025) study this hypothesis using a mismatch in the presence of crop-specific pests and pathogens as a shifter of technology's inappropriateness and investigate its effect on global innovation, technology diffusion, and productivity. Their findings provide support for each pillar of the inappropriate technology hypothesis and demonstrate how the direction of innovation underlies disparities in global agricultural productivity.

Following the "inappropriate technology hypothesis," the impact of Western agricultural knowledge on Chinese agriculture is uncertain. This is because there are significant differences between Chinese and Western agriculture and amongs different regions of China. In the 1930, Chinese agriculture was characterized by small farms with intensive human labor and manure inputs, whereas Western agriculture was dominated by large farms with extensive use of agricultural machinery, commercial fertilizers, and chemical fertilizers. In Section III, we estimate the production function to depict the characteristics of Chinese agriculture in the 1930s. The estimated function shows that due to the lack of large farms and agricultural technology, Chinese agriculture relied on investing more labor and organic fertilizers in smaller farmland to enhance farm productivity during that time. Additionally, staple crops varied depending largely on geography and environment. For example, rice dominated southern China, wheat dominated northern China, while Western Europe and the United States were dominated by barley, wheat, and corn. These discrepancies imply that the "useful" knowledge based on Western agriculture may not be directly applicable to Chinese farms.

In this paper, we first investigate whether the diffusion of Protestantism had a positive impact on Chinese agricultural productivity in the 1930s. We use the number of communicants per 10,000 people in 1920 as a proxy for Protestantism in a prefecture and match it with the yields of various important food crops that occupied at least one percent of the crop hectares. We collected information on 147 sampled counties from 114 prefectures in 18 provinces from 1929 to 1933. Our baseline results show that the presence of Protestantism indeed had a significant and positive effect on grain production at that time. Specifically, one additional communicant per 10,000 people led to a 0.6% increase in agricultural productivity. Additionally, we employ the duration of Protestant missions in 1920 as another proxy variable for Protestantism to test its impact on agricultural output. Robustness checks further support the positive influence of Protestantism on agricultural output. These results suggest that overall, Protestantism encouraged agricultural development in 1920s–1930s China.

Since the choice of located counties when missionaries entered China was not randomly assigned, the endogeneity issue is a major concern. Missionaries may have preferred to settle in regions with higher grain productivity, and these counties may have remained relatively prosperous in the 1930s. Hence, our baseline results may not provide valid evidence for a positive impact of Protestantism on agricultural output. We conducted two checks to address this concern. First, we examined the correlation between Protestantism and the average grain yield during the early period, namely the Qing dynasty. Our rationale was that if the result was caused by the missionaries' preference for prosperous locations, the counties with initially higher agricultural output in the Qing dynasty should have attracted more missionaries. Our results show that there is no significant correlation between the two. Therefore, we can conclude that our baseline results are not due to reverse location selection. Second, in the baseline specification, we further controlled for the initial level of agricultural production in each county during the Qing dynasty, and the effect of Protestantism remained.

To test whether the "inappropriate technology hypothesis" matters, we examined the heterogeneity in the effects of Protestantism on agricultural productivity. Specifically, we investigated whether the effects depended on agricultural factor inputs and crop varieties. Two findings stand out. First, the effect is weakened by organic fertilizer inputs and strengthened by plot size (without controlling for labor and fertilizer inputs). Second, the effect of Protestantism is significantly positive for wheat (0.010), while the effect for rice is very small (−0.002). Moreover, there is no significant difference between the effect for wheat and the effect for other crops such as corn, millet, beans, kaoliang, and roots. All these results indicate that Western missionaries could not efficiently manage small-plot and organic-fertilizer-intensive agriculture and were better at growing wheat than rice. This is not surprising since most of them came from Europe and America, where organic fertilizer is less used, and the staple crops are barley and wheat due to the specific natural environment.

The heterogeneity findings are also consistent with the classic work on induced innovation in agricultural development by Yujiro Hayami and Vernon Ruttan (1985). Their works specifically argued that American type of agricultural technology was not well-suited to Japanese agriculture and rice cultivation in the nineteenth and twentieth centuries. Similar to Chinese agriculture, Japanese agriculture was also characterized by limited land supply and infavorable people-land ratios in the 1900s. While China still relied on traditional crops and natural fertilizers, Japan had already adopted advanced chemical fertilizers and increasing fertilizer application as well as seed improvements to increase yields. As a result, in the twentieth century, Japan experienced rapid growth in agricultural production and productivity similar to that of the United States by increasing land productivity under severe land constraints. Ma (2004) also shows that Japan surpassed China in sericulture in the 1930s through developing appropriate technology to overcome resource limitations.

In addition, we further examine the effect of Protestantism on the wages (or costs) of hired laborers in rice and wheat regions. We measure labor wages at two levels: one includes total labor costs, which not only covers wages but also food expenses and other labor costs, and the other focuses solely on labor wages. We divide labor into two categories, long-term laborers (year laborers), and short-term farm laborers (month and day laborers during peak seasons). The results show that, regardless of the type of laborer, Protestantism increased labor wages (or costs) only in the wheat region and had little effect on labor wages in the rice region. This result aligns with the heterogeneous effect of Protestantism on the yields of rice and non-rice crops in China. Agricultural labor wages are correlated with agricultural production. Western agricultural knowledge brought by Protestantism increased wheat yields, thus benefiting agricultural laborers in wheat-producing areas, while laborers in rice-producing areas did not experience significant changes.

This paper complements the research on the contributions of Protestantism. Existing Protestant research focuses on its impact on economic development and offers a range of possible channels of influence (as shown in footnote 1). The most relevant paper is Bai and Kung (2015). They find that Protestantism promoted urbanization in China through the dissemination of Western knowledge by establishing hospitals and schools between 1840 and 1920. Our paper further examines whether the spread of Western useful knowledge promoted agricultural productivity in 1920s China. We draw on the "inappropriate technology hypothesis" and pay attention tos the differences in agricultural characteristics between China and the West. We find that although Protestantism increased agricultural output in 1930 China, its effects varied considerably across regions with different agricultural inputs and crop varieties. Our findings fill a gap in the literature on the impact of Protestantism on agricultural development and support the inappropriate technology hypothesis from a religious diffusion perspective.

The rest of the paper is organized as follows. In Section II, we briefly describe the development of Protestantism in China and compare the characteristics of Chinese and Western agriculture. In Section III, we introduce the data sources and define the variables used in the analysis. In Section IV, we present an empirical analysis of the impact of Protestantism on agricultural production in 1930s China. Section V summarizes and concludes this study.

## 12.2 Historical Background

### *12.2.1 The Development of Protestantism in China, 1840–1920*

With the sign of a series of unequal treaties during the First Opium War (1839–1842), the Qing government was forced to open its doors to the Western powers. Western missionaries and other foreigners were admitted to enter China but were initially only allowed to reside in the five earliest treaty ports. After the Second Opium War (1856–1860), they were granted access to the Chinese inland areas. Thereafter, Protestantism experienced fast expansion in China, from 60 missionaries in 1860 to nearly 2,500 missionaries in 1900 (Thompson 2009). By 1920, the Protestantism had reached its peak, with missionary presence recorded in 94% of Chinese counties, 84% had records of Protestant communicant numbers, and 78% had established Protestant congregations or evangelistic centers (Stauffer 1922). Figure 12.1 depicts the development of missionary work in the late Qing Dynasty. We can see that by 1920 over 70% of the counties had recorded missionary work. Figure 12.1 directly demonstrates the wide penetration of Protestantism in China in the 1920s.

The spread of Protestantism sparked growing hostility and conflicts between the Chinese people and foreign missionaries. The conflicts culminated in the Boxer Rebellion of 1900, which led to the death of 5,000 Chinese communicants and 188 foreign Protestant missionaries and their children (Esherick 1988). To mitigate hostility and build trust with Chinese residents, missionaries took the educational and medical missions as the primary means of disseminating the Gospel. They worked to establish Western hospitals to control diseases and introduced Western medicine into China (Bays 2011; Elman 2006). They also erected Protestant schools to introduce some new Western-based curriculum and taught a variety of novel subjects ranging from mathematics and astronomy to English, history, and geography (Gu 2010; Richard 1916).

However, by the early twentieth century, although Protestantism's penetration was wide it was not deep. According to Stauffer's survey (1922), fewer than 0.1% of Chinese people had converted to Protestantism. Some missionaries criticized the concentration of educational and medical missions in urban areas at the expense of rural areas, where more than three-quarters of Chinese population lived at the time (Reisner 1924; Groff 1924). Then from the 1910s, missionaries began to give importance to agricultural missions. They shifted their focus from urban to rural areas, in the hope of winning the faith of Chinese peasants and ultimately achieving "the Christian occupation of China" through ruralizing the church. Ting Shu-Ching, a general secretary of the Y.W.C.A of China had said that "We need missionaries

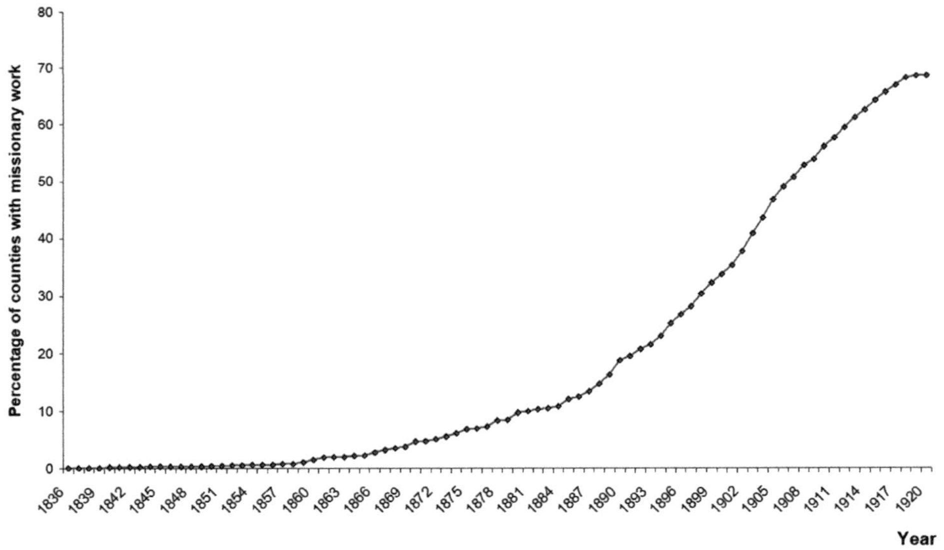


**Fig. 12.1** Percentage of counties with Protestant Missionary Work (*Source* The Christian occupation of China: a general survey of the numerical strength and geographical distribution of the Christian forces in China [Stauffer 1922])

trained in rural and agricultural work to come out as experts to help our farmers [...] Through the improvement of seeds, new methods of agriculture, and through spiritual contact with the farmers, the village might be won to Christ" (Cheng 2018). Thus, in addition to spreading "useful" Western educational and medical knowledge in urban areas, Protestant missionaries also facilitated the spread of advanced Western agricultural techniques in rural China at that time.

## *12.2.2 Characteristics of Chinese Agriculture*

### 12.2.2.1 Comparisons: Chinese Agriculture vs. Western Agriculture

There were great differences between Chinese and Western agriculture in the early twentieth century. First, farm size and labor input intensity varied greatly. In comparison to the large, less labor-intensive farms of Western countries, Chinese agriculture was characterized by small, labor-intensive farms in the absence of abundant farmland and effective labor markets (Wang et al. 2016; Cook 1999). According to the survey on 16,786 farmlands across 22 provinces by Buck (1937), the average size of farm plots in 1930s was only 0.38 hectares, and the crop area per capita was 0.25 hectares.[2] While in the UK, the average size of all types of farms was already over 40 hectares in 1800 (Allen 1994) and the cultivated area per agricultural population was around 2.8 hectares in 1910 (van Zanden 1991). As for the United States, in 1910, the average farm size was about 56.25 hectares, and the farmland per farm population was about 11.12 hectares.[3]

Second, there were differences in the adoption of chemical fertilizers. In contrast to the high dependence of Chinese farmland on manure, Western countries rely mainly on commercial chemical fertilizer to increase land productivity. Even though fertilizer consumption in Western European countries has increased rapidly since 1900, due to the spread of fertilizer technology and the increase in agricultural prices (van Zanden 1991), most European countries only consumed less than 20 kg/ha of fertilizers (represented by $N, P_2O_5, K_2O$).[4] In contrast, the manure produced on Chinese farms averaged up to 7400 kg/ha[5]in the 1930s, while chemical fertilizer production was very low until the 1970s, due to a lack of resources and technology (Li et al. 2013; Wang et al. 1996).

Third, China had very little agricultural mechanization. Unlike Chinese agriculture, which was dominated by manual labor and traditional tools, labor-saving

---

[2] LUC, Statistics, Chapter II, Table 15; Chapter XL, Table 3.

[3] Data source: United States. Bureau of the Census. (1975). Historical statistics of the United States, colonial times to 1970 (No. 78). Table: Series K 1–16.

[4] For US, the commercial fertilizer consumed in 1910 is approximately 14.11 kg/ha. (Data source: Historical statistics of the United States, colonial times to 1970 (No. 78). Table: Series K 192–194).

[5] Data source: LUC, Statistics, Chapter IV, Table 11.

agricultural machinery such as threshers, reapers, and seeders, were widely used on European and American farms in the 1930s (Olmstead and Rhode 1988; Binswanger 1986; Pingali 2007), partly because larger farms are more easily adapted to mechanization for higher productivity (Qiu and Luo 2021; Foster and Rosenzweig 2022). For example, in the United States, the storage of tractors had expanded to around one million units in 1930, and about 13.5% of farms reported owning tractors (Olmstead and Rhode 2001). While in China, the agricultural mechanization began in the 1950s, the first agricultural machinery factories were established during the First Five-Year Plan (1953–1957) (Stavis 1978).

In short, there were huge differences between the Chinese and Western agriculture in the 1930s. In contrast to the Western advanced mechanized agriculture, Chinese agriculture was featured by scattered farmland plots, intensive labor input and organic fertilizer usage, and the absence of mechanization at that time.

#### 12.2.2.2 Production Function Estimation

We attempted to estimate the production function of Chinese agriculture in the 1930s in order to characterize Chinese agriculture accurately and directly. Specifically, we use the Cobb–Douglas production function with four conventional agricultural inputs: labor, organic fertilizer (manure), irrigation rate, and farm plot size. The estimation specification as:

$$\begin{aligned} lnY_{cijt} = {} & \beta_1 \ln Labor_{ijt} + \beta_2 \ln Fertilizer_{ijt} + \beta_3 Irrigated_{ijt} \\ & + \beta_4 \ln Farmsize_{ijt} + MainCrop_c + CropZone_i \\ & + Prov_j + Year_t + \varepsilon_{cijt} \end{aligned} \tag{12.1}$$

where $Y_{cijt}$ is the yield of crop $c$ in county $i$, prefecture $j$ and year $t$. $MainCrop_c$ indicates which of the seven main crop categories[6] the crop c belongs to. $CropZone_i$ is the agricultural area[7] in which county $i$ is located. $Prov_j$ and $Year_t$ control for fixed effects for the province in which prefecture $j$ is located and the year in which the $Y_{cijt}$ is surveyed, respectively.

Table 12.1 shows the contribution of each input on Chinese agricultural productivity. Column (1) shows that the three major inputs, labor, organic fertilizer, and irrigation, as expected, have significant positive contributions on crop yield. In terms of magnitude, the crop production per hectare will increase around 0.41% (0.16%, 0.32%) with 1-percentage-point (0.01) increase in effective labor (fertilizer, irrigation

[6] The seven main crop categories are shown in Table 12.2, including Wheats, Maize, Sorghum, Millets, Rice, Legumes and Tuber and Roots.

[7] Buck (1937) divides the surveyed regions into eight agricultural areas based on their staple crops, including Spring wheat area, Winter wheat-millet area, Winter wheat-kaoliang area, Yangtze-rice–wheat area, Rice-tea area, Sichuan Rice area, Double cropping rice area, and Southwestern rice area.

**Table 12.1** Production function estimation

| Dependent Var | Yield (ln) | | |
|---|---|---|---|
| | (1) | (2) | (3) |
| Labor (ln) | 0.406*** | | 0.368*** |
| | (0.102) | | (0.112) |
| Fertilizer (ln) | 0.163* | | 0.157* |
| | (0.093) | | (0.092) |
| Irrigated | 0.317** | | 0.324** |
| | (0.146) | | (0.142) |
| Farm plot size (ln) | | −0.200*** | −0.048 |
| | | (0.057) | (0.062) |
| MainCrop FE | Y | Y | Y |
| Year FE | Y | Y | Y |
| Province FE | Y | Y | Y |
| Agricultural area FE | Y | Y | Y |
| Observations | 779 | 779 | 779 |
| R-squared | 0.762 | 0.716 | 0.763 |

*Note* Standard errors are clustered at prefecture level. Constant terms are not reported. * Significant at 10%; ** Significant at 5%; *** Significant at 1%

rate). Column (2) shows a significant "inverse relationship" (IR) between agricultural productivity and farm plot size in the 1930s in China. The inverse relationship is common in developing Asian countries in the twentieth century, in which agriculture is dominated by small farms (Fan and Kang 2005; Fleisher and Liu 1992). There are several main explanations for IR[8] in developing countries. One important reason is the imperfect labor market, which limits non-farm employment opportunities (Benjamin and Brandt 2002). Lacking sufficient farmland and off-farm sources of income, Chinese farmers have had to invest more labor and fertilizer in small farms to maximize agricultural production. Usually, the less arable land there is, the more intensive the inputs. Figure 12.2 visually depicts the significant negative correlations between farm size and labor and fertilizer inputs in Chinese agriculture in the 1930s. In addition, the absence of agricultural machinery makes the management of large farms less efficient than that of small farms. As a result, we see that the larger the farm, the lower the crop yield per hectare.

Then we combine the impacts of the three agricultural inputs and farm size together. As shown in column (3) in Table 12.1, the positive impacts of labor, organic fertilizer (manure), and irrigation remain, with only a slight decline compared with those in column (1). However, the IR between crop yield and farm size decreases sharply (from −0.182 to −0.048) and becomes insignificant. This means that the

[8] Such as the omitted land quality (Benjamin 1995), imperfect factor markets (Foster and Rosenzweig 2022), and measurement errors (Lamb 2003; Desiere and Jolliffe 2018).

**Table 12.2** Main Crop Categories

| Category | Included Crops | Observations |
|---|---|---|
| 1. Wheat | Wheat, barley, barley (hulless), buckwheat, spring wheat | 219 |
| 2. Maize | Maize | 49 |
| 3. Sorghum | Sorghum | 63 |
| 4. Millet | Millet, millet (proso), millet (non-glutinous proso) | 98 |
| 5. Rice | Rice, glutinous rice, early rice, late rice | 134 |
| 6. Legumes | Green beans, fava beans, peas, soybeans, black beans | 171 |
| 7. Tubers and roots | Potatoes, sweet potatoes, winter radish | 89 |

intensive use of labor, fertilizers, and increased irrigation are the root causes of high crop yields per hectare on small farms. In summary, lacking large farms and advanced agricultural technology, Chinese agriculture is characterized by investing more labor and organic fertilizers on smaller farmland to enhance farm productivity in the 1930s. Therefore, Chinese farmers may be inclined to adopt labor-intensive techniques that made heavy use of organic fertilizers.

## 12.3 Data

To explore the effect of Protestantism on agricultural output, we construct a dataset on the spatial distribution of Protestant activities in 1920 and the output of some important grain crops between 1929 and 1933. Our Protestantism data are obtained by digitalizing Stauffer's (1922) survey, a statistical report that comprehensively records Protestant activities in China during the period 1840–1920. Our output data are drawn from the statistics version of Land Utilization in China (Buck 1937), a study depicts the status of land use in China from 1929 to 1933 by collecting various information on 16,786 farms in 168 localities and 38,256 farm families in 22 Chinese provinces at that time. After combining these two resources, we end up with a dataset with 823 crop samples covering 147 counties located in 114 prefectures in 18 provinces. Figure 12.3 depicts the distribution of 114 sampled prefectures on the 1820 Qing Dynasty map of China. In the following sections, we provide definitions of the specific variables employed in the empirical analysis.

### *12.3.1 Agricultural Output in 1930s*

We use the yields per hectare of different food crops to proxy the level of agricultural productivity in each county from 1929 to 1933. Buck (1937) surveyed the output of 28 important crops in the 1930s, including 22 food crops such as rice, wheat, and beans, and six cash crops such as cotton, rapeseed, and tobacco. We focus on

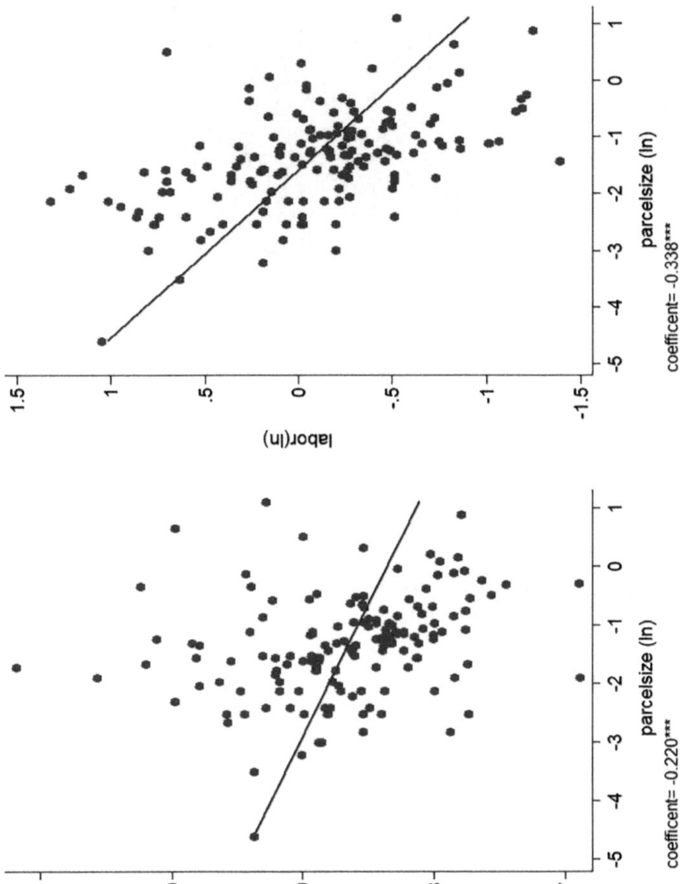


**Fig. 12.2** Correlation between farm parcel size and agricultural inputs per hectare (*Source* Land utilization in China, statistics [Buck 1937])

**Fig. 12.3** Distribution of 114 sampled prefectures

food crops in this paper. In specific, these food crops could be broadly classified into seven categories based on their crop attributes: wheat, maize, sorghum, millet, rice, legumes, and tubers and roots. Table 12.2 provides detailed information on the crops included in each category.

#### 12.3.1.1 Protestantism

Following Bai and Kung (2015), we primarily use the number of communicants per 10,000 people to represent the level of Protestantism in each prefecture. Besides, we take the Protestant duration by 1920 in each prefecture (measured from the recorded year the missionary work began) as another measure of Protestantism to test the robustness of the results. Figure 12.4 shows the distribution of Protestant duration (measured from the recorded year the missionary work began) by 1920 in our sampled 114 prefectures.

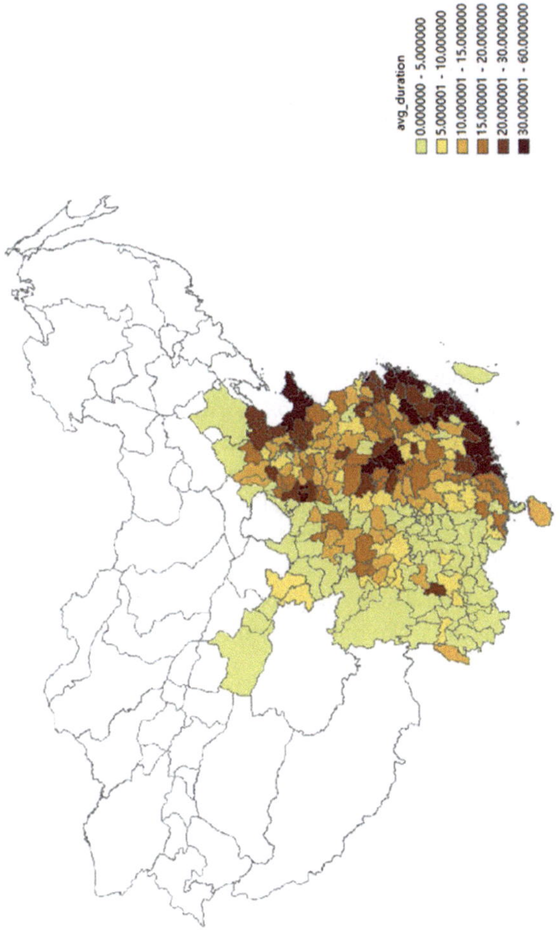


**Fig. 12.4** Distribution of protestantism average duration in 1920 (*Source* The Christian Occupation of China: a general survey of the numerical strength and geographical distribution of the Christian forces in China [Stauffer 1922])

#### 12.3.1.2 Control Variables

In addition to the key explanatory variable of Protestantism, we control for the potential effects from some other factors, including agricultural inputs (during the 1930s and the Qing period), Western penetration, prefecture size, population density, provincial capital, and urbanization.

*Agricultural inputs.* According to agricultural production function, agricultural output is directly determined by factor inputs, such as farm labor, fertilizer, and land. This information can be obtained from LUC (Buck 1937). Specifically, we use the number of effective farm labor per hectare, i.e., the number of workers who work 12 months a year, to proxy for labor input. Fertilizer input is measured by the amount of manure produced on farms per hectare. Land input is proxied by the size of the farm plots. We also control for the effect of irrigation rates, as irrigation is a key determinant of land quality.

*Western penetration.* Catholicism had been active for many years before Protestantism entered China. The potential effects of other Western religions must be taken into consideration. We use the number of Catholic churches per one million people to proxy for the status of Catholicism activities in each prefecture. Besides, we employ the duration of treaty port and railway in a prefecture to control for the possible effects of western economic penetration.

*Political center, prefecture size, and population density.* To the extent that prefectures with a provincial government appear to be more economically prosperous and appealing to foreigners, political centrality influences the development of Protestantism. We control for the location of provincial capital using a dummy variable, indicating whether the prefecture is a provincial capital or not. In addition to political centrality, prefectures with larger regions or more population are also attractive to foreigners. Therefore, the prefectural size and population density may also affect the growth of Protestantism in the area. We directly control for these two factors in our empirical estimation.

*Initial agricultural output inQing dynasty.* Initial differences in agricultural productivity across regions affect not only the choice of location for foreign missionaries, and thus the spread of foreign religions, but also the subsequent development of agriculture. It is therefore necessary to control for the initial level of agricultural output in each region. The data on initial agricultural output are based on digitalizing a statistical report on grain production during the Qing Dynasty, which is published on a book entitled "Agricultural development in Qing China, a quantitative study, 1661–1911" (Shi 2017). These data record 2,633 cases of grain production in 677 counties during the different emperors of the Qing dynasty. Unfortunately, only 74 of these counties still have production records in the 1929–1933 agricultural production data. We use the average grain yield per hectare of a county throughout the Qing dynasty to represent the initial grain production level of the county. The summary statistics, definitions and sources of these relevant variables are shown in Table 12.3.

**Table 12.3** Variable definitions and summary statistics

| Variable | Definition | Obs | Mean | S.D | Data sources |
|---|---|---|---|---|---|
| *(1) Agricultural output (by county)* | | | | | |
| | Output of important grain crops per hectare *in 1929–1933* (locality, log term) | 823 | 7.188 | 0.913 | A |
| | Grain output per hectare during different emperors of *theQing dynasty* (log term) | 2,633 | 7.635 | 0.904 | E |
| *(2) Protestantism (by prefecture)* | | | | | |
| | Total communicants per 10,000 people | 823 | 7.566 | 9.448 | B |
| | Duration of the protestant missionary work by 1920 | 823 | 34.944 | 16.370 | B |
| *(3) Agricultural inputs (by county)* | | | | | |
| | Labor: Man-equivalents per crop hectare (exclude idle time, log term) | 790 | -0.117 | 0.523 | A |
| | Fertilizer: Amount of fertilizer produced per crop hectare (log term) | 779 | 8.637 | 0.618 | A |
| | Irrigated: Percent of crop area irrigated | 823 | 0.421 | 0.381 | A |
| | Parcel size: Average size of parcels of land (hectare, log term) | 823 | -1.356 | 0.843 | A |
| *(4) Western penetration (by prefecture)* | | | | | |
| | Catholicism: Number of Catholic missionary stations per 1 million population | 823 | 3.342 | 3.220 | B |
| | Railway duration (by 1929) | 823 | 8.109 | 10.717 | C |
| | Treaty port duration (by 1929) | 823 | 9.420 | 21.307 | C |
| *(5) Demographic and political factors (by prefecture)* | | | | | |
| | Prefecture size in 1920 ($km^2$, log term) | 823 | 9.423 | 0.586 | D |
| | Population density in 1910 (log term) | 823 | 4.935 | 0.827 | F |
| | Provincial capital location | 823 | 0.122 | 0.327 | D |

*Note* The data sources are the following: A, Buck (1937); B, Stauffer (1922); C, Yan (1955): D, CHGIS (2007); E, Shi (2017); F,Ge (2000)

## 12.4 Results

### 12.4.1 Baseline Results

We first use the OLS approach to examine the impact of Protestantism on agricultural output in the 1930s. The dependent variable is the output per hectare of different crops in a county, and the key independent variable is the Protestantism of the prefecture in which the county is located. The baseline specification is given by,

$$lnY_{cijt} = \beta P_{j,1920} + Input_{ijt}\prime\gamma + X_j\prime\varphi + MainCrop_c + CropZone_i + Prov_j + Year_t + \varepsilon_{cijt} \quad (12.2)$$

where $P_{j,1920}$ is a proxy for Protestantism in in prefecture $j$, including the number of communicants per 10,000 people in 1920 and the duration of Protestant missionary work by 1920. $Input_{ijt}\prime$ is a vector of agricultural inputs in county $i$, including labor, fertilizer, irrigated rate and farm plot size; $X_j\prime$ is a vector of control variables of prefecture $j$, including Catholicism, the duration of railway and treaty ports, population density, the prefecture size, and whether the prefecture is a provincial capital. $Y_{cijt}$, $MainCrop_c$, $CropZone_i$, $Prov_j$, and $Year_t$ are same as the definitions in Eq. (12.1).

Table 12.4 reports baseline results. There is a significant and positive relationship between Protestantism in 1920 and agricultural output in 1929–1933. Specifically, column (1) shows that Protestantism has the effect of significantly increasing grain yield per hectare after controlling crop dummies, provincial dummies, and year dummies. In column (2), we additionally control for the possible effect of penetration of other Western religions (i.e., Roman Catholicism). The positive impact of Protestantism on crop yields is held constant. In terms of magnitude, one additional communicant per 10,000 people in 1920 could have increased the crop yield per hectare by 1 percentage point (0.01) in the 1930s. However, unlike Protestantism, the impact of Catholicism on crop yields is smaller (0.008) and statistically insignificant. This implies that it is Protestantism that positively affects agricultural output rather than other Western religions such as Roman Catholicism that play a role.

In column (3), we add agricultural input controls and agricultural area[9] dummy variables, which to some extent represent regional agricultural characteristics. The positive impact of Protestantism remains significant, but the magnitude decreases slightly, from 0.010 (column (2)) to 0.007 (column (3)). As for the factor inputs, not surprisingly, more labor, fertilizer inputs and higher irrigation rates result in higher agricultural outputs. Farmland size has a negative effect on crop yield but not significant. These effects are consistent with the conclusions we reached in the production function estimates in Table 12.1 and are of comparable magnitude. Column (4)

[9] LUC (Buck 1937) divides the surveyed regions into 8 agricultural areas based on their staple crops, including Spring wheat area, Winter wheat-millet area, Winter wheat-kaoliang area, Yangtze-rice–wheat area, Rice-tea area, Sichuan Rice area, Double cropping rice area and Southwestern rice area.

**Table 12.4** Effects of protestantism on agricultural production in 1930s

| | ln Yield per hectare | | | | |
|---|---|---|---|---|---|
| | (1) | (2) | (3) | (4) | (5) |
| Protestantism | 0.010** | 0.010** | 0.007** | 0.007** | 0.006** |
| | (0.004) | (0.004) | (0.003) | (0.003) | (0.003) |
| Catholicism | | 0.008 | −0.009 | −0.007 | −0.008 |
| | | (0.015) | (0.011) | (0.012) | (0.011) |
| Labor (ln) | | | 0.364*** | 0.370*** | 0.369*** |
| | | | (0.105) | (0.100) | (0.101) |
| Fertilizer (ln) | | | 0.174* | 0.208** | 0.214** |
| | | | (0.095) | (0.094) | (0.094) |
| Irrigated | | | 0.333** | 0.359*** | 0.374*** |
| | | | (0.140) | (0.136) | (0.138) |
| Parcel size (ln) | | | −0.034 | −0.021 | −0.017 |
| | | | (0.064) | (0.067) | (0.068) |
| Prefecture size (ln) | | | | 0.035 | 0.026 |
| | | | | (0.061) | (0.060) |
| Population density 1910 (ln) | | | | 0.133* | 0.113 |
| | | | | (0.080) | (0.080) |
| Provincial capital | | | | −0.120 | −0.102 |
| | | | | (0.101) | (0.104) |
| Railway duration (1929) | | | | | −0.001 |
| | | | | | (0.003) |
| Treaty port duration (1929) | | | | | 0.002 |
| | | | | | (0.002) |
| MainCrop FE | Y | Y | Y | Y | Y |
| Year FE | Y | Y | Y | Y | Y |
| Province FE | Y | Y | Y | Y | Y |
| Agricultural area FE | | | Y | Y | Y |
| Observations | 823 | 823 | 779 | 779 | 779 |
| R-squared | 0.687 | 0.688 | 0.766 | 0.768 | 0.769 |

*Note* Standard errors are clustered at prefecture level. Constant terms are not reported. * Significant at 10%; ** Significant at 5%; *** Significant at 1%

additionally controls for demographic and political factors, including prefecture's size, population density, and political center status. The significant positive effect of Protestantism on agricultural output remains and is constant (0.007). With the inclusion of other two Western influence factors, the duration of railway and treaty port in a prefecture, column (5) presents the final model with all control variables included. We can see that, one additional communicant per 10,000 people results in a significant increase in crop yields of 0.6 percent. That is, a one-standard-deviation increase in the density of communicants (9.488) in a prefecture could promote 5.693 ($0.6 \times 9.488$) percentage points increase in grain production. Or to put it another way, compared to prefectures with no Protestantism penetration, agricultural productivity is 4.5% higher in the prefectures with average level of Protestantism (7.566 per 10,000 people as shown in Table 12.3).

We perform some robustness and placebo tests using Qing agricultural output in Table 12.5. Column (1) is the baseline results shown in column (5) of Table 12.4 for comparison purposes. In column (2), we control for differences in initial Qing agricultural output across counties. Of the 147 counties with production records for 1929–1933, only 74 counties have Qing grain production records. Besides, column (2) excludes root and tuber samples because the Qing data does not record root and tuber production. As a result, the number of observations is reduced by more than half, from 779 to 341, compared to the baseline estimate. After controlling for the initial average grain yield in the Qing dynasty, the positive impact of Protestantism remains significant, and the magnitude (0.008) is consistent with the baseline estimates in column (1). In column (3), we use the subsample of 74 counties with records of crop yields both in the 1930s and the Qing dynasty for robustness tests. The positive impact of Protestantism remains evident, and the magnitude of the coefficients is stable (0.007). In addition, the impact of Catholicism on agricultural production is still insignificant.

**Table 12.5** Robust and Placebo Test: Qing agricultural output

| | ln Yield per hectare | | | |
|---|---|---|---|---|
| | (1) | (2) | (3) | (4) |
| | 1930s | | | Qing |
| Protestantism | 0.006** | 0.008** | 0.007** | 0.002 |
| | (0.003) | (0.003) | (0.004) | (0.002) |
| Catholicism | −0.008 | 0.007 | 0.013 | −0.002 |
| | (0.011) | (0.012) | (0.011) | (0.010) |
| AverageYield (Qing) | | 0.102 | | |
| | | (0.063) | | |
| Control variables | Y | Y | Y | Y |
| MainCrop FE | Y | Y | Y | \ |
| Year/Emperor FE | Y | Y | Y | Y |
| Province FE | Y | Y | Y | Y |
| Agricultural area FE | Y | Y | Y | \ |
| Observations | 779 | 341 | 341 | 2,448 |
| R-squared | 0.769 | 0.780 | 0.774 | 0.616 |

*Note* Standard errors are clustered at prefecture level. Control variables include all variables in column (5) of the baseline regression Table 12.4

One major concern for the causality between Protestantism and agricultural output is the possible endogeneity. Specifically, the choice of located counties when missionaries entered China is not random. Missionaries may have preferred to settle in the regions with higher agricultural output, and that these counties were still relatively prosperous in the 1930s. To determine whether the endogeneity exists, we conduct a placebo test using Qing dynasty agricultural output as the dependent variable. In column (4), we study the effect of Protestantism in 1920 on the initial output in the Qing dynasty. The dependent variable is grain yield per hectare of different farmlands in a county during different emperors of the Qing dynasty. The Protestantism coefficient is not significant and has a small value (only 0.002). This result suggests that Protestantism in the 1920s had no effect on agricultural yields per hectare in the Qing Dynasty (mainly before 1840). Therefore, the positive impact of Protestantism on crop yields is not due to the choice of location at the time of missionary entry. It can be argued that the introduction of Protestantism did contribute to agricultural production in the 1930s.

Furthermore, we take another proxy of Protestantism to test the robustness of Protestant impacts. We take the duration of missionary work in each prefecture by 1920 as an alternative measure of Protestantism. The results are shown in Table 12.6. The effect of Protestantism duration on agricultural output is positive and significant with an effect size of 0.007 (column (1)), which is close to the baseline result (0.006) in column (1) of Table 12.4. In addition, column (2) adds control for average agricultural output in Qing dynasty, column (3) is a 74-counties subsample estimation, and column (4) is a placebo test using Qing grain yield per hectare as the dependent variable. The estimates in columns (2) to (4) are also robust to the results in the corresponding columns of Table 12.5. Thus, the positive impact of Protestantism on agricultural output can be said to be robust and credible.

### *12.4.2 Heterogeneities Analysis*

The impact of Protestantism on agriculture may vary across regions with different agricultural characteristics. According to the "inappropriate technology hypothesis," the role played by Protestant technologies in agriculture may be related to specific agricultural characteristics or crop categories. Based on the characteristics of Chinese agriculture presented in Sect. 2.2, we explore the heterogeneity of Protestant impacts on agricultural output in terms of fertilizer and labor inputs, farm plot size, as well as crop varieties.

#### 12.4.2.1 By Agricultural Inputs: Labor, Fertilizer, and Farm Plot Size

Based on the baseline estimation in column (5) of Table 12.4, we further examine the heterogeneous impact of Protestantism in terms of agricultural inputs in Table 12.7. Specifically, we interact the amount of organic fertilizer produced, effective labor,

**Table 12.6** Robustness Test: Protestant Duration

| | ln Yield per hectare | | | |
|---|---|---|---|---|
| | (1) | (2) | (3) | (4) |
| | 1930s | | | Qing |
| Protestant Duration | 0.007** | 0.012*** | 0.012*** | -0.001 |
| | (0.003) | (0.003) | (0.003) | (0.002) |
| Catholicism | −0.010 | 0.007 | 0.012 | −0.001 |
| | (0.011) | (0.012) | (0.011) | (0.011) |
| AverageYield (Qing) | \ | Y | \ | \ |
| Control variables | Y | Y | Y | Y |
| MainCrop FE | Y | Y | Y | \ |
| Year/Emperor FE | Y | Y | Y | Y |
| Province FE | Y | Y | Y | Y |
| Agricultural area FE | Y | Y | Y | \ |
| Observations | 779 | 341 | 341 | 2,448 |
| R-squared | 0.771 | 0.791 | 0.787 | 0.616 |

*Note* Standard errors are clustered at prefecture level. Control variables include all variables in column (5) of the baseline regression Table 12.4

and farm plot size with Protestantism. We are interested in the coefficients of the interaction terms. Columns (1)–(3) of Table 12.7 show the interaction results of Protestantism with labor, fertilizer, and farm plot size separately. Column (1) indicates that the effect of Protestantism does not significantly vary with labor inputs. Column (2) shows that the effect of Protestantism is weaken by fertilizer usage, while column (3) shows that the effect of Protestantism is strengthened by farm plot size (without controlling fertilizer). In terms of magnitude, a 1% increase in the intensity of fertilizer use is associated with a 0.015% decrease in the positive effect of one additional communicant per 10,000 people, and a 1% increase in the farm plot size is associated with a 0.007% increase in the positive effect.

Columns (4) and (5) incrementally add interaction terms between Protestantism and agricultural inputs. Column (4) includes heterogeneity in labor and fertilizer use. Column (5) captures heterogeneity across all agricultural inputs, including labor, fertilizer, and farmland size. Although the estimates of the interaction term are of the same magnitude as those in the first three columns, the heterogeneity remains significant only for fertilizer. The results show that the western agricultural knowledge introduced by the Protestant missionaries worked mainly in places where the area of cultivated land was larger, and the production of organic fertilizers was smaller. This suggests that the new agricultural knowledge was to some extent incompatible with the traditional agriculture of China at that time, in line with the "inappropriate technology hypothesis."

**Table 12.7** Heterogeneity: Labor, fertilizer, and farm plot size

| | ln Yield per hectare | | | | |
|---|---|---|---|---|---|
| | (1) | (2) | (3) | (4) | (5) |
| Protestantism | 0.006** | 0.135** | 0.018*** | 0.146** | 0.146** |
| | (0.003) | (0.052) | (0.007) | (0.072) | (0.069) |
| Protestantism × Labor (ln) | −0.009 | | | 0.002 | 0.012 |
| | (0.007) | | | (0.009) | (0.012) |
| Protestantism × Fertilizer (ln) | | −0.015** | | −0.016* | −0.015* |
| | | (0.006) | | (0.008) | (0.008) |
| Protestantism × Parcel size (ln) | | | 0.007* | | 0.007 |
| | | | (0.004) | | (0.006) |
| Labor (ln) | 0.459*** | 0.388*** | 0.398*** | 0.365*** | 0.296** |
| | (0.108) | (0.100) | (0.099) | (0.117) | (0.125) |
| Fertilizer(ln) | 0.222** | 0.343*** | 0.232** | 0.352*** | 0.349*** |
| | (0.095) | (0.109) | (0.095) | (0.114) | (0.114) |
| Parcel size (ln) | −0.015 | −0.021 | −0.055 | −0.021 | −0.061 |
| | (0.066) | (0.065) | (0.073) | (0.065) | (0.077) |
| Control variables | Y | Y | Y | Y | Y |
| MainCrop FE | Y | Y | Y | Y | Y |
| Year FE | Y | Y | Y | Y | Y |
| Province FE | Y | Y | Y | Y | Y |
| Agricultural area FE | Y | Y | Y | Y | Y |
| Observations | 779 | 779 | 779 | 779 | 779 |
| R-squared | 0.770 | 0.773 | 0.772 | 0.773 | 0.774 |

*Note* Standard errors are clustered at prefecture level. Control variables include all variables in column (5) of the baseline regression Table 12.4

#### 12.4.2.2 Crop Varieties

Due to specific natural circumstances, the food crops in Europe and the United States in the twentieth century were mainly barley, wheat, and corn rather than rice. Western agricultural techniques may be more applicable to wheat cultivation but are not equally effective for rice. In addition, Western missionaries may have more agricultural experience with wheat cultivation than with rice. Thus, the impact of Protestantism on agricultural output may be heterogeneous across crop varieties, especially for rice and other non-rice crops.

Table 12.8 presents the heterogeneity of the effect of Protestantism among different crops. In column (1), we interact Protestantism with a full set of crop dummies and set wheat as the reference crop. Unsurprisingly, the positive impact of Protestantism on crop yields comes mainly from increased wheat yields, rather than increased rice yields. Specifically, an increase of one Protestant per 10,000 people is associated with a significant increase of 1 percentage point (0.01) in wheat yield per hectare. In contrast, the effect of Protestantism on rice is significantly smaller than on wheat, almost zero (0.010–0.012 = -0.002). Column (2) divides crops into three categories, namely wheat, rice, and other crops. The difference in the effects of Protestantism on wheat and rice is the same as in column (1). As a result, the introduction of Protestantism greatly increased wheat yields while having little effect on rice yields, which is in line with our expectations. In addition, the effects of Protestantism on other crops are not significantly different from the effects on wheat.

**Table 12.8** Heterogeneity: Crop varieties

| | ln Yield per hectare | |
|---|---|---|
| | (1) | (2) |
| Protestantism | 0.010*** | 0.010*** |
| | (0.004) | (0.004) |
| Protestantism * Rice | −0.012*** | −0.012*** |
| | (0.004) | (0.004) |
| Protestantism * Other Grain | | −0.001 |
| | | (0.004) |
| Protestantism * Corn | −0.013 | |
| | (0.009) | |
| Protestantism * Sorghum | 0.007 | |
| | (0.006) | |
| Protestantism * Millet | 0.003 | |
| | (0.005) | |
| Protestantism* Beans | −0.002 | |
| | (0.003) | |
| Protestantism* Tubers/Roots | −0.003 | |
| | (0.006) | |
| Control variables | Y | Y |
| MainCrop FE | Y | Y |
| Year FE | Y | Y |
| Province FE | Y | Y |
| Agricultural area FE | Y | Y |
| Observations | 779 | 779 |
| R-squared | 0.773 | 0.772 |

*Note* Standard errors are clustered at prefecture level. Control variables include all variables in column (5) of the baseline regression Table 12.4

### *12.4.3 Labor Wages*

Appropriate Western agricultural technologies have increased crop yields and thus the marginal productivity of agricultural labor, which is reflected in labor wages. Since the effect of Protestantism is significantly positive for the wheat rather than rice, Protestantism is likely to raise the farm labor wages in wheat-growing regions. Buck (1937) provides information on agricultural areas to which the sample counties belonged, based on the staple crops grown locally. There are eight agricultural regions in total, three are wheat regions and the other five are rice regions. We define a dummy variable to indicate whether the county located in rice regions or not. In addition, Buck (1937) also documents the total labor costs and wages for farm laborers, including year laborers, and short-time farm laborers (month and day laborers during peak seasons). Total labor costs include not only wages but also food expense and other labor costs. After matching with the data on Protestantism and other control variables, we end up with year labor wages for 121 counties, month labor wages for 101 counties, and day labor wages for 127 counties.

Table 12.9 shows the heterogeneity of the effect of Protestantism on farm labor wages in different agricultural regions. In the wheat regions, Protestantism has a significant and positive effect on total labor costs and wages for all types of farm workers. In contrast, for short-term laborers, the positive impact of Protestantism on their income is significantly smaller in rice regions than in wheat regions. Take month laborers for example (shown in columns (2) and (5)), one additional communicant per 10,000 people increases the total labor cost (or wages) in the wheat regions by 1.9 (or 2.0) percentage points. However, in the rice region, the effect is almost zero (0.019–0.020 = −0.001), as indicated by the coefficient of the interaction term. The results imply that the introduction of western agricultural knowledge increases the wheat yields and benefits the farm laborers in the wheat regions, while it has no effect on rice production and the laborers working in the rice regions.

## 12.5 Conclusions

Bai and Kung (2015) provide evidence that Protestantism significantly promoted Chinese economic prosperity in the period from 1840 to 1920. Effective channels are Western knowledge diffusion activities associated with schools and hospitals erected by missionaries. Given the importance of agriculture to economic growth in the historical China, we further investigate whether the Western knowledge introduced by missionaries is "useful" in promoting Chinese agricultural production in the 1930s.

However, the impact of specific agricultural technology largely depends on local agricultural characteristics, such as environment, endowments, and socioeconomic factors. There were huge differences between Western and Chinese agriculture in thes 1930. Western agriculture was characterized by large farms, low use of organic fertilizers, and advanced agricultural machinery. Chinese agriculture, on the other

**Table 12.9** Effects of Protestantism on Farm Labor Wages

| | Total labor cost | | | Wage only | | |
|---|---|---|---|---|---|---|
| | (1) | (2) | (3) | (4) | (5) | (6) |
| | Year | Month | Day | Year | Month | Day |
| Protestantism | 0.018** | 0.019*** | 0.007*** | 0.017** | 0.020*** | 0.006*** |
| | (0.007) | (0.007) | (0.002) | (0.008) | (0.007) | (0.001) |
| Protestantism* Rice Area | −0.015 | −0.020* | −0.007*** | −0.000 | −0.026*** | −0.006*** |
| | (0.010) | (0.011) | (0.002) | (0.024) | (0.010) | (0.002) |
| Control variables | Y | Y | Y | Y | Y | Y |
| Province FE | Y | Y | Y | Y | Y | Y |
| Agricultural area FE | Y | Y | Y | Y | Y | Y |
| Observations | 121 | 101 | 127 | 121 | 101 | 127 |
| R-squared | 0.651 | 0.681 | 0.623 | 0.550 | 0.650 | 0.633 |

*Note* Standard errors are clustered at prefecture level. Control variables include all variables in column (5) of the baseline regression Table 12.4

hand, was characterized by small farm sizes and intensive usage of labor and organic fertilizers. In addition, at that time, the main food crops in the West were wheat, barley, and corn, while the main food crops in China were wheat and rice. Therefore, according to the "inappropriate technology hypothesis," useful knowledge based on Western agriculture may not be useful for Chinese agriculture.

We use missionary density and the duration of missionary work as two proxies for Protestantism, and food crop production per hectare as the dependent variable. The baseline results show that Protestantism had a significant positive effect on agricultural productivity in 1930s China. But the effect is smaller for the crops with more fertilizer usage and smaller farm plot size. This may be because Western agriculture is characterized by low fertilizer use and large cultivated areas. Their agricultural techniques are not applicable to traditional Chinese agriculture, which is characterized by intensive cultivation. In addition, since Western missionaries specialized in growing the wheat and corn, the main food crops of Western countries, the impact of Protestantism on rice is significantly smaller than on wheat. Further, the spread of Protestantism contributed to the increase in the wages of farm laborers in wheat areas, whereas it had little effect on the wages of farm laborers in rice areas. Our findings suggest that useful knowledge may not be appropriate under some circumstances, because such knowledge is often customized for specific conditions and production.

**Acknowledgements** Ying Bai acknowledges financial support from the University Grants Committee/Research Grants Council of the Hong Kong Special Administrative Region, China (project no. AoE/B-704/22-R).

## References

Acemoglu, Daron, and Fabrizio Zilibotti. 2001. Productivity Differences. *The Quarterly Journal of Economics*116 (2): 563–606.

Allen, Robert. 1994. Agriculture during the Industrial Revolution. In *The Economic History of Britain since 1700*, 3rd ed., 96–123. London: Publisher.

Atkinson, Anthony B., and Joseph E. Stiglitz. 1969. A New View of Technological Change. *The Economic Journal* 79 (315): 573–578.

Bai, Ying, and James Kai-sing Kung. 2015. Diffusing Knowledge While Spreading God's Message: Protestantism and Economic Prosperity in China, 1840–1920. *Journal of the European Economic Association* 13 (4): 669–698.

Barro, Robert J. 2004. Spirit of Capitalism: Religion and Economic Development. *Harvard International Review* 25 (4): 64–68.

Basu, Susanto, and David N. Weil. 1998. Appropriate Technology and Growth. *The Quarterly Journal of Economics* 113 (4): 1025–1054.

Bays, Daniel H. 2011. *A New History of Christianity in China*. Malden, MA: John Wiley & Sons.

Becker, Sascha O., and Ludger Woessmann. 2009. Was Weber Wrong? A Human Capital Theory of Protestant Economic History. *Quarterly Journal of Economics* 124 (2): 531–596.

Becker, Sascha O., and Ludger Woessmann. 2010. The Effect of Protestantism on Education before the Industrialization: Evidence from 1816 Prussia. *Economics Letters* 107 (2): 224–228.

Benjamin, Dwayne. 1995. Can Unobserved Land Quality Explain the Inverse Productivity Relationship? *Journal of Development Economics* 46 (1): 51–84.

Benjamin, Dwayne, and Loren Brandt. 2002. Property Rights, Labour Markets, and Efficiency in a Transition Economy: The Case of Rural China. *Canadian Journal of Economics/Revue canadienne*d'économique 35 (4): 689–716.

Bessin, Ric. 2019. Bt-Corn: What It Is and How It Works. Entfact 130, University of Kentucky College of Agriculture, Food and Environment. https://entomology.ca.uky.edu/ef130.

Binswanger, Hans. 1986. Agricultural Mechanization: A Comparative Historical Perspective. *The World Bank Research Observer* 1 (1): 27–56.

Buck, John Lossing. 1937. *Land Utilization in China: Statistics*. Chicago: University of Chicago Press.

Campagne, Pascal, et al. 2017. Genetic Hitchhiking and Resistance Evolution to Transgenic Bt Toxins: Insights from the African Stalk Borer Busseola Fusca (Noctuidae). *Heredity* 118 (4): 330–339.

Cheng, Mengliu. 2018. *New Agricultural Gospel: Protestant Agricultural Missions in China in the Early Twentieth Century*. PhD diss.: Duke University.

CHGIS. 2007. Version 4. Cambridge, MA: Harvard Yenching Institute and Fudan Center for Historical Geography.

Cook, Scott. 1999. Surplus Labour and Productivity in Chinese Agriculture: Evidence from Household Survey Data. *The Journal of Development Studies* 35 (3): 16–44.

Desiere, Sam, and Dean Jolliffe. 2018. Land Productivity and Plot Size: Is Measurement Error Driving the Inverse Relationship? *Journal of Development Economics* 130: 84–98.

Elman, Benjamin A. 2006. *A Cultural History of Modern Science in China*. Cambridge, MA: Harvard University Press.

Esherick, Joseph W. 1988. *The Origins of the Boxer Uprising*. Berkeley: University of California Press.

Fan, Shenggen, and Connie Chan-Kang. 2005. Is Small Beautiful? Farm Size, Productivity, and Poverty in Asian Agriculture. *Agricultural Economics* 32: 135–146.

Fleisher, Belton M., and Yunhua Liu. 1992. Economies of Scale, Plot Size, Human Capital, and Productivity in Chinese Agriculture. *Quarterly Review of Economics and Finance* 32 (3): 112–124.

Foster, Andrew D., and Mark R. Rosenzweig. 2022. Are There Too Many Farms in the World? Labor Market Transaction Costs, Machine Capacities, and Optimal Farm Size. *Journal of Political Economy* 130 (3): 636–680.

Gallego, Francisco A., and Robert Woodberry. 2010. Christian Missionaries and Education in Former African Colonies: How Competition Mattered. *Journal of African Economies* 19 (3): 294–329.

Ge, Jianxiong. 2000. *China Population History*, vol. 6. Shanghai: Fudan University Press.

Glaeser, Edward L., and Bruce I. Sacerdote. 2008. Education and Religion. *Journal of Human Capital* 2 (2): 188–215.

Griliches, Zvi. 1957. Hybrid Corn: An Exploration in the Economics of Technological Change. *Econometrica* 25 (4): 501–522.

Groff, George W. 1924. The Rural Church. *The Chinese Recorder* 55 (12): 775.

Gu, Weimin. 2010. *Christianity and Modern Chinese Society*. Shanghai: Shanghai People's Press.

Hayami, Yujiro, and Vernon W. Ruttan. 1985. *Agricultural Development: An International Perspective*. Baltimore: Johns Hopkins University Press.

Lamb, Russell L. 2003. Inverse Productivity: Land Quality, Labor Markets, and Measurement Error. *Journal of Development Economics* 71 (1): 71–95.

Li, Yuxuan, et al. 2013. An Analysis of China's Fertilizer Policies: Impacts on the Industry, Food Security, and the Environment. *Journal of Environmental Quality* 42 (4): 972–981.

Lipset, Seymour Martin, and Gabriel Salman Lenz. 2000. Corruption, Culture, and Markets. In *Culture Matters*, edited by Lawrence E. Harrison and Samuel P. Huntington. New York: Basic Books.

Ma, Debin. 2004. Why Japan, Not China, Was the First to Develop in East Asia: Lessons from Sericulture, 1850–1937. *Economic Development and Cultural Change* 52 (2): 369–394.

McCleary, Rachel, and Robert Barro. 2003. Religion and Economic Growth Across Countries. Working Paper No. 3708464.

Moscona, Jacob, and Karthik A, Sastry. 2025. Inappropriate Technology: Evidence from Global Agriculture. No. w33500. National Bureau of Economic Research.

Olmstead, Alan L., and Paul W. Rhode. 2001. Reshaping the Landscape: The Impact and Diffusion of the Tractor in American Agriculture, 1910–1960. *The Journal of Economic History* 61 (3): 663–698.

Olmstead, Alan L., and Paul Rhode. 1988. An Overview of California Agricultural Mechanization, 1870–1930. *Agricultural History* 62 (3): 86–112.

Pingali, Prabhu. 2007. Agricultural Mechanization: Adoption Patterns and Economic Impact. In *Handbook of Agricultural Economics*, vol. 3, 2779–2805. Amsterdam: Elsevier.

La Porta, Rafael, et al. 1998. Law and Finance. *Journal of Political Economy* 106 (6): 1113–1155.

Qiu, Tian, and Biliang Luo. 2021. Do Small Farms Prefer Agricultural Mechanization Services? Evidence from Wheat Production in China. *Applied Economics* 53 (26): 2962–2973.

Reisner, John H. 1924. The Church and China's Rural Population. *The Chinese Recorder* 55 (12): 762.

Richard, Timothy. 1916. *Forty-Five Years in China: Reminiscences*. New York: Stokes Company Publishers.

Stauffer, Milton T. 1922. *The Christian Occupation of China: A General Survey of the Numerical Strength and Geographical Distribution of the Christian Forces in China*. Shanghai: China Continuation Committee.

Stavis, Benedict. 1978. *The Politics of Agricultural Mechanization in China*. Ithaca, NY: Cornell University Press.

Stewart, Frances. 2016. *Technology and Underdevelopment*. London: Springer.

Shi, Zhihong. 2017. *Agricultural Development in Qing China, a Quantitative Study 1661–1911*. Beijing: Social Sciences Academic Press.

Stross, Randall E. 1986. *The Stubborn Earth: American Agriculturalists on Chinese Soil, 1898–1937*. Berkeley: University of California Press.

Thompson, Larry Clinton. 2009. *William Scott Ament and the Boxer Rebellion: Heroism, Hubris and the "Ideal Missionary."* Jefferson, NC: McFarland.

United States Bureau of the Census. 1975. *Historical Statistics of the United States, Colonial Times to 1970*. Washington, DC: US Department of Commerce, Bureau of the Census.

van Zanden, Jan Luiten. 1991. The First Green Revolution. *Economic History Review* 44 (2): 215–239.

Wang, Qiang, Catherine Halbrendt, and Stanley R. Johnson. 1996. Grain Production and Environmental Management in China's Fertilizer Economy. *Journal of Environmental Management* 47 (3): 283–296.

Wang, Xiaobing, et al. 2016. Wage Growth, Landholding, and Mechanization in Chinese Agriculture]. *World Development* 86: 30–45.

Woodberry, Robert D. 2012. The Missionary Roots of Liberal Democracy. *American Political Science Review* 106 (2): 244–274.

Yan, Zhongping. 1955. *Selected Statistical Materials on Modern Chinese Economic History*. Beijing: Ke Xue Press.

**Ying Bai** is a Professor in the Department of Economics at The Chinese University of Hong Kong and co-director of CUHK-UC San Diego Joint Laboratory on Chinese Economy. He earned his Ph.D. degree at The Hong Kong University of Science and Technology. His research interests encompass development economics, economic history, and the political economy of China. He employs cutting-edge statistical techniques and novel datasets to address historical issues of paramount importance in China's development, such as the causes and consequences of conflict, the impact of the West (especially Protestantism) on modern economic growth, and the political and economic consequences of China's most important institutions—the imperial civil exam system and the hierarchical administration system. Much of his research has been disseminated in prestigious journals, such as the *Quarterly Journal of Economics, Econometrica*, the *Review of Economics and Statistics*, the *Economic Journal, the International Economic Review*, and *the Journal of the European Economic Association*. His paper received the 2018 Distinguished CESifo Research Affiliate Award and the 2021 Masahiko Aoki Award. Additionally, in 2018, he was honored with the CUHK Young Researcher Award.

**Xiaoyu Bian** is a Ph.D. student in Economics at The Chinese University of Hong Kong. Her primary fields of study include economic history, political economy, development economics, and labor economics. Xiaoyu's research examines the influence of religions (especially Protestantism) on China's modern agricultural development and employs market access to assess the effects of national capital relocation and the diversion of the Grand Canal on China's economic growth in historical contexts. Currently, she is investigating China's historical environmental changes and their implications for modern sustainable development.

# Author Index




Z. Chen et al. (eds.), *Quantitative History of China*, Studies in Economic History,
https://doi.org/10.1007/978-981-96-8272-0

## L



## M



## N

# Subject Index





Z. Chen et al. (eds.), *Quantitative History of China*, Studies in Economic History,
https://doi.org/10.1007/978-981-96-8272-0

GPSR Compliance

*The European Union's (EU) General Product Safety Regulation (GPSR) is a set of rules that requires consumer products to be safe and our obligations to ensure this.*

*If you have any concerns about our products, you can contact us on ProductSafety@springernature.com*

In case Publisher is established outside the EU, the EU authorized representative is:

Springer Nature Customer Service Center GmbH
Europaplatz 3
69115 Heidelberg, Germany

**Batch number: 10725823**

Printed by Printforce, the Netherlands